Frank Keuper / Christian Oecking / Andreas Degenhardt (Eds.)

Application Management

Frank Keuper / Christian Oecking
Andreas Degenhardt (Eds.)

Application Management

Challenges – Service Creation – Strategies

GABLER

Bibliographic information published by the Deutsche Nationalbibliothek
The Deutsche Nationalbibliothek lists this publication in the Deutsche Nationalbibliografie; detailed bibliographic data are available in the Internet at http://dnb.d-nb.de.

Prof. Frank Keuper holds the chair in business administration, especially convergence management and strategic management at Steinbeis University, Berlin. He is also academic head and director of the Sales & Service Research Center (partner of Telekom Shop Vertriebsgesellschaft mbH) and the T-Vertrieb Business School (partner of Telekom Deutschland GmbH).

Christian Oecking is Chairman of the Management Board at Siemens IT Solutions and Services GmbH.

Andreas Degenhardt is Head of Global Application Management at Siemens IT Solutions and Services GmbH.

1st Edition 2011
Revised reprint 2011

Editorial Office: Barbara Roscher | Jutta Hinrichsen

Gabler Verlag is a brand of Springer Fachmedien.
Springer Fachmedien is part of Springer Science+Business Media.
www.gabler.de

Cover design: KünkelLopka Medienentwicklung, Heidelberg
Printed on acid-free paper
Printed in Germany

ISBN 978-3-8349-1667-9

Foreword

Double-digit growth rates clearly illustrate the growing importance of Application Management. Information and telecommunication technology is essential to the success of modern business, but only with the help of IT applications users can access the required IT systems. In particular, companies in the consumer market are feeling the impact of this trend. For example, applications ("apps") are critical to the success of telecommunications providers and, often enough, they even stimulate the need for new Web experiences. Here it is important to note that applications have to be easy to install and easy to use. Then, the wish to use the technology will arise.

The corporate world presents a similar picture. Depending on their functionality, applications will determine whether IT and business can align. Today, information technology is only a vehicle and not an end in itself. Its role is to serve the company's goal by supporting and developing business processes in order to meet future requirements. Companies expect IT applications to run smoothly in the background and to be user friendly, the same way as consumers expect that apps act like a "push on a button".

This trend means increasing challenges for Application Management Services (AMS). On the one hand, these services have to fully manage a complex application landscape consisting of multiple solutions and systems from different manufacturers. On the other hand, AMS always have to take the latest trends in technology into account such as cloud computing, Software as a Service (SaaS), grid computing or mobility solutions. In view of short innovation cycles in information and telecommunication technology, decision makers are facing an essential question: How do we accomplish the diverse requirements and new concepts to form an AMS business model that will yield lasting benefits for the involved parties?

One key to solving this dilemma is to standardize and automate AMS processes. After all, the efficiency with which an AMS company performs its job is the best way for the provider's differentiation. IT providers can assure high quality at competitive prices by industrializing service processes and can pass on the economies to customers.

Implementing a comprehensive knowledge management system is one way to reap the potential of efficiency for the benefit of customers. Systematically storing and providing up-to-date knowledge and expertise is a real advantage in highly competitive markets. This fact becomes particularly apparent with IT systems that are critical for business processes. Often they are based on decades-old software solutions and, in addition, the developers of these solutions are gradually approaching retirement. This change period gives rise to a slew of questions which ask for innovative short-term solutions. One consequence is to combine development and maintenance of software on the one hand and incorporating this software into current operations on the other.

This book illustrates how intermeshing Service Creation (developing applications) and Service Management (operating applications) can lead to lasting success for Application Management Services. The authors build a bridge between theory and practice. Case studies from Europe, India and South America illustrate aspects of the growing AMS market – providing a valuable orientation for professionals and scientists alike.

Wolfsburg, March 2011

KLAUS HARDY MÜHLECK

Head of Group IT and Group CIO (Chief Information Officer)
General Representative of the Volkswagen Aktiengesellschaft

Introduction

Application Management (often also referred to as Application Lifecycle Management) is a combination of provider services for applications and support for applications systems across their entire lifecycle. By 2015 analysts expect business models relying heavily on Application Lifecycle Management and based increasingly on cloud computing will make up half of all new enterprise IT concepts. The objective of this collection of articles is to demonstrate the close links between service creation and service management.

To present and analyze the many different aspects of application management, this volume has been subdivided into four parts.

Part 1	Application Management – Challenges and Chances
Part 2	Application Management – Service Creation and Quality Management
Part 3	Application Management – Strategies and Instruments
Part 4	Application Management – Case Studies

Figure 1: *Structure*

In the first part the article of *CHRISTIAN OECKING* and *ANDREAS DEGENHARDT* pays attention here to the organizational variant of transferring application management in the narrower sense to an external third-party provider in the form of an outsourcing solution. Against this backdrop, the standardized procedure model of *SIEMENS IT SOLUTIONS AND SERVICES* was outlined for shaping the evolution from Application Management 1.0 to Application Management 2.0. *MARKUS BÖHM, STEFANIE LEIMEISTER, CHRISTOPH RIEDL* and *HELMUT KRCMAR* focus in their article on the IT provisioning perspective of cloud computing. They examine the evolution from outsourcing to cloud computing as a new IT deployment paradigm. In doing so, they highlight the effects on the outsourcing value chain, summarize market players and their roles within a new cloud computing value network, and, finally, discuss potential business models for IT service providers.

The first paper in the second part from *BHASWAR BOSE* focuses on essential elements in quality management. The article by *PETRA ENDHOLZ* highlights the significance of the human element in the IT business, while also considering operative and cost aspects as well as strategic elements. She outlines general activities necessary to face the challenges of the market. Furthermore, the paper provides an insight into initiatives for resource management – with the focus on competence management.

Part three starts with the paper by *BENEDIKT SCHMIDT,* in which he describes the importance of knowledge management for application management. Beginning with the fundamental theories and approaches in relation to knowledge management, he goes on to talk about instruments and methods for knowledge transfer. *BENEDIKT MARTENS* and *FRANK TEUTEBERG* introduce a reference model for risk and compliance management of IT services in cloud computing environments. They also describe the implementation of this reference model by means of the ADOit software tool. *IRVATHRAYA B. MADHUKAR* and *FLORIAN A. TÄUBE* show the advantages of integrated service creation and service management. They study the interrelation between software application development and application management and have conducted a case study with interviews in India. *KATJA WOLTER'S* paper shows the link between cloud computing and competitive intelligence and describes the process of analyzing the market and the competitors. The article by *CHRISTIAN SCHULMEYER* and *FRANK KEUPER* highlights the potential of morphological psychology for deriving requirements for design recommendations of Web applications using examples of customer self-service applications.

Part four begins with the paper by *ANJALI ARYA* presenting a successful case study where outsourcing of application management support was deployed for a pharmaceutical industry major. The article by *LAURENT CERVEAU* and *FREDDIE GEIER* aims to show that application of a software methodology requires multiple small steps in many areas across the project team. Last but not least, *MAXIMO ROMERO KRAUSE* analyzes the market for global production centers for application management in Latin America.

A special thanks to our authors without whose contributions this book would not have been possible. Despite the tight schedule, the authors demonstrated extraordinary commitment in putting together their practical and theoretical contributions. As always, delivery of the final proofs to *Gabler Verlag* was only possible thanks to the many "helping hands" in the background. We would like to take this opportunity of expressing our thanks.

Another special thank you from the editors goes out to *KATJA WOLTER*, as research assistant within the faculty of economics, with a special focus on convergence management and strategic management, at *Steinbeis-University Berlin*. The editors wish to express a further special note of thanks to *BARBARA ROSCHER* und *JUTTA HINRICHSEN* of *Gabler Verlag* for their help and cooperation in publishing this book.

Hamburg/Munich, December 2010

PROF. DR. FRANK KEUPER, ANDREAS DEGENHARDT and CHRISTIAN OECKING

Call for Papers

Business + Innovation (B+I) as a new double-blind-review journal is both to contribute substantial scientific knowledge for dissemination and to offer useful guidelines for management practice.

Interested authors are welcome to submit **original empirical or conceptual papers (**targeting an appropriate balance of theory and practice) in **German or English** for one of the following subject areas: Strategy (e.g. strategic/organizational/HR management, business modelling), Innovation (e.g. innovation/knowledge/technology/I&C/e-business management) or Global view (cross-sector trends and current market developments). Further **information on the formal and contentual requirements** is provided at www.businessundinnovation.de.

B+I proudly supports:

Pull a(t)traction!

We are currently looking for partners and sponsors , wanting to participate in bringing this prestigeous, international sports event to life.

Interested? Contact us at

steuermann hamburg GmbH · Schanzenstraße 70 · 20357 Hamburg · Tel 0049 40 432 08 45 0

Table of Contents

Part 3:

Part 4:

Part 1:

Application Management – Challenges and Chances

Application Management 2.0

CHRISTIAN OECKING and *ANDREAS DEGENHARDT*

Siemens AG – Siemens IT Solutions and Services

1 Introduction

As 'informatization'[1] has increasingly spread to encompass more and more of our everyday business activities, the role of the Chief Information Officer (CIO) has also undergone radical changes. Whereas in the past the 'Head of IT' was often regarded by their colleagues and superiors as barely more than a strange technology geek, in recent years the CIO has become a key figure in many organizations. This change is reflected in more than simply the new title following the Anglo-American CxO convention[2]. The CIO is a managerially trained generalist who, among other things,

- thinks along business (process)-oriented, results-driven and competitive lines,
- possesses the relevant business information,
- is not so much driven by user departments, but rather considers themselves to be a driver of product and/or process innovations, and
- sees information technologies (IT) as a means to an end rather than the central focus of their activities.[3]

This new role makes the CIO a key actor in strategic management because, as information technology increasingly permeates the processes in enterprises and consequently the concomitant design and control of the IT problem resolution process, the relationship between companies and the market also changes. The relationship between a market and a company is characterized by a complexity differential[4] which must be overcome[5] in order to achieve the overriding objective of a company – its continued existence in the long term. The continued existence of companies in private enterprise that are in it for the long term is ensured when they are able to sell their products and services profitably – i.e. when they succeed on the market. A company succeeds on the market when the products and/or services it sells are competitive and are economically viable. Accordingly, if a company is able to improve its competitiveness and profitability (foremost corporate objective), this also helps it maximize success and ultimately safeguard its long-term viability.[6]

Since a company has no control over market complexity, it follows that the only option available to it is to master its own level of complexity. It does this by focusing on its core competencies.[7] Consequently CIOs must ask themselves, or must be able to answer the question, how they can provide IT services effectively and efficiently within a wider strategic remit of focusing on core competencies. It is in this context that the company must decide the optimum balance between sourcing IT services inhouse and procuring them externally.[8] IT services that can be better provided by external providers from the point of view of effect-

---

1 *DANOWSKI* (2008), p. V.

2 Cf. *BRENNER/WITTE* (2007), p. 31.

3 Cf. *PIETSCH* (2009), p. 393, with reference to *HARTERT* (2000), p. 652.

4 Cf. *KEUPER* (2004) and *KEUPER* (2005).

5 Cf. *KEUPER* (2004), p. 3.

6 Cf. *HERING* (1995), p. 5.

7 Cf. (also for the following statements in this paragraph) *KEUPER/OECKING* (2006), p. VII ff.

8 Cf. *MÄNNEL* (1981).

tiveness or efficiency should then of course also be procured externally. IT services must therefore be examined to determine whether it is still necessary to provide them. If so, in view of the wide range of IT service provision options ranging along the continuum from internal to external providers, the CIO is faced with an extremely difficult choice.[9] Inhouse and external procurement are at the ends of the IT service provider continuum, but nowadays there are a vast array of hybrid options in between these two extremes.[10]

The provision of and support for an effective and efficient IT infrastructure for the various user departments is a core element of the service portfolio of internal IT organizations. In view of the above, the CIO must systematically identify which options are potentially viable and document this in the IT infrastructure strategy as a key part of the IT functionality strategy.[11] The aim of an infrastructure strategy of this type is to standardize and harmonize the corporate information system environment in order to drive down infrastructure costs while at the same time maintaining or improving infrastructure performance. This information system environment includes hardware, operating systems, networks, and in particular applications.

Stipulating the type and manner of provision of IT infrastructure components (hardware, applications, etc.) usually greatly affects the organizational and operational structure of a company and has a significant influence on its agility and its ability to flexibly adapt to changing circumstances, which in turn has a lasting impact on safeguarding the company's existence in the long term.[12] CIOs are well aware of these business-critical impacts. Over recent years they have therefore made considerable efforts to press ahead with the harmonization, consolidation and standardization of IT infrastructures. In some cases the results are highly sobering however. According to a recent study conducted by Actinium Consulting, only 29% of IT managers surveyed (N = 219) claimed they were able to account for all the infrastructure components in their companies at all times. The lack of transparency with regard to licenses and maintenance contracts is a further problematic area. Only 28% of those surveyed had immediate full access to all the license and maintenance contracts along with the relevant supplier information. Even more alarmingly, 69% of those surveyed reported that changes to technical systems, processes and responsibilities were either documented only partially or not documented at all.[13] As a consequence, this lack of transparency creates performance risks that threaten to reduce customer satisfaction with the services of the IT organization (reduced effectiveness). Moreover, the lack of knowledge regarding the content of existing maintenance contracts, in some cases coupled with licenses that are still valid for obsolete systems no longer in use, may create unnecessary costs (reduced efficiency).

---

9 Cf. *VON GLAHN/OECKING* (2007), p. 29.

10 von *GLAHN/KEUPER* (2008), p. 9.

11 *COHEN/YOUNG* define 'sourcing strategy' as follows: "A sourcing strategy is the set or portfolio of plans, directives, and decisions (what we call sourcing action plans) that define and integrate internally and externally provided services to fulfill an enterprise`s business strategy. The challenge of a sourcing strategy is to continuously deliver to the organization the exact combination of internal and external resources and services that are necessary to support business objectives." *COHEN/YOUNG* (2006), p. 38.

12 Cf. for this paragraph *HOLTSCHKE/HEIER/HUMMEL* (2009), p. 93.

13 For a summary of the findings of the *ACTINIUM CONSULTING* study, cf. *PÜTTER* (2010).

In summary, it can be seen that optimizing the existing IT infrastructure and the IT application landscape are two important ways of increasing the value added of the internal IT organization. In many companies however, the IT application landscape still resembles a giant construction site. The reason for this is that existing systems have often become increasingly complex over time, as a result of mergers, takeovers or other expansionary moves for example, while at the same time becoming more and more difficult to control. Among many IT managers, the lack of knowledge about the existing level of complexity of their own IT landscapes gave rise to the motto: 'Never change a running system.' As a consequence, defects tended to be rectified in a makeshift way and expensive legacy applications were maintained because of their importance for keeping the business going, while more and more new applications had to be integrated by means of costly interfaces. The ever higher costs for managing the application portfolio threatened to wipe out the laboriously created added value of the internal IT organization.

The magic words 'IT industrialization' would seem to point to the way out of this effectiveness/efficiency dilemma of IT application management outlined above. From the point of view of the CIO, the goal is to apply the principles of IT industrialization – and above all the principle of standardization – to the field of application management, both to exploit the inherent effectiveness and efficiency potential in the existing application environment and to gear up the IT application portfolio and ultimately the internal IT organization for the future.

2 Application Management in the Light of the IT Industrialization Megatrend

2.1 Application Management

2.1.1 Definition

There is no standard definition of application management in the literature.[14] This would seem an appropriate point, therefore, to examine the concept in order to better understand the remainder of this article. We will first decompose the term into its individual constituents 'management' and 'application', then combine these to arrive at a definition of the term as a whole.

The management process is primarily concerned with controlling operational problem resolution processes. The problem that triggers the problem resolution process usually arises from a divergence between an actual state in reality which is perceived to be negative from a planned state which is considered desirable by management in the institutional sense (variance between actual and plan). Overcoming this variance involves analyzing the initial situation (including problem identification, description, analysis and assessment), defining the objectives, the measures and the means, execution and evaluation of the results.[15] Control of the problem resolution process is a matter for management in the functional sense and

---

[14] Cf. *Marggi* (2002), p. 21 f.

[15] Cf. *Thommen/Achleitner* (2009), p. 49 f.

comprises the following aspects: planning, decision-making, assignment of tasks, and monitoring.[16]

Information systems are 'socio-technical (man/machine) systems comprising human and machine components (subsystems) used to optimally provide information and communication according to economic criteria.'[17] Man and machine thus constitute the subsystems of an information system where, to be more precise, machines should be thought of as applications that can only run in a specific hardware environment. The applications process data for internal company processes.[18] From the point of view of business informatics, however, the starting point is not an all-encompassing information system. An information system can rather be broken down into a defined number of subsystems. Depending on the respective purpose, therefore, *KRCMAR* makes a distinction between application systems for administration, for planning and for supporting decision-making.[19] The problems associated with planning and provision in relation to application systems in their entirety are then the responsibility of IT management.[20]

Application management forms part of this remit. Two definition approaches can be distinguished according to the envisaged scope of the remit. *KAISER* defines application management to be the 'combination of operational services for applications as well as project and implementation services and (further) development activities by an external IT service provider on a long-term basis. Generally, fixed price elements and service level agreements (SLAs) form the contractual basis for these services.'[21] This is application management in the wider sense because it also includes application development services. Like *KAISER*, *MARGGI* also bases his definition on the application lifecycle: application management encompasses all controlling activities concerned with planning, building and running an application.[22] *MARGGI* makes a distinction between this and *application operation*. This refers to "sub-services of the overall operation which include operational activities for the operation of applications."[23] One criticism of *MARGGI'S* definition is that it does not cover the entire lifecycle; the end of life of an application, its retirement, is simply ignored.

In consideration of the above, therefore, for the purposes of this article application management refers to the lifecycle-oriented control of the problem resolution process for operational application systems excluding any fundamental application development services. In particular, application management encompasses user support and the further development of applications already in use. This definition can also be seen as application management in the narrower and functional sense.

---

16 Cf. *RÜHLI* (1996) and *THOMMEN/ACHLEITNER* (2009), p. 48 ff.

17 *WKWI* (1994), p. 80.

18 Cf. *KRCMAR* (2005), p. 25.

19 Cf. *KRCMAR* (2005), p. 26. In addition, application systems can be differentiated according to where they are used as operational or supra-operational applications and by industry focus.

20 Cf. *KRCMAR* (2005), p. 27.

21 *KAISER* (2005), p. 10.

22 Cf. *MARGGI* (2002), p. 24.

23 *MARGGI* (2002), p. 24.

2.1.2 Forms of Application Management

In practice, application management takes many different forms. In principle, however, certain application-related IT services, e. g. the maintenance of an application, are outsourced to third parties. If the external provider, the application service provider, only takes over the longer-term responsibility for maintaining an application without taking responsibility for the infrastructure, this is known as stand-alone application management. In the case of application hosting, only the infrastructure underlying the application and its maintenance is outsourced to a third party. Often IT services that are allocated to application management are part of extensive outsourcing activities which include, for example, third-party provision of IT infrastructure services. This is referred to as embedded application management. These activities may even extend to full outsourcing, i.e. the complete outsourcing of infrastructure and application support (first and second-level support) by a company to a specialist third party.[24]

2.1.3 Advantages of Application Management Outsourcing from the Company's Perspective

There are a whole host of reasons why companies delegate control of the problem resolution process for all or parts of their operational application systems to an application service provider. From the strategic point of view, external application management enables the company to focus on its own core competencies. As a rule this does not include the operation and maintenance of application systems. By leveraging specialization, transaction volume and factor cost gains, companies can generate cost savings and free up financial resources for more lucrative uses. Kaiser further argues that the IT budget accounts for between 2% and 4% of turnover in most companies depending on the industry concerned. In turn, up to half of this is spent on application support. Assuming that the IT budget remains constant, efficient application management thus creates the necessary financial leeway to drive forward IT innovation. Moreover, companies need to devote fewer resources to coordination and administrative tasks. A further argument for outsourcing application management activities is the greater cost transparency as the vendor's comprehensive monitoring or development services to be provided over the period are factored into the total cost of ownership or the service level agreements. Another benefit for companies is that application service providers are themselves interested in maximizing their economies of scale and synergy effects, and are therefore constantly investing in improving their own technologies. As a consequence, companies not only enjoy greater technology security, if contracts are carefully drafted, they can also benefit from the resulting efficiency gains without having to make any investment themselves.[25]

---

[24] Cf. for the whole paragraph *KAISER* (2005), p. 10 f.

[25] Cf. for the whole paragraph *KAISER* (2005), p. 13 f.

2.2 IT Industrialization and Application Management

The era of industrialization stands for “the spread of high-productivity industrial methods of production and service provision in all sectors of the economy.”[26] For many decades already, application of the industrialization principles of, for example, standardization, automation and modularization to IT has been debated by academics and practitioners. Depending on which method of counting is used, IT industrialization is even referred to as the second or third industrial revolution.[27] *HOLTSCHKE/HEIER/HUMMEL* define IT industrialization as “the application of industrial approaches, methods and processes to IT, and in particular to IT management [...], in order to improve the effectiveness of internal IT organizations and external IT service providers.”[28] This definition’s exclusive focus on effectiveness should, however, be extended to include the perspective of efficiency, because an effective IT organization is not necessarily efficient and vice versa. Effectiveness and efficiency represent the two equally relevant dimensions of a successful IT organization over the long term.

Historically speaking, *HOLTSCHKE/HEIER/HUMMEL* group the evolution of IT “from individual entity into bulk commodity” into three phases: the “handmade IT” phase, the “manufactured IT” phase, and the “IT commodities” phase.[29] The first phase is characterized by the respective IT organization making its products available on request. This implies a low level of standardization plus greatly limited reusability of product components. In addition, the lack of flexibility of these “customer products” coupled with their low modularity leads to comparatively high deployment and maintenance costs for companies on the one hand and high margins for IT service providers on the other hand.

In the following phase, which coincided approximately with the start of the 1990s, the first industrialization principles began gaining a foothold in IT as well. For instance, IT production processes were separated out into individual steps and employees began to specialize. This rationalized “manufactured IT” produced or configured standard IT applications according to customers’ needs: “Characteristic are ready-made, preconfigured, scalable, repeatable and stable (i.e. reliable) solutions.”[30]

With his publication “Does IT Matter? – Information Technology and the Corrosion of Competitive Advantage”, *CARR* made a major contribution to the start of the third phase – “IT commodities” – in which he compares the development of IT with that of the steam engine, the railways or the telephone. He argues that over time IT loses its effect as a competitive differentiator: “History reveals that IT needs to become ordinary – needs to lose its strategic importance as a differentiator of companies – if it is to fulfill its potential.”[31] IT is becoming more and more of a commodity, i.e. “generally available mass produced goods with largely standardized features that can be virtually bought off the shelf.”[32]

26 *MEYERS LEXIKONVERLAG* (2007).

27 Cf. *HOLTSCHKE/HEIER/HUMMEL* (2009), p. 18.

28 *HOLTSCHKE/HEIER/HUMMEL* (2009), p. 18.

29 Cf. *HOLTSCHKE/HEIER/HUMMEL* (2009), p. 17 ff.

30 *HOLTSCHKE/HEIER/HUMMEL* (2009), p. 19.

31 *CARR* (2004), p. 11.

32 *HOLTSCHKE/HEIER/HUMMEL* (2009), p. 20.

If IT services have only a limited, if any, impact as a competitive differentiator, it would thus seem an obvious step to critically examine all areas of IT management services from a cost/benefit perspective – including application management. It therefore comes as no surprise to find that for many years the level of IT services provided inhouse has been steadily falling in companies in German-speaking countries. This is documented by a recent empirical study conducted by *DUMSLAFF/LEMPP*. For this study a total of 133 decision-makers in German, Austrian and Swiss companies took part in an online survey between October and November 2009. They answered questions on their IT organization, the level of IT industrialization, innovation, current IT trends and budgets for the coming years.[33] According to the study, internal production by IT organizations with respect to the operation and maintenance of applications had fallen 16.5% from the previous year.[34] In addition, respondents indicated they planned to reduce their inhouse production further in the area of application management over the coming two years to arrive at a target value of around 43% on average. 123 respondents said they were actively pushing to reduce the internal production proportion. From the point of view of the companies, key areas for action are the implementation of standards and the restructuring of partner and service provider management.[35] A more differentiated picture emerges when one examines the changes to the internal production percentages by industry. While internal production for application management in the financial services sector is still up around 56%, retailers report a figure of only 39%. The forecasts are also interesting: the financial services companies surveyed plan to reduce their inhouse production by 13% within the next five years, while those in the retail sector anticipated a fall of only 4% during the same period. Depending on the turnover of the companies surveyed, it appears that internal production is currently running at around 47% for application management, with this value being set to drop to 42% over the coming five years. This reduction is being driven primarily by companies having a turnover between EUR 500 million and EUR 5 billion (from 54% to 48%) and enterprises with a turnover of more than EUR 5 billion (from 36% to 28%).[36]

2.3 Drivers of the Industrialization of Application Management

There are essentially two groups of potential drivers of industrialization in application management: company-external drivers and company-internal drivers.

IT commoditization brackets the company-external drivers. Along with increasing globalization, above all it includes consumerization and a wider range of products.[37]

- As yet no generally valid definition of globalization has emerged. In his definition based on a scientific interdisciplinary approach, *KESSLER* describes globalization as follows: "Globalization refers to processes of increase and geographic expansion of cross-border social interaction."[38] This cross-border social interaction rests to a high degree on the maturity of IT, which has come a long way in the meantime. It enables human-machine

---

[33] Cf. *DUMSLAFF/LEMPP* (2010), p. 10 f.

[34] Cf. *DUMSLAFF/LEMPP* (2010), p. 20.

[35] Cf. *DUMSLAFF/LEMPP* (2010), p. 20.

[36] Cf. *DUMSLAFF/LEMPP* (2010), p. 21.

[37] Cf. *HOLTSCHKE/HEIER/HUMMEL* (2009), p. 21 f.

[38] *KESSLER* (2007), p. 8.

communication completely independently of location and time. At the same time, more and more IT service providers are entering the market for IT services because the knowledge barriers to providing IT services that previously existed are being increasingly eroded. There are also significant factor price differences between the various regions.[39] Companies are exploiting these factor price differences to procure their IT services externally, e. g. from India or China. As a consequence, the costs of providing IT services are falling, and a separation is emerging between the location at which the IT service is produced and the location at which it is consumed. Exploitation of these factor price advantages in other regions necessitates the greatest possible standardization of IT services production, because only in this way is it possible to ensure a constant IT service quality, which in turn may be crucial to the running of the IT service user's business. In general the global procurement of IT services for economic reasons has also revolutionized application management and contributed to the rise of application commoditization.

- Not least due to globalized IT service procurement, companies are taking a new look at their internal IT organizations and what they offer. Besides the fulfillment of customers' needs, IT service users are increasingly taking cost/benefit ratios into account. This trend is also reinforced by the fact that, as a result of standardization, IT service users can choose from a wide range of off-the-peg IT services, literally from all over the world. The internet creates the necessary transparency for this to function. Ultimately, IT industrialization is driving application management providers to focus much more strongly on solutions. They are increasingly being required to offer customers highly integrated, high-availability, transparent and inexpensive application management services – 24 hours a day around the globe.

- The attitude of end users towards IT is changing both in their work and in their private lives. As a result of the growing diffusion of internet technologies and the (mobile) terminals required to use them, demands on performance and usability are also rising. In addition, it should be possible to obtain IT services inexpensively. Today's private consumer may become tomorrow's employee and vice versa. As a consequence, a generally demanding attitude towards IT prevails which no longer stops at the company's door. For instance, end users expect the same level of user friendliness, the same breadth and depth of service, the same security and availability of services from their work applications as they are used to having on mini-apps on their mobile phones. The "consumerization" of IT is driving application management to become more effective and more efficient – while at the same time applications perceived to be effective and efficient by users are pushing up their expectations. In some cases, work applications that do not meet this level of expectation are not used by employees, or are not used by them in the way intended. New applications are sometimes not accepted by business end users. Ignoring the consumerization trend thus hinders the exploitation of effectiveness and efficiency potentials, which in turn jeopardizes the long-term future of the company.[40]

---

39 Cf. *HOLTSCHKE/HEIER/HUMMEL* (2009), p. 21.

40 Cf. for the entire paragraph *HOLTSCHKE/HEIER/HUMMEL* (2009), p. 23.

A company-internal driver for the increasing importance of application management is the desire of companies to "focus on IT tasks close to their core business".[41] The intention is to combine such IT services provided into billable services charged on a usage basis (utility principle). This is based on positive experiences from IT infrastructure which companies now wish to carry over to application management as well.[42] Moreover, as already mentioned above, the complexity of the IT application landscape has dramatically increased in many companies over the past decades. Applications which have already been in use for a long time and were designed for other IT architectures altogether, but which are still operable and still critical for the business, must be prepared for data transfer and data integration with new application solutions. In addition, it must be possible to use the applications across different companies and national borders (interoperability). Companies must also provide intensive support for application maintenance. IT suppliers are constantly improving their applications and, besides new functionality, also offer better security and stability. It is necessary to plan upgrades carefully, roll them out during operations, and keep them running. At the same time, end users must be trained to use the IT applications to ensure that no competitive disadvantage is suffered.

2.4 Effectiveness and Efficiency Potential of Industrialized Application Management

The strategic success factor of quality correlates to effectiveness, whereas the strategic success factor of costs is connected to efficiency. As a third strategic success factor, time is of a hybrid nature, i.e. it has an impact on both effectiveness and efficiency.[43]

Costs, quality and time are also the relevant success factors for effective and efficient – and consequently successful – application management. The global support concept of *SIEMENS IT SOLUTIONS AND SERVICES* (SIS) as an application management provider therefore also focuses on achieving simultaneous effectiveness and efficiency gains for the buyers of its application management services.[44] The background to this is the general move away from placing the primary focus on efficiency and costs in IT management towards simultaneously increasing both effectiveness and efficiency levels. For modern application management, this means that the balance of the strategic success factor triangle, comprising the cornerstones of costs, quality and time, has shifted considerably (see Figure 1).

---

41 *STRUMBERGER* (2009), cited according to *PREHL* (2009).

42 Cf. *PREHL* (2009).

43 Cf. *KEUPER* (2001), p. 11 ff., and the literature cited there.

44 Cf. *CLOER* (2010).

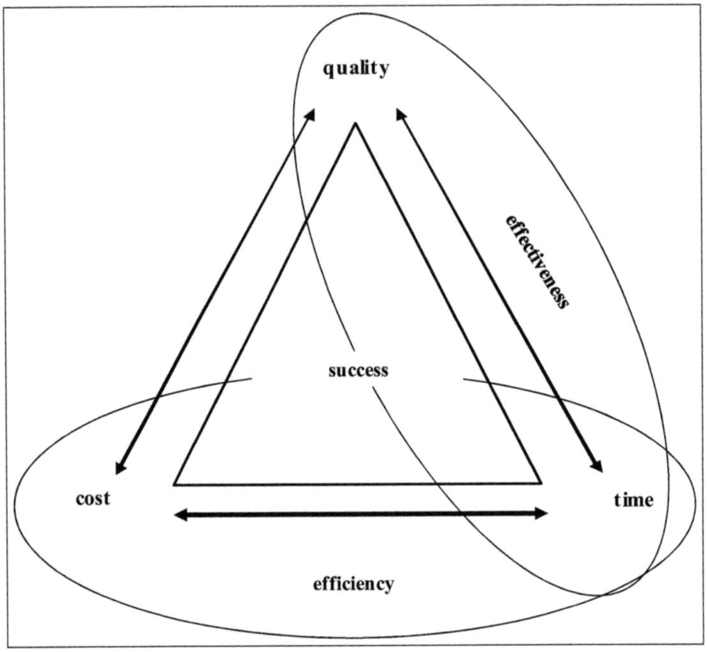

Figure 1: Triangle of strategic success factors quality, cost and time[45]

Empirically, this claim is supported by a recent study by *THE HACKETT GROUP* (see Figure 2). Among the group of top performers, in particular this study identified effectiveness gains, in terms of lower defect rates and greater responsiveness to business demands, as a result of outsourcing application management to an external provider. With respect to the efficiency aspect of costs, the top performers achieved savings primarily in relation to application maintenance. Finally, the success of application management among the top performers is also demonstrated by the hybrid strategic factor of time – in this case the completion of project tasks on time.

45 *KEUPER/HANS* (2003), p. 73.

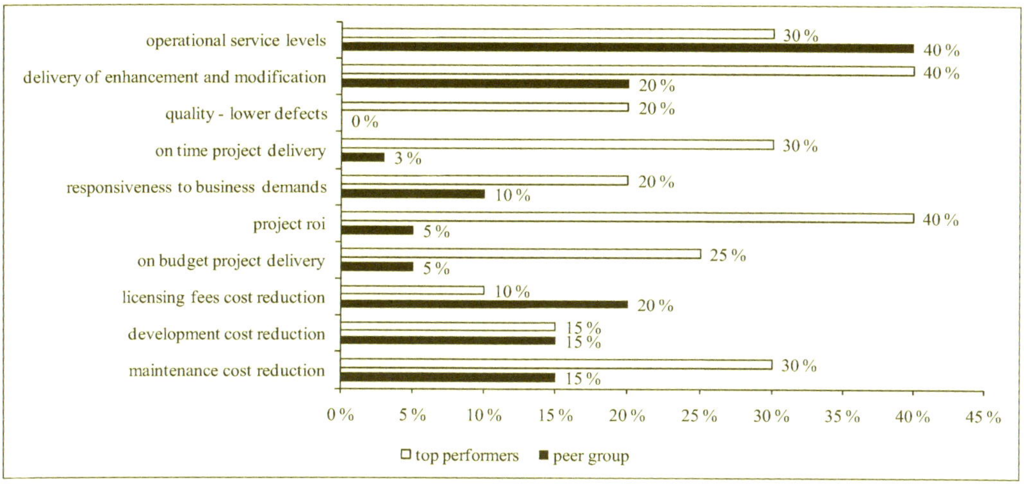

Figure 2: Application management outsourcing performance impact[46]

3 Reference Models for the Industrialization of Application Management

Reference models are used to map the key processes necessary for the provision of IT services in IT organizations, the activities and roles associated with the processes, the interdependencies between the processes, and the relationships to external entities.[47] This creates a baseline for future IT service delivery (reference).[48] In general reference models have the following features:[49]

- Universality, i.e. the reference model possesses a level of abstraction that enables it to be used for companies of different sizes, in different industries, etc.
- Completeness, i.e. the reference model contains all relevant processes, roles, interaction relationships, metrics, etc.

Unless reference models are used, there can be no process transparency for the purposes of IT management. This would make a "targeted, structured adaptation to changing conditions [...] and enterprise-wide benchmarking more difficult."[50] As a result of the internal IT organization evolving from a function-focused silo mentality into a cross-functional (internal) IT

---

46 *The Hackett Group* (2010).

47 Cf. *Zarnekow/Brenner/Pilgram* (2005), p. 53, *Krcmar* (2005), p. 107 ff., *Walter/Böhmann/Krcmar* (2007), p. 9 and *Röder/Schomann* (2010), p. 139.

48 In particular, this makes the technical/organizational interdependencies transparent, as a result of which the measures for standardization can be better planned, and implementation can be better controlled and directed.

49 Cf. *Karer* (2007), p. 28.

50 *Zarnekow/Brenner/Pilgram* (2005), p. 53.

service provider, a number of service-oriented reference models have become established. Figure 3 shows an overview of common reference models for IT (service) management.

Of particular relevance to industrialized application management are the IT Infrastructure Library (ITIL) and Application Services Library (ASL) reference models.

Reference Models (Frameworks) for IT Service Management	
ASL – Application Services Library	ISPL – Information Services Procurement Library
BDM – IT-enabled Business Development and Management Methodology	IT Management – the threefold IT Management model
BiOOlogic	IT Process Model
BiSL – Business Information Services Library	IT Service Capability Maturity Model
CMM – Capability Maturity Model	ITIL – IT Infrastructure Library
CobiT – Control Objectives for Information and related Technology	KPMG Maturity Model
EBIOS – Expression of Needs and Identification of Security Objectives	MIP – Managing the Information Provision
eSCM-SP v2 – eSourcing Capability Model for Service Providers	MOF – Microsoft Operations Framework
eTOM – the Enhanced Telecom Operations Map	OSI model
Generic Framework for Information Management	PERFORM
HP IT Service Management Reference Model	PRINCE2
IIM – Information Infrastructure Management	SDLC – System Development Life Cycle
IMM – IT Management Model	SIMA – Standard InterAccess Management Approach
IPW – Introducing Process-oriented Working Methods	TOGAF – The Open Group Architecture Framework
ISM – Integrated Service Management	UPF – the Unified Process Framework

Figure 3: Selected reference models for IT service management[51]

[51] *ITSM-PORTAL* (2006).

3.1 IT Infrastructure Library (ITIL)

ITIL has become established as the de-facto standard for service-oriented IT management. The history of this reference model dates back to the end of the 1980s. At that time the British government instructed the Central Computer and Telecommunications Agency (CCTA) – today the Office of Government Commerce (OCG) – to optimize public administration through the use of IT. ITIL was thus born.

ITIL is a collection of best practices concerned with the provision of cost-effective IT services of an adequate quality[52] by an IT organization to its customers.[53] These initially confusing and comparatively unstructured collection of best practices has in the meantime been extensively revised and adapted in line with the changed conditions. The third version of ITIL (ITIL V3), was condensed into five core publications:[54]

- *Service Strategy* contains approaches for the strategic design, development and deployment of IT service management in (IT) organizations. The Service Strategy volume thus contains principles, guidelines and processes that are also used in the other volumes. These aspects are supplemented by relevant IT service management topics such as financial management, portfolio management, organization development and risk management. In summary, the Service Strategy makes clear what the objectives of the IT organization are, how it is positioning itself with respect to its internal and external stakeholders, and especially with respect to competitors, as well as the measures used or potentially used to manage costs and risks.
- *Service Design* defines principles and procedures for implementing the strategic goals in the form of portfolio elements as services. In addition to the creation of new services, this also includes adapting and developing services already in use.
- *Service Transition* focuses on the planned deployment of new or adapted services. The primary focus is on minimizing failure risks and service outages. The main aspects covered by this volume are therefore program management, release management and risk management.
- *Service Operation* covers both reactive and proactive methods, instruments and tools for maintaining IT service provision. This volume thus addresses, inter alia, the safeguarding of stable IT service provision and the adjustment of service levels.
- *Continual Service Improvement* is concerned with the ongoing improvement of IT service management. In particular, this volume focuses on service design, service transition and service operation.

With respect to lifecycle-oriented application management, what is most significant is that ITIL V3 is based on a service lifecycle approach which explicitly postulates the alignment of IT and business objectives as guiding maxims for the IT organization, and which in particular takes cognizance of the latest (IT) compliance rules.

---

52 For the concept of quality in relation to IT services and ITIL Cf. *ITSMF* (2005), p. 15 ff.

53 Cf. *ITSMF* (2005), p. 37.

54 Cf. *ITSMF* (2008). A detailed description of the contents of ITIL V3 will not be given at this point. For an introduction, cf. *GRIMM* (2010), p. 83 ff.

ITIL essentially addresses three processes that are relevant to the industrialization of application management:[55]

➢ *The incident management process*: This process encompasses all the faults, queries and problems reported to the user help desk by end users. Incidents may however also be triggered by support staff at the application service provider or be generated by certain tools.

  ITIL can be used to help standardize incident resolution. To this end, *SIEMENS IT SOLUTIONS AND SERVICES* uses a standard process worldwide which is based on the experiences gathered by expert groups and which has been placed in a central repository for reference. Staff receive appropriate training in webinars and case studies are used to simulate real situations. When generated, incident resolution tickets are forwarded directly to the available experts in each case. This process is subject to continual service improvement.

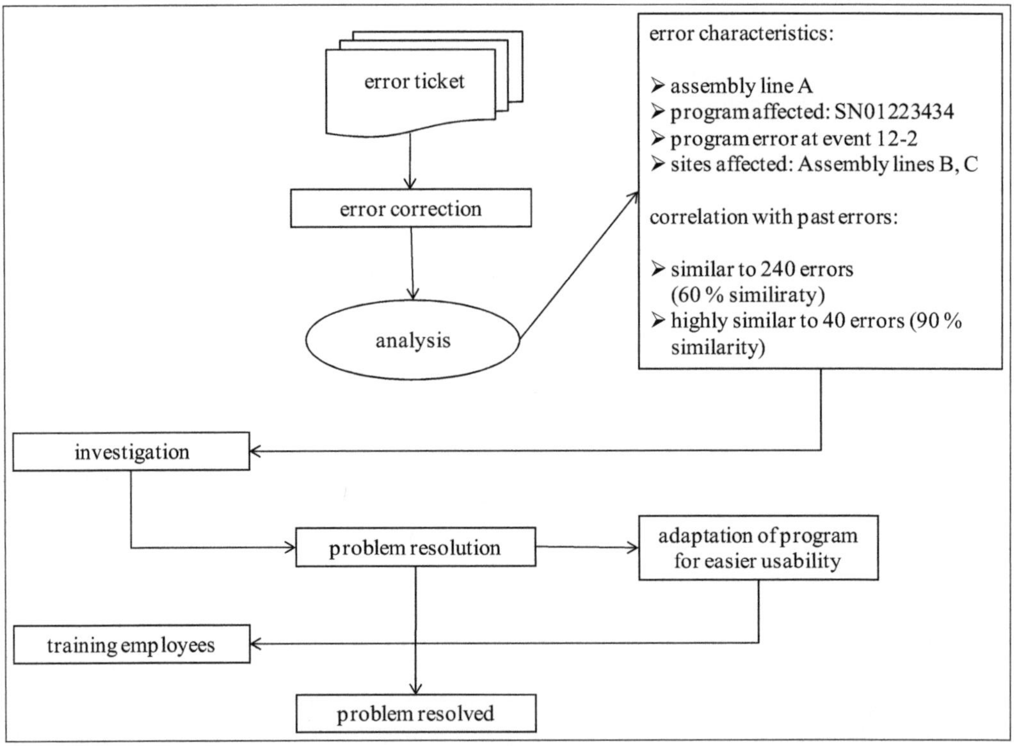

Figure 4: Example of ITIL-based standardization of an incident resolution process[56]

[55] For a detailed description cf. *SCHMIDT* (2009), p. 142.

[56] *SIEMENS IT SOLUTIONS AND SERVICES* (2010a).

- *Problem management process*: This process is used to avoid new problems, prevent repeated incidents, and minimize the impact of errors or incidents as far as possible.
- *Change management process*: This process is closely allied to the problem management process and focuses on solving problems by means of configuration changes, which in turn must be approved and implemented on the basis of change requests.

3.2 Application Services Library (ASL)

There is a link between the ITIL and ASL reference models inasmuch as ASL was developed for supporting applications on the basis of ITIL V2.[57] ASL can stand alongside ITIL as an independent reference model or can be thought of simply as a more detailed specification of ITIL for modern application support.[58]

ASL itself is freely available to companies and application service providers under a public domain license. ASL focuses on:[59]

- Support for business processes
- Providing a conceptual framework
- Best practices for practical implementation and greater alignment with business processes

With ASL, support is provided over the entire application lifecycle. ASL also contains a maturity model for determining the lifecycle phase of an application. In contrast to ITIL, ASL does not have an explicit problem management process, but rather considers this part of quality management.

ASL is divided into three levels: the strategic, the tactical and the operational level. These levels are closely linked to the internal and external company circumstances relevant to application management. ASL assigns Applications Cycle Management and Organization Cycle Management to the strategic level. The management processes are found on the tactical level in ASL. The operational level includes the Maintenance and Enhancement/Renovation components.[60]

One criticism that may be leveled is the relatively arbitrary assignment of components. For instance, from a business point of view it is not clear why the management processes should be assigned to the tactical level. In any case, the differentiation between operational, tactical and strategic management levels is somewhat contested among business management academics. Moreover, ASL remains a highly abstract model and must be adapted to suit the particular requirements in each case. It is important here to use clearly defined concepts from the outset in order to avoid subsequent misinterpretations and misunderstandings. However, this criticism may also be countered by the observation that ITIL was also initially formulated

57 Cf. *Schmidt* (2009), p. 142.

58 Cf. *Schmidt* (2009), p. 142.

59 *Schmidt* (2009), p. 143.

60 The individual components are not discussed in detail here. For an introduction cf. *Schmidt* (2009), p. 145.

with a high level of abstraction and specifics were gradually added over time – not least as a result of the steadily rising experience curve of IT managers in the companies and at the IT service providers.

Currently the greatest merit of ASL is that it provides a way of clearly structuring the processes relevant to effective and modern application management, and consequently provides both IT organizations and external application service providers with starting points for success-oriented mapping of the company's organizational and operational structure.

Figure 5 shows the three ASL levels and the assignment of the respective level components.

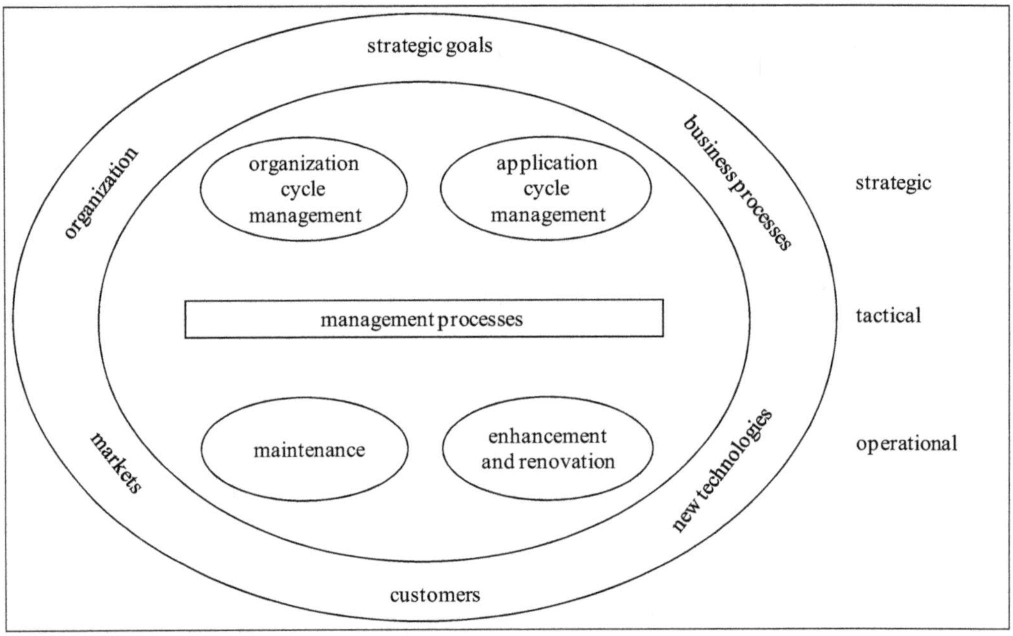

Figure 5: Application Services Library[61]

[61] SCHMIDT (2009), p. 144.

4 Application Management Service Roadmap – Shifting from Application Management 1.0 to Application Management 2.0

The observance and incorporation of best practices from the above reference models facilitates the transformation of traditional application support (Application Management 1.0) into a best-fit environment (Application Management 2.0). Figure 6 shows the Application Management Service Roadmap and the associated IT services that enable this transformation.

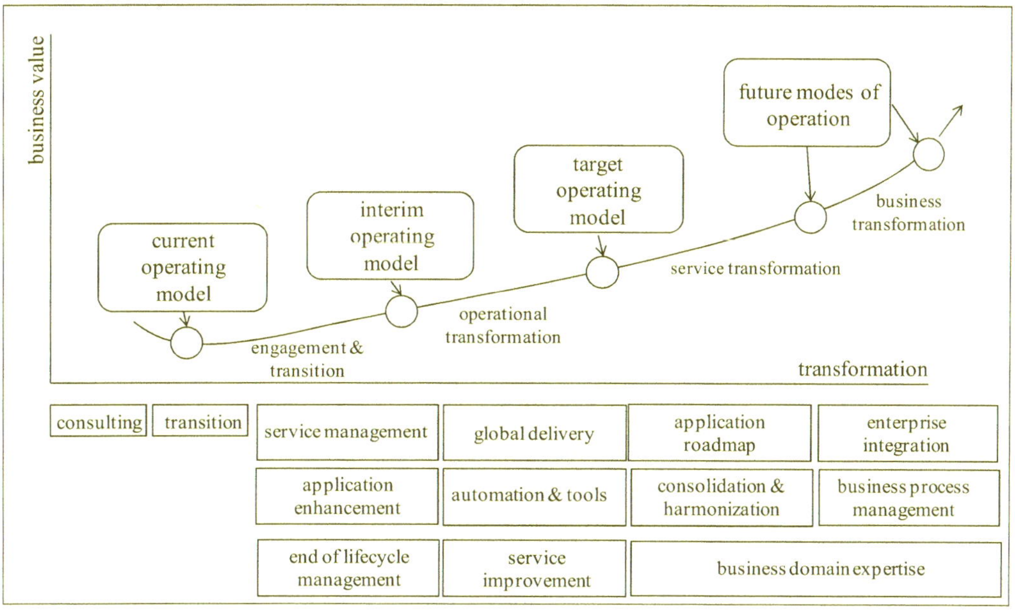

Figure 6: Application Management Service Roadmap[62]

The benefits for companies of using the roadmap outlined in Figure 6 when modernizing are manifold. The following effectiveness and efficiency potentials are created depending on the particular transformation phase:

- Current Operating Model
  - Transparent Baseline: Value Comparison Assessment establishes transparency of baseline cost, saving potential, and business-aligned transformational priorities.
  - Demonstrable Return on Investment: Business case demonstrates return on investment in outsourcing application management to third party providers, such as Siemens IT Solutions and Services.
  - Low-Risk Transition: Rapid, low-cost, low-risk transfer of service delivery from inhouse or incumbent outsource provider (e. g. Siemens IT Solutions and Services).

---

62 *Siemens IT Solutions and Services* (2010b).

- Interim Operating Model
  - Cost Efficiency and Commercial Framework: Immediate reduction in cost of service delivery and cost predictability, enhanced commercial transparency
  - Service Excellence: High-quality core services realized through best-practice processes and business-aligned SLAs, continual service improvement
  - Partnership: Enhanced partnership-based approach to relationship management and governance to drive improvement and transformation.
- Target Operating Model:
  - Economies of Scale: Transparent year-on-year cost reductions and realized through ongoing productivity and efficiency measures at industrialized delivery centers.
  - Improved User Experience: Service delivery automation and tools to improve user experience through self-service and real-time service performance monitoring.
  - Lean Six Sigma: Leverage Lean Six Sigma to drive service delivery and customer business process improvements.
- Future Modes of Operation
  - Business-driven Technology Transformation: Enhancement, consolidation, and rationalization of your application portfolio to minimize cost, simplify use, avoid obsolescence and improve agility.
  - Business Performance and Competitive Edge: Continual improvement and innovation program leverages customers' industry know-how and investment in relevant technology innovation.
  - SOA and Business Process Excellence: Core business processes optimized through Lean Six Sigma, automated through Service-Oriented Architecture (SOA) work-flows.

The following diagram shows the benefits that may be gained by companies who transfer their application management to an external application service provider. In addition, the exploitation of the individual potential benefits is shown using the example of Siemens IT Solutions and Services (see Figure 7).

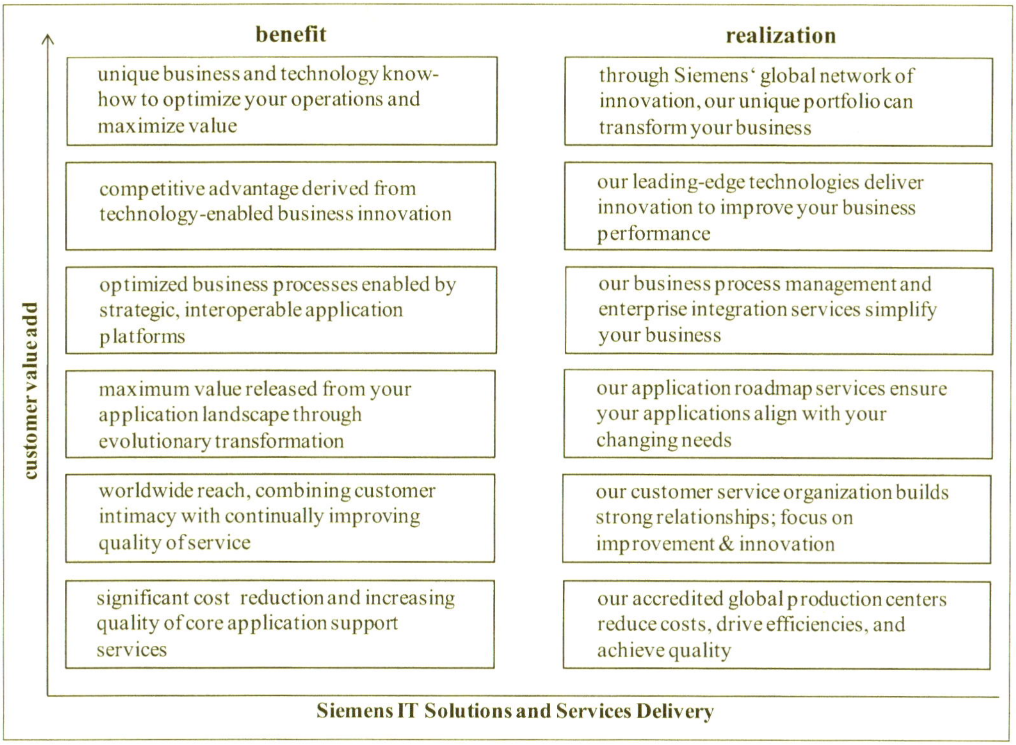

Figure 7: *Benefits of application management delivery by Siemens IT Solutions and Services and its realization*[63]

5 Success factors for the Transition to Application Management 2.0

As already mentioned, alongside efficiency, effectiveness is the second relevant success dimension if the transformation from Application Management 1.0 to Application Management 2.0 is to succeed. Since effectiveness equates to quality as a strategic success factor, it is particularly the quality-influencing factors that must be identified and managed during the transformation. Previous experience of *Siemens IT Solutions and Services* in the area of application management has shown that the following factors in particular are decisive for the customer's quality perception, and consequently for the success of Application Management 2.0:

---

63 *Siemens IT Solutions and Services* (2010a).

- *Use of a globally standardized toolset*: The application service provider must use a highly integrated toolset which is standardized worldwide. First and foremost this includes automation tools. For instance, the use of a standardized ticketing tool enables the average resolution time for a support request to be cut from six hours to less than three hours. It also enables a significant lowering of response times. The use of an estimation tool for the ex ante analysis of application extensions also offers enormous effectiveness potential because it avoids time-consuming misspecifications while at the same time ensuring that the customer receives the service originally expected. The implementation of a central knowledge database containing, for example, standard resolution procedures for regularly recurring inquiries is also highly relevant. The added value for the end customer is above all clear when the knowledge assets are linked to the ticketing tool, which in turn significantly cuts customer inquiry resolution times.

  The toolset should also include a performance management tool such as the Verint tool from *Siemens IT Solutions and Services*. This makes it possible to automatically measure how long it takes to resolve a problem. It shows

  - whether a solution to the problem was found without using the knowledge database,
  - how often existing solution suggestions were used to resolve problems,
  - which knowledge assets were used by support staff in the customer service organization to resolve the problem,
  - which knowledge assets were used which did not have anything to do with the eventual problem resolution,
  - how high the first solution rate is, and
  - how often a ticket was opened and closed without resolving a problem, only to be subsequently opened again.

- *Expertise*: The application service provider should possess unique business know-how across a variety of industries. In addition it should have a detailed understanding of the heterogeneity of the business and technical requirements of its customers. This expertise is demonstrated, inter alia, by an extensive track record with blue-chip clients worldwide. The application service provider should also be familiar with the reference models, instruments, tools and methods for standardizing, harmonizing and consolidating heterogeneous IT landscapes. This includes, for example, in-depth knowledge of modular enterprise resource planning systems.

- *Standardized employee training worldwide*: The quality driver expertise is also closely linked to the training of staff. The same level of training, based on standardized education and training standards, ensures that customers will receive the same quality they are used to, around the clock everywhere in the world.

- *Know-how transfer*: The application service provider should have suitable methods, instruments and tools at its disposal in order firstly to learn from the experiences gained, and secondly to derive process improvements from these experiences. It must then be possible to transfer these process improvements across to the customer's organization in a suitable way.

- *Global reach, yet regional proximity*: The quality perception of the application service provider's end customers is also influenced by the cultural fit between the end customer and the application service provider's employees.[64] A study by *Accenture* in 2008 showed that 69% of outsourcing agreements were unable to achieve initially anticipated effectiveness and efficiency potentials because of a cultural incompatibility between the vendor and client.[65] *Vantage Partners* identified "culture" as posing the greatest challenge for outsourcing deals (N = 378).[66] It is therefore vitally important for the application management provider to also have employees locally, i.e. specifically implementing a single point of customer contact for all communications.[67] The customer must not get the impression of being served from "somewhere far away". This contact person should also have the necessary industry know-how (see also quality driver expertise) and the ability to make changes to the information flow without having to contact the customer, other countries or the regional support management.[68] The actual production of the services takes place in global production centers, to enable better economies of scale for example.

- *Contactability*: Customers must be able to contact the application service provider 24/7, 365 days of the year. The provider must be able to answer inquiries competently and resolve problems effectively and efficiently.

- *Accreditation*: The application service provider should possess the following accreditations: ISO 2000-1 IT Service Management, ISO 27001 Information Security, ISO 9001:2000 Quality Management and SEI CMMI Level 3–5.

- *Change management in the customer's organization*: Previous project experience has shown that in the course of application management outsourcing, the necessary investment in change management measures cannot be underestimated.[69] By outsourcing IT services previously provided inhouse, e. g. application extensions, to external third parties, jobs in the customer organization are lost and entire careers change. The technophile programmer who was previously respected for his COBOL know-how must now become an application manager at the interface between the customer and the provider organization. He changes from being a problem solver into an internal advisor or a provider management or release management coordinator. To cope with this changed role, the Application Manager 1.0 himself requires help to become Application Manager 2.0. In future Application Manager 2.0 will be measured on his ability to enable the customer organization to cooperate effectively and efficiently with the application service provider. Ideally, as part of a holistic service approach the application service provider will have appropriate training concepts in place, will hold workshops and offer focused coaching.

---

64 Cf. *Weschke* (2008) and *Kvedaraviciene/Boguslauska* (2010).

65 Cf. *Accenture* (2008).

66 Cf. *Ertel/Enlow/Bubman* (2009).

67 *Degenhardt/Godard/Rauch* (2010), p. 9.

68 Cf. *Degenhardt/Godard/Rauch* (2010), p. 9.

69 Cf. *Degenhardt/Godard/Rauch* (2010), p. 12.

In our experience, it is well worth setting up a Change Advisory Board (CAB). Representatives of the application service provider should also sit on the CAB, on the one hand to support the necessary communication measures, and if necessary bring in experience from other projects, but above all to facilitate the adaptation of the change management framework to the transition and transformation progress.[70]

Finally, it should be noted that the change management process should already form part of the contract negotiations. This will enable the expectations of both parties to be defined from the outset, and above all will avoid ineffective communication both internally and externally.

6 Summary

This article has shown that IT industrialization is proceeding apace. Like the industrial revolution, it is changing the lives of people, and in turn also the way in which value added is created in companies. Without the effective and efficient provision of IT services to support core competencies, however, in many companies it would not be possible to create added value at all. Of crucial importance here is the control of the problem resolution process for IT applications which is directed to increasing both effectiveness and efficiency. The problems and challenges for the CIO in relation to application management are manifold. Similarly there are numerous solution options that include both organizational and operational structure components. Both of these are addressed by reference models, with ITIL and ASL in particular focusing on problems in the context of application management. It was shown how effectiveness and efficiency potentials can be exploited on the basis of application management for enterprises "industrialized" on the basis of ITIL and ASL. Particular attention was paid here to the organizational variant of transferring application management in the narrower sense to an external third-party provider in the form of an outsourcing solution. Against this backdrop, the standardized procedure model of *SIEMENS IT SOLUTIONS AND SERVICES* was outlined for shaping the evolution from Application Management 1.0 to Application Management 2.0. In addition, we identified the potential benefits associated with such a procedure for companies who outsource their application management to *SIEMENS IT SOLUTIONS AND SERVICES*, as well as the success factors for achieving application management excellence. It remains to note that IT industrialization in general and industrialization of application management in particular are making great strides forward. The further development of the reference models by academics and practitioners must however keep pace with this development. There is still much to be done by everyone!

---

70 Cf. *DEGENHARDT/GODARD/RAUCH* (2010), p. 12.

References

ACCENTURE (2009): Driving high performance outsourcing. Best practices from the Masters, online:http://www.accenture.com/NR/rdonlyres/C625415D-5E2B-4EDE-9B65-77D635 365211/ 0/driving_outsourcing.pdf, publication date: not stated, retrieved: 28.08.2010.

BOGASCHEWSKY, R./ROLLBERG, R. (1998): Prozessorientiertes Management, Berlin/Heidelberg 1998.

BRENNER, W./WITTE, C. (2007): Erfolgsrezepte für CIOs, München/Wien 2007.

CARR, N. G. (2004): Does IT Matter? – Information Technology and the Corrosion of Competitive Advantage, Boston 2004.

COHEN, L./YOUNG, A. (2006): Multisourcing – Moving beyond outsourcing to achieve growth and agility, Boston 2006.

CLOER, T. (2010): Siemens beauftragt SIS mit Application Management, online: http:// www.computerwoche.de/management/it-services/2350574/, publication date: 03.08.2010, retrieved: 24.08.2010.

DANOWSKI, M. (2008): Foreword in: *HOLTSCHKE, B./HEIER, H./HUMMEL, T.*, Quo vadis CIO?, Berlin/Heidelberg 2008, pp. v–vii.

DEGENHARDT, A./GODARD, A./RAUCH, F. P. (2010): Top 10 Pitfalls of Application Management Services, Whitepaper, online: http://www.it-solutions. siemens.com/b2b/ it/en/global/Documents/Publications/white-paper-Pitfalls_PDF_e.pdf, publication date: 08/2010, retrieved: 28.08.2010.

DRUCKER, P. F. (1993): Management: Tasks, Responsibilities, Practices, London et al. 1993.

DUMSLAFF, U./LEMPP, P. (2010): Studie IT-Trends 2010 – Die IT wird erwachsen, online: http://www.ch.capgemini.com/m/ch/tl/IT-Trends_2010. pdf, publication date: 2010, retrieved: 24.08.2010.

ERTEL, D./ENLOW, S./BUBMAN, J. (2010): Managing Offshoring Relationships – Governance in Global Deals, online: http://www.vantagepartners.com/ResearchAndPublicationsviewpub lications.aspx?id=2638, publication date: 2010, retrieved: 28.08.2010.

VON GLAHN, C./KEUPER, F. (2008): Shared-IT-Services im Kontinuum der Eigen- und Fremderstellung, in: *KEUPER, F./OECKING, C.* (Eds.), Corporate Shared Services – Bereitstellung von Dienstleistungen im Konzern, 2nd edition, Wiesbaden 2008, pp. 3–26.

VON GLAHN, C./OECKING, C. (2007): Transition und Transformation von Shared-IT-Services, in: *KEUPER, F./OECKING, C.* (Eds.), Corporate Shared Services – Bereitstellung von Dienstleistungen im Konzern, 2nd edition, Wiesbaden 2008, pp. 27–51.

GRIMM, R. (2010): Der operative IT-Strategie-Ansatz, in: *KEUPER, F./SCHOMANN, M./ZIMMERMANN, K.* (Eds.), Innovatives IT-Management – Management von IT und IT-gestütztes Management, 2nd edition, Wiesbaden 2010, pp. 71–97.

HERING, T. (1995): Investitionstheorie aus der Sicht des Zinses, Wiesbaden 1995.

HARTERT, D. (2000): Informationsmanagement im Electronic Business am Beispiel der Bertelsmann AG, in: *WEIBER, R.* (Eds.), Handbuch Electronic Business, Wiesbaden 2000, pp. 643–654.

HOLTSCHKE, B./HEIER, H./HUMMEL, T. (2008): Quo vadis CIO?, Berlin/Heidelberg 2008.

ITSMF (2005): IT Service Management basierend auf ITIL, 2005.

ITSMF (2008): ITIL, online: http://www.itsmf.de/itsm_itil.html, publication date: not stated, retrieved: 13.03.2008.

KAISER, S. (2005): Application Management in Deutschland, online: https:// www.pac-online.com/backoffice/servlet/fr.pac.page.download.document.DocumentView?docId=WhitePaper_AM_DE_Oct_05&dtyId=white_paper&pathFile=%2Fhome%2Fpac%2FLenya%2Fbuild%2Flenya%2Fwebapp&fileName=WhitePaper_AM_DE_Oct_05.pdf&mth=open, publication date: 2005, retrieved: 24.08.2010.

KARER, A. (2007): Optimale Prozessorganisation im IT-Management – Ein Prozessreferenzmodell für die Praxis, Berlin 2007.

KEUPER, F. (1999): Fuzzy-PPS-Systeme – Einsatzmöglichkeiten und Erfolgspotentiale der Theorie unscharfer Mengen, Wiesbaden 1999.

KEUPER, F. (2001): Strategisches Management, München/Wien 2001.

KEUPER, F. (2004): Kybernetische Simultaneitätsstrategie – Systemtheoretisch-kybernetische Navigation im Effektivitäts-Effizienz-Dilemma, Berlin 2004.

KEUPER, F. (2005): Gestaltung der Unternehmenskomplexität im Lichte von *ASHBY* und *LUHMANN*, in: ZP – Zeitschrift für Planung und Unternehmenssteuerung, Vol. 16 (2005), pp. 211–237.

KEUPER, F./HANS, R. (2003): Multimedia-Management – Strategien und Konzepte für Zeitungs- und Zeitschriftenverlage im digitalen Informationszeitalter, Wiesbaden 2003.

KEUPER, F./OECKING, C. (2008): Foreword in: *KEUPER, F./OECKING, C.* (Eds.), Corporate Shared Services – Bereitstellung von Dienstleistungen im Konzern, 2nd edition, Wiesbaden 2008, pp. XI–XVIII.

KEUPER, F./OECKING, C. (2008): Shared-Service-Center – The First and the Next Generation, in: *KEUPER, F./OECKING, C.* (Eds.), Corporate Shared Services – Bereitstellung von Dienstleistungen im Konzern, 2nd edition, Wiesbaden 2008, pp. 475–502.

KESSLER, J. (2007): Globalisierung oder Integration. Korrespondenzprobleme bei der empirischen Erfassung von Globalisierungsprozessen, TranState Working Papers, No. 53, Bremen 2007.

KRCMAR, H. (2005): Informationsmanagement, Berlin/Heidelberg 2005.

KVEDARAVICIENE, G./BOGUSLAUSKAS, V. (2010): Underestimated Importance of Cultural Differences in Outsourcing Arrangements, in: Inzinerine Ekonomika-Engineering Economics, Vol. 21 (2010), No. 2, pp. 187–196.

MÄNNEL, W. (1981): Die Wahl zwischen Eigenfertigung und Fremdbezug, 2nd edition, Stuttgart 1981.

MARGGI, R. (2002): Application Operation – Definition, Prozesse, Organisation und Erfolgsfaktoren, Intake 2002.

Meyers Lexikonverlag (2007): Industrialisierung, in: *Bibliographisches Institut & F. A. Brockhaus AG* (Eds.), online: http://lexikon.meyers.de/ index.php?title=Industrialisierung &oldid=157563, publication date: 27.02.2007, retrieved: 20.02.2008.

Pietsch, T. (2010): Der CIO 2.0 – Schlüsselfigur für das Enterprise 2.0, in: *Keuper, F./Hamidian, K./Verwaayen, E./Kalinowski, T.* (Eds.), transform IT, pp. 377–397.

Prehl, S. (2009): MLP übergibt Application-Management an HP, online: http://www.Computerwoche.de/management/it-services/1903616/, publication date: 18.08.2009, retrieved: 24.08.2010.

Pütter, C. (2010): Kein Durchblick in der IT-Infrastruktur, online: http://www.cio.de/ strategien/2238635/index.html, publication date: 27.07.2010, retrieved: 18.08.2010.

Röder, S./Schomann, M. (2010): Chancen und Grenzen der Industrialisierung von IT-Services, in: *Keuper, F./Schomann, M./Zimmermann, K.* (Eds.), Innovatives IT-Management – Management von IT und IT-gestütztes Management, 2nd edition, Wiesbaden 2010, pp. 125–150.

Schmidt, B. (2009): Wettbewerbsvorteile im SAP-Outsourcing durch Wissensmanagement – Methoden zur effizienten Gestaltung des Übergangs ins Application Management, Berlin 2009.

Siemens IT Solutions and Services (2010a): IT Industrialization and beyond – How we work together, Part IV, München 2010.

Siemens IT Solutions and Services (2010b): Application Management by Siemens IT Solutions and Services, München 2010.

The Hackett Group (2010): Application Management Outsourcing Performance Impact, online: http://www.thehackettgroup.com/studies/appout/, publication date: 2010, retrieved: 24.08.2010.

Ulrich, H. (1995): Führungsphilosophie und Leitbilder, in: *Kieser, A./Reber, G./Wunderer, R.* (Eds.), Handwörterbuch der Führung, 2nd edition, Stuttgart 1995, pp. 798–808.

Walter, S. M./Böhmann, T./Krcmar, H. (2007): Industrialisierung der IT – Grundlagen, Merkmale und Ausprägungen eines Trends, in: *Fröschle, H.-P./Strahringer, S.* (Eds.), IT-Industrialisierung, HMD – Praxis der Wirtschaftsinformatik, Vol. 44 (2007), No. 256, pp. 6–16.

Weschke, K. (2008): Kulturelle Passung als Erfolgsfaktor im Kontext von HR Shared Services, Diplomarbeit, Universität Mannheim 2008.

WWKI (1994): Profil der Wirtschaftsinformatik, Ausführungen der Wissenschaftlichen Kommission der Wirtschaftsinformatik, in: Wirtschaftsinformatik, Vol. 36 (1994), No. 1, pp. 80–81.

Zarnekow, R./Brenner, W./Pilgram, U. (2005): Integriertes Informationsmanagement – Strategien und Lösungen für das Management von IT-Dienstleistungen, Berlin/Heidelberg 2005.

Cloud Computing – Outsourcing 2.0 or a new Business Model for IT Provisioning?

Markus Böhm, Stefanie Leimeister, Christoph Riedl and *Helmut Krcmar* [1]

Technische Universität München

[1] The authors gratefully acknowledge the financial support for this research from Siemens IT Solutions & Services in the context of the Center for Knowledge Interchange at Technische Universität München (TUM), Germany. This research is part of the SIS-TUM competence center "IT Value Innovations for Industry Challenges". The responsibility for the content of this publication lies with the authors.

1 Introduction

The term cloud computing is sometimes used to refer to a new paradigm – some authors even speak of a new technology – that flexibly offers IT resources and services over the Internet. Gartner market research sees cloud computing as a so-called “emerging technology”[2] on its way to the hype. When looking at the number of searches for the word pair “cloud computing” undertaken with the Google search engine one can get an imagination of the high interest on the topic. Even terms like “outsourcing”, “Software-as-a-Service (SaaS)” or “grid computing” have already been overtaken[3].

Cloud computing can be seen as an innovation in different ways. From a technological perspective it is an advancement of computing, which’s history can be traced back to the construction of the calculating machine in the early 17th century[4]. This development continued with the invention of the analytical engine (1837), the logical engine (1885) and the tabulating machine (1890)[5]. The actual history of modern computing began with the invention of the first computers (Z3 in 1941 and ENIAC in 1945)[6]. Since then advancements emerged at a good pace. The sixties and seventies were the ages of mainframe computing. Central computing resources were harnessed through terminals that provided just the input and output devices to interact with the computer. With the development of the first microprocessor (1969) hobbyists began to construct the first home computers, before mail-order kits such as the Altair 8800 were sold in 1975. Other computer manufacturers like Apple, Atari or Commodore entered the market for computer home users, before IBM introduced its personal computer (PC) in 1981[7]. Since then the development paced up, the diffusion of PCs increased significantly and an increasing miniaturization lead to the development of laptop computers and mobile devices.

Another important technology, which paved the way for cloud computing was the development of the ARPAnet (1969), a fail-proof communications network which became today’s Internet[8]. Soon, services like e-mail or the world wide web, a hypertext based information management system, gained popularity. Technologies like Java, Ajax, WebServices and many more supported the development of rich, interactive websites. Eventually whole applications could be deployed over the Internet, which was around the year 2000 referred to as Software-as-a-Service[9]. In analogy to the provision of software via the web, computing resources could also be accessed via the Internet. Especially for scientific purposes grid computing got established in the early 1990ies[10]. When looking at this brief history of computing, one can easily see the different streams from local calculating machines, to central mainframes, via personal computers and handheld devices to the new quasi centralization trend that can be seen in cloud computing.

2 Cf. *Fenn* et al. (2008).

3 Cf. *Google* (2009).

4 Cf. *Freytag-Löringhoff/Seck* (2002).

5 Cf. *Babbage* (1864) and *Burack* (1949).

6 Cf. *Goldstine/Goldstine* (1946), *Rojas* (1997).

7 Cf. *Freiberger/Swaine* (2000), p. 325 et seqq.

8 Cf. *Freiberger/Swaine* (2000), p. 206 et seqq.

9 Cf. *Bennett* et al. (2000) and *Finch* (2006).

10 Cf. *Foster/Kesselman* (2003).

Yet a different point of view is to look at cloud computing from an IT provisioning perspective. In this sense cloud computing has the potential to revolutionize the mode of computing resource and application deployment, breaking up traditional value chains and making room for new business models. Many providers like Amazon, Google, IBM, Microsoft, Salesforce or Sun positioned themselves as platform and infrastructure providers in the cloud computing market. Beside them there emerge more and more providers, who build their own applications or consulting services upon infrastructure services offered by other market players.

Our contribution shall focus on the IT provisioning perspective of cloud computing. It will start with a literature review on current definitions of cloud computing and a conceptual framework of different service layers. It will further examine the evolution from outsourcing to cloud computing as a new IT deployment paradigm. Hereby it highlights the effects on the outsourcing value chain, summarizes market actors and their roles within a new cloud computing value network, and finally discusses potential business models for IT service providers.

2 The Cloud Computing Concept: Definition of a new Phenomenon

Due to the current fashion, the term cloud computing is often used for advertising purposes in order to revamp existing offerings with a new wrap. Larry Ellison's (CEO of Oracle) statement at the Analysts' Conference in September 2007 provides a felicitous example: *"We've redefined cloud computing to include everything that we already do. I can't think of anything that isn't cloud computing with all of these announcements. The computer industry is the only industry that is more fashion-driven than women's fashion"*[11]. In the following chapter we try to clarify the term to provide a common understanding.

2.1 State of the Art

To date there are few scientific contributions which strive to develop an accurate definition of the cloud computing phenomenon. Youseff et al. were among the first who tried to provide a comprehensive understanding of cloud computing and all its relevant components. They regard cloud computing as a "*collection of many old and few new concepts in several research fields like Service-Oriented Architectures (SOA), distributed and grid computing as well as Virtualization*"[12]. According to Youseff et al. "*cloud computing can be considered a new computing paradigm that allows users to temporary utilize computing infrastructure over the network, supplied as a service by the cloud-provider at possibly one or more levels of abstraction*"[13]. When speaking about levels of abstraction, the authors refer to their proposed cloud computing ontology which will be described in Chapter 2.3 of this contribution.

---

11 *FOWLER/WORTHEN* (2009), p. 2.

12 *YOUSEFF* et al. (2008), p. 1.

13 *YOUSEFF* et al. (2008), p. 1.

According to Armbrust et al. "*Cloud Computing refers to both the applications delivered as services over the Internet and the hardware and systems software in the datacenters that provide those services. The services themselves have long been referred to as Software as a Service (SaaS). The datacenter hardware and software is what we will call a Cloud. When a Cloud is made available in a pay-as-you-go manner to the general public, we call it a Public Cloud; the service being sold is Utility Computing. We use the term Private Cloud to refer to internal datacenters of a business or other organization, not made available to the general public. Thus, Cloud Computing is the sum of SaaS and Utility Computing, but does not include Private Clouds*"[14]. In this way the authors as well understand cloud computing as a collective term, covering preexisting computing concepts such as SaaS and utility computing. Armbrust et al. especially perceive the following aspects as new: (1) the illusion of infinite computing capacity available on demand, (2) the elimination of up-front commitment to resources on the side of the cloud user, and (3) the usage-bound pricing for computing resources on a short-term basis[15].

Being grid computing scholars, Buyya et al. postulate a more technical focused approach, regarding cloud computing as a kind of parallel and distributed system, consisting of a collection of virtualized computers. This system provides resources dynamically, whereas Service Level Agreements (SLA) are negotiated between the service provider and the customer.[16] In an attempt to provide a generally accepted definition, Vaquero et al. have derived similarities, based on Geelan's collection of expert opinions.[17] They claim that "*clouds are a large pool of easily usable and accessible virtualized resources (such as hardware, development platforms and/or services). These resources can be dynamically reconfigured to adjust to a variable load (scale), allowing also for an optimum resource utilization. This pool of resources is typically exploited by a pay-per-use model in which guarantees are offered by the Infrastructure Provider by means of customized SLAs*"[18].

The majority of definitions however originate from cloud computing service providers, consulting firms and market research companies. The market research company IDC for example defines cloud computing very general as "*an emerging IT development, deployment and delivery model, enabling real-time delivery of products, services and solutions over the Internet*"[19]. In that sense, cloud computing is the technical basis for cloud services, offering consumer and business solutions that are consumed in real-time over the Internet. The technological foundation of cloud computing includes infrastructure, system software, application development and deployment software, system and application management software as well as IP-based network services. IDC also mentions usage-bound pricing as a core characteristic[20]. Another example of a market research company's declaration is Gartner's definition of cloud computing as "*a style of computing where massively scalable IT-enabled capabilities are delivered 'as a service' to external customers using Internet technologies*"[21].

---

14 *ARMBRUST* et al. (2009), p. 4.

15 *ARMBRUST* et al. (2009), p. 4.

16 Cf. *BUYYA* et al. (2008), p. 2.

17 Cf. *GEELAN* (2009).

18 *VAQUERO* et al. (2009), p. 51.

19 *GENS* (2008).

20 Cf. *GENS* (2008).

21 *PLUMMER* et al. (2008), p. 3.

Autor[22]	**Service**	**Hardware**	**Software**	**Data**	**(Development) Platform**	**Pay-Per-Use**	**off-premise (public)**	**Scalability**	**No Upfront Commitment**	**Virtualization**	**SLA**	**Deterministic Performance**	**Internet/network**	**Automation**
ARMBRUST et al. [1]	x	x	x			x	x	x	x				x	
BREITER/BEHRENDT [2]	x	x				x		x		x				x
BRISCOE/MARINOS [3]	x	x	x					x		x			x	
BUYYA [4]		x						x		x	x			
FOSTER et al. [5]	x	x	x		x			x		x			x	
GARTNER [6]	x	x	x					x					x	
GROSSMAN/GU [7]	x	x		x				x					x	
GRUMAN/KNORR [8]	x	x	x		x								x	
IDC [9]	x	x				x		x					x	
KIM [10]	x	x	x	x		x		x	x				x	
MCFREDRIES [11]	x	x	x	x						x				
NURMI et al. [12]	x	x	x					x				x		
VAQUERO et al. [13]	x	x			x	x		x		x	x			
VYKOUKAL et al. [14]	x	x				x		x					x	
WANG et al. [15]	x	x	x	x										
WEISS [16]	x	x	x					x						
YOUSEFF et al. [17]	x	x			x	x		x		x	x			
Nominations	**16**	**17**	**10**	**4**	**4**	**7**	**1**	**14**	**2**	**7**	**3**	**1**	**9**	**1**

Table 1: *A comparison of various cloud computing definitions*

22 [1] *ARMBRUST* et al. (2009) [2] *BREITER/BEHRENDT* (2008) [3] *BRISCOE/MARINOS* (2009) [4] *BUYYA* et al. (2008) [5] *FOSTER,* et al. (2008) [6] *PLUMMER* et al. (2008) [7] *GROSSMAN/GU* (2009) [8] *GRUMAN/KNORR* (2008) [9] *GENS* (2008) [10] *KIM* (2009) [11] *MCFREDRIES* (2008) [12] *NURMI* et al. (2008) [13] *VAQUERO,* et al. (2009) [14] *VYKOUKAL* et al. (2009) [15] *WANG* et al. (2008)[16] *WEISS* (2007) [17] *YOUSEFF* et al. (2008).

2.2 A Definition of Cloud Computing

Table 1 summarizes key characteristics of cloud computing as they are understood by the respective authors. The list of definitions was compiled in May 2009 based on database queries and web search. It is restricted to scientific contributions and statements of selected market research companies. The largest consent among the authors is spanning around the features service, hardware, software, scalability and Internet/network. Furthermore, usage-bound payment models and virtualization are frequently mentioned as well. The latter, however, is considered a fundamental prerequisite[23] and is thus not explicitly mentioned by many authors.

Based on our literature review and our perception of cloud computing, we provide a definition that regards the concept holistically, from both the application and infrastructure perspective. Hereby we focus on the deployment of computing resources and applications, rather than on a technical description. Furthermore our definition stresses the ability of service-composition, allowing service providers to create new services by aggregating existing services, enabling customized solutions and varying distribution models. These two aspects might be driving forces, through which cloud computing could change the IT-Service Business. Thus, we define *cloud computing as an IT deployment model, based on virtualization, where resources, in terms of infrastructure, applications and data are deployed via the internet as a distributed service by one or several service providers. These services are scalable on demand and can be priced on a pay-per-use basis.*

2.3 The Layers of Cloud Computing

Cloud computing is based on a set of many pre-existing and well researched concepts such as distributed and grid computing, virtualization or Software-as-a-Service. Although, many of the concepts don't appear to be new, the real innovation of cloud computing lies in the way it provides computing services to the customer. Various business models have evolved in recent times to provide services on different levels of abstraction. These services include providing software applications, programming platforms, data-storage or computing infrastructure.

Classifying cloud computing services along different layers is common practice in the industry[24]. Wang et al. for example describe three complementary services, Hardware-as-a-Service (HaaS), Software-as-a-Service (SaaS) and Data-as-a-Service (DaaS). These services together form Platform-as-a-Service (PaaS), which is offered as cloud computing[25]. In an attempt to obtain a comprehensive understanding of cloud computing and its relevant components, Youseff, Butrico and Da Silva were among the first who suggested a unified ontology of cloud computing[26]. According to their layered model (see Figure 1), cloud computing systems fall into one of the following five layers: applications, software environments, software infrastructure, software kernel, and hardware. Each layer represents a level of abstraction, hiding the user from all underlying components and thus providing

[23] Cf. *Armbrust* et al. (2009).

[24] Cf. *Kontio* (2009), *Reeves* et al. (2009) and *Sun Microsystems* (2009).

[25] Cf. *Wang* et al. (2008).

[26] Cf. *Youseff* et al. (2008).

simplified access to the resources or functionality. In the following section we are going to describe each layer of Youseff's Butrico's and Da Silva's model.

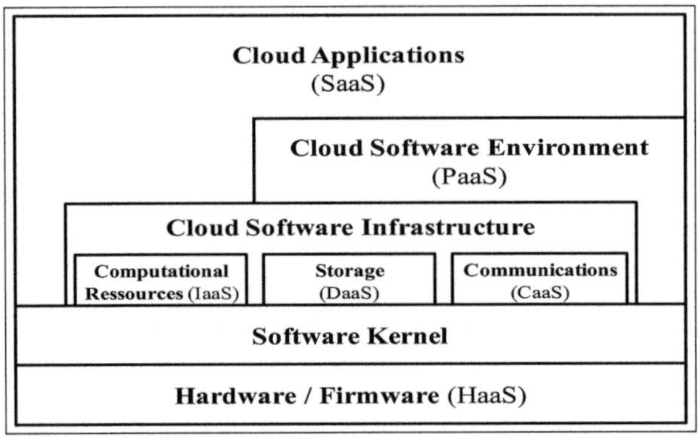

Figure 1: The layers of cloud computing27

2.3.1 Cloud Application Layer

When it comes to user interaction, the cloud application layer is the most visible layer to the end-customer. It is usually accessed through web-portals and thus builds the front-end, the user interacts with when using cloud services. A Service in the application layer may consist of a mesh of various other cloud services, but appears as a single service to the end-customer. This model of software provision, normally also referred to as *Software-as-a-Service*, appears to be attractive for many users. Reasons for this are the reduction of software and system maintenance costs, the shift of computational work from local systems into the cloud, or a reduction of upfront investments into hardware and software licenses. Also the service provider has advantages over traditional software licensing models. The effort for software upgrades is reduced, since patches and features can be deployed centrally in shorter cycles. Depending on the pricing model a continuous revenue stream can be obtained. However, security and availability are issues that still need to be addressed. Also the migration of user data is a task that should not be underestimated.

Examples for applications in this layer are numerous, but the most prominent might be Salesforce's Customer Relationships Management (CRM) system[28] or Google's Apps, which include word-processing, spreadsheet and calendaring[29].

2.3.2 Cloud Software Environment Layer

The cloud software environment layer (also called software platform layer) provides a programming language environment for developers of cloud applications. The software environment also offers a set of well-defined application programming interfaces (API) to utilize cloud services and interact with other cloud applications. Thus developers benefit from features like automatic scaling and load balancing, authentication services, communication

---

27 In imitation of *YOUSEFF* et al. (2008), p. 4.

28 Cf. http://www.salesforce.com.

29 Cf. http://apps.google.com.

services or graphical user interface (GUI) components. However, as long as there is no common standard for cloud application development, lock-in effects arise, making the developer dependent on the proprietary software environment of the cloud platform provider. This service, provided in the software environment layer is also referred to as *Platform-as-a-Service*.

A known example of a cloud software platform is Google's App Engine[30], which provides developers a phyton runtime environment and specified APIs to develop applications for Google's cloud environment. Another example is Salesforce's Apexchange platform[31] that allows developers to extend the Salesforce CRM solution or even develop entire new applications that runs on their cloud environment.

As we will highlight in Chapter 4.1 one can also look at the cloud platform from a value network or business model perspective. In that sense, the cloud platform can act as a market place for applications.

2.3.3 Cloud Software Infrastructure Layer

The cloud software infrastructure layer provides resources to other higher-level layers, which are utilized by cloud applications and cloud software platforms. The services offered in this layer are commonly differentiated into computational resources, data storage, and communication.

Computational resources in this context are usually referred to as *Infrastructure-as-a-Service (IaaS)*. Virtual Machines are the common form of providing computational resources to users, which they can fully administrate and configure to fit their specific needs. Virtualization technologies can be seen as the enabling technology for IaaS, allowing data center providers to adjust resources on demand, thus utilizing their hardware more efficiently. The downside of the medal is the lack of a strict performance allocation on shared hardware resources. Due to this, infrastructure providers cannot give strong performance guarantees which result in unsatisfactory service level agreements (SLA). These weak SLAs propagate upwards in the cloud stack, possibly leading to availability problems of cloud applications. The most prominent examples of IaaS are Amazon's Elastic Compute Cloud[32] and Enomalism's Elastic Computing Infrastructure[33]. There are also some academic open source projects like Eucalyptus[34] and Nimbus[35].

In analogy to computational resources data storage within the cloud computing model is offered as *Storage-as-a-Service*. This allows users to obtain demand-flexible storage on remote disks which they can access from everywhere. Like for other storage systems, trade-offs must be made between the partly conflicting requirements: high availability, reliability, performance, replication and data consistency, which in turn are manifested in the service providers SLAs.

---

30 Cf. http://code.google.com/intl/de-DE/appengine.

31 Cf. http://sites.force.com/appexchange/home.

32 Cf. http://aws.amazon.com/ec2.

33 Cf. http://www.enomalism.com.

34 Cf. http://www.eucalyptus.com.

35 Cf. http://workspace.globus.org.

Examples of Storage-as-a-Service are Amazon's Elastic Block Storage (EBS)[36] or its Simple Storage Service (S3)[37] and Rackspace's Cloud Files.[38] In addition, to simple storage space, data can be offered as service as well. Amazon for example offers the human genome or the US census as public data sets to use for other services or analytics[39].

A fairly new idea is *Communication-as-a-Service (CaaS)*, which shall provide quality of service ensured communication capabilities such as network security, dedicated bandwidth or network monitoring. Audio and video conferencing is just one example of cloud applications that would benefit from CaaS. So far this service is only a research interest rather than in commercial use. However, Microsoft's Connected Service Framework (CSF)[40] can be counted into this class of services.

As Figure 1 shows, cloud applications must not necessarily be developed upon a cloud software platform, but can also run directly on the cloud software infrastructure layer or even the software kernel, thus bypassing the aforementioned layers. Although this approach might offer some performance advantages, it is directly dependent on lower level components and does not make use of development aids such as the automatic scaling provided by the cloud software platform.

2.3.4 Software Kernel Layer

The software kernel layer represents the software management environment for the physical servers in the datacenters. These software kernels are usually implemented as operation system kernel, hypervisor, virtual machine monitor or clustering middleware. Typically, this layer is also the level where grid computing applications are deployed. Globus[41] is an example of a successful grid middleware. At this layer, cloud computing can benefit from the research already undertaken in the grid computing research community.

2.3.5 Hardware / Firmware Layer

At the bottom end of the layered model of cloud computing is the actual physical hardware, which forms the backbone of any cloud computing service offering. Hardware can also be subleased from datacenter providers to, normally, large enterprises. This is typically offered in traditional outsourcing plans, but in a as-a-service context also referred to as *Hardware-as-a-Service (HaaS)*. One example of this is IBM's Managed Hosting Service[42].

With regard to the layered model of Youseff, Butrico and Da Silva described above, cloud computing can be perceived as a collection of pre-existing technologies and components. Therefore we see cloud computing as an evolutionary development and re-conceptualization, rather than a disruptive technological innovation. In our opinion cloud computing is rather an innovation in the delivery model of IT services, as we have highlighted it in our definition

36 Cf. http://aws.amazon.com/ebs.

37 Cf. http://aws.amazon.com/s3.

38 Cf. http://www.rackspacecloud.com/cloud_hosting_products/files.

39 Cf. http://aws.amazon.com/publicdatasets/.

40 Cf. http://msdn.microsoft.com/en-us/library/bb931207.aspx.

41 Cf. http://www.globus.org.

42 Cf. http://www-935.ibm.com/services/de/index.wss/offering/ebhs/a1007253.

(see Chapter 2.2). Therefore we are showing the evolution of cloud computing in the context of IT provisioning in the following chapter.

3 Differences between Cloud Computing and the Traditional Provision of IT

The provision of IT resources in enterprises is closely linked with the general consideration whether information and communication technology should be kept inside the firm or whether it should be sourced from external providers – a question that has been established as a prominent research topic in business administration research for quite a while under the term "make or buy" decision or vertical design[43]. In recent years, the option to outsource IT services to an external service provider has grown in importance due to a variety of positive aspects associated with the outsourcing decision, such as, e.g., cost, quality, flexibility, and competitive advantages. Outsourcing has become one of the most important organizational concepts in recent decades, especially in the light of the rapid development of information technology[44].

To understand the evolution from traditional IT provisioning models towards new concepts of IT service provision such as cloud computing, a short summary of the history of outsourcing research will be given. This might also help to contrast and evaluate the new concept of cloud computing in the context of IT service provisioning.

3.1 The Evolution from Outsourcing to Cloud Computing

Although outsourcing has been an established topic for decades and one of the essential research issues is, the focus of the research has shifted over time. At the beginning of the outsourcing phenomenon the focus laid on the *decision between an internal or external provision of IT services* and the *subject of outsourcing* (infrastructure, applications and processes). Later, the strategic outsourcing decision of Kodak in 1989 led to a more differentiated approach, addressing the topic of *vertical design*. As a first step the motivation behind the *pro or contra of outsourcing decisions* was investigated. The central motives for outsourcing decisions are still mainly economical benefits, in particularly flexibility of costs and cost savings, technological advantages, innovation, strategic aims, and business-oriented advantages, such as an increasing service quality or an increasing flexibility of the business[45].

Following the discussion about outsourcing motives and potential benefits and risks the question of the appropriate *scope of outsourcing* became an issue that led to the distinction between selective and total outsourcing[46]. Within short time this has led to the consideration of what benefits and what performance advantages can be gained through an external

43 Cf. *Behme* (1995) and *Dillmann* (1996).

44 Cf. *Matiaske/Mellewigt* (2002).

45 Cf. *Bongard* (1994) and *Grover* et al. (1994).

46 Cf. *Lacity/Hirschheim* (1993).

sourcing of IT services. It was investigated, which *efficiency gains* could be obtained through outsourcing, compared to the internal operation of IT[47]. These questions often remained unanswered and the efficiency of outsourcing was very difficult to prove, which resulted in a backward movement towards *insourcing* or *backsourcing*. Despite criticism the organizational concept of outsourcing has become an established management practice and further, the design parameters of a successful outsourcing project have gained particular interest. So far the focus has mainly been on the *design of the contract* between the outsourcing partners[48]. Only recently, the awareness has been increased that the contract alone is not able to completely cover and specify the complexity of an outsourcing project. This is especially true, because the subject-matter of the contract, "information technology", is a very volatile, fast changing asset and therefore requires flexibility during the outsourcing relationship[49]. Since that, new approaches to the "relationship management", i.e., the maintenance of a good outsourcing relationship, are now seen as the key factor to a successful outsourcing project[50]. Figure 1 summarizes the evolution of the outsourcing concept.

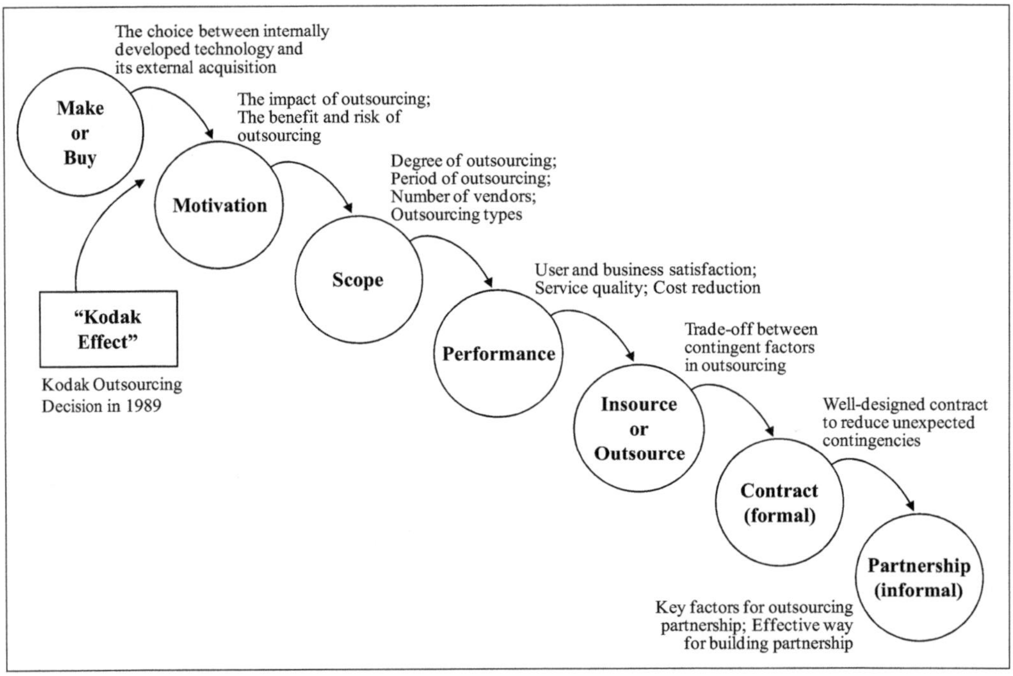

Figure 2: The evolution of external IT provisioning51

The relation between cloud computing and outsourcing is best illustrated by taking current challenges of outsourcing into account: On the one hand, customers expect a cost-effective, efficient and flexible delivery of IT services from their service providers, at a maximum of

47 Cf. *LOH/VENKATRAMAN* (1995).

48 Cf. *SAUNDERS* et al. (1997).

49 Cf. *HÄBERL* et al. (2005).

50 Cf. *GOLES/CHIN* (2005) and *LEIMEISTER* et al. (2008).

51 In accordance with *LEE* et al. (2003).

monetary flexibility (i.e., pay-per-use models). At the same time, more and more customers demand innovations or the identification of a customer-specific innovation potential from their service providers[52]. Out of these challenged and constraints posed by clients, the new phenomenon of cloud computing has emerged. Cloud computing aims to provide the technical basis to meet customer's flexibility demands on a business level. Interestingly, new cloud computing offers to meet these business demands were first addressed by providers that have not been part of the traditional outsourcing market so far. New infrastructure providers, such as Amazon or Google, that were previously active in other markets, developed new business models to market their former by-products (e. g., large storage and computing capacity) as new products. With this move, they entered the traditional outsourcing value chain (see Figure 2) and stepped into competition with established outsourcing service providers. These new service providers offer innovative ways of IT provisioning through pay-per-use payment models and help customers to satisfy their needs for efficiency, cost reduction and flexibility. In the past the physical resources in traditional outsourcing models have been kept either by the customer or the provider. On the contrary, cloud computing heralds the paradigm of an asset-free provision of technological capacities.

3.2 A Comparison of Outsourcing and Cloud Computing Value Chains

A value chain describes the interactions between different business partners to jointly develop and manufacture a product or service. Here, the manufacturing process is decomposed into its strategically relevant activities, thus determining how competitive advantages can be achieved. Competitive advantages are achieved by fulfilling the strategically important activities cheaper or better than the competition.[53] A value chain does not only contain different companies but also different business units inside one organization that jointly produce a product or service. The manufacturing process is seldom strictly linear and, thus, is often not seen as a value chain but rather as a value network. It is a network of relationships that generates economical value and other advantages through complex dynamical exchanges between companies.[54] Especially with regard to new Internet services, value networks are often understood as a network of suppliers, distributors, suppliers of commercial services and customers that are linked via the Internet and other electronic media to create values for their end customers.[55]

3.2.1 Traditional IT Service Outsourcing Value Chain

In traditional IT service outsourcing the value chain is usually divided into the areas infrastructure, applications and business processes, which can be complemented by strategy and consulting activities (see Figure 2). In each of these four value chain steps the whole cycle of IT-services, often referred to as "plan, build, run", must be supported and implemented. Thus, single aspects of individual value chain steps may be outsourced, such as the development of applications. Purchasing and operating IT hardware as well as hosting can be further divided into services that are done by the customer himself and such that use

52 Cf. *LEIMEISTER* et al. (2008).

53 Cf. *PORTER* (1985).

54 Cf. *ALLEE* (2002).

55 Cf. *TAPSCOTT* et al. (2000).

resources of a hosting provider. Here, the myriad possibilities of combination may lead to complex outsourcing relationships.

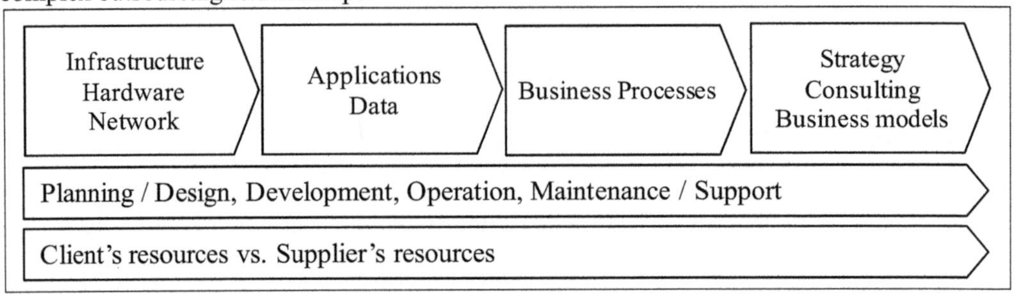

Figure 3: A traditional IT service outsourcing value chain

3.2.2 Cloud Computing Value Chain

A general trend from products to services can be observed[56]. This trend is not only restricted to the IT world, but becomes evident also in many other industries. In the transport industry, for example, the service offering is mobility, instead of solely cars. The trend does not only lead to more outsourcing, but also from the classical hardware-based outsourcing of data centers to computing as a service (see Chapter 2.3.3). A similar trend can be found in the software business, which leads away from delivering software products off the shelf towards offering software as a service (see Chapter 2.3.1). Cloud computing links these two areas of a stronger service-oriented hardware outsourcing to the "as-a-service" concept for software. Here, cloud computing shows two big facets: infrastructure-based services are now offered dynamically to the needs of customers, often referred to as utility computing, where the customer is charged according to its actual usage.

Secondly, new cloud computing platforms emerged, to integrate both hardware and software as-a-service offerings. These platforms allow creating new, single as well as composed applications and services that support complex processes and interlink multiple data sources. From a technical point of view these platforms provide programming and runtime environments to deploy cloud computing applications (see Chapter 2.3.2). Looking at these platforms from a value chain perspective, they can be perceived as some kind of market place, where various cloud computing resources from different levels (infrastructure, platform services and applications) are integrated and offered to the customer. By composing different services, complex business processes and can be supported and accessed via a unified user interface. The as-a-service concept of cloud computing allows to develop new complex service-oriented applications that consist of a mixture of on-premise and off-premise services as well as pure cloud applications. Examples, how different business models utilize the new concept provided with cloud computing are given in Chapter 4.

From the layers of the cloud computing services model, described in Chapter 2.3, we can derive three major actors within the value network: the service provider, the platform provider and the infrastructure provider. The infrastructure provider supplies the value network with all the computing and storage services needed to run applications within the cloud. The platform provider offers an environment within which cloud applications can be

56 Cf. *JACOB/ULAGA* (2008).

deployed. He also acts as some kind of catalogue or market within which applications are offered to the customer through one simple portal. The service provider develops applications that are offered and deployed on the cloud computing platform. As we especially want to highlight the aspect of service composition, we have added the aggregator role to the simplified cloud computing value network depicted in Figure 4. The aggregator is a specialized form of the service provider, offering new services or solutions by combining pre-existing services.

Within this value network value is created by providing services that are valuable for other participants of the network. Infrastructure services for example are essential for all other actors within the value network, who consume this service to provide their service offering. All the actors within the value network exchange services for money add value for other actors through service refinement and eventually provide services that fulfill the customers' needs. As it can be observed in practice, one company can of course act in more than one role. Salesforce for example is a platform provider (AppExchange) and application provider (CRM) at the same time[57]. It can also host its own infrastructure or partly source it from third party infrastructure providers. Various service providers can offer their applications on the Salesforce platform which customers can utilize in conjunction with or separately of Salesforce's CRM solution. Aggregators might combine different services to easily provide a customized solution for the customer.

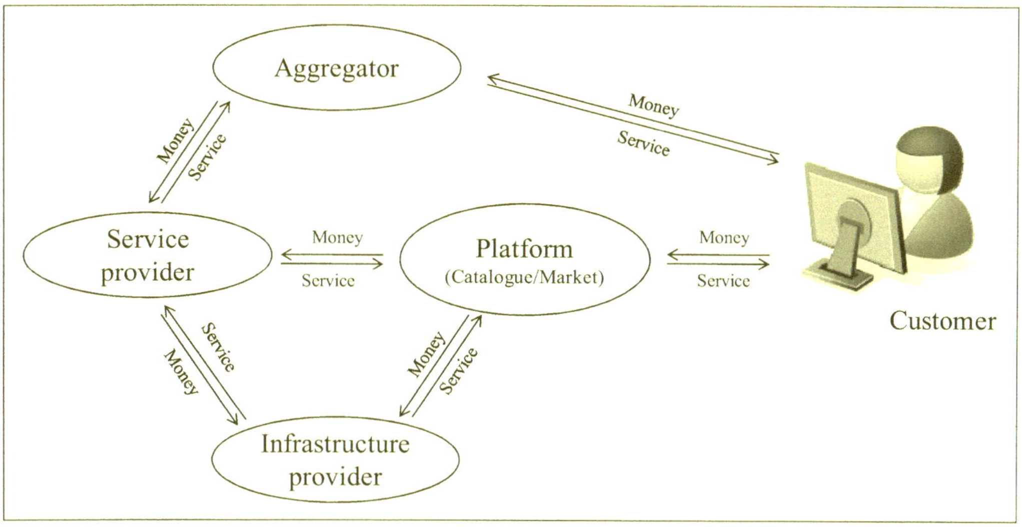

Figure 4: A simplified value network of cloud computing[58]

3.2.3 Comparison

Through an increased service orientation and a continuing technical standardization, the classical value chain has broken up. The model of "single-provider, one-stop provision of

[57] Cf. http://www.salesforce.com.

[58] A more elaborate, generic value network of cloud computing is presented and discussed in *BÖHM* et al. (2010).

outsourcing" is replaced by a network of different service providers, offering a wide range of services and products on different levels.

The main characteristics of cloud computing, from a users perspective, compared to traditional IT outsourcing is the flexible deployment of virtual and asset-free resources and services. This model allows the implementation of flexible, pay-per-use business models. Comparing cloud computing with classical outsourcing shows how the value chain has broken up and how fine-grained services can be offered. This allows service providers, to provide existing customers a new flexibility, and to access entirely new customer groups with new services and business models. In addition, the cloud computing model allows modifying existing services without large investments, extending them and offering them with new business models. JungleDisk[59] for example uses the hardware-related infrastructure services of Amazon to offer user-friendly storage services for end-users.

4 Cloud Computing Business Models

Through the increased service orientation and the opportunities of offering services on general cloud computing platforms provided by other providers as well as the new opportunities to integrate individual component services to create value-added, complex services gave rise to a set of new roles and business models that can be found in cloud computing. The following sections discuss these new roles in cloud computing and the business models that offer opportunities for those new market players.

4.1 Actors and Roles in Cloud Computing

Cloud computing services are often classified by the type of service being offered. For example, Youseff et al. distinguish between five levels with corresponding services in their ontology: applications (SaaS), cloud software environment (PaaS), cloud software infrastructure (IaaS, DaaS, CaaS), software core and finally the hardware (HaaS).[60]

In contrast to this layer model, that is quite common in the IT domain, the outsourcing market can also be seen from a more business-oriented perspective, namely from a value chain or value network perspective (see Chapter 3.2.2). Based on the analysis of providers of cloud computing services we could identify the following actors in the cloud market:

The *customer* buys services through various distribution channels, for example, directly from the service provider or through a platform provider. Corresponding roles are found, for example, in *BARROS* and *DUMAS*[61], *RIEDL ET AL.*[62] or *HAUPT*[63].

---

59 Cf. http://www.jungledisk.com.

60 Cf. *YOUSEFF* et al. (2008).

61 Cf. *BARROS/DUMAS* (2006).

62 Cf. *RIEDL* et al. (2009b).

63 Cf. *HAUPT* (2003).

Service providers, also labeled IT vendors, develop and operate services that offer value to the customer and an aggregate services provider respectively. They access hardware and infrastructure of the infrastructure providers. For example, *TAPSCOTT* et al. call this role "content provider"[64] and *HAUPT* "manufacturer"[65].

Infrastructure providers provide the technical backbone. They offer the necessary, scalable hardware for the services[66] upon which the service providers offer their services. Infrastructure providers are sometimes also called IT vendors.

Aggregate services providers (aggregators) combine existing services or parts of services to form new services and offer them to customers. Therefore, they are both a customer (from the perspective of the service provider) and a service provider (from the perspective of the customer). *BARROS* and *DUMAS* call that role "service broker"[67], *HAUPT* calls that an "assembler"[68]. Aggregators that focus on the integration of data rather than services are called *data integrators.* They ensure that already existing data is prepared and is usable by different cloud services and can be regarded as a sub-role of aggregators with a straightforward focus on technical data integration. A similar concept is called "system integrator" or "business process integrator" by *MUYLLE* and *BASU*[69] or "service mediator" by *BARROS* and *DUMAS*[70]. With these terms these authors refer, in general, to aggregators that focus more on the technical aspects necessary for data and system integration while (service) aggregators in a broad sense also include the business aspects of merging services to offer new service bundles.

The *platform provider* acts as a kind of catalog in which different service providers offer services. Often the services are based on the same development platform but also completely open, platform-independent development directories are possible. The platform provider offers the technical basis for the marketplace where the services are offered.

Last, the *consulting* for the customers serves as a support for the selection and implementation of relevant services to create value for their business model[71].

4.2 The Platform Business Model

The platform provider is the fundamental player in the cloud computing environment. It provides the central platform and market place where all other actors come together, trade their services, and interact with each other. The platform provides a central registry of

64 Cf. *TAPSCOTT* et al. (2000).

65 Cf. *HAUPT* (2003).

66 Cf. *TAPSCOTT* et al. (2000).

67 Cf. *BARROS/DUMAS* (2006).

68 Cf. *HAUPT* (2003).

69 Cf. *MUYLLE/BASU* (2008).

70 Cf. *BARROS/DUMAS* (2006).

71 Cf. *CURRIE* (2000).

services offered on the platform.[72] Service providers can then register their services with the central service registry which can be browsed by customers to discover the services they need. Thus, the platform provider brings service providers and service consumers closer together. There are several options how the platform provider can generate revenue from the services provided through the platform. Most common, as in the examples of Salesforce, the Apple Store, or Amazon, is a fee or subscription based system: either for the provider to register the service, the service consumer to access the registry, or both.

As the example of Salesforce later on shows, it is also common for the platform provider to offer its own services on the platform as well. These are often basic delivery functions necessary for third-party providers to create marketable services such as billing and payment services.[73] These platform services allow others to easily create tradable services from their "raw" services. It is also quite common for the platform provider to offer infrastructure services as well. In such a way, they hope to expand the range and portfolio of their platform by offering rather simple ways through which service providers can offer their services.

The aim of the platform business model is to increase value and revenue through attracting as many other providers and customers to interact through their platform and thus achieving network effects.[74] They generate value through their brokering activities of bringing supply and demand closer together as well as through their value added services that allow others to create service offering easily. The following paragraphs illustrate the platform business model using Salesforce as an example.

Based in the United States, Salesforce[75] is a supplier of applications for the customer relationship management (CRM) and the automation of the sales organization. However, these applications are not sold as software for on-premise operation, but as a service via Salesforce's cloud computing platform. In a monthly subscription companies provide their sales staff with flexible access to Salesforce applications without having to purchase new additional hardware resources or software licenses. This allows companies to respond flexibly to constantly changing business requirements, increasing or reducing their user-basis. Companies are not required to commit to any up-front investments and expensive implementation projects.

Next to offering its own CRM and sales organization automation applications, Salesforce opened its platform for third party service providers. Thus, other service providers are able to offer specialized extensions and entirely new applications that are seamlessly integrated into Salesforce's applications. For example, the service provider *Print SF*[76] offers an application that allows users to create, print and mail letters and other postal items. Thus a value network between customers, Salesforce and various third-party providers is established (see Figure 5).

---

72 Cf. *RIEDL* et al. (2009a).

73 Cf. *BARROS/DUMAS* (2006).

74 Cf. *ECONOMIDES* (1996).

75 Cf. http://www.salesforce.com.

76 Cf. http://www.printsf.com.

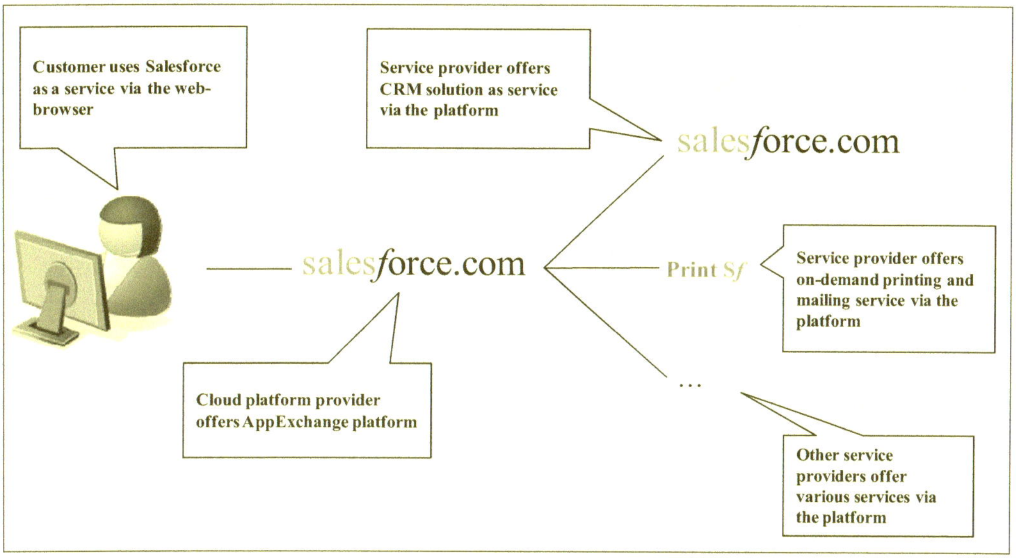

Figure 5: Example of the Salesforce value network

4.3 The Aggregator Business Model

Aggregation and composition are used to describe services that contain other services as sub-services.[77] In the business domain, an aggregation would comprise multiple services and provide access to them in a single location. Aggregation and composition are core characteristics of the value networks and ecosystems that evolve around cloud computing. Service aggregations are quite ubiquitous and can be found in business-to-business as well as business-to-consumer markets for products, services and information.[78] In a similar definition, service aggregators are defined as entities that "group services provided by other providers into a distinct value-added service and can themselves act as providers"[79]. Thus, service aggregators have a dual role. On the one hand, they offer the aggregated services and thus act as a service provider who can enforce their own policies for the aggregated service. On the other hand, they rely on external services offered by other parties within the ecosystem. Hereby, they act as a service consumer.[80]

Similar to a digital retailer, aggregators choose suitable services that are offered by various service providers, make decisions about different market segments, determine prices, and control the transaction. Due to market volume and market power, aggregators can decrease their transaction costs and thus generate value. Aggregators can, for example, be found in the area of logistics where they allow their customers to outsource complete business processes.

---

[77] Cf. *O'Sullivan* et al. (2002).

[78] Cf. *Tapscott* et al. (2000).

[79] *Papazoglou/van den Heuvel* (2007).

[80] Cf. *Riedl* et al. (2009b).

In the aggregator business model, an entity acts as an intermediary between service consumers and providers. Through the aggregator role certain services are combined based on the aggregators detailed domain knowledge which adds additional value to the resulting aggregate service. The main goal is to offer services that provide a solution to a customer-specific need. Thus, aggregators re-brand, re-purpose and re-factor services for a specific or anticipated customer demand. The value proposition includes selection, organization, matching, price, convenience, and fulfillment.[81] One might assume and further investigate when analyzing the value chain of cloud computing, that a fair amount of the value is captured by the service aggregator – compared to other cloud roles.

Related to the integration of data, a specialization of the aggregator role is the data integrator. The data integrator operates under a similar business model as the aggregator, but its focus lies more on the integration and provision of data rather than on the integration of service components. Data integrators would, for example, act as entities that "can transparently collect and analyze information from multiple web data sources"[82]. This process requires in particular resolving the semantic or contextual differences in the information. Based on post-aggregation analysis where the integrated data is combined with the integrator's domain, knowledge value-added information is synthesized.

5 Conclusion and Perspectives

Considering the historic development of providing IT resources, cloud computing has been established as the most recent and most flexible delivery model of supplying information technology. It can be seen as the consequent evolution of the traditional on-premise computing spanning outsourcing stages from total to the selective, and from the multi-vendor outsourcing to an asset-free delivery. While from a technical perspective, cloud computing seems to pose manageable challenges, it rather incorporates a number of challenges on a business level, both from an operational as well as from a strategic point of view. As laid out above, cloud computing in its current stage also holds a number of contributions for both theory and practice that this article could reveal and that will be addressed below.

5.1 Contribution to Research

The field of cloud computing research is only just emerging. Existing research focuses particularly on the technical aspects of the provision of a cloud, particularly in the area of grid computing and virtualization. Business models and value chains have been studied only to a limited degree. In this respect, this article takes a first step by systematically bringing together the various definitions of cloud computing and combining them under one coherent definition. As a major result, this article could elaborate on the building blocks of understanding the substantial elements of the cloud computing concept, i.e., the characteristics of service, hardware, software, scalability and Internet/network. Also pay-per-use billing models and virtualization belong to the core elements of the new cloud concept.

---

81 Cf. *TAPSCOTT* et al. (2000).

82 *MADNICK/SIEGEL* (2002).

In addition, the article could contribute to a systematic description of major actors (such as, e. g., customer, service provider, infrastructure provider, aggregator, platform, consulting and data integrators) entering the cloud computing market. Such a description can provide a first step towards systematically investigating the value network of cloud actors and can also shed light on analyzing where the value of cloud services is captured.

5.2 Contribution to Practice

The development of outsourcing and cloud computing towards a more flexible delivery model laid out in this paper has a strong impact not only from an academic point of view, but also particularly on practical business issues. Thereby, both the client and provider perspective of cloud computing and outsourcing services have to be taken into consideration.

5.2.1 Perspectives for Customers

Cloud computing is closely related to the general question of whether IT resources should be provided internally or externally and in both cases *how* they should best be delivered. Holding their own IT resources, such as, e. g., a datacenter does often not make sense for many customers and is too much effort, especially for small or startup companies. In Armbrust's words, this "would be as startling for a new software startup to build its own datacenter as it would for a hardware startup to build its own fabrication line"[83]. Here, externally sourcing IT resources in a cloud computing model provides new opportunities for a flexible, usage-dependent sourcing of IT resources. Besides start-up companies, also established organizations can take advantage of the elasticity of cloud computing regularly. Similar to the underlying idea of selective sourcing or on-demand outsourcing models, cloud computing can provide flexibility and efficiency in terms of cost variabilization (monetary flexibility) and also in terms of availability of IT resources (IT flexibility).

Moreover, the flexibility associated with cloud computing can also be used in settings where clients keep their IT in-house. So-called private clouds allow clients to efficiently manage their IT resources and balance peak loads and idle time in an optimal way. These opportunities should be considered in future decisions. However, the potential gains in flexibility and efficiency come along with some risks, for example, in the field of data security that needs to be taken into account. Breaking up the traditional outsourcing value chain uncovers a variety of new configurations and different actors which may result in the development of complex value networks that need to be identified and managed accordingly.

5.2.2 Perspectives for Service Providers

For service providers new opportunities arise from both a technical as well as from a business view. From a technical view, the construction of very large data centers using commodity computing, storage, and networking resources facilitated the opportunity of selling those resources on a pay-per-use basis below the costs of many medium-sized datacenters, while at the same time serving a large group of customers. From a business view, the challenges and opportunities are even more interesting. Here, service providers benefit from breaking up the outsourcing value chain to position themselves in the market and to offer new services. As the

---

83 *ARMBRUST* et al. (2009).

market for cloud computing services has not yet a clear shape we now observe a phase of experimentation where new and viable business models are explored. Especially in the field of service aggregation and integration new opportunities for service providers emerge. Even without large investments in infrastructure reliable and powerful services can be offered that use the infrastructure of established providers such as Amazon or Google. This has implications for innovation aspects such as time-to-market and offering of service prototypes. In addition, there are new businesses fields in the area of accompanying services such as data integration and consulting that will evolve in the next years.

5.3 Outlook and Further Research

In a broad understanding, cloud computing can be regarded as an evolution in the development of outsourcing models, i.e., the provision of IT resources. The business challenges of the user and the specific customer requirements for cost reduction, flexibility, and innovation are met in a more granular and mature way. At the same time, cloud computing as a new technological concept asks the same basic question as outsourcing does: *How are IT resources provided for the customer?* Consequently, the same problems, challenges, and issues are raised that have already been posed in the various stages of the development of outsourcing (see Figure 1). In analogy to the evolution in outsourcing, cloud computing is in the initial phase where asking for the participation ("if or if not"), for the motivation ("why cloud computing", "cui bono?") and for the subject ("what should be done externally") is relevant.

While cloud computing might be regarded as the consequent development of the established organizational concept of outsourcing on the basis of a new technological concept, it states an even more holistic claim. Extending many aspects of IT outsourcing, cloud computing shifts the focus from an exclusive technological perspective to a broader understanding of business needs. It addresses the most prevailing business needs of flexibility, availability, and reliability, as well as economies of scale and skill and lays out how the technological concept of cloud computing can meet (both in an aligning and enabling claim) these business challenges.
However, these considerations are only just beginning and focus primarily on the causes and manifestations of cloud computing.

From an academic perspective, future research should focus on two major topics in this context: First of all, many practitioners label cloud computing as a disruptive innovation. Although uncovering a number of new features, one has to investigate further whether cloud computing can live up to these expectations and deserves the label disruptive technology. By drawing analogies from other business models and technologies that were successful or not successful in the past, one can evaluate the sustainability of the new cloud computing paradigm.

A second promising research stream focuses on the business challenges associated with the rise of the new computing paradigm. New players – formerly active in other core markets – entered the cloud computing market and are now in competition with established IT (service) providers. As one major consequence, the traditional value chain breaks up and develops a complex value network with a myriad of established and new players on different layers in the cloud computing stack. It has to be investigated what the newly evolving value network looks like and where the value of cloud computing is captured in the long-run. Within the context of evolving value networks, the implications of cloud computing on service level agreements and the relationship between the actors will become a further research topic. Since future software solutions might be composed of several modular cloud services the complexity increases and possibly inhibits serious impacts on service level agreements and liability issues.

References

ALLEE, V. (2002): The future of knowledge: Increasing prosperity through value networks, Burlington 2002.

ARMBRUST, M. et al. (2009): Above the Clouds: A Berkeley View of Cloud Computing, Berkeley 2009.

BABBAGE, C. (1864): Passages from the life of a philosopher, London, 1864.

BARROS, A. P./DUMAS, M. (2006): The Rise of Web Service Ecosystems, in: IT Professional, 2006, Vol. 8, No. 5, pp. 31–37.

BEHME, W. (1995): Outsourcing, in: Das Wirtschaftsstudium, 1995, Vol. 24, No. 12, p. 1005.

BENNETT, K. et al. (2000): Service-based software: the future for flexible software, Seventh Asia-Pacific Software Engineering Conference (APSEC), Singapore 2000, pp. 214–221.

BÖHM, M./KOLEVA, G./LEIMEISTER, S./RIEDL, C./KRCMAR, H. (2010): Towards a Generic Value Network for Cloud Computing, in: *ALTMANN, J./RANA, O. F.* (Ed.) 7th International Workshop on the Economics and Business of Grids, Clouds, Systems, and Services (GECON), Heidelberg, pp. 129–140.

BONGARD, S. (1994): Outsourcing-Entscheidungen in der Informationsverarbeitung. Entwicklung eines computergestützten Portfolio-Instrumentariums: Unternehmensführung & Controlling, Wiesbaden 1994.

BREITER, G./BEHRENDT, M. (2008): Cloud Computing Concepts, in: Informatik Spektrum, 2008 Vol. 31, No. 6, pp. 624–628.

BRISCOE, G./MARINOS, A. (2009): Digital Ecosystems in the Clouds: Towards Community Cloud Computing, in: Arxiv preprint arXiv:0903.0694, 2009.

BURACK, B. (1949): An Electrical Logic Machine, in: Science, 1949 Vol. 109, No. 2842, pp. 610–611.

BUYYA, R./YEO, C. S./VENUGOPAL, S. (2008): Market-oriented cloud computing: Vision, hype, and reality for delivering it services as computing utilities, International Conference on High Performance Computing and Communications 2008.

CURRIE, W. (2000): The supply-side of IT outsourcing: the trend towards mergers, acquisitions and joint ventures, in: International journal of physical distribution and logistics management, 2000 Vol. 30, No. 3/4, pp. 238–254.

DILLMANN, L. (1996): Outsourcing in der Produktentwicklung. Eine transaktionskosten-theoretische Betrachtung der zunehmenden Fremdvergabe pharmazeutischer Produkt-entwicklungsaufgaben in der BRD, Dissertation, Frankfurt 1996.

ECONOMIDES, N. (1996): The economics of networks, in: International journal of industrial organization, 1996 Vol. 14, No. 6, pp. 673–699.

FENN, J. et al. (2008): Hype Cycle for Emerging Technologies, 2008, Research Report, Gartner, Stamford 2008.

FINCH, C. (2006): The Benefits of the Software-as-a-Service Model, in: Computerworld Management, online: http://www.computerworld.com/s/article/107276/The_Benefits_of_the_Software_as_a_Service_Model, last update: 2006-01-02, date visited: 2009-07-03.

FOSTER, I./KESSELMAN, C. (2003): The grid: blueprint for a new computing infrastructure, 2nd edition, Amsterdam 2003.

FOSTER, I./ZHAO, Y./RAICU, I./LU, S. (2008): Cloud Computing and Grid Computing 360-Degree Compared, Grid Computing Environments Workshop (GCE), Austin 2008, pp. 1–10.

FOWLER, G. A./WORTHEN, B. (2009): The Internet Industry Is on a Cloud - Whatever That May Mean, in: The Wall Street Journal, online: http://online.wsj.com/article/SB123802623665542725.html, last update: 2009-03-26, date visited: 2009-04-09.

FREIBERGER, P./SWAINE, M. (2000): Fire in the valley: the making of the personal computer, 2nd edition, New York 2000.

FREYTAG-LÖRINGHOFF, B. V./SECK, F. (2002): Wilhelm Schickards Tübinger Rechenmaschine von 1623, 5th edition, Tübingen 2002.

GEELAN, J. (2009): Twenty-One Experts Define Cloud Computing, in: Virtualization Journal, online: http://virtualization.sys-con.com/node/6123752009, date visited: 2009-04-09.

GENS, F. (2008): Defining "Cloud Services" and "Cloud Computing", in: IDC eXchange, online: http://blogs.idc.com/ie/?p=1902008, date visited: 2009-04-08.

GOLDSTINE, H. H./GOLDSTINE, A. (1946): The electronic numerical integrator and computer (ENIAC), in: Mathematical Tables and Other Aids to Computation, 1946, pp. 97–110.

GOLES, T./CHIN, W. W. (2005): Information systems outsourcing relationship factors: detailed conceptualization and initial evidence, in: SIGMIS Database, 2005 Vol. 36, No. 4, pp. 47–67.

GOOGLE (2009): Insights for Search, online: http://www.google.com/insights/search/2009, date visited: 2009-04-08.

GROSSMAN, R. L./GU, Y. (2009): On the Varieties of Clouds for Data Intensive Computing, in: IEEE Computer Society Bulletin of the Technical Committee on Data Engineering, 2009 Vol. 32, No. 1, pp. 44–51.

GROVER, V./CHEON, M. J./TENG, J. T. C. (1994): A Descriptive Study on the Outsourcing of Information Systems Functions, in: Information & Management, 1994 Vol. 27, No. 1, pp. 33–44.

GRUMAN, G./KNORR, E. (2008): What cloud computing really means, in: Infoworld, online: http://www.infoworld.com/print/340312008, date visited: 2009-04-08.

Häberle, O./Jahner, S./Krcmar, H. (2005): Beyond the On Demand Hype: A Conceptual Framework for Flexibility in Outsourcing, European Academy of Management Annual Conference (EURAM), Germany, May 4th – 7th 2005, TUM Business School Munich 2005.

Haupt, S. (2003): Digitale Wertschöpfungsnetzwerke und kooperative Strategien in der deutschen Lackindustrie, Dissertation, St. Gallen 2003.

Jacob, F./Ulaga, W. (2008): The transition from product to service in business markets: An agenda for academic inquiry, in: Industrial Marketing Management, 2008 Vol. 37, No. 3, pp. 247–253.

Kim, W. (2009): Cloud Computing: Today and Tomorrow, in: Journal OF Object Technology, 2009 Vol. 8, No. 1, pp. 65–72.

Kontio, M. (2009): Architectural manifesto: An introduction to the possibilities (and risks) of cloud computing, online: http://www.ibm.com/developerworks/library/ar-archman10/, date visited: 2009-07-30.

Lacity, M. C./Hirschheim, R. A. (1993): Information Systems Outsourcing – Myths, Metaphors and Realities, Chichester, New York 1993.

Lee, J.-N. et al. (2003): IT Outsourcing Evolution – Past, Present and Future, in: Communications of the ACM, 2003 Vol. 46, No. 5, pp. 84–89.

Leimeister, S./Böhmann, T./Krcmar, H. (2008): IS Outsourcing Governance in Innovation-Focused Relationships: An Empirical Investigation, 16th European Conference on Information Systems, Galway, Ireland 2008.

Loh, L./Venkatraman, N. (1995): An empirical study of information technology outsourcing: Benefits, risk and performance implications, Sixteenth International Conference on Information Systems, Amsterdam 1995, pp. 277–288.

Madnick, S./Siegel, M. (2002): Seizing the opportunity: Exploiting web aggregation, in: MIS Quarterly Executiue, 2002 Vol. 1, No. 1, pp. 35–46.

Matiaske, W./Mellewigt, T. (2002): Motive, Erfolge und Risiken des Outsourcings – Befunde und Defizite der empirischen Outsourcing-Forschung. (With English sum-mary), in: Zeitschrift für Betriebswirtschaft, 2002, pp. 641–659.

McFredries, P. (2008): Technically speaking: The cloud is the computer, in: Spectrum IEEE, 2008 Vol. 45, No. 8, p. 20.

Muylle, S./Basu, A. (2008): Online support for business processes by electronic intermediaries, in: Decision Support Systems, 2008 Vol. 45, No. 4, pp. 845–857.

Nurmi, D. et al. (2008): The Eucalyptus Open-source Cloud-computing System, Cloud Computing and Its Applications, Chicago 2008.

O'Sullivan, J./Edmond, D./Ter Hofstede, A. (2002): What's in a Service?, in: Distributed and Parallel Databases, 2002 Vol. 12, No. 2, pp. 117–133.

Papazoglou, M./van den Heuvel, W. (2007): Service oriented architectures: approaches, technologies and research issues, in: The VLDB Journal The International Journal on Very Large Data Bases, 2007 Vol. 16, No. 3, pp. 389–415.

PLUMMER, D. C. et al. (2008): Cloud computing: Defining and describing an emerging phenomenon, Research Report, Gartner, Stamford 2008, pp. 1–9.

PORTER, M. E. (1985): Competitive Advantage: Creating and Sustaining Superior Performance, New York 1985.

REEVES, D. et al. (2009): Cloud Computing: Transforming IT Midvale 2009.

RIEDL, C. et al. (2009a): A Framework for Analysing Service Ecosystem Capabilities to Innovate, Proceedings of 17th European Conference on Information Systems (ECIS'09) 2009.

RIEDL, C. et al. (2009b): Quality management in service ecosystems, in: Information Systems and e-Business Management, 2009 Vol. 7, No. 2, pp. 199–221.

ROJAS, R. (1997): Konrad Zuse's legacy: the architecture of the Z1 and Z3, in: IEEE Annals of the History of Computing, 1997 Vol. 19, No. 2, pp. 5–16.

SAUNDERS, C./GEBELT, M./HU, Q. (1997): Achieving Success in Information Systems Outsourcing, in: California Management Review, 1997 Vol. 39, No. 2, pp. 63–79.

SUN MICROSYSTEMS (2009): Take your Business to a Higher Level 2009.

TAPSCOTT, D./TICOLL, D./LOWY, A. (2000): Digital capital: harnessing the power of business Webs, Boston 2000.

VAQUERO, L. M. et al. (2009): A break in the clouds: towards a cloud definition, in: ACM SIGCOMM Computer Communication Review, 2009 Vol. 39, No. 1, pp. 50–55.

VYKOUKAL, J./WOLF, M./BECK, R. (2009): Service-Grids in der Industrie – On-Demand-Bereitstellung und Nutzung von Grid-basierten Services in Unternehmen, in: WIRTSCHAFTSINFORMATIK, 2009 Vol. 51, No. 2, pp. 206–214.

WANG, W. et al. (2008): Scientific Cloud Computing: Early Definition and Experience, High Performance Computing and Communications, 2008. HPCC '08. 10th IEEE International Conference on 2008.

WEISS, A. (2007): Computing in the clouds, in: netWorker, 2007 Vol. 11, No. 4, pp. 16–25.

YOUSEFF, L./BUTRICO, M./DA SILVA, D. (2008): Toward a Unified Ontology of Cloud Computing, Grid Computing Environments Workshop 2008, pp. 1–10.

Part 2:

Application Management
– Service Creation and Quality Management

Essential Bits of Quality Management for Application Management

Bhaswar Bose

Siemens AG – Siemens IT Solutions and Services

1 Introduction

This article on quality management has been possible by putting together my experiences around the subject while being a practitioner myself.

The word quality, as per ISO 9000 definition is "Degree to which a set of inherent characteristics fulfils requirements"[1]. The *quality* of something can be determined by comparing a set of inherent characteristics with a set of requirements. If those inherent characteristics meet all requirements, high or excellent quality is achieved. If those characteristics do not meet all requirements, a low or poor level of quality is achieved

Be it a manufactured product or a service, the set of requirements mentioned above are always given explicitly or implicitly by the customer. Hence the customer also determines whether the product or service meets the requirement. For the supplier, practicing stringent quality management processes alone helps to bridge the gap between what is provided and what is expected.

Quality management is one of the key pillars of success for application management just as it is for other forms of manufacturing or service businesses, whether big or small. Without strong quality management practices, achievement of both short term goals and objectives like meeting customer requirements and Service Level Agreement (SLA) and long term goals like business growth and market establishment get impacted.

There are many elements of quality management. However, the essential elements of quality management useful for the application management business are:

- Quality planning
- Quality control
- Quality assurance and
- Quality improvement

JOSEPH M JURAN[2], the quality Guru of the 20th century had mentioned about the three managerial processes, i.e. quality planning, quality control and quality improvement. List of books written by *JURAN* are listed at the end of this article. All of these *Essential Bits of Quality Management* put together in the correct manner ensures success for the application management business.

Let us now look closely at each of the topics in question here.

---

[1] TC 176/SC (2005). *ISO 9000:2005, Quality management systems -- Fundamentals and vocabulary*. International Organization for Standardization. For more on ISO 9000, please refer to http://www.iso.org/iso/home.html.

[2] For more on *JOSEPH M. JURAN*, please refer to http://www.juran.com/about_juran_institute_our_founder.html and http://en.wikipedia.org/wiki/Joseph_M._Juran.

2 Quality Planning

The quality planning process has to consider few key elements of the organization and business unit guidelines and business plans that include goals and objectives. Quality planning should be done systematically and therefore should follow a process. Figure 1 below shows the process.

Figure 1: Process for Quality Planning

2.1 Understanding the Customers' Quality Requirements

The starting point of quality planning is to develop understanding of the quality requirements of the customer. In the case of application management, the customer typically specifies the required service levels in the contract document. The service levels form part of the Service Level Agreement or SLA.

The SLA will contain the details of metrics (including their operational definition), the targets and reporting frequency. A typical SLA of a customer for application management would have metrics like

- % of Incident tickets responded to within a stipulated time
- % of Incident tickets resolved within a stipulated time

The stipulated time and % may vary as per the Priority of the ticket

There could however be unspecified or implicit needs of the customer which would need to be taken into account too. These needs would be mostly qualitative in nature. Typical of these could be:

- Ease of communication with the service provider
- Suggestions of innovation for the customer processes
- Suggestions for changes at the customer end that could lead to reduction in incidents
- Quick turnaround time for actions requested

2.2 Considering the Organizational or Corporate Quality Standards

Since the application management business would typically be a business unit or segment of the organization, the business unit or segment would have to consider the corporate quality guidelines and standards that would be binding on the unit for preparing the quality plan.
Some of the typical quality standards that could come from corporate level quality management group could be:

- Guidelines for project quality management
- Guidelines for supplier quality management
- Guidelines for documentation and maintaining records

Since there are many quality system standards available for implementation and getting certified on, the choice could be left to the business unit to determine the correct quality standard that is suitable to the business. However, here again, the organization could recommend adopting certain Quality Standards purely from a standardization perspective. Some of these typical standards are:

- ISO/IEC 9001:2008 – *Quality management systems – Requirements*
- ISO/IEC 27001:2005 – *Information technology – Security techniques – Information security management systems – Requirements*
- ISO/IEC 20000:2005 – *Information technology – Service management*
- ISO/IEC 14001:2004 – *Environmental management systems*[3]

2.3 Considering the Organizational Business Goals and Objectives

The quality planning process should be completely aligned with the organizational business goals and objectives. This is necessary, as the success of the organization in achieving the goals and objectives, both short term and long term, can only be achieved with an aligned quality management program.

[3] For more details on the above management standards, please refer to www.iso.org.

Most organizations nowadays carry out the planning aligned to the four dimensions of the Balanced Scorecard[4]. These dimensions are:

- Customers
- Processes
- Financial
- Employees

While carrying out the quality Planning exercise, the quality management team would need to understand the goals and objectives of the organization, along the above-mentioned dimensions. Post this, planning of the quality program to support achievement of the specific goals and objectives that would be impacted by a program of quality management, need to be done.

One of the examples here could be an objective from the customer segment – SLA fulfillment. Even though SLA fulfillment is not achievable by sole effort of the quality management group, it should include this objective while carrying out the quality planning exercise. This is because the quality management group can put programs to analyze performance, analyze reasons for SLA non-fulfillment, assess and improve the business processes that impact SLA fulfillment which in turn would enable achievement of the target.

After considering all the organizational goals and objectives, the quality management team would need to arrive at the quality management goals and objectives. The quality management group can develop some additional goals and objectives. These may not have been considered by the organization for its planning, but could help the organization in the long term. Examples of such goals could be training of employees on quality improvement techniques like Six Sigma[5] or quality management standards like ISO 20000 or ITIL[6] (IT Information Library) etc.

2.4 Determine Methods, Tools, Metrics, Reports and Review Mechanisms to achieve the Quality Objectives

Once the quality goals and objectives have been created, it is extremely important to have the quality planning exercise consider the items that will help achieve the objectives or take corrective actions when deviations from the plan occur. These are:

- methods and tools,
- metrics and
- reports and review mechanisms

---

4 For more detailed information on Balanced Scorecard see *KAPLAN/NORTON* (1996).

5 For more information on Six Sigma, please refer to www.isixsigma.com.

6 For more information on ITIL, please refer to http://www.itil-officialsite.com/home/home.asp accessed on 17th July 2010.

Some of the methods that can be applied for the application management business could be "Documentation of the business processes" that can be used by the employees when necessary or for training purposes, implementation of ISO standards like ISO/IEC 9001:2008, ISO/IEC 20000:2005 and ISO/IEC 27001:2005 etc. There can be numerous tools for documentation but flowcharting is, practically speaking, the easiest way of clearly documenting processes as it appears more like a picture rather than a written text.

Two types of metrics can be used for measurement of the progress towards the objectives.

These are:

- Effectiveness metrics
- Efficiency metrics

Effectiveness metrics measure the degree to which the objective has been achieved, that is how close to the desired position is the achievement. Effectiveness metrics are therefore mostly like "%-achievement of an objective" or "%-fulfillment" etc.

Efficiency metrics measure the amount of resources that have been used to reach the position mentioned above. Efficiency metrics are mostly like "Resource utilization", "Cost per project", "Effort per ticket" etc.

"Reports and review mechanism" is the backbone for the success of any program. With effective reports that highlight issues clearly and a review mechanism that ensures a periodic review and course correction, achievement of stretched goals and objectives can become easy. The types of reports that are mostly useful are:

- daily reports like SLA monitoring reports, backlog reports, utilization reports, attendance reports
- weekly reports like performance summary reports, trend reports
- monthly reports like business unit and project performance summary reports, financial performance reports

Reviews of performance need to be done regularly. Reviews can again be daily, weekly and monthly and mostly with the daily, weekly and monthly reviews published. Quarterly business reviews are also done depending on a need basis. Reviews are never complete without capturing the minutes of meeting and creation of action plans for bridging gap between actual performance and target. Action plans need to have owners who needs to drive closure of the action points.

2.5 Create Quality Control, Quality Assurance and Continuous Improvement plans

The quality planning exercise needs to plan for quality control, quality assurance and continuous improvement. These are explained separately over the next few pages.

3 Quality Control

Quality control for application management business consists of processes that ensure that the service provided to the customer is error free and the processes followed for delivering such services are controlled.

Figure 2 below summarizes the quality control mechanism:

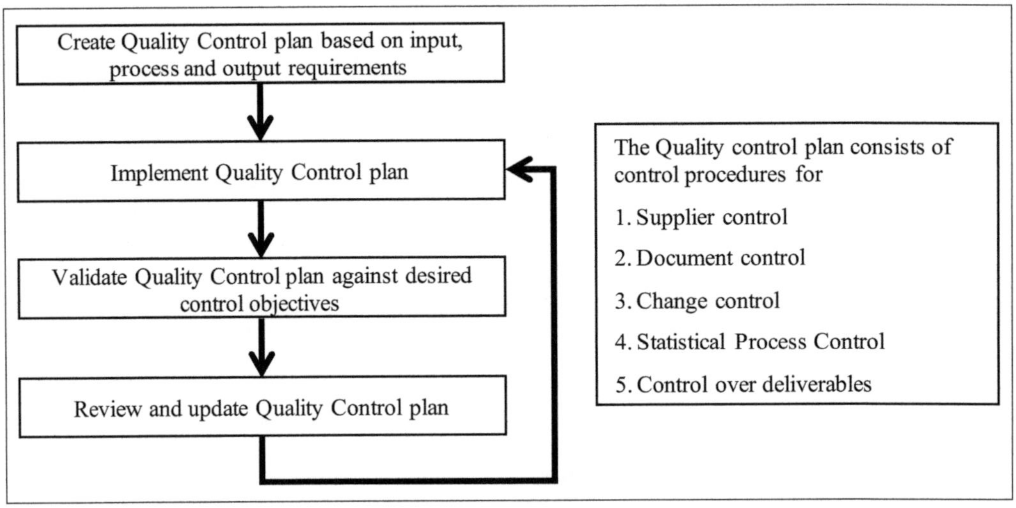

Figure 2: Process for Quality Control

3.1 Creation of the Quality Control Plan based on the Input, Process and Output Requirements

For any business process, the process can be effectively displayed at high level, in the form of a SIPOC[7], where

S = Supplier
I = Input
P = Process
O = Output
C = Customer

The suppliers provide the inputs, which get processed to generate the outputs which are then consumed by the customers. Figure 3 below depicts this. Customers either explicitly or implicitly express the requirements from the output. Similarly, for the process to generate the output, specific requirements are generated.

---

7 For more information on SIPOC and SIPOC templates please refer to http://www.isixsigma.com/index.php?option=com_k2&view=item&id=1013&Itemid=1&Itemid=1.

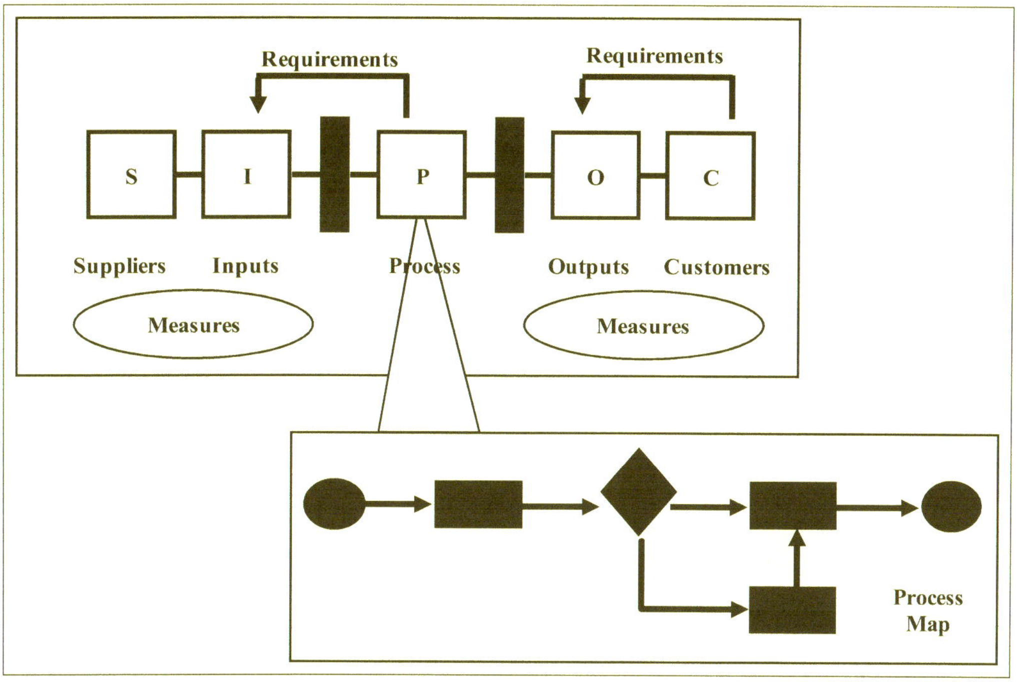

Figure 3: SIPOC diagram

Typical suppliers in the case of application management are the support functions, for example the Resource Management Group (RMG) which is responsible for recruiting manpower for projects. Typical process in case of application management would be the incident management process and the typical output would be a resolved incident ticket. Measures are the metrics that need to be put in for suppliers, inputs, process, output and customer requirements that help in validating the effectiveness of each towards meeting the customer requirements.

Quality control based on the above concept requires control plans to be created for suppliers, process and outputs. Control plans for suppliers need to take into account the quality of inputs that would come from the suppliers as well as process control methods being adopted by the suppliers for generating the inputs. For the process, statistical process control plans should be deployed which act- as a forewarning system. The control plan for the deliverables would need to take into account the customer specified requirements e. g. the SLA.

For application management business, document control and change control plans are also important so that the correct documents are available for use and non-standardized documents are removed. Since changes to an application do happen frequently, it is important to have change control plans that control the way the changes are carried out in the application.

Details of the above-mentioned plans including the means to create them have been kept outside the purview of this article. For more information, the reader is requested to refer to the end of article reference section.

3.2 Implementation of the Quality Control plan

Once the quality control plans are ready and can be implemented, it is necessary to plan the implementation well. Communication and training about the control plans is very important for effective implementation.

The implementation of the plans needs to be communicated to all the stakeholders including customers in some cases so that the customers gain confidence in the services provided.

Training on the control plans needs to be provided to all the persons who would be using them, so that the controls are effectively understood and implemented.

3.3 Validation of the Quality Control Plan against the desired Objectives

As has been mentioned earlier, quality controls are put in place with objectives of control on the inputs, process and outputs of a process. It is therefore imperative to validate whether the desired objectives of control have been achieved or not.

The starting point for such validation needs to be at the output level. In case defective output is reaching the customer, review and change of the control plan for outputs need to be done.

In case no defective outputs are reaching the customer but the process still generates defects that get trapped at the output inspection stage, the statistical process control plans as well as quality assurance plans need to be revisited.

In case defects or failures are generated because of inputs, revalidation of the supplier control plans needs to be done.

3.4 Review and Update of the Quality Control Plans

Post validation of the quality control plans, if review and update of the plans are necessary, should be done by bringing together the subject matter experts, the users of the control plans and the quality management people.

Before finalization of the revised control plans, it is always better to test out the effectiveness once more. If desired objectives are met, plans can be frozen and may not be reviewed till there are changes in the process or customer requirements.

4 Quality Assurance

More and more organizations, be it engineering or service based, have either moved or are moving to a quality assurance model from a quality control model. This applies to application management services as well. The quality assurance process puts in methods and tools that ensure that the process becomes robust to prevent defects from getting generated. Since supplier's processes are not controlled by the organization, it is still important to have a quality control mechanism for suppliers.

Figure 4 depicts the process of quality assurance.

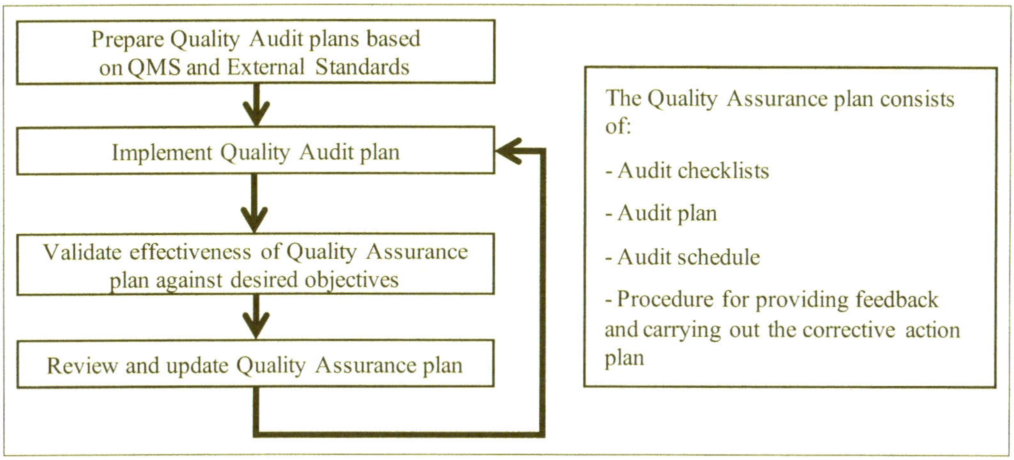

Figure 4: Process for Quality Assurance

Quality assurance for application management is carried out mainly through implementation of requirements of the ISO/IEC standards like ISO 20000 etc referred earlier in this article.

Of these three standards, ISO 20000, which is based on information technology service management principles outlined in Information Technology Information Library (ITIL) V2, is the most applicable and useful standard. ISO 20000, which is based on process management concepts, helps in managing all the relevant business processes of application management using ITIL practices and process management concepts.

Since data security is also of primary importance both to the customer and the service provider, application of ISO 27001 requirements becomes important.

ISO 9001:2000 standard is not always necessary if ISO 20000 standard has been applied. However, the business unit can still apply ISO 9001:2000 practices for the more systematic business management and assured quality of service for the customer.

4.1 Preparation of the Quality Audit plans

4.1.1 Quality Audits for ensuring Application of Quality Standards

Post implementation of the requirements of the ISO standards, audit plans need to be created. The ISO standards recommend that internal audits are carried out before the external audits. The best practice is to have two internal audits in a year, followed by closure of the identified observations and non-conformances.

It is better to get quality management persons from other parts of the organization to carry out internal audits. This is because it brings in a completely impartial view as in the case of an external audit.

Internal audits, however, are sample based audits and therefore not all the application management projects are picked up for auditing to check application of the quality standards. A good way to manage and ensure application of the quality standards is to apply a mechanism of periodic auditing of all the projects by the quality management team of the business unit. This kind of audit can be termed as a project audit. The periodicity of these audits needs to be planned taking into consideration the business importance of the project. Therefore, more important projects would need to be audited more and the less important ones need to be audited less.

4.1.2 Quality audits to check Application of process Steps at Transaction Level

Project audits, internal and external audits ensure that implementation and adherence to the requirements of the international quality standards are adhered to. These audits check for process management and application of requirements at a high level. To ensure that written down work instructions and Standard Operating Procedures (SOP) are followed, it is good to audit the transactions that take place in a typical application management business.

These audits should be sample based to use minimal auditor time and again focus on a plan that is based on performance of the consultants (who are people working on transactions in an application management business) in the previous audits. However, at the starting stage of implementation of the audit mechanism, all consultants need to be audited equally.

An audit sheet for this type of transaction audit would capture all the important steps that are mentioned in the SOP. The auditor needs to audit the transaction either "live", i.e. while the transaction is taking place or "post facto", i.e. when the transaction has been completed. For example, if the transaction is with incident management, the auditor could check whether all the documented steps are followed by the consultant while the ticket is being resolved, or could check the ticketing tool and other supporting tools post resolution.

These audits help to highlight individual level, team level or unit level failures and knowledge gaps. To close the loop, feedback and trainings are conducted so that the failures do not repeat.

4.2 Implementation, validation, review and updating of Quality Plans

Quality plans implementation, validation and updating follow the exact process as has been explained earlier in the section for quality control. Hence, these are not repeated again in this section.

5 Quality Improvement

For any business and therefore equally applicable for application management, is the implementation of a process of quality improvement. A quality improvement program in some organizations may also be termed as a continuous improvement program to include improvements that may be not quality oriented, e. g. an improvement program to reduce costs. Since application management business involves repetitive work, there is an increased scope of process improvement through a structured quality improvement program.

Almost all of the well known quality improvements processes follow standard steps. These steps could be as has been depicted in Figure 6.

Key for implementation of a quality improvement program in any organization is the management buy-in and commitment. This is because all such programs involve training of people to carry out improvement projects, time of these resources on the project which would not be billable in most cases and also involvement of external consultants as methodology experts. All of these require expenditure and the Return on Investment (ROI) would happen over some months and in some cases a few years. Hence without management buy-in and commitment a quality improvement program cannot be launched or cannot succeed.

Quality improvement programs should ideally be led by quality management team people who have had prior experiences in implementing such programs. This is because such persons can combine their knowledge of the improvement methodology with their experience of handling the change management process that the organization typically goes through while implementing the new or changed processes.

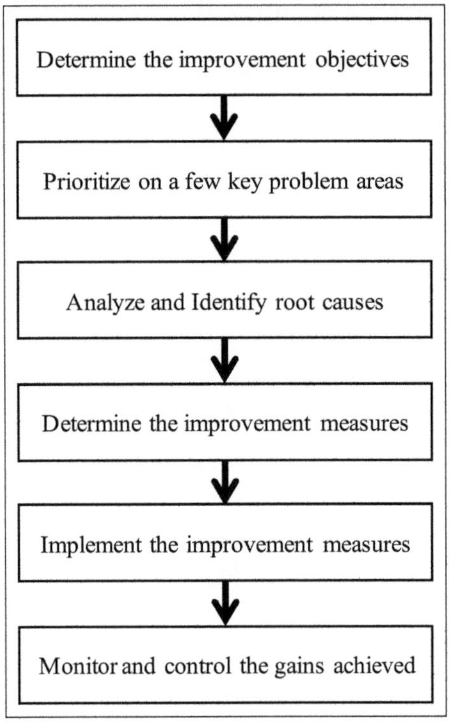

Figure 5: *Process for Quality Improvement*

5.1 Determination of the Opportunities for Quality Improvement

Identification of the areas where quality improvement is required is the first step in the process.

For application management business, the most convenient starting point of such an identification process is the fulfillment of the SLA with the customers. If there are failures in fulfillment of any or all the parameters / metrics of the SLA and causes of the problems are not clearly known, the requirement for quality improvement is easily observed.

If SLA fulfillment is being achieved and the customer is satisfied with the output he is receiving, there could be variations in the process that may need to be corrected or there could be higher lead time or cycle time[8] issues that may need to be corrected. Such variation problems or higher cycle time issues can become candidates for quality improvement.

[8] Lead time is the time taken to complete a set of activities that is from the start of the set of activities to the end of the set of activities. Cycle time is the time to complete a cyclical operation. For example, in a car assembly line, the cycle time to fix four doors in the car could be 30 min but the time taken to completely roll out a car from the assembly line would be the Lead time which typically could be five hours.

In case process variations are due to variations in the inputs, the quality control processes for suppliers need to be taken up for quality improvement.

Other sources of requirements for quality improvement projects are employee issues or issues identified by the management based on the business needs.

All the improvement requirements need to be converted to a "Measurable Problem" using a measurement framework before the prioritization can be carried out. Figure 7 below depicts the sources of quality improvement requirements.

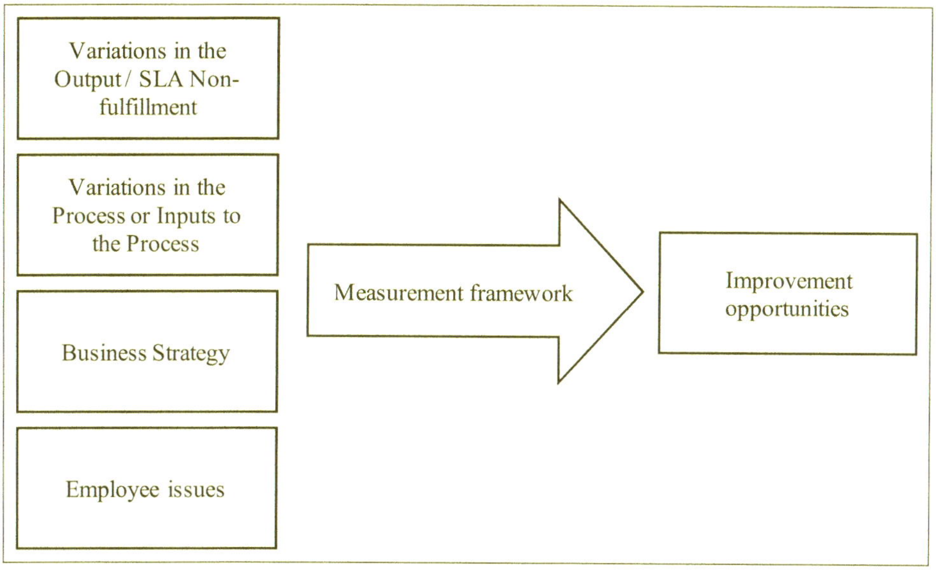

Figure 6: Identification of opportunities for Quality Improvement projects

5.2 Prioritization of Opportunities

Since resources are always limited, it is important to prioritize the opportunities for quality improvement. There are a few methods or criteria that can be used for prioritization of the opportunities. These are:

- Cost – benefit analysis
- Short-term or long-term business impact
- Customer need
- Employee need
- Expected time to complete the project

Prioritization of opportunities should be done by the quality management team along with subject matter experts. The recommendations from this team should then be placed to the management team for final prioritization. This helps in having complete management focus and support for the projects.

5.3 Analysis for Root Cause Identification and Determination of the Solutions

Analysis for root cause identification can be done using several methods and it should left to the quality management team experts to determine the most suitable method. Statistical techniques deployed in the well known Six Sigma DMAIC[9] approach helps to determine root causes with data and statistical validation. Easier approaches can also be adopted, especially if the project team members are not trained enough on statistical tools and techniques. For example, Ishikawa (Fish bone) diagram[10] is one of the most common tools used for finding out root causes.

Once the root causes have been identified and validated, it is necessary to find out the solutions that will either remove the root causes or at least reduce the impact of them. Just as the root causes need to be validated to be true root causes, the solutions also need to be validated to be effective solutions. Determination and validation can also be done using well known methods and tools. Details of these methods and tools are not covered in this article.

5.4 Implementation of the Solution

In the application management business, the interaction of the process directly happens with the end-users (who are mostly the *customers* in the case of application management business). This means that services provided are directly consumed by the end-users. Hence changes made in the process can be directly felt by the end-users. Therefore, before implementation of the solution, it is absolutely important to do a *piloting* of the solution.

A pilot or a test-run helps in restricting the impact of any unanticipated problem. Since end-users (customers) can still get impacted by the test-run, it is important to keep them informed at all times.

Once the pilot has been termed as "successful", it is ok to roll out the improvement across all areas that come under the scope of the project.

---

9 Six Sigma DMAIC is a structure problem solving methodology using statistical tools and techniques. The acronym DMAIC stands for Design, Measure, Analyze, Improve & Control which are the five phases of the problem solving process in the same order. For more information on Six Sigma DMAIC methodology, please refer to http://www.isixsigma.com/index.php?option=com_k2&view=itemlist&layout=category&task=category&id=35&Itemid=106.

10 Cf. *ISHIKAWA* (1986). *ISHIKAWA* or fish-bone is a root cause determining technique created by *KAORU ISHIKAWA* and gets the name of a fish-bone as the diagram looks like one. For more info on *ISHIKAWA* diagram, please refer to http://en.wikipedia.org/wiki/Ishikawa_diagram.

5.5 Monitoring and Controlling the Gains Achieved

It is often seen that even though the improvement is observed during pilot run and also after full-scale implementation, it does not get sustained. The way to tackle this is to monitor the related measurable parameter closely and control it.

Statistical control is widely used as a tool as control charts can be used to identify common cause and special cause variations.

Regular review of the results, new or changed process by the management also helps in sustaining the gains. This is because any change in a set process always faces resistance and one of the most effective ways of ironing out such resistances is use the management support on the improvement project.

There are other measures that can be used for monitoring and control and the reader is requested to refer to the internet as a lot of information on the same exists there.

6 Conclusion

Application management being a very standardized and commoditized practice, thus requires many or all of the techniques of quality management mentioned in this article for achieving the goals and objectives set for carrying out application management.

Application management is highly people dependant to start with and therefore challenges always are to make it more and more people independent through setting up of standardized processes, measurement of these processes and continuous improvement. Businesses therefore have to continuously focus on the objective of setting and improving processes. Quality management practices have to play a very important part in helping businesses attain that objective.

While it is always easier to understand the essential bits of quality management, the challenge lies in implementation. The most suited approach is the "Top-down approach" where the management sets up processes and supports implementation. Success does not come immediately in most businesses, including application management, but that should not be taken as a deterrent. However, a strong base of quality management ensures an early success and a long term continued dominance in the ever challenging markets of application management.

References

CROSBY, P. B. (1979): Quality is Free, New York 1979.

GITLOW, H. S./GITLOW, S. J. (1987): The Deming Guide to Quality and Competitive Position, Englewood Cliffs, New York 1987.

ISHIKAWA, K. (1986): Guide to Quality Control, New York 1986.

JURAN, J. M. (1967): Management of Quality Control, New York 1967.

JURAN, J. M. (1970): Quality Planning and Analysis, New York 1970.

JURAN, J. M. (1989): Juran on Leadership for Quality – An Executive Handbook, New York 1989.

JURAN, J. M. (1995): Directions of Managing for Quality, Milwaukee, Wisc. 1995.

JURAN, J. M. (1999): Quality Control Handbook, 5th edition, New York 1951.

KAPLAN, R. S./NORTON, D. P. (1996): The Balanced Scorecard: Translating Strategy into Action, Boston, Massachusetts 1996.

SCHERKENBACH, W. W. (1986): The Deming Route to Quality and Productivity, Washington 1986.

Resource and Competency Management – Know and manage your People

PETRA ENDHOLZ

Siemens AG – Siemens IT Solution and Services

1 The Market defines the Demand for Resource and Competency Management

The Information Technology (IT) market has been developing rapidly since its emergence. Hardware and software, network and storage media, programming languages and new data warehouse concepts demonstrate an evolution that was not considered possible a few years ago. With these developments the standards towards IT service provider are increasing and changing. Traditionally, keywords like ‚Business Process Outsourcing (BPO)' or 'On-site, offshore delivery' were formative for this business. Nowadays, a companies' strategy needs to incorporate trends such as 'Green IT' or 'Cloud computing'. The latter being known as singular IT services which are flexibly retrievable and scalable[1], e. g., Software as a Service (SaaS)' or, Platform as a Service (PaaS)'[2].

For these rather technology driven and 'hands-on' topics, customers expect from IT service provider in general competitive pricing including continuous price reductions, meeting or exceeding service level agreements, and ensuring a high level of quality along standards set by the industry.

Even more challenging aspects show up on the strategic side. For every IT provider it is crucial to know and to understand customer's decision criteria. In general IT service decisions are made by the customers IT department head together with the board, mainly the Chief Information Officer.

What criteria or measurements do the board members of a company apply to define the success of IT nowadays? Most companies direct and align the internal IT services towards their business goals. Target achievements are still mostly measured solely by reduction of IT costs. An analysis of IDC discloses that the second most often selected key performance indicator is the cycle time of IT processes. Business-IT-alignment such as the reduction of end-to-end business processes targets rank third. This shows that short-term cost reduction goals are still the dominant aspect for decisions. However, this endangers long-term, sustainable value aspects for the customer as it focuses on one delimited domain, but does not take the impact on the companies' overall business processes and targets into account.[3]

IT service providers cannot limit their value contribution to high quality, cost efficient IT delivery. This will not be sufficient to sustain one's position in the market. To create a long-term partnership with the customer, the IT provider needs to consult the customer on the strategic impact of IT services on its core business goal and processes to build a durable alliance.

This holds true for Application Management in particular. Providing application management services involves a combination of technology know-how linked with a good understanding of customers' business processes.

---

1 *GILLETT* (2008), p. 10, and cf. *SMITH/CEARLEY* (2008), p. 3 et seq.

2 *MARRIOTT* (2008), p. 21.

3 Cf. online *COMPUTERWOCHE* (2008).

This article will highlight the significance of people in the IT business, while also considering operative and cost aspects as well as strategic facets. It will outline general activities to face the market challenges. Thirdly, the paper will provide an insight to initiatives on resource management - with the focus on competence management - chosen and implemented for *Siemens IT Solution and Services*, Global Operations, Global Application Management.

2 Resource and Competence Management as a Critical Factor of Success

Why should an IT service provider focus on his employees or so called 'human capital'? Is it because it's part of the company value system and consequently an image building activity? Or is it a business demand to accomplish a cost-efficient IT service delivery or even to provide a competitive advantage?

To answer this question in practice, it is worth looking at the company's values as well as the operational and strategic business rational.

2.1 Defining the Appropriate Business Strategy supported by the VRIO Model

Each company follows long-term profit objectives with the ultimate goal of ensuring the existence of its business. To safeguard the company, strategies are defined based on internal and external market information. Internal business reviews concentrate mainly on accounting data. Over years the focus was on *strategic external analysis*; primarily environmental analysis. This resulted in more and more similar strategies of companies active in the same market and in decreasing margins. Hence *strategic internal analysis* increased in significance. This builds a more stable foundation from which to select the appropriate strategy particularly in quickly changing markets and times with volatile customer expectations.[4]

The VRIO framework will be only briefly introduced. It is a tool to conduct strategic internal business analysis. Resource and capability within the framework embrace all types, such as patents, unique assets, brand loyalty, employee satisfaction, reputation, economies of scale to name only a few.

VRIO is an acronym of the four question framework. It asks about a resource or capability to determine its competitive potential from a strategic business point of view:[5]

- The Question of Value: "Is the firm able to exploit an opportunity or neutralize an external threat with the resource/capability?" Valuable resources contribute to an organization's efficiency, quality, customer responsiveness, and innovation. If a resource helps bring about any one of these four things then it is valuable.[6]

---

4 *HOSSFELD* (2005), p. 1 et seq.

5 Cf. online *WIKIPEDIA* (2009).

6 Cf. *HILL/JONES* (1998).

- The Question of Rarity: "Is control of the resource/capability in the hands of a relative few?" A resource is rare simply if it is not widely possessed by other competitors.
- The Question of Imitability: "Is it difficult to imitate, and will there be significant cost disadvantage to a firm trying to obtain, develop, or duplicate the resource/capability?" Generally, intangible resources or capabilities, like corporate culture or reputation, are very hard to imitate and therefore inimitable.
- The Question of Organization: "Is the firm organized, ready, and able to exploit the resource/capability?" Organizational focus refers to integrated and aligned managerial practices, routines, and processes. It also connotes managerial leadership and decisions that support key assets in terms of how these assets are developed and sustained.

Valuable?	Rare?	Costly to Imitate?	Exploitable by the Organization?	Competitive implications	Economic performance	Strengths or Weaknesses
No	-	-	No	Competitive Disadvantage	Below normal	Weakness
Yes	No	-	to	Competitive Parity	Normal	Strength
Yes	Yes	No		Temporary competitive advantage	Above normal	Strength and distinctive competence
Yes	Yes	Yes	Yes	Sustained competitive advantage	Above normal	Strength and sustainable distinctive competence

Figure 1: Schematic illustration of the VRIO Model of Barney[7]

Within the VRIO framework, if a resource is only valuable, it leads to competitive parity. Both value and rarity are required for a temporary competitive advantage. Value, rarity, and inimitability are required for a sustained competitive advantage[8], and an organizational focus is necessary to both develop a competitive advantage and sustain it.[9]

Even if the terminology of resource and capability within the framework is defined in a broader scope, it can also be applied with a narrow focus on 'human resources' or 'human assets'. Thus it sheds a different light onto the significance and potential impact of 'human capital' for the company.

The topic 'Transition and Transformation Management' shall serve as a practical sample to illustrate the above:

Global Application Management offers customers highly developed and innovative service offerings. This entails not only the transition, i. e. taking over application management services under a current Operating Model, but also the systematic transformation of the IT landscape for the continued market competitiveness of the customer. A methodology and specific

[7] BARNEY (1996), p. 163.

[8] Cf. BARNEY/WRIGHT (1998), p. 31 et seqq.

[9] Cf. JUGDEV (2005), p. 7.

portfolio element was designed to continuously increase the business value for the customer; it matures in stages from Interim Operating Model, Target Operating Model, to Future Modes of Operation.

This service portfolio element itself is to be considered a valuable and rare capability. In the VRIO model it would most likely be ranked as providing at least a temporary competitive advantage.

However, this element cannot be offered without adequately skilled resources. Therefore, the role Transition and Transformation Project Manager was established. This resource needs to fulfill multiple requirements: A Transition and Transformation Project Manager leverages a deep technical expertise along with industry-specific process and market knowledge (i. e. Business-IT-alignment), highly developed project management skills, building onto internal methodologies, external quality and industry standards such as Lean & Six Sigma and intercultural savvy. Furthermore, the resource needs to speak 'both languages' to communicate successfully to the customer – IT and business.

The VRIO model delimits a sustained competitive advantage with the question of Imitability. The resource of a Transition and Transformation Project Manager can to a great extent only be developed within a company. To answer this question, the combination of an innovative service portfolio element, implementing the required structures globally to provide and market the service, developing underlining methodologies and training frameworks, and identifying and educating the adequate people who have for example a well established network must be considered.

The combination of factors just mentioned indicates that this service offering is difficult to imitate. It further emphasizes the importance of the role 'Transition and Transformation Project Manager' as well as the role of the 'Portfolio Manager' to achieve a sustained competitive advantage.

2.2 Economic Impact of People

Next to strategy, the operative aspects are in general more present in day-to-day business. Two statements of the analyst *GARTNER*[10] will serve as a short introduction to the two main aspects:

- Cost drivers continue to be a key consideration for global delivery.
- Quality and consistency challenges will continue in particular in offshore locations.

This section will consider the impact of people in relation to cost and service quality. Both factors are not surprising for any player in the IT market, however, both are still the two most important decision factors for customers.

---

[10] *MARRIOTT* (2008), p. 32 et seq.

- An IT company's balance sheet contains only few capital assets, mainly properties, office equipment and hardware. Compared to this, the P/L includes costs related to software, infrastructure and personnel. The P/L has a much bigger impact on the overall valuation of the company. *Depending on the type of IT services, here IT application management services, the personnel costs is likely to have the greatest single source impact compared to the total costs.*

- When taking on new outsourcing deals for new or existing customers, an important step of this process is the design phase for a new business transition or a new transformation. Internal studies reveals that this planning and concept phase has a great impact on the overall cost management. In other words, errors or inaccuracies in the design phase which are detected at a later stage are difficult and costly to be straitened out. Furthermore, a trustful and long-term partnership with the customer depends on the design and consulting skills of the supplier. The appropriate solution for the specific customer demand needs to be analyzed, proposed and duly implemented. *To deploy the right people with the required skill set especially when designing a new deal is crucial for overall success and profit of the business.*

- Achieving and maintaining high quality standards nationally and internationally is important for the success of an outsourcing deal. Industry standards, e. g., Information Technology Infrastructure Library (ITIL) provide concepts and policies for managing information technology infrastructure, development and operations[11,12]. Methodologies and frameworks are in place. The key aspect is to have those fully implemented in all delivery units of all countries on the same quality level. The operation processes are executed by employees who need the right skill set. *The right set of competencies in service operations is a prerequisite to achieve quality standards and continuous improvement as demanded by customers.*

- Delivering IT services out of multiple locations is a challenge in itself. It means establishing the same processes and standards for different cultures in countries with extremely diverse circumstances, e. g., educational background, demographic environment, economic situation. This complex delivery network is an interaction between multiple locations. For each of these locations the analysts of Gartner denote: "The 'perfect' offshore location does not exist – vigilance and active management are essential"[13]. An IT service provider needs to clearly define roles and responsibilities and decide where to physically locate these, to have information on hand in order to balance work distribution, and to manage staff turnover rates. *Clear organizational structures, defined roles and a meaningful management information system including qualified staff data is a prerequisite for managing complexity across locations.*

---

11 Online *WIKIPEDIA* (2009).

12 Cf. online *ITIL* (2009).

13 *MARRIOTT* (2008), p. 34.

2.3 Leverage of the company's value system and business relationship

Selected strategy and operative aspects were mentioned. Both exist within and are influenced by the culture of the company. In technology-intensive industries the approach to people is typically technocratic. Strategies relate more to hard facts than to cultural or value aspects. However, a competitive advantage can only be sustainable if it is in line with the company culture. In the following, two selected points are presented; on how values can impact the companies' success and an example of relationship management during an outsourcing deal.

In general it is difficult to measure the impact of a company's value system on the identification and motivation level of employees and how it impacts profit. Studies in western companies indicate that about 70% of an employee's motivation level is impacted by the manager[14]. Another analysis reveals the correlation of the company's culture and values and its success. It is remarkable that the more successful companies do not have 'overly engineered' structures and controls but rather win by values such as trust. Other successful values are 'Complimentary approaching on each other' (i. e. accepting and knowing own strengths and weaknesses, conscious approaching of others to complement each other and achieve top results) or 'Uniqueness' (i. e. convinced and willing to achieve uniqueness by all internal and external actions). Employee satisfaction surveys or customer satisfaction surveys are in general used to make these impacts transparent. Surveys can be used to translate a gut instinct into figures to convince management and to make sound management decisions.

The key message is that a management team implementing and living a culture of 'successful values' impacts the overall success of a company.

A second point outlined and one example of living internal company values is experienced every day. One of the mayor challenges faced by service providers and service recipients when conducting offshore deals is to establish a true business partnership by understanding the roles of trust and control in the management of these partnerships[15]. This can be difficult even after many years of experience.

---

14 *BARBER/HAYDAY/BEVAN* (1999).

15 Cf. *MARRIOTT* (2008), p. 32.

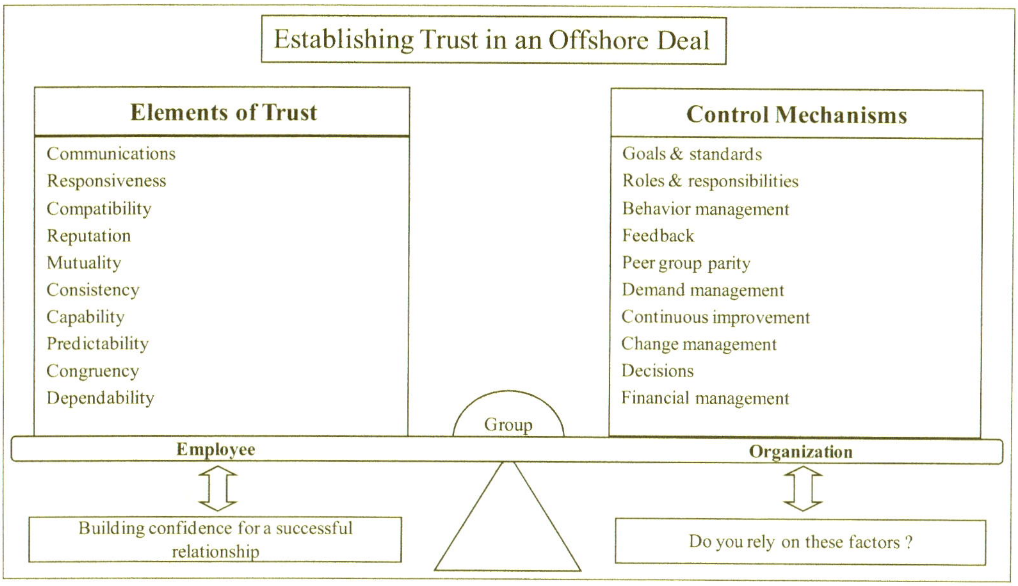

Figure 2: Elements in an Offshore Deal[16]

- *GARTNER* refers to "Elements of Trust" on the employee level. Not only intercultural facets need to be considered to communicate effectively. Moreover, a 'global culture' needs to emerge which incorporates the aspects of consistency, responsiveness, mutual appreciation, confidence by predictability and as a result of trust.
- On the organizational level the appropriate "Control Mechanism" needs to be in place. This includes setting global goals, frequent feedback, conducting change management and behavior management to establish standards.

A successful global IT delivery incorporates the organizational aspects, such as transparent controls, as well as individual elements realized by a trust-based collaboration.

So far the impact of human resources towards the short- and long-term success of an IT service provider has been illustrated. The following main part of this article will include general topics of Resource Management and present a particular initiative, Competency Management for Global Application Management of *Siemens IT Solution and Services*, in more detail. This shall provide an insight on how strategic and operative challenges are operationalized in day-to-day business.

16 *MARRIOTT* (2008).

3 Competency Management at Global Application Management of *Siemens*

This section will first introduce Global Application Management of *Siemens IT Solution and Services* in its global structure and set up. It will then give a general introduction and definition of Resource Management as it is applied in practice. Following this is a more detailed demonstration of Competency Management as one part of Resource Management; outlining the development of a competency structure, the concept of Competency Management and surrounding conditions when implementing a global initiative.

At first the organizational background will be illustrated to support a better understanding of the subsequent sections.

Global Application Management (GAA) is a part of Global Operations with *Siemens IT Solution and Services*. GAA has developed its organizational structure along with market demands; starting with offshore activities in the beginning of this century mainly due to cost reasons. Initially, the tasks were structured in the form of an 'extended workbench' with colleagues in Russia for example.

Nowadays, Global Application Management has matured into a true global system. One organizational structure, which was developed with and through the international management team, sets the framework. The defined model, called 'Target Operating Model' includes the organizational structure, definition of roles and responsibilities, and describes the way of working. Most important is that the international management team achieved a thorough implementation across all countries. Also the type of relationship and the work performed in the lower costs countries – often referred to as 'Offshore locations' – has changed. Former 'extended workbenches' were enriched with a wider spectrum of tasks and responsibilities up to taking over full service provisions.

GAA is structured in two organizational subunits as defined in the Target Operating Model. The Global Production Center (GPC) hosts and is responsible for the operational delivery especially for standardized services in the most efficient way and at a continuous quality level. The service delivery is to a notable share out of lower costs countries such as Russia or India. The Customer Service Organization (CSO) represents Application Management in multiple, mostly higher-cost countries and is the customer interface in cooperation with other *Siemens* units. CSO is responsible for the fulfillment of customer contracts and is responsible for the operational service delivery of customer specific, non-standardized services in an effective and profitable way.

The organizational set up and development towards a global culture provide a very good groundwork for initiatives in the field of Resource or Competence Management.

3.1 Overview of Resource Management

There is not one single definition of Resource Management. In the way it is applied here is to be understood in the sense of people management, representing the active management of employees also referred to as 'human capital'.

Resource Management ensures short- and long-term the availability of resources in the right number with the required set of competencies as per business demand.

The main goal following this definition is to have 'the right person at the right time in the right function'. This reflects on the following factors from a business standpoint:

- Adequate qualification of the person/s, meaning the right level of competence for the assigned task
- Availability of the person/s, including number of resources, time, and location, e. g. in the required country
- Conducting the assignment of the task and the underlining business process from two angles:
  - Assigning project related tasks, e. g. for transition projects or for proposal work, which have in general a short- or mid-term planning interval
  - Deploying delivery related roles or functions, e. g. technical expert or production line manager, to fill temporary or permanent positions within the line organization
- Transparency by availability of information for the organization to plan and develop the organization accordingly, often referred to as 'strategic planning' and 'strategic competence management'

As defined for Global Application Management, the function Resource Management coordinates activities related to global resource planning, skill structure, resource development and assignment management for the unit and has a governance function for respective processes, tools and activities. In particular, Resource Management will focus on establishing a global structure for resource management activities to enable and support global business needs. Resource Management is an integrated part of the business with a strong interlink to Human Resources Department. Selected topics of resource management are outlined in a few words in the following:

- Quarterly rolling resource forecast: The Global Production Center (GPC) delivers operational IT services to customers in multiple countries (see also section 3). To support the GPC head in the decision for a future resource demand, e. g. to ramp up personnel, a forecast process was established. This process is conducted quarterly with monthly updates in case of major changes. It collects information of the Customer Service Organization (CSO) units of all countries on current and on potential new customer contracts. The information includes the next twelve months and lists not only the number of resources but also the type of service and competencies required (e. g. particular SAP Modules or Remedy). The information is aggregated and allocated to the particular GPC. When introducing this process one lessons learned session was conducted at the end of each quarter. The learnings helped to quickly enhance the process and to increase the level of acceptance.

- Short-term resource deployment: The staffing of projects, e. g. for transition and transformation projects or for proposal, is another task of Resource Management. A global tool is in place for *Siemens IT Solution and Services* which is managed by another unit outside Global Operations. Therefore, the task focuses on operative assignment management which is conducted by trained resources around the globe. The central team conducts quality checks of the data, supports countries in case of questions or escalations and fosters a regular exchange by leading a global community.

Other topics relevant for Resource Management are structured development initiatives, such as training concepts or global expert communities, skill landscapes, job code or role concepts also outlining job paths and career opportunities, or supporting processes to ensure compliant set up of staff deployment across countries. Most of these activities are developed or provided in close cooperation with and sometimes also mandated by other departments, e. g. Human Resources, International Human Resources or Corporate Accounting.

In relationship to the above listed topics competency management is understood as a fundamental building block. Therefore, this topic was elected to be introduced and outlined in more detail in the following.

3.2 Introduction to Competency Management – a Part of Resource Management

Literature defines the terminology ‚competence' as well as competency management' itself from different angles.[17]

One definition is: Competency management refers to the analysis of existing competencies, the identification of missing competencies and the timely development of those.[18]

Siemens classifies competency management as "the identification and closure of competency gaps in human resources necessary to implement strategic business unit decisions." *Siemens* implemented one uniform worldwide competency model, the *Siemens* Competency Model. The model comprises the three elements Knowledge, Experience and Capabilities[19]. The *Siemens* Competency Model defines the framework and details the element Capabilities. It leaves expansion space in the areas Knowledge and Experience to fulfill the specific business requirements of a sector or unit.

---

17 *BREITNER* (2005).

18 Cf. *BIESALSKI* (2006).

19 *ROSENSTIEL/PIELER/GLAS* (2004).

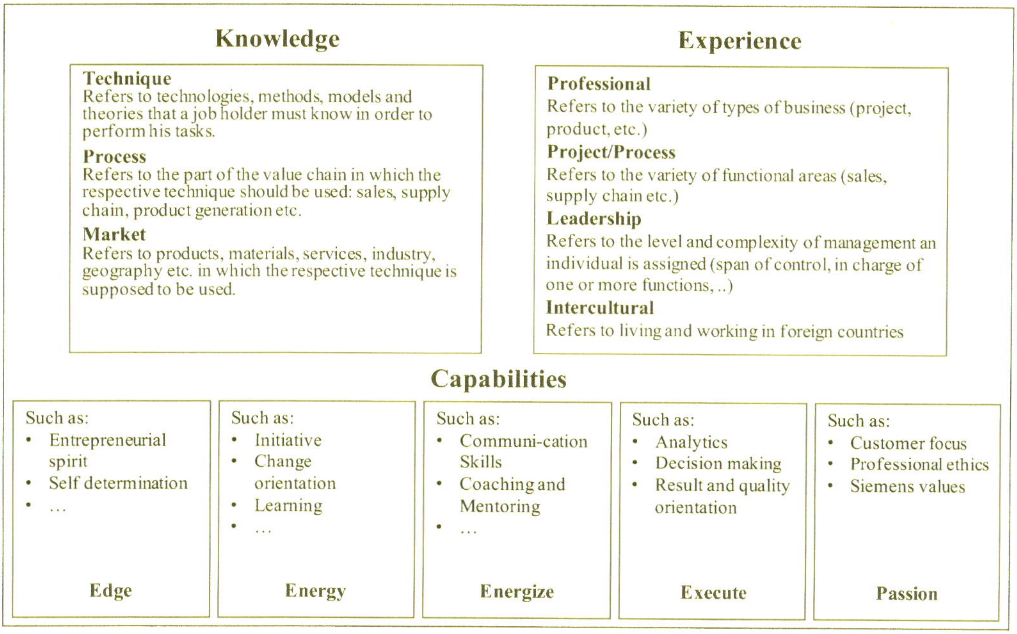

Figure 3: *Siemens Competency Model*

Building on the standards of *Siemens* and considering the particular demand for IT service provider, the goal of the initiative Competency Management was set as follows:

Enhancing the individual and thereby the organizational core competencies for optimizing service delivery is the overall purpose of introducing a uniform global Competency Management.

The two main objectives are transparency and an active personnel and organizational development. The information gathered adds value in various aspects for the organization, e. g. it supports and enables management to balance work load between countries also short-term, and it allows individuals to become known across the organization for highly developed competencies or to conduct trainings for other employees.

The project comprised two mayor deliverables which are introduced in the following; the competency structure and the underlining operative processes defined in the competency concept.

3.3 Development of a Competency Structure

The first deliverable was the development of a comprehensive yet specific Competency Structure for the company's Global Operations delivery.

In this step it is essential to analyze the strategic facets in order to define the goal and the scope of the competency structure, e. g. groups of employees, regional focus. The overall target for the unit Global Application Management was to have a uniform global structure in place to obtain additional transparency of the organization. The content and with this the broadness of the structure had its focus on the experts of the company, e. g. not including commercial competencies or competencies of other support functions in detail. At a later stage the target group was widened to also include managerial competencies.

The following lists the core requirements for the concept of the structure:

- Development of a structure based on the company-wide *Siemens* Competency Model
- Hierarchical concept of the structure based on dimension and sub-dimensions
- Uniform levels with objective criteria to define the level for a particular competence

As outlined before, the specified competency structure is based on the *Siemens* Competency Model which comprises three elements: Knowledge, Experience and Capabilities. The structure is build up systematically by separating these three elements. Upon detailing this structure for the IT delivery the focus was placed onto 'applied knowledge', recognizing the blend of these three elements, in particular increasing the level of knowledge through work experience.

3.3.1 Hierarchical Model

The basis for competence management is the competency structure, also denoted as competency catalogue[20]. It is constructed in a hierarchical model. The upper layers are called 'Element' and 'Dimension'.

The development of the structure was conducted as a top-down approach for the layers 'elements' and the 'dimensions'. This allowed for a structure in line with *Siemens* guidelines and with business requirements of the organization. After that the first and second layer of the sub-dimension was created together with experts of the organization in the particular fields in workshop. The expert exchange was also considered a quality gate for the logic of the predefined upper structure. In the course of this process, one adjustment was made in the upper layer 'dimension' until it passed the quality gate.

---

20 Cf. BIESALSKI (2006).

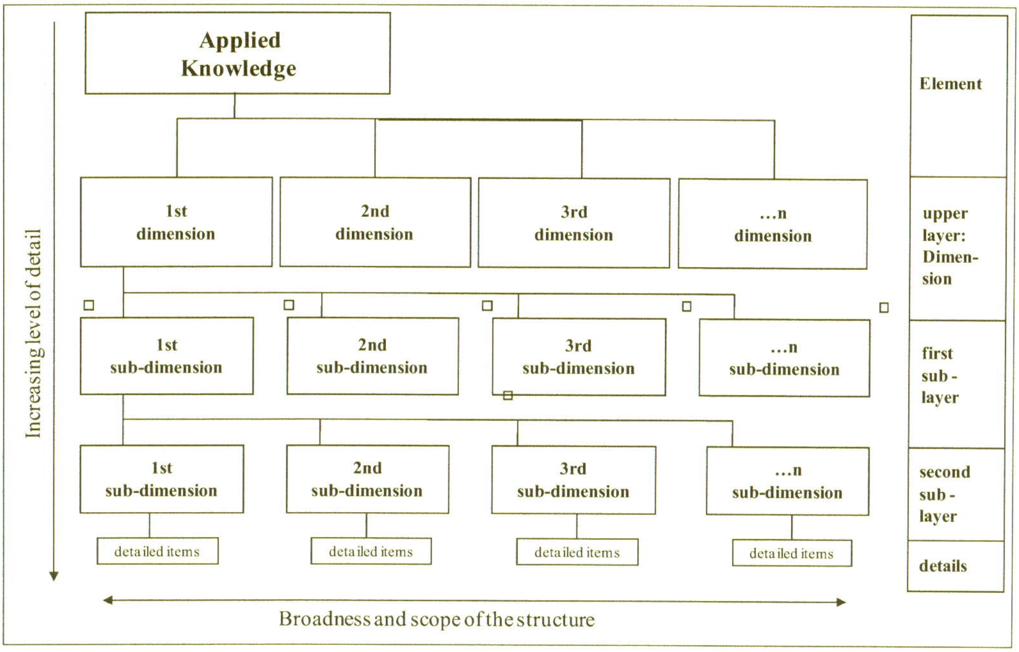

Figure 4: Hierarchy model of the competency structure

It is clustered into six knowledge dimensions:

- *Operational Excellence*: The dimension "Operational Excellence" covers the knowledge of how our services are provided and maintained, including processes, methods / frameworks, tools, requirements as well as service level management and project management.
- *Technology*: The dimension "Technology" covers knowledge regarding hardware architecture and software, especially business process related software (e. g. *SAP*, *Siebel)* which is separated from other software (e. g. Java, HTML). It includes knowledge ranging from application "consult / design" to "build" to "operate" to "maintain", as well as "test management".
- *Business Processes*: The dimension "Business Process" covers process knowledge that is generally applicable to all industries - for example, the financial, logistics, and human resources processes. It also includes knowledge of taking over customer IT processes (ITO) and customer business processes (BPO).
- *Market / Vertical*: The dimension "Market / Vertical" covers the knowledge of a specific industry (with respect to industry specific processes, IT-architecture and branch specific types of enterprise organization, industrial environment and business models, e. g. legal regulations etc).
- *Sales & Business Development*: The dimension "Sales & Business Development" covers the knowledge needed to win new customers and maintain and develop existing customers. This includes application of marketing techniques and the development and maintenance of portfolio elements.

- *People & Organizational Excellence*: The dimension "People & Organizational Excellence" covers the knowledge of strategic orientation for self, team and internal organizational development. It includes establishment of structures and development of the organization, of a team or person, e. g. training, change management, communication, languages.

The focus is to evaluate knowledge which is currently applied or could be utilized in the near future without additional training efforts. Each knowledge dimension is divided into several subdimensions and up to two hierarchy levels. These three layers add up to 100 different knowledge competencies.

The depth of the competency structure depends on the overall target. This structure aims to inventory competencies to utilize for organizational and personnel development. Therefore, the core competencies, such as 'Operational Excellence' or 'Technology' were outlined in more detail, e. g. for *SAP* know-how as far as listing of the individual modules of *SAP*.

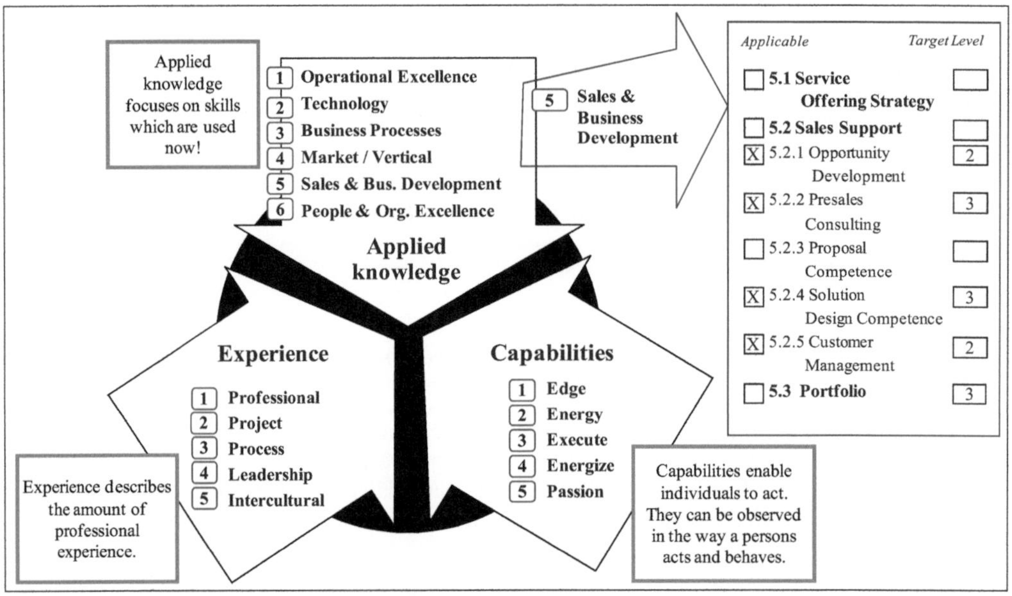

Figure 5: Global Operations Competency Structure

3.3.2 Level Model

The levels are akin to a metric system. These define to which extent the specific competency is existent. Models in the industry and in literature reach from three levels, e. g. basic, advanced, expert, up to seven or even nine levels.[21]

21 GROTE/KAUFFELD/EKKEHART (2006).

It was decided to have one rating option "no evaluation" and then five different levels reaching from Level 1 'Beginner' to Level 5 'Master'.

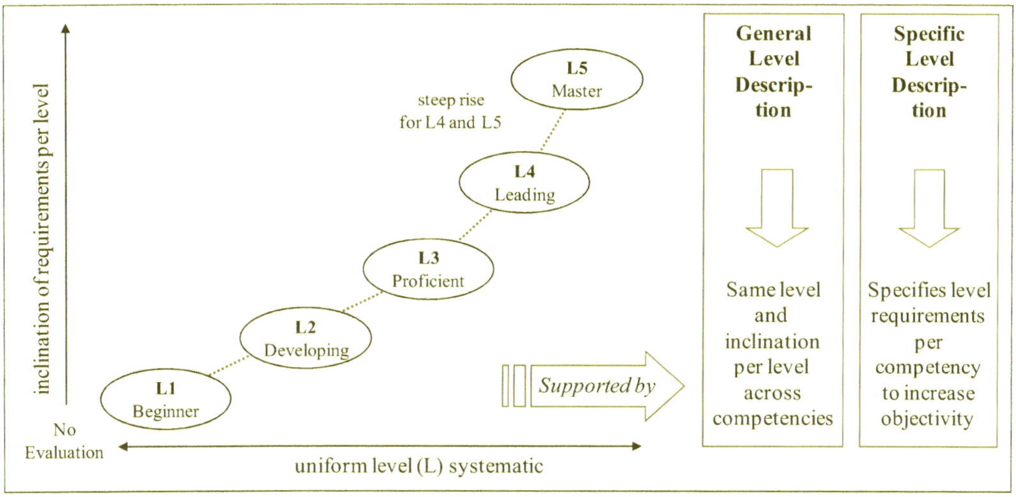

Figure 6: Level model of the competency structure

Three main reasons were the basis for choosing the scale of five:

- Sufficient number in scale to ensure clear and distinctive competency levels as the structure is applied globally. It shall provide a uniform language specific enough to fulfill customer requirements, e. g. a Level 2 in ITIL[22] for 'Service Level Management' is recognized in the same way in India, USA, or Brazil.
- Development steps of an employee can be specified in more detail and may be reached faster than in a level scale of three. This provides options to develop and, therefore, has a positive impact on the employee's motivation to improve in a particular field.
- The upper two levels are exceptional levels. It was important to identify internationally the "stars" (meaning outstanding experts) in a particular field. At the same time it demonstrates to employees that development opportunities are possible in two directions; in an expert profile (high level of expertise in one or very few competencies) or in a general profile (multiple competencies on a lower to medium level).

The unique requirements for a particular level of the element Knowledge follow a 'general level description' outlining breadth and depth of a competency. This ensures that a Level 3 for the competency 'Opportunity development' follows the same guidelines as a Level 3 for the competency 'Process knowledge: Data content management'

22 *ITIL.ORG* (2009).

Guidelines were set for the participants giving guidance on how to conduct the level rating. A requirement is that competencies are up-to-date, meaning current and valid. Competencies shall be rated on the level that a competency is used at present or could be used in the foreseeable future. In other words, competencies that have aged or are no longer relevant are not to be rated.

The structure covers technical know-how, methods and also social competencies. Considering the constant changes in the IT business and a continuous need to adapt the skills of the organization, one important competence is 'Training'. This competence will exemplify the specific level description. For this particular competence the description of the levels are addressed to two target groups: to the 'classical' trainer and people responsible for training concepts and secondly to (technical) experts of the organization who are also capable of conducting trainings for their field of expertise.

Description of the competence "Training"
This competence covers training concepts, program design, implementation and training analysis for strategic or daily business to foster "a learning organization".

L1 Beginner	L2 Developing	L3 Proficient	L4 Leading	L5 Master
- Schedules and coordinates with internal stakeholders for execution of training programs - Helps in identifying training needs or - Conducts brief knowledge transfer sessions within own work environment	- Identifies training needs - Supports development of training curriculum - Performs vendor management for training programs and related initiatives - Helps in end-to-end execution of training program including issue of certifications or - Conducts trainings for own knowledge field / area of expertise	- Performs diagnostic study of identified needs - Actively supports development of training curriculum and communication plan in line with business needs - Actively helps in the design and execution of training initiatives - Is responsible for end-to-end execution of training programs or - Conducts trainings for several knowledge fields / areas of expertise	- Designs and executes training programs - Creates train-the-trainer concepts - Is responsible for driving value-added initiatives like e-learning and innovative programs like opinion polls, quiz shows, training fairs, exhibitions, etc. - Adapts training measures and develops services for specific situations and demands	- Advises top management on learning initiatives - Manages alliances, partner management for training and value-added initiatives like e-learning - Validates train-the-trainer concepts and recommends the type, method and process for training programs - Establishes a culture of learning in the organization - Identifies learning requirements that will support successful implementation of corporate, regional, and group business strategies

Figure 7: Sample of a specific level description of the "Training" competence

3.4 Concept of Competency Management

The second mayor deliverable of the project is introduced next. The Concept of Competency Management defines and interlinks the operative assessment process and its results to two main processes which are existent in the organization:

- *Annual personnel development process*: *Siemens* has processes in place to conduct the development of an individual efficiently. The focus of competency management is to have the competency data available, to intensify the dialogue between manager and employee even further, to stress competency as a core management topic and to use the transparent information to develop the individual in line with the organization and with this in line with the market. The Operative Competency Management Cycle describes this process.

- *Annual strategy process*: The link of competency management towards the company-wide strategy process goes in two directions. One is to provide input on the competency landscape of a unit or country as information to define next year's strategy. The second is to apply the finalized strategy in respect to competencies as input for the organization and to break down the future requirements for a unit, country or group of employees. The Integration into strategic planning cycle outlines this subject.

Both processes and the interrelation are presented in the following two sections.

3.4.1 The Operative Competency Management Cycle

Probably the most challenging part of Competency Management is the data gathering, the assessment process itself. For the here presented initiative the operative Competency Management Cycle is linked up to the standardized annual personnel development process of *Siemens*, called Performance Management Process.

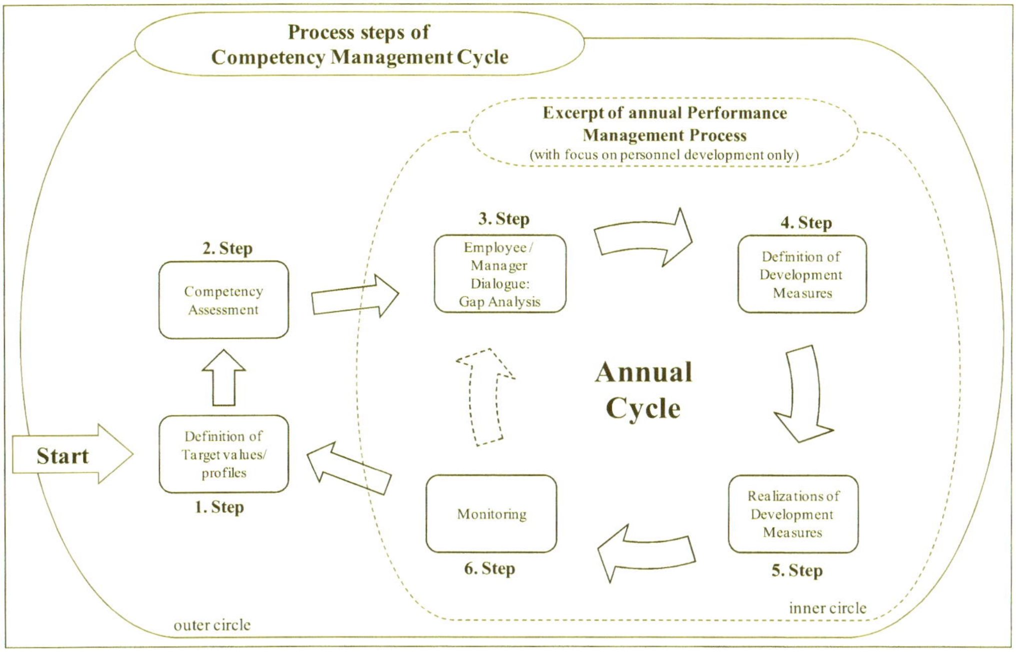

Figure 8: Operative annual Competency Management Cycle

The goal was to implement a sustainable process and to integrate it into the existing process landscape. The inner circle (Figure 8, step 3 to 6) represents an excerpt of the worldwide established Performance Management Process. This process is mandated by Human Resources and conducted in all units and countries of the organization. In entails various aspects such as annual target setting, monitoring of target achievement, definition of development measures, career planning, income/benefits review. The figure above lists only the aspects in regard to personnel development and is, therefore, an extract only.

In this case sustainability of the outer circle is achieved by tying the additional steps required to conduct the assessment (Figure 8, step 1 and 2) into the existent, mandatory annual process.

A brief overview of the process steps:

1. Step: Definition of Target Values / Profiles
From an organizational point of view target values can be predefined before the assessment starts, e. g. , by specifying profiles for a group of employees. Target values can be alternatively identified by analyzing the as-is data after the assessment is conducted (step 2) and by comparing it to future business requirements. Target values and profiles are defined and updated annually for the respective organizational units and represent the future business requirements. They are determined by the respective top management together with experts.

2. Step: Online Competency Assessment
This step represents the assessment process itself. It is most vital to focus on obtaining high quality data, meaning comparable and accurate data across countries based on the same objective criteria. This involves two parallel activities:

→ Self-analysis: The employee evaluates his/her current level of competency and provides reasoning which proves and makes the selected level transparent to any third party.

→ Analysis by manager: The manager evaluates the employee's competencies and seeks to arrive at the most correct estimate of the employee's competencies.

3. Step: Employee and Manager Dialogue / Gap Analysis
The focus is to further increase the dialogue between manager and employee and to drive and anchor the strategically important topic of personnel development. It is understood that both parties involved – the manager as well as the employee - have a responsibility towards the person's development. Employee and manager compare the results with target values and discuss deviations in this personal dialogue with the objective of identifying and articulating the employee's developmental needs. This personal dialogue is integrated into the companies annual Performance Management Process. Please refer to step 1 on the definition of target values from an organizational standpoint. From an individual point of view manager and employee should additionally define individual targets based on specific job requirements considering planned development or career steps.

4. Step: Definition of Development Measures
Concrete developmental measures for competency development are defined along with timelines and responsibilities, and integrated the annual Performance Management Process.

Competency development within a function means the actualization journey from the as-is competency profile to the identified target values. Typical development measures include deployment on projects, specific practical experiences, on the job training, self-learning, learning through training programs. Competency development into another function means the development effort to take on new and/or challenging tasks or graduating to another position.

5. Step: Realizations of Development Measures
The manager and the employee track the progress of development measures through a continuous dialogue. It is part of the target setting process. The implementation of measures including adjustments and modifications are duly documented.

6. Step: Monitoring
Target achievements are monitored in frequent monitoring sessions. The implementation of an effective competency management is incorporated in the objectives for manager. The realization of individual measurements is reviewed accordingly. The development measures are again examined by the manager and the employee and documented accordingly.

3.4.2 Integration into Strategic Planning Cycle

The annual competency cycle as well as the outlined assessment process focuses more on the individual level. It provides feedback to the employee on his/her current set of competencies and on development opportunities through a structured procedure; it further provides transparency of the individual and the team to the respective manager.

Aiming towards an integrated competency management concept, the strategic junction is introduced: At the company level, it assists in the competency development of the organization as a whole. It contributes valuable information for mid- and long-term planning and to integrate the personnel management activities with the strategic business needs.

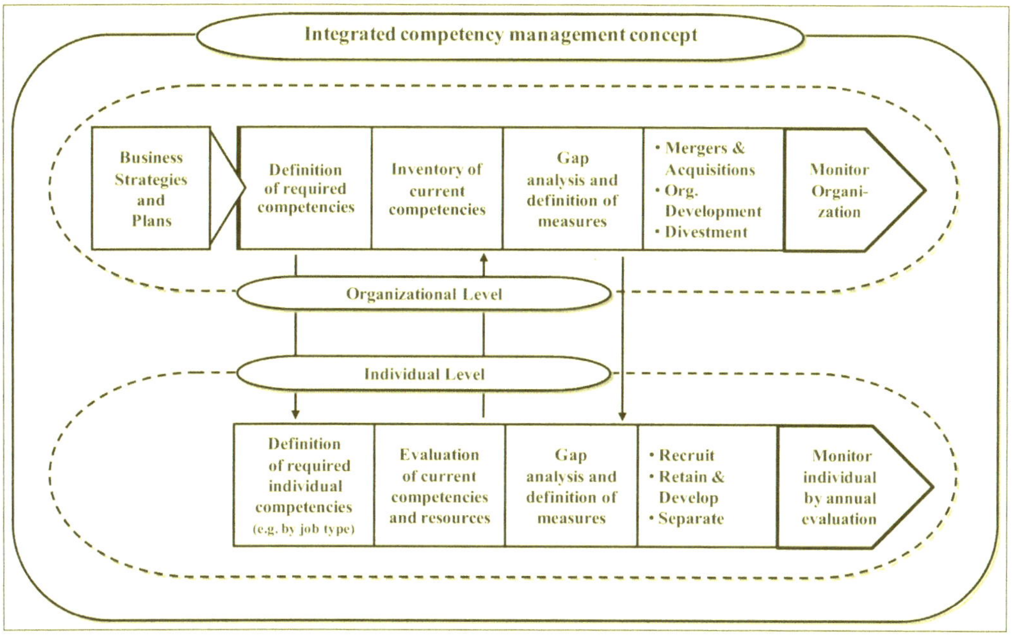

Figure 9: Link between organizational and individual competency development

The figure shows that the organizational and the individual level are interlinked. Both require input and provide output to each other. Based on business strategies, core competencies for the organization are defined. This is broken down to units and groups of employees. The individual knows the competency requirements. Evaluating the current competencies through an assessment and aggregating the data provides information to the organization on the as-is situation. Measurements can be defined accordingly. A measurement may be that a core competency is required for the future and not available at all in the organization (e. g. for a new product or technology). The management can then make a decision if cooperation with strategic partners is feasible to close the gap. Another option might be to hire several key experts of the specific topic and set up internal training programs to achieve the required goal.

A company needs to decide if it addresses the individual and organizational level subsequently or in parallel when introducing a competency management. The question can be reduced to where to start the process – on the individual or the organizational level. The decision depends mainly on what the prior target of the organization was. It is important to communicate the steps and the overall approach to employees, manager and other process partners, including workers council.

Global Application Management decided to start in the first cycle with the inventory of competencies. Based on the as-is information, measures and decisions for the organization follow.

3.5 Surrounding Conditions

Next to the information on resource and competency management this section shall outline practical aspects which need to be considered when developing and implementing a global initiative such as Competency Management. These type of initiatives or activities hold an often underestimated complexity.

Global organizations struggle with balancing central governance and country or unit autonomy. The challenge is to define an approach which can be implemented in a timely manner, considering local laws and regulations, which finds acceptance and which is an adequate solution for the defined objective.

In the case of Competency Management, an "evolving" project approach was chosen. It was originally defined for one part of the organization. First pilots in three countries were conducted. With increasing maturity it was adapted to suit a larger part of the organization. Again pilots to test two different assessment processes were conducted and again an improved approach combining the advantages of both pilots was defined.

As in any system that combines automated and manual steps, the manual part – competency assessment – can be the weak link.[23]

Data quality aspects as well as data security should be planned and considered right from the start. The goal is to achieve an objective measurement across countries. If the data is not comparable, is not worth to spending time gathering it. For Competency Management the employee is asked to provide reasoning for the chosen level. Within the self-assessment tool

---

23 Online *INTELLIGENTENTERPRISE* (2009).

text fields are to be filled. In these text fields the employee lists facts in an objective manner which relate directly to the specific level description in bullet point style. All points of the level description must be attested. Otherwise, the next lowest level is to be selected.

People related initiatives also need to consider the change management aspect. There is a high risk involved if managers or employees do not accept the new procedure. This may either affect the data quality negatively or even jeopardize the overall implementation.

The implementation of Competency Management does not impact the organizational set-up as is, but it changes the interaction within the organization by emphasizing the management of the organizational key assets: people, their knowledge and the ability to deploy that in a way which aims at a continuous improvement of people excellence. For the initiative of Competency Management it was decided that the organization needs to be accompanied in transition from the old to the new cultural pattern by focusing on the following key elements:

- Underlining the need and benefits of actively managing employee competencies
- Subsequently consistently re-enforcing and acknowledging the new behavior
- Building the competencies necessary to assimilate the new pattern across the entire organization

The above is an excerpt only which shall illustrate the various aspects of people related initiatives in general and how these topics were approached for Global Application Management.

4 Conclusion

The IT market and its developments will not slow down. Operative and strategic aspects will continue to be a challenge. The only way for companies to face this challenge is to develop a suitable and competitive strategy and to enable the organization to keep up with the market.

Adequate organizational structures and global standardized processes are important. A competency structure and assessment process is such a structural element and provides guidance. However, to truly meet the market requirements means that the organization is enabled to learn on its own. Therefore, Competency Management is considered a building block to implement active and continuous people management worldwide.

The results of the competency analysis for Global Application Management will be applied for multiple activities. Some of those listed below have started; others are in the planning stage:

- Identify experts (e. g. employees with competency level 4 or 5) globally, e. g. for strategic important customer deals, projects and proposals
- Use information to staff projects, e. g. transition and transformation projects, with the adequate skill level and cost rate, including mix of junior and senior consultants as well as onshore and offshore resources

- Set up global training plans based on the identified gaps for key roles of the Global Delivery Network
- Identify country or unit specific training or other development measures and use information to calculate the training budget; check training success based on next year's data
- Structure and standardize induction plans for Global Production Center to ensure quick ramp up of resources and same quality of skills at same job level
- Link jobs to specific competency level globally and build up an expert career framework; provide transparency to employees on competency requirements for roles and jobs within the organization and empower individuals to take responsibility for their own development

The above are single operative objectives focusing on particular benefits for the organization.

Referring once more to the VRIO Model (see section 2.1), the Question of Organization refers to integrated and aligned managerial practices, routines, and processes. The 'human resource' is receiving more and more attention in the IT business. This will provide a long-term sustained competitive advantage to the company.

Working in a technology-intensive industry, these single objectives need to be united in a greater model. The identification of key assets and their development has to become an integral part of managerial leadership and to be internalized by the organization.

The first steps on this path have been taken. The journey of Global Application Management of *Siemens IT Solution and Services* remains stimulating and interesting.

References

BARBER, L./HAYDAY, S./BEVAN, S. (1999): From People to Profits: The HR link in the service-profit chain, Report 355, Institute for Employee Studies (IES Research Networks), Brighton 1999.

BARNEY, J. B. (1996): Gaining and sustaining competitive advantage, 1st ed., New Jersey 1996.

BARNEY, J.B./WRIGHT, P.M. (1998): On becoming a strategic partner: The role of human resources in gaining competitive advantage, in: Human Resource Management, 1998, Vol. 37, No. 1, pp. 31–46.

BIESALSKI, E. (2008): Kompetenzmanagement & Personalentwicklung, online: http://kompetenzmanagement.wordpress.com/, last update: 25.11.2008, date visited: 22.05.2009.

BREITNER, M. H. (2005): Kompetenzmanagement: Aktuelle Konzepte und Methoden. Kompetenzmanagement als Schlüssel integrierter wertschöpfender Verfahren, in: 3. Symposium Kompetenzmanagement und Business Value Chain. Schloss Birlinghoven, Sankt Augustin/Bonn on 07.-.08.09.05, 2005.

COMPUTERWOCHE.DE (2008): Kostenfokus behindert IT-Business-Alignment, online: http://www.computerwoche.de/heftarchiv/2008/42/1224952/, 2008, No. 42, 10.10.2009.

GBI.DE (2006): Suche nach klaren Strukturen – Die Forderung nach Kompetenzmanagement mach die Runde – doch wie geht's?, in: Stuttgarter Zeitung, 17.06.2006.

GROTE, S./KAUFFELD, S./FRIELING, E. (2006): Kompetenzmanagement, Grundlagen und Praxisbeispiele, Stuttgart 2006.

GILLETT, F. E. (2008): Future View: The New Tech Ecosystems Of Cloud, Cloud Services, And Cloud Computing, Forrester 2008.

HOßFELD, O. (2005): Hauptseminararbeit: Strategische Unternehmensanalyse unter besonderer Berücksichtigung des Wertkettenmodells von Porter und des VRIO Modells von Barney, Kiel 2005.

HILL, C. W. L./JONES, G. R. (1998): Strategic Management Theory: An Integrated Approach, 4th ed., Boston 1998.

ITIL.ORG (2009): ITIL ®, online: http://www.itil.org/en/, Glenfis Ltd., last update: not disclaimed, date visited: 03.06.2009.

INTELLIGENTENTERPRISE.COM (2009): IBM - Optimizing the Human Supply Chain by Michael Voelker, online: http://www.intelligententerprise.com/showArticle.jhtml;jsessionid=2F0W02VF2TS2EQSNDLRSKH0CJUNN2JVN?articleID=175002433, United Business Media LLC, published: 01.01.2006, date visited: 26.03.2009.

JUGDEV, K. (2005): The VRIO Framework of Competitive Advantage: Preliminary research implications for innovation management, PICMET, Portland State University, Portland 2005.

MARRIOTT, I. (2008): Outsourcing Market / Environment – Overview, Gartner, 2008.

VON ROSENSTIEL, L./PIELER, D./GLAS, P. (2004): Strategisches Kompetenzmanagement, Wiesbaden 2004.

SMITH, D. M./CEARLEY, D. W. (2008): Contrasting Perspectives on Cloud Computing; Gartner, 2008.

WIKIPEDIA (2009): online: http://en.wikipedia.org/wiki/ITIL, last update: 07.08.2009, date visited: 07.08.2009.

WIKIPEDIA (2009): online: http://en.wikipedia.org/wiki/VRIO, last update: 29.04.2009, date visited: 28.05.2009

Part 3:

Application Management – Strategies and Instruments

Knowledge Management Strategies and Instruments as a Basis for Transition to Application Management

Benedikt Schmidt

Siemens AG – Siemens IT Solution and Services

1 Introduction

This article describes aspects of knowledge management and its significance for application management. It presents instruments and methods for knowledge transfer on the basis of fundamental knowledge management approaches and theories. In application management, knowledge is transferred when responsibility passes to another party, especially when an implementation project is completed or when the operation of applications is outsourced or outtasked.

This presentation of knowledge management instruments is followed by a look at the governance that is needed in the author's opinion to control and monitor transition projects.

2 Knowledge Management

Knowledge plays an important role in all walks of life, including the support of applications. Only if support staff know how a system is supposed to respond are they able to answer questions and deal with problems and errors reported by users. The key to this is the transfer of knowledge from the previous organization to the new provider of support. This article describes approaches to knowledge structuring and explains the importance of implicit or tacit knowledge for support activities.

2.1 Basics and Definitions

The most widespread definition of knowledge in the literature makes a distinction between data, information and knowledge.[1]

Data denotes a collection of symbols to describe a thing or person in elementary terms. Data can be recorded, classified and stored but it is not structured to indicate specific contexts.

Information can be regarded in two ways: firstly as organized data in which individuals see a meaning and which they interpret and use to draw conclusions, and secondly as the result of the interpretation of data that people get and give a meaning on the basis of the context and their personal knowledge.

Knowledge comes from linking various pieces of information on the basis of a context and against the background of an individual's experiences.[2] According to *NONAKA* et al., information becomes knowledge when it is interpreted by individuals and is placed in a context – anchored in their beliefs and actions.[3]

---

1 Cf. *DAVENPORT* (1998), *NONAKA* (2001), *KRCMAR* (2003), *MERTINS* (2003), *MAIER* (2005), and *PROBST* (2006).

2 Cf. *MAIER* (2005), p. 4.

3 Cf. *NONAKA* (2001), p. 15.

DAVENPORT describes the transition from data to information in terms of different methods:

- *Contextualization* – the purpose of data collection is known
- *Categorization* – the analysis unit or main component of the data material is known
- *Calculation* – the data can be analyzed mathematically
- *Correction* – errors have been eliminated from the data
- *Condensation* – the data has been consolidated[4]

In this context, knowledge is defined as "[...] a fluid mix of framed experience, values, contextual information, and expert insight that provides a framework for evaluating and incorporating new experiences and information".[5] Knowledge is therefore dynamic and keeps changing, depending on the context in which it was considered or acquired. According to *DAVENPORT*, knowledge in organizations is not just kept in documents or electronic repositories but is gradually embedded in organizational routines and processes so knowledge must be understood both as a dynamic process and as a static substance. *DAVENPORT* states that the creation of knowledge – that is the transformation of information into knowledge – must be seen in the following context:

- *Comparison* – assessment of one item of information against other, known information
- *Consequences* – the implications of decisions and actions based on this information
- *Connections* – the relationships between knowledge elements
- *Conversation* – assessment of this information by others[6]

When it comes to knowledge and its management, *DAVENPORT* focuses in part on the interaction between individuals and regards interpersonal relationships as playing a major role in the creation of knowledge.

2.2 Concept of Knowledge Management according to *NONAKA* and *TAKEUCHI*

According to NONAKA et al., knowledge in organizations is created in a dynamic process consisting of action and reaction. This concept holds that knowledge is created in a spiral that involves a dialectic debate on existing knowledge and comes about in the social interaction between individuals and organizations (cf.).

4 Cf. *DAVENPORT* (1998), p. 30.

5 *DAVENPORT* (1998), p. 32.

6 Cf. *DAVENPORT* (1998), p. 32 ff.

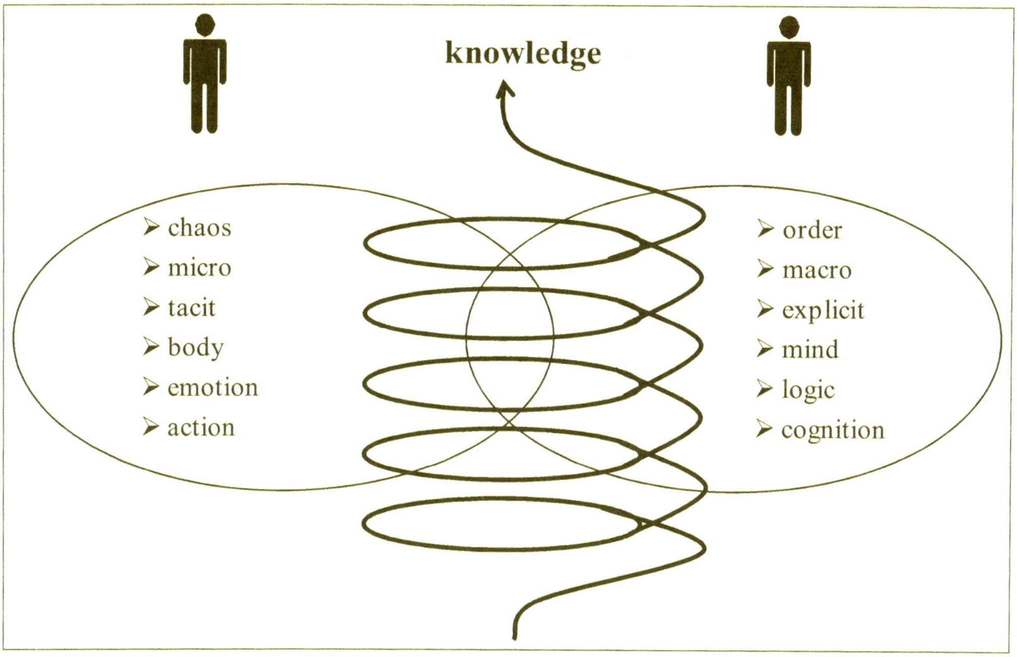

Figure 1: Creation of knowledge in the knowledge spiral[7]

NONAKA et al. categorize knowledge as explicit and tacit. *Explicit knowledge* has the following characteristics:

- It can be articulated in formal and systematic language
- It can be kept in the form of data, scientific formulae, specifications and manuals
- It is easy to process, transfer and store

This is contrasted with implicit or *tacit knowledge*, which has the following characteristics:

- It is strongly tied to people and hard to formalize
- It is deeply anchored in actions, procedures, routines, values and emotions
- It is hard to transfer to others[8]

The interaction of these two types of knowledge creates new knowledge. New knowledge can only be created when explicit knowledge is joined by tacit knowledge. *TAKEUCHI* extends the definition of tacit knowledge by adding a cognitive dimension. This is based on the values, beliefs, ideals, emotions and mental models that are ingrained in everybody's perception.[9]

7 Cf. *NONAKA*, (2001), p. 13.

8 Cf. *NONAKA* (2001), p. 15.

9 Cf. *TAKEUCHI* (2001), p. 319.

2.3 Concept of Knowledge Management according to *PROBST*, *RAUB* and *ROMHARDI*

PROBST et al. describe a knowledge management model consisting of individual building blocks which together form a comprehensive approach to the implementation of knowledge management. The individual blocks are not isolated from each other but are closely linked (cf. Figure 2).

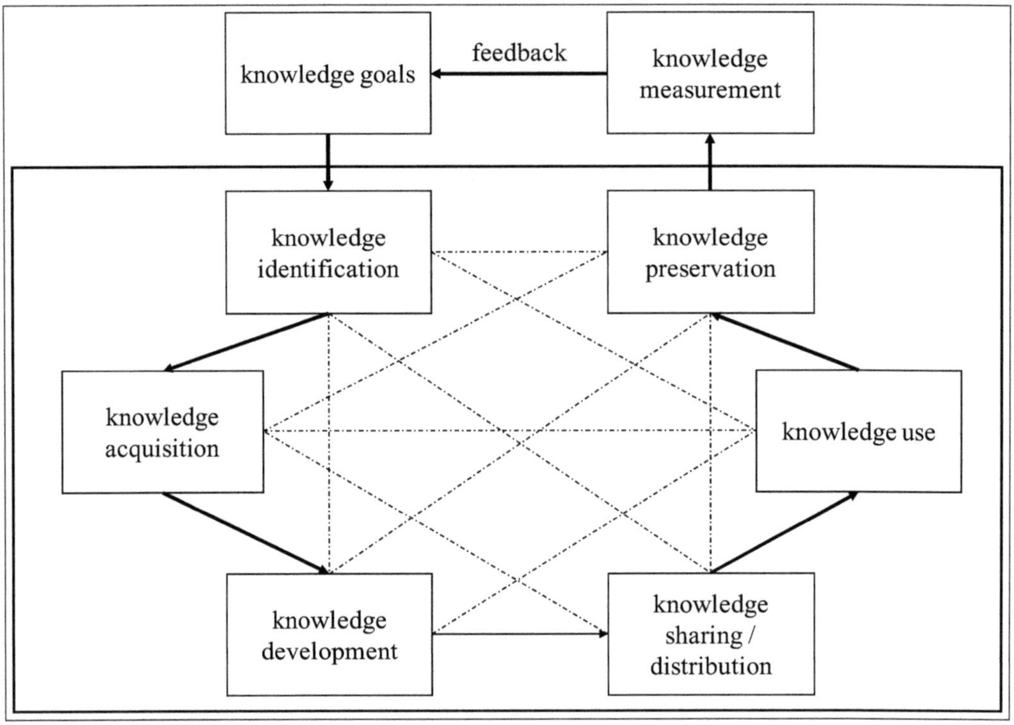

Figure 2: Knowledge management according to PROBST et al.[10]

Two of these building blocks (knowledge goals and knowledge measurement) clearly indicate the strategic significance of knowledge management whereas the other six describe operational tasks.

The process of defining *knowledge goals* points the way for knowledge management and establishes the frame of reference for arrangements and activities. Knowledge that is important for the company's success now and in the future is determined here, and a concrete link to the knowledge factor is added to the strategic corporate goals. Goals are defined on three levels. The normative level creates a knowledge-sensitive corporate culture, the strategic level defines long-term programs to achieve corporate goals, and the operational level describes how to realize the strategic knowledge goals (i.e. the day-to-day procedures and activities relating to knowledge as a resource).

10 Cf. *PROBST* (2006), p. 32.

The success of knowledge management activities is assessed in the *knowledge measurement* process. Knowledge management activities are recorded and the success or failure of action is shown, for instance by using a balanced scorecard model.

The *knowledge identification* block provides transparency about internal and external data. When enough information is available, it is possible to make purposeful decisions in line with the corporate goals and avoid, for example, setting up redundant resources. Knowledge sources can be identified and evaluated on the basis of clear knowledge goals. Internal identification helps in the search for experts but also spells out the collective knowledge of processes, relationship networks and values throughout the enterprise. External identification covers experts, suppliers, customers as well as information in databases and trade journals and from the Internet.

Knowledge acquisition helps to reach decisions on the type of knowledge that ought to be obtained externally. In this process, knowledge is acquired, for example, from knowledge products such as CD-ROMs and from knowledge bearers and by making use of stakeholders such as customers and partners.

The development of new ideas, products and skills at the company itself is the subject of the *knowledge development* process. Gaps between the organization's existing knowledge and its knowledge goals must be closed. On the individual level, this is based on learning processes that support the employee's creativity and problem-solving capacity. On the collective level, new knowledge components are created through interaction, communication and integration, individual knowledge blocks within learning groups, think tanks, communication forums and lessons learned.

The *knowledge distribution* block defines who needs to know what and to which degree of detail, and how the distribution processes can be shaped. This block is not confined to distribution but also covers sharing in the sense of teamwork, and extends to mergers, acquisitions and disinvestments. Knowledge multipliers and knowledge networks are used as instruments for this.

Putting knowledge users in touch with the required sources of knowledge is the organizational part of *knowledge use*. From the technical viewpoint, the focus is on the presence of an infrastructure and the necessary access facilities. This process focuses on individual employees as knowledge management customers.

Knowledge preservation is intended to prevent loss of knowledge when people join another company or retire or when stored knowledge becomes outdated. This process consists of the selection, storage and updating phases. In the selection phase, data, information and knowledge components are split up into valuable and worthless parts. The valuable parts are kept for later use. The kind of preservation is defined in the storage phase. According to *PROBST*, preservation can be individual, collective or electronic. In the updating phase, the organizational knowledge base is managed so that it can act as a basis for decision-making. This includes editing to delete outdated elements and correct any bad content.[11]

---

[11] Cf. *PROBST* (2006), p. 27 ff.

2.4 Concept of Process-oriented Knowledge Management

According to *GRONAU* et al., this concept looks at knowledge-intensive processes in addition to activities relating to business processes. The aim is to consider those processes describing the requirements for and acquisition and use of the knowledge that is needed to execute business processes.

Business processes involve input and output (of the flow of goods for example) and implicitly assume the presence of the necessary knowledge. On the other hand, knowledge management activities take place independently of business processes, for example supporting the company's learning and communication processes or creating knowledge maps. The link between knowledge management and business process is not set up automatically. The objective of business process-oriented knowledge management is therefore to establish synergies between business processes and knowledge management.[12]

HEISIG describes the assumptions below as the basis of his approach to business process-oriented knowledge management:

- An individual's knowledge is used in conjunction with the know-how of colleagues, customers, suppliers and competitors to cope with day-to-day work and solve problems that occur.
- Lack of time is the most common barrier that is raised to reject knowledge management activities so these activities must be integrated in daily tasks and business processes.
- Knowledge is created, stored, distributed and used in different ways, depending on the business process in question. These specific requirements need to be taken into account when managing knowledge.
- The business process forms the framework for knowledge management so knowledge must be created and used on a user-oriented basis with the focus on corporate activities.
- Since the corporate culture in different departments is inhomogeneous owing to their different functions, business process-oriented knowledge management therefore provides the opportunity to consider knowledge-intensive activities and their links within the company instead of arguing about shared values within the framework of a corporate culture.
- Business process-oriented knowledge management involves individual employees to a greater extent because knowledge activities are geared to their daily work and the intrinsic motivation of these employees can be increased by improvements to these activities.[13]

According to *GRONAU*, business process-oriented knowledge management is achieved through sustained, efficient conversion of knowledge with regard to the goals of the organization and its processes. To map the link between knowledge processes and business processes, Gronau has developed the Knowledge Modeling and Description Language (KMDL; cf. Figure 3).

---

12 Cf. *GRONAU* (2005), p. 2.

13 Cf. *HEISIG* (2003), p. 15 ff.

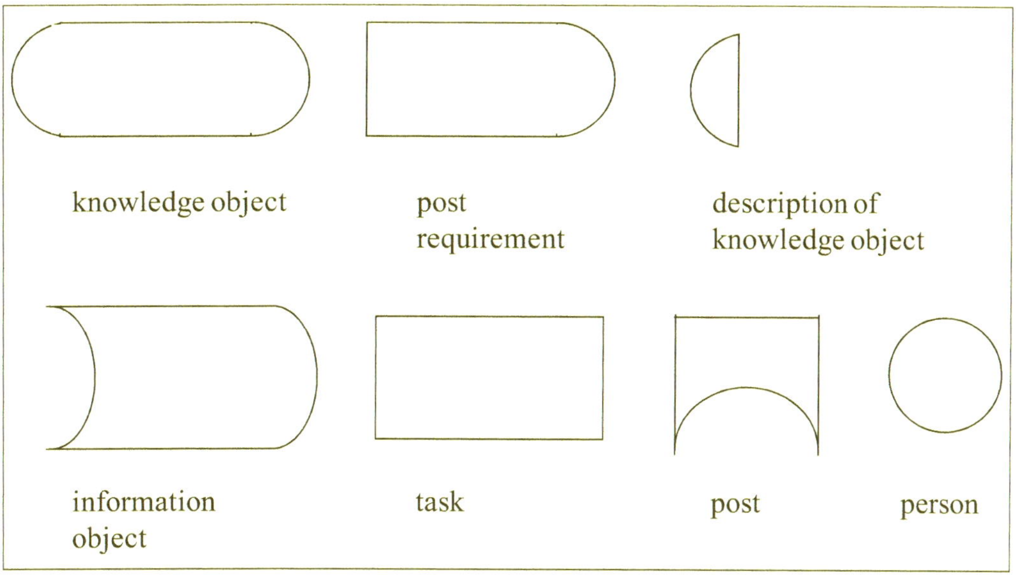

Figure 3: Knowledge Modeling and Description Language (KMDL)[14]

KMDL provides this object library with the following content:

- *Information objects* stand for explicit knowledge and represent, for example, documents in which explicit knowledge is recorded.
- A *task* denotes a processing step on the way from inputs to outputs.
- Tasks are associated with *posts*. The corporate structure can be mapped by associating employees and tasks with a post.
- *Persons* are the individuals who have knowledge objects, i.e. tacit knowledge.
- A *knowledge object* describes the tacit knowledge of the person with whom it is associated. The total of all knowledge objects is the individual's knowledge base.
- A *post requirement* represents the tacit knowledge that is required to perform the task in question.

Knowledge conversions can be represented by linking information objects and knowledge objects via KMDL. It is also possible to map conversion properties from which the competencies required of the individual can be derived so that these conversions can take place. The knowledge conversions are represented via KMDL, showing the points in the organization where knowledge is required, created, stored and used.[15]

14 *Gronau* (2005), p. 6.

15 Cf. *Gronau* (2005), p. 6 ff.

With this representation it is possible to map knowledge flows that are needed to execute business processes. The points at which knowledge is needed and used become clear and the tacit knowledge required of the persons involved can be mapped. Consequently KMDL can be used, on the one hand, to initiate specific training and improvement measures resulting in greater process efficiency and, on the other hand, to act as a knowledge transfer instrument, which will be demonstrated later in this article.

2.5 Structured Framework for Knowledge Management

The *Potsdam knowledge management model* structures the tasks of knowledge management and helps to formulate a clear knowledge strategy.[16]

This model aims to build a framework for knowledge management tasks and to foster its implementation with the aid of technical, cultural and organizational steps. The task of knowledge management is sustained conversion of knowledge that is tied to persons or documents, taking the goals of the organization and its processes into account.

The model describes three dimensions. The first dimension is *reach*, which defines how far knowledge activities extend – ranging from a knowledge-intensive activity on its own to the network level linking various knowledge activities. The *actor dimension* relates to the persons taking action – beginning with an individual and extending to groups and entire organizations. This dimension defines the level on which knowledge management is relevant or on which corresponding steps ought to be taken.

The *management dimension* describes management's view of knowledge management, i.e. of the individual actor, the knowledge manager and corporate management. This dimension deals with those in charge – those who define, implement and embody the company's knowledge strategy.

Knowledge activities can be clearly structured and measured against the background of these three dimensions. It is possible to identify gaps and take action to close them. A clear strategy can be drawn up, including the implementation of knowledge tasks.

These knowledge tasks include *determining knowledge requirements*, i.e. recording tacit and explicit knowledge, *identifying knowledge* as an overview of knowledge sources, and *measuring knowledge*, i.e. assessing the value of knowledge for processes or the company. *Cleaning up knowledge* is the task of removing unnecessary knowledge parts and thus avoiding bad decisions based on outdated or incorrect information. When it comes to *knowledge acquisition*, the focus is on acquiring knowledge that is required but is not yet available in the organization. The goal of *knowledge editing* is to describe knowledge in a way that is clear and uniquely identifiable and to make it easy to find. This results in *knowledge transparency*, which helps to disseminate meta knowledge with the aid of technical resources such as subject-specific portal sites. *Knowledge use* should be *fostered* by means of processes and by implementing incentive systems. *Knowledge distribution* should be fostered directly, for example via training courses, and indirectly, for example through a knowledge-oriented corporate culture. The last task of knowledge management is regarded as *knowledge preservation*, which covers shaping of the organizational knowledge base to

---

16 Cf. GRONAU (2008).

ensure that present and future requirements can be met and that the knowledge can be reused (cf. Figure 4).

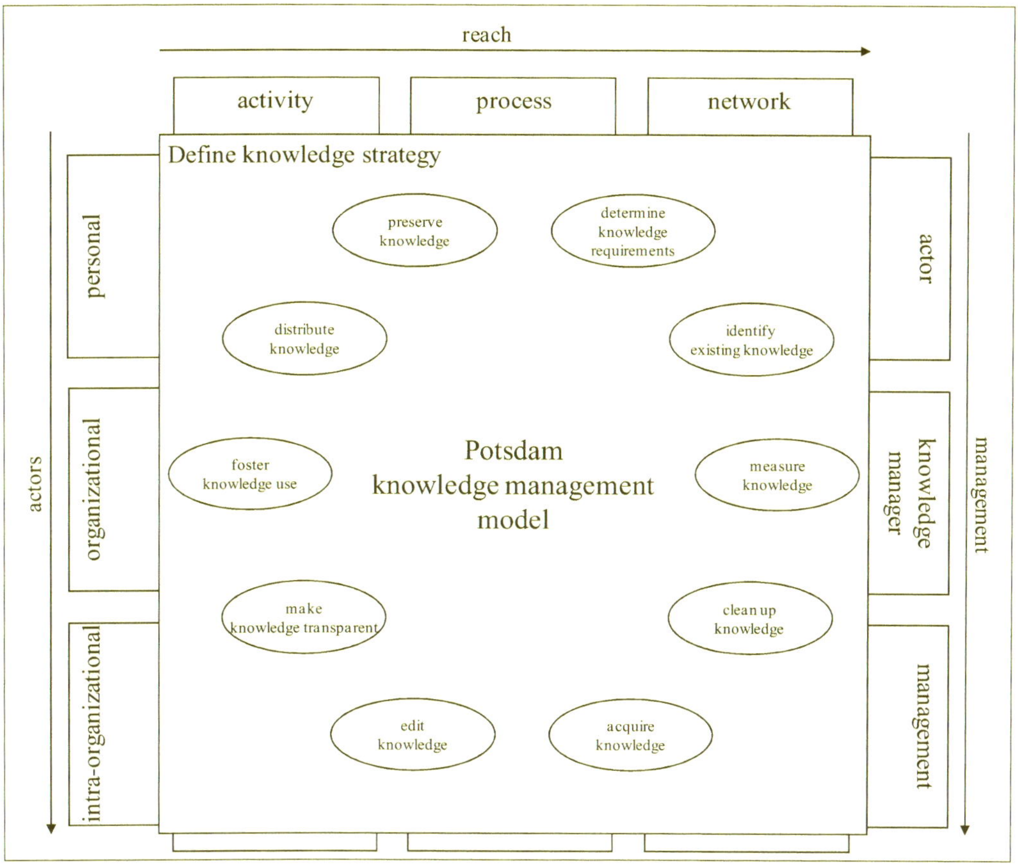

Figure 4: Potsdam knowledge management model – holistic understanding of knowledge management[17]

This knowledge management model can serve as a basis for developing a structured approach to knowledge transfer in which the parties involved are identified, clear goals are defined and focused methods of tackling knowledge tasks can be derived.

This chapter showed that knowledge is created dynamically and should be transferred dynamically, that individuals should be at the center of knowledge transfer and that a holistic approach is required when considering knowledge management activities. Against the strategic background of knowledge use it is necessary, in application management, to focus on imparting knowledge. The transition to a new service provider, in particular, is a critical phase that requires special attention. The next chapter gives a structured view of this knowledge transfer phase.

---

17 GRONAU (2008).

3 Knowledge Transfer

ITIL sees the goal of knowledge management as providing the right information at the right time to the right contact or right location. The added value for the organization is seen in the points below:

- Knowledge transfer as a critical success factor for operations
- Training of users, service providers and support staff
- Recording of errors discovered in the transition phase and their workarounds
- Documentation of implementation and test information
- Reuse of existing instruments for testing, training and documentation
- Compliance with legal requirements
- Support for decision-making through availability of all relevant information

Achieving this added value requires a knowledge management strategy that incorporates a governance model, planning for organizational changes, the definition and implementation of knowledge management roles, and key indicators to measure effectiveness.

This strategy can act as a basis for concrete implementation in the form of knowledge transfer aiming to move so-called knowledge packages from one organization to another in a way that is tailored to and can be easily used by the receiving organization. As a result, the receiving organization should be able to provide the services in its remit and to understand the knowledge management requirements. The delta between understood requirements and observed knowledge is the so-called knowledge gap.[18]

This view sees knowledge transfer as a one-way street and one-off action with the focus on the externalization of knowledge. As presented above, though, it is an iterative and dynamic process that creates new knowledge and is thus a continuous activity in application support.

The knowledge transfer process is influenced by various factors. These cannot be regarded separately as they interact with each other. For example, motivation of the parties involved depends, among other things, on the individual's previous experiences with knowledge transfer and the openness of the parties involved is affected by the general corporate culture. VON KROGH et al. presents the following factors:

The *type of knowledge* (whether tacit or explicit) has an effect on the method of knowledge transfer and consequently on its course and speed. The *type of transfer* should be geared to the knowledge to be transferred. Personal interaction provides many options for internal knowledge transfer. *Earlier experiences* will either impede or facilitate matters, depending on the type of experiences involved. If individuals have had positive experiences, for example, they will be more open when it comes to knowledge transfer. The *ability to perceive and learn* and the *will to learn* are other factors that affect transfer. Content can be transferred more easily when building on existing knowledge. The *motivation* of the parties involved has

[18] Cf. TAYLOR (2007), p. 145 ff.

a very strong impact on the success or failure of knowledge transfer. A transfer project can only be completed successfully with motivated individuals. *Trust* and the resultant *interactions* between individuals are two additional factors that can have a positive or negative impact on the transfer of information. The *openness* of the parties involved and the underlying *corporate culture* can have a positive effect on knowledge transfer. When knowledge sharing is seen as positive in an undertaking and knowledge is not viewed under *power aspects*, this can lead to openness on the part of those involved in the process. *Explicit management support*, the creation of an adequate *organizational structure* and the provision of enough *time* for knowledge transfer are other aspects that can have a positive impact. *Incentive systems*, which need not necessarily be of a financial nature, can induce individuals to pass knowledge on to others.[19] It is conceivable that the person passing on knowledge will get new knowledge in return, for example by having the opportunity to take part in training for new technology.

VON KROGH et al. describe corporate culture as having a medium impact. In the author's opinion, this is true for internal knowledge transfer within a company but this aspect becomes very important when knowledge is transferred to another organization, such as in the case of outsourcing to an external service provider. There will be some difficulties when members of two organizations meet that have a conflicting understanding of knowledge management. When it comes to knowledge transfer during a transition, it is necessary to deal with a variety of potential conflicts. This begins with different terminology concerning the subject, extends to the concrete approach to identifying and sharing knowledge and goes on to the willingness of individuals to pass on their knowledge.

Structured knowledge transfer should start with the fact that the new application supporters must familiarize themselves with the application and special aspects of the business in question. This includes considering the respective tasks in the application area, describing them and carrying them out regularly as planned. Knowledge transfer meetings should be held to analyze existing documentation about systems and processes and to collaborate on incidents that are not critical in terms of time. In this respect it is important to establish the context between the application (i.e. technical mapping) and business requirements (i.e. business processes). The progress of these activities should be monitored at weekly status meetings and open points should be escalated and decided in good time so as not to hinder overall progress.

The Potsdam knowledge management model can be used to structure knowledge transfer. The *reach dimension* defines the focus and objective of knowledge transfer activities. When an IT system is being handed over, knowledge transfer relates to the handover of existing networks (e.g. linking application supporters to users) and their integration in the new support landscape that is being set up. Groups in existing organizations can be identified as *actors*. Here, it is a matter of an intra-organizational transfer of knowledge. The *management dimension* is considered at the end of this article in respect of governance to control and monitor knowledge transfer.

In addition to these dimensions, there are organizational approaches and technical methods and resources to support transfer. The next sections look at these two subjects.

---

[19] Cf. *VON KROGH* (1998), p. 243 ff.

3.1 Organizational Aspects of Knowledge Transfer

The organizational aspects of knowledge transfer deal with the individuals involved and their interactions. It is necessary to consider ways of handling knowledge transfer between organizations efficiently or to see which organizational levers have a positive impact on the transfer of tacit knowledge between organizations.

According to *TAYLOR* et al., application management employees play a special role in the creation of information about the applications used. Staff at the user help desk must understand the importance of knowledge management. Only then will they document incidents and problems in detail and, above all, record the solutions, such as in the shape of workarounds, so that they can be used by downstream support instances and users.[20] On the organizational level, change and the acceptance associated with it play an important role in the organization. *TAYLOR* et al. present five factors that impact on readiness to change:

- Need for change
- Vision
- Plan
- Resources
- Competence[21]

Employees must understand the *need* for pending changes, for example the pressure of costs and the lack of inhouse resources, which can be the main reason for outsourcing an application to an external provider. The external partner must provide a clear *vision* of the added value that the service creates for the organization and what that means in concrete terms. The *plan* is the detailed approach, including milestones. Project planning and communicating this are the key to success. In particular when the reason for involving an external partner is a lack of internal *resources*, the provider's employees must be available for the customer and have the required *competence*. This will become apparent during the transition project. Two of the most frequent questions to check the resources and their competence are likely to be: are the provider's staff always available during the transition and do they understand our business?

ANDERSON et al. state that transfer of knowledge is equivalent to loss of control if knowledge is seen to be power and power is exercised in the form of control. Behind this lies the fear of losing power or a position in the company, and the associated loss of standing. This is shown in the statement "What I know and why I'm an important part of the operation".[22] Here, the individual's standing is defined by his or her knowledge and not by the added value that he or she generates for the organization. The assumption that knowledge is power and should therefore be protected and hidden if possible is wrong in the author's opinion. In a knowledge-intensive society, only those people will ultimately develop further who are willing to share and pass on their knowledge. In respect of transition, this means that only those will be successful who pass on their knowledge about the applications, organization,

---

20 Cf. *TAYLOR* (2007), p. 153.

21 Cf. *TAYLOR* (2007), p. 162.

22 *ANDERSON* (2007), p. 3.

data and business processes. With this view of knowledge, current supporters can show their technical competence on the one hand and can present their networks reaching into the organization on the other hand. This will most likely cause these employees to be regarded as important resources for this customer and for the provision of services. As a consequence of this, there can be several options for a future activity:

- These *employees stay in the company* and coordinate the external partner, especially at the interface to lines of business and in supplier management. They take on the role of an intermediary and translator between IT (in this case the external provider) and business. This means that they understand the requirements of business processes and translate them in respect of the technical provider and, together with the provider, develop concepts and solution approaches to implement the changes that are wanted. They thus initiate permanent system changes and continuously improve the systems in use.
- Another option is to *move to the external service provider*. There they can act as business solution managers for their former employer and ensure a smooth, trouble-free transition from the status quo to the new provider. With their existing networks and deep system knowledge, they make things easier for the new provider and, as business solution managers, will add value for both organizations.
- The third option is to *move to the new provider with the goal of working there for other customers* and to use the technical competence there.

But these options are only available to those employees who willingly share their knowledge and consequently give others the chance to recognize and assess their skills and, on the basis of these competences, keep them as key persons for the existing customer or win them for other customers. From the viewpoint of knowledge transfer and under financial aspects, the best possible option may be a combination; that is working for the current customer for a while and then moving on to a new customer.

In a knowledge society, employees who hang on to their knowledge will lose out. In the short term, their tacit, hidden knowledge can be advantageous for them but, in the medium to long term, they will fail with this strategy of hanging on to their knowledge. When key persons in organizations do not share their knowledge, they cannot be recognized as such. This means, on the one hand, that the internal employer will underestimate their significance and will consequently not rate them as critical or important resources and, on the other hand, that the external provider will assess them incorrectly and will consequently not put them on the list of potential candidates for transfer to the company as part of the contract.

Transferring employees as part of an outsourcing project can overcome major barriers to knowledge transfer. Individuals who see a perspective in the new job will be motivated and will in turn motivate colleagues to share their knowledge too. Moreover, there is less risk of losing tacit knowledge because critical resources, and with them the knowledge of critical business processes and applications, move to the new provider. It is important not to underestimate the significance of networks and communities that existing employees would bring with them to the benefit of the new provider. The relationship level to the customer's users would therefore already exist for some of the future application supporters. External supporters would find it easier to join these networks or start to collaborate with them on the basis of existing trust.

ANDERSON et al. do not see knowledge transfer as a one-off issue during a transition but as an ongoing process which will help to turn the outsourcing contract into a success. The partners' willingness to collaborate and keep sharing information is the critical success factor.[23] *SANTHANAM* et al. confirm this in an empirical study. In the course of operations, knowledge is not only transferred between IT experts but also between users and application supporters. This is not a one-way street from IT to users; all parties involved gain knowledge. Users learn more about the technical configuration by taking part in training and asking questions, and application supporters learn more about business processes and their requirements by interacting with users. As instruments to support this knowledge transfer, *SANTHANAM* et al. suggest setting up user forums where users can meet personally and have the opportunity to discuss system use with users and supporters from other areas. Another aspect mentioned in this study is the identification of experts for the different types of available knowledge. Problems can be linked to the right expert faster on this basis.[24]

Organizational and technical barriers can be taken down in this way, which will foster the creation of new knowledge. Personal meetings will create a basis of trust, increase the trust in the competence and character of others, establish a joint basis for interaction and thus give rise to new knowledge.

The transfer of tacit knowledge can therefore be fostered by socializing and using networks. However, this does not consider the points at which tacit knowledge is created during a transition and in the subsequent support phase.

Here, KMDL can help to point out the transfer of knowledge and place the focus on the critical points of a transition project. In the author's opinion, the resources presented in the next section should be combined and used in a transition so as to foster the transfer of tacit knowledge.

3.2 Technical Aspects of Knowledge Transfer

This section on technical aspects looks at existing approaches or components which, in the author's practical experience, have been used in combination to support the best possible transition to a new service provider.

3.2.1 Service Knowledge Management Base

According to ITIL, it is essential to set up a service knowledge management system (SKMS) for a transition to be able to provide services throughout the world across various locations and time zones. This system is a portal that is available to the service provider organization itself, and also to customers and partners, and delivers information about the service. This portal consists of four layers, of which one is the presentation layer; that is the actual portal in which users can generate various items of information. Information about governance, quality management, fixe assets and the user help desk can be generated here. Self-help is also available in the shape of FAQs. The next layer maps the processes relevant for the processing of information, for example reporting and monitoring functions. Beneath that is the layer on

23 Cf. *ANDERSON* (2007), p. 6.

24 Cf. *SANTHANAM* (2007), p. 185 ff.

which information is integrated. According to ITIL, this is the actual service knowledge management base in the form of a database. The fourth layer comprises the data sources. Data from ERP systems, event/alert and configuration management databases are administered here.

The goal of this portal is to increase efficiency, for example by allowing users to search for solutions themselves, and to minimize the risk through standardized, proven error handling processes (cf. Figure 5).[25]

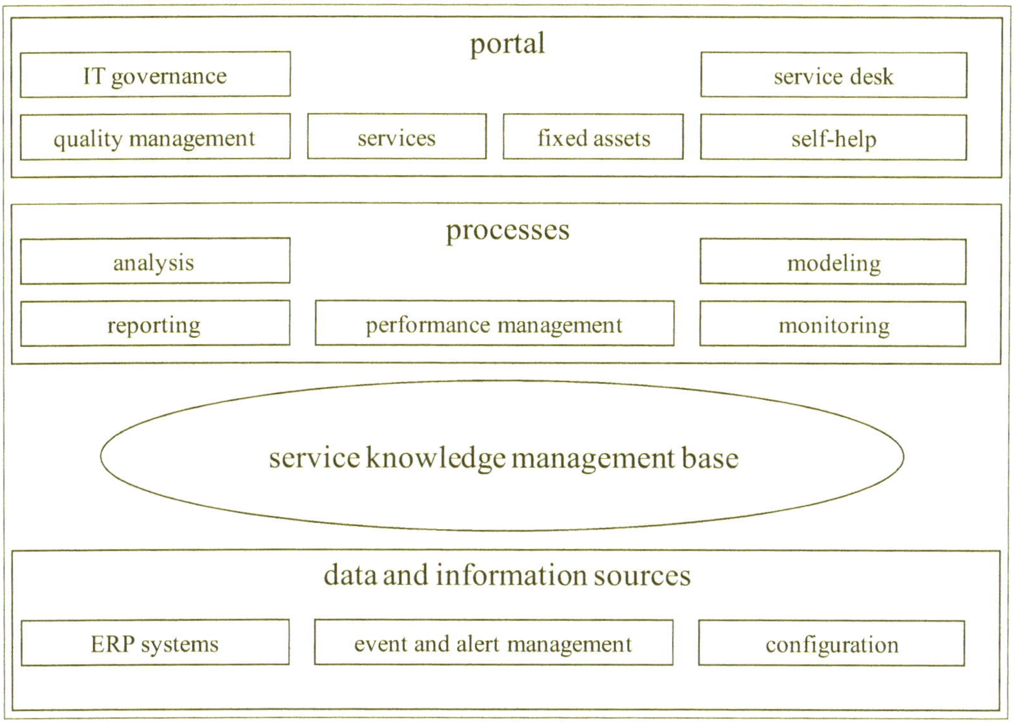

Figure 5: Service knowledge management system[26]

The prerequisites for using such a system are maintenance and identification of relevant data. The effort seems to be very high, especially when such a system does not yet exist and has to be built from scratch for a transition. In the author's opinion, such a portal should be set up in the medium term for every customer; in the short term, though, the new provider should focus on trouble-free transfer of operations.

25 Cf. *TAYLOR* (2007), p. 151.

26 Cf. *TAYLOR* (2007), p. 151.

3.2.2 Reverse Business Engineering

Reverse business engineering is one method to systematically analyze existing ERP systems. It identifies which processes, transactions and master data are used, including how often and how exactly. Conversely, the configuration of the process model and the actual use of the system, in this case SAP R/3, can be derived from this data.[27]

An example of an RBE analysis shows which types of information can be generated automatically (cf. Figure 6). It becomes clear that a large part of the customer-specific configuration is not used in production mode. 70 % of the customer's own transactions and 72 % of reports are not used according to this analysis. In the Siemens-specific situation[28], 89 % of transactions and 92 % of reports are not in use. This may have been caused by failure to adapt applications to changes in the business environment. Analysis of the most frequent transactions shows that there is overlapping in the maintenance of customer master data. Master data is maintained both in the Sales and Finance modules as well as in the central Master Data Management module. This indicates failure to exploit potential synergies (adequately).

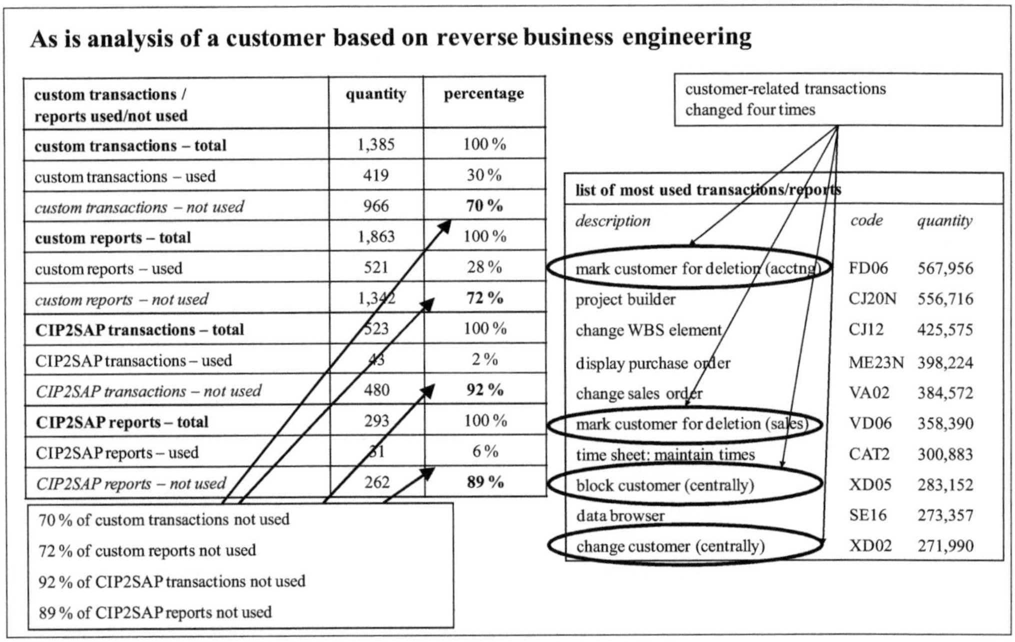

Figure 6: Extract from the results of an RBE analysis[29]

---

[27] Cf. *HUFGARD* (1999), p. 429 ff.

[28] CIP2SAP stands for Corporate Information and Processes to SAP and contains guidelines and rules that are specific to Siemens as a group and are integrated in the SAP modules Logistics and Finance.

[29] *SCHMIDT* (2010), p. 214.

These analyses and evaluations can help during transition to focus knowledge transfer on the system parts that are actually in use. In addition to the relevance of the used objects, the new provider, who has collected this data, should also have the opportunity to start continuous improvement of the SAP system. Unused program parts can be removed, making the system more readily convertible. This also makes it easier to carry out upgrades or implement hot packages. It is also possible to address the unclear master data maintenance situation and initiate a more detailed analysis of processes as possible action. The new provider organization can present its competence and motivation with these actions.

3.2.3 Live Tools

Siemens IT Solutions and Services and IBIS Prof. Thome AG have developed a system that can be used, among other things, to process data collected by means of an RBE analysis. The extracted data – i.e. the used transactions, organizational structure, customizing information, master data and documents – is processed with the aid of Live Tools. The business processes are then visualized (cf. Figure 7).

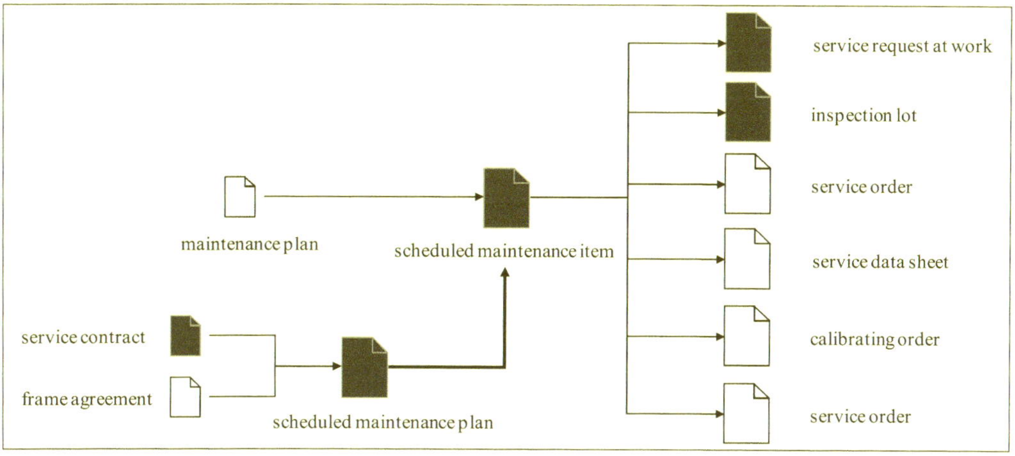

Figure 7: Presentation of processes with Live Tools[30]

Colors show the status of the respective components. Black objects indicate active process documents; that is to say parts of the process that are actively used. Light gray components are part of the standard system but are not used for this customer. Similar coding applies to upstream and downstream process documents, which are shown on the right or left of a Black document. In this way it is possible to clearly present the document flow in the organization and to ensure in a transition project that all relevant areas are considered and analyzed systematically.

[30] SCHMIDT (2010), p. 215.

3.2.4 Knowledge Maps

To analyze the relevant areas, it is not sufficient to consider technical aspects only. Knowledge bearers in the respective organizations should be identified and brought together so that they can transfer their knowledge in an efficient communication process. Knowledge maps are regarded as an instrument for this and can be used in a transition project. They make it possible to identify the knowledge bearers and to map the interaction between individuals and issues. Transition managers and the customer get a compressed overview of the persons taking action in the transition project and individuals can find the right contact.

The prototype of this knowledge map shows where the knowledge bearers are located and the issues that they work on. This is indicated by the colors of the individual points on the map. The system provides detailed information about the individual knowledge bearers, including their roles, specific subject areas, skills, location and contact data. In a transition project, this allows work groups or subject areas to be shown. If the database is maintained properly, it is also possible to identify the knowledge bearers on the customer's and provider's side.

3.2.5 Support Matrix

Another tool is the support matrix, which can show the services and the service providers (cf. Figure 8). On the macro level, responsibilities for the applications should be defined on the basis of the services to be provided. Services are shown vertically and applications horizontally. Responsibility is shown at the intersection of the respective fields – in this case with color indicating the different providers. For the SAP-relevant services there is a homogeneous supplier structure. User help desk, application problem resolution and application enhancement services come from one provider and key user support and administration, including monitoring, come from a second provider. In the case shown, responsibilities for interfaces lie with the different parties throughout the service chain.

	SAP FI	SAP CO	SAP SD	SAP HR	SAP Basis	interfaces		
services						**101**	**102**	**103**
service desk	service provider A							
key user support	customer							
application problem resolution	service provider A							
application enhancements	service provider A							
application administration & monitoring	customer						**"black hole"**	
other services								
training	"white spot"	service provider E						
consulting	service provider A							

Figure 8: *Support matrix for SAP R/3*[31]

The simple form of the support matrix is intended to make it possible to map complex support scenarios. The variety of the existing support landscape, including all applications and persons responsible, can result in a sort of patchwork in which the different providers can be responsible for a whole range of services and applications. The actual state of support in a transition project can be mapped in this way. It is possible to identify responsibilities and discover white spaces (missing responsibilities) or black holes (multiple assignment). A target matrix can be generated in another step, i.e. help in developing a future support structure.

On the micro level, the support matrix can be used as another form of knowledge map. The contacts responsible for a particular service and application can be entered in the respective fields to help find the right contact.

3.2.6 Knowledge Modeling and Description Language

The technical and organizational aspects of knowledge transfer presented above can help to identify key support persons, focus correctly on the system parts in use and plan and initiate the future deployment of staff. KDML can be used to present the transfer of tacit knowledge.

The creation and use of knowledge can be made transparent by representing the existing support processes. In a project with the University of Potsdam, the support processes and required information at Siemens IT Solutions and Services were visualized with the aid of KMDL (cf. Figure 9).

---

31 *SCHMIDT* (2010), p. 218.

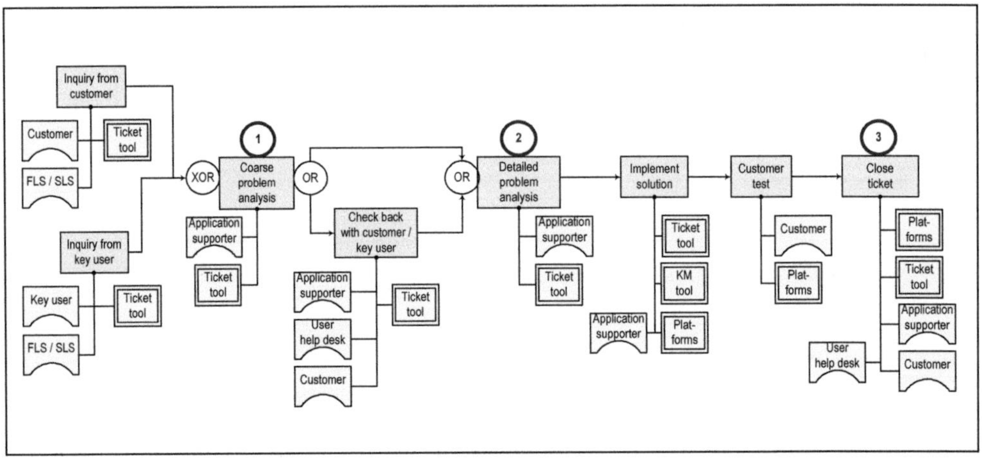

Figure 9: Problem management in the KMDL process view[32]

Various suggestions for improvement can be derived from this chart in conjunction with discussions among the experts involved in the process. The *search* process should identify whether a similar problem already exists. Colleagues should be asked on the one hand and the trouble ticket system should be searched on the other hand. Then an analysis should be conducted to see whether existing solutions can be adapted. This *adaption* phase should cover the existing solution and searching across areas. When the solution has been completed, the focus should be on *reuse*. The documentation should be checked and keywords should be implemented.[33] Using KMDL to analyze support processes makes it possible to hold purposeful discussions with the application supporters and to identify potential for improvement within the existing processes.

Schmid shows how the different views of KMDL can be used in a knowledge-based maintenance organization. The *KMDL process view* shows the chronology of individual process steps and the allocation of resources. To do this, the process is split up into individual tasks which are in turn linked to roles. Only organizational processes are considered in this view.

The *KMDL activity view* shows knowledge conversions within the support process. These knowledge conversions are linked to the persons / roles and mapped.[34]

Analyzing the processes shown in KMDL makes it possible to draw conclusions about the knowledge-intensive processes in a support organization. An *occurrence report* shows the frequency of individual objects in a process. This allows frequently used objects as well as persons and roles to be identified. The *externalization report* shows the information created in the course of knowledge conversion. In this report it is possible to identify objects that are either created from various information objects or are used to create many information objects. These knowledge objects can be critical for the entire process. The *relevancy report* evaluates which knowledge conversions are used and how often. This allows people to

---

32 *SCHMIDT* (2010), p. 224.

33 Cf. *SCHMIDT* (2010), p. 224.

34 Cf. *SCHMID* (2009), p. 100 ff.

identify, for example, the great importance of personal knowledge exchange in the shape of socialization. The *competence report* documents the knowledge contained in the activities. It illustrates the tasks for which knowledge is used and allows knowledge profiles to be created.[35]

Using KMDL in a transition project is intended to help to identify important nodes in the existing maintenance organization. This method enables knowledge monopolies and key resources to be identified and action to be taken to keep these key players (cf. section 0). Critical knowledge objects should be identified via KMDL. In conjunction with tools such as reverse business engineering and Live Tools they enable the activities in a transition project to be prioritized. Application components that are used in various business processes and are often involved in knowledge conversions should be given high priority in a transition. The results of these two methods can be presented as a four-field matrix that can help to prioritize the approach (cf. Figure 10).

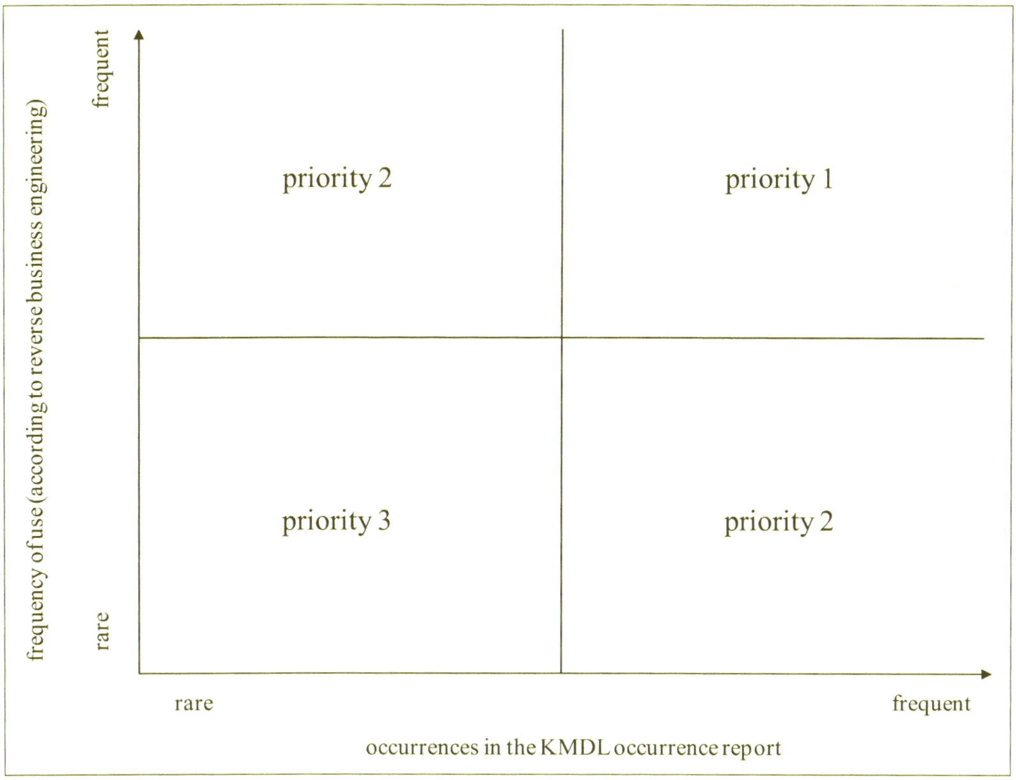

Figure 10: Prioritization of activities on the basis of KMDL and RBE[36]

[35] Cf. SCHMID (2009), p. 107 ff.

[36] SCHMIDT (2010), p. 221.

Accordingly, top priority should be given to those components of the application that are both used frequently in the RBE technical analysis and occur frequently in the KMDL occurrence report. When it comes to knowledge transfer, priority level 2 should be given to application components used frequently either in transactions or in knowledge conversions. The lowest priority should be given to any components used only rarely in processes or in the creation and transfer of knowledge. If only a limited amount of time is available for the transition, the focus should be on those components with priority level 2 that occur often in KMDL. If the employee of the existing provider wants to leave the company, he or she would only be available to pass on knowledge for the short period of the transition. In contrast, the RBE analysis can be used for any period and can therefore be treated with a lower priority.

The two other KMDL reports should be used to identify the knowledge culture of the surrendering company and to define an approach to the transfer. In organizations with a high level of socialization, particular importance should be attached to personal interaction between the organizations surrendering and receiving knowledge. This should create a basis of trust and the surrendering organization can transfer its knowledge in its normal way. In organizations with a high level of knowledge externalization, the focus of the transition should be on analyzing existing documents. The *competence report* should help to identify suitable employees for taking over important support roles. In conjunction with other methods and tools, KMDL should help to enable the transfer of tacit knowledge. The next section deals with the interaction between the right contact and the organizational environment.

3.3 Significance of Communication

LINNARTZ et al. define the significance of a communication concept in setting up a support organization in terms of the control of the information flow. Who receives what information and when is defined. Accordingly, information can be placed in three classes. Strategic, tactical and operational information is relevant in the various phases of support initialization. Management's *strategic decisions* concerning the expansion of business or a change of supplier should also be communicated to employees. *Tactical information* is based on strategic decisions and includes, for example, information from regular user surveys based on strategic goals to make the use of applications more efficient. *Operational information* is relevant for actual operations. For example, the failure of important system functions is communicated to users quickly here.

Tactical and operational information should be communicated regularly as and when required. A newsletter is ideal for tactical information about support, for instance. Communication should provide users with the following content:

- Setting the mood
- Notification of all contacts
- Notification of tasks and authorizations in 1st level support
- Definition and notification of forwarding to 2nd level support
- Notification of tasks and authorizations in 2nd level support
- Definition and notification of approaches to 3rd level issues

- Definition and notification of the escalation plan
- Definition and notification of rules for approvals and acceptance processes[37]

This structured approach should also include the relationship level. The method and options of (bidirectional) communication have an impact on the success of a transition. For example, management of the company and of the old and new service providers should ideally attend the first information events in order to demonstrate unity. This signals a uniform approach to users. The opportunity of entering into a dialog with decision-makers is intended to increase acceptance of the change of provider.

Control of the transition and, in particular, communication of the same messages to the outside should be governance tasks. The next section examines this in more detail, together with critical success factors and their measurability.

3.4 Governance

RÜTER et al. state that IT governance combines principles, procedures and measures which aim to achieve business goals, use resources responsibly and minimize the risk with the aid of IT.[38] These goals can be transferred to a transition project. Continuity should be ensured when there is a transition of applications, i.e. the customer can keep working with the systems despite the change of provider. During the transition the resources needed for this must be used responsibly in the company's interests, potential risks must be monitored and action must be taken to reduce the risk.[39] In addition to these activities, *JOHANNSEN* et al. see the measurement of success as a governance task. As far as they are concerned, the difference to IT management is that governance covers a broader spectrum. In governance, the focus begins with the harmonization of IT strategy with business strategy and extends to the operational control of information systems. The strategic orientation of IT to future requirements, stakeholder management and a business-based view of the added value of IT are the main differences between governance and pure IT management.[40]

TORNBORN et al. point out that it is not only the provider who is responsible for these activities. The customer and the provider bear joint responsibility for monitoring and protecting the transition plan that they drew up together. Governance activities should include monitoring of the transition project via weekly status meetings covering the following:

- Report on ongoing activities and critical points
- Review of the transition plan and any changes needed
- Analysis of the delta between planned and actual deadlines and activities
- Management of unplanned issues and action planning
- Allocation of resources

---

[37] Cf. *LINNARTZ* (2004), p. 192 ff.

[38] Cf. *RÜTER* (2006), p. 28.

[39] Cf. *TORNBORN* (2007), p. 4.

[40] Cf. *JOHANNSEN* (2006), p. 14.

- Escalations in the event of hindrances[41]

In addition to these aspects, *TORNBORN* et al. find it necessary for senior management to be available and have the required powers to make decisions. If a transition project is not proceeding as planned, the decision-makers should be notified on the customer and provider sides so that they can decide about possible on-the-spot action. In extreme cases, this action should even include suspension of the transition for a certain period. This shows the level of decision-making competence that senior managers involved in governance need to have.[42] In the author's opinion, the body in charge of governance activities should be a steering committee composed of representatives of the customer, the previous provider and the new provider. This body can control a transition and ensure its success. This governance structure should reflect the special significance of knowledge transfer and use the third dimension of the *Potsdam knowledge management model.* The management dimension defines clear responsibilities for knowledge management activities and aims to anchor them in the organization. The next section looks at the key indicators used to measure a transition.

3.4.1 Key Indicators to Measure a Transition

In the author's opinion, the proof of the success of a transition should always be that the service is still available and usable and that the requirements for support of business processes are satisfied. There are various factors on top of that which can be used to measure a transition. Measurements with key indicators can be carried out at two times: during the transition for operational control and after the transition to show the result.

According to *SCHMIDT*, it is necessary to monitor and check ongoing activities during a transition project in addition to measuring the project when the transition has been completed. The following key indicators can be used to control and monitor *during a transition*:

- Availability of resources on the side of the customer, the previous provider and the new provider
- Number of activities completed in comparison with plans
- Status of activities for the infrastructure used (PBX, trouble ticket system etc.)[43]

ITIL defines various factors that can indicate success or failure *after a transition*:

- Use of resources compared with capacity
- Employee skills
- Compliance with service levels
- Comparison of actual costs with the budget
- Time taken for the transition in comparison with plans
- Quality of service, for example user satisfaction

---

41 Cf. *TORNBORN* (2007), p. 4 ff.

42 Cf. *TORNBORN* (2007), p. 8.

43 Cf. *SCHMIDT* (2010), p. 226 ff.

- Added value for the organization
- Problems and incidents
- Risks[44]

According to *Schmidt* , there are not only these general key indicators but also others that can be used to measure whether knowledge was successfully transferred to support a complex application. The *immediate solution rate at the user help desk* indicates the extent to which support staff have understood the business processes and their mapping in the system. The more inquiries they were able to answer directly, the better knowledge transfer seems to have been. The *times to process incidents and problems* show how well application supporters have understood the system configuration within the framework of knowledge transfer. The faster they solved problems, the less time they needed to find the cause; this can indicate good understanding of the configuration. The *throughput times and number of open problems* show how efficiently problems can be processed and whether tacit knowledge was transferred in all areas of the software. Frequent problems and many unprocessed cases can indicate poor knowledge transfer. The *actual processing time for change requests compared with the estimated time* shows how reliable the application supporters are in configuring the application. The fewer differences up or down, the more they have mastered the system and the more efficiently knowledge was transferred. The last key indicator, the *number of support employees compared with previous employees*, can show the synergy potential that the new provider exploited during the transition.[45]

The last part of this chapter summarizes the critical success factors for a transition.

3.4.2 Risks and Critical Success Factors

As far as the new provider is concerned, there are risks that can have a negative impact on performance, especially in the start phase, i.e. from the milestone when support went live. These include the risk that employees will no longer be available because they leave the company and take their tacit knowledge with them. From the organizational viewpoint, there is the risk that the existing organization is unwilling to hand over resources and raises organizational or political barriers that could prevent the transfer of employees.

These risks can also be accompanied by technological risks including, for example, the type of technology used. If the technology is old, it may be hard to find experts on the free market. If the applications involve very complex configurations, there is the risk that shared resources will not be available for support, culminating in a 1-to-1 assignment of employee to application. This makes it impossible for the provider to achieve economies of scale and meet financial targets.

Alongside technical aspects, which can be measured objectively, the critical success factor can be the individual looking after the application at present and in the future. In the author's opinion, one way of minimizing employee-related risk is to identify key resources in the existing organization at an early stage and take action to give them a perspective in the new provider's company. To make this transfer of employees possible, there should be strong

---

44 Cf. *Taylor* (2007), p. 18.

45 Cf. *Schmidt* (2010), p. 228.

governance pursuing the shared goal of turning this transition of responsibility for applications into a success. Existing political or organizational barriers can only be torn down by clear decisions on the management level.

The transfer of tacit knowledge to the new provider is the factor which, in the author's opinion, should have top priority. The methods and approaches presented here should help to make the transition to the new provider efficient.

4 Summary

Knowledge transfer, which is essential during the transition to a new service provider, is the task that poses the biggest challenge in application management. In supporting the applications, operations must not be disturbed in any way and tacit knowledge must be recorded and transferred systematically.

Existing support staff must be exchanged seamlessly. It is necessary to identify key resources and give them a perspective in the new company and to transfer the tacit knowledge of those who do not have a future at the new service provider's company.

This article presented methods and approaches to work out a clear knowledge management strategy for this phase of a transition and to identify the required knowledge and transfer it systematically to the new service provider. The actors play a key role. A clear and understandable approach is needed to make this critical transition possible – from the individual knowledge worker right up to a top manager.

The Potsdam knowledge management model is a good basis for systematic development of an approach and can be used purposefully with the support of the methods and tools presented here to identify and transfer tacit knowledge.

Against this background, transition to a new service provider gives opportunities to those knowledge workers who are willing to share their knowledge. With this attitude, they have the chance to position themselves with the future managers.

References

Anderson, D./Huntley, H. (2007): Addressing Knowledge Transfer in Outsourcing, in: Gartner Research, online: http://www.gartner.com/DisplayDocument?id=500915&ref=g_sitelink, published: 07.02.2007, accessed: 29.06.2010.

Davenport, T./Prusak, L. (1998): Wenn Ihr Unternehmen wüßte, was es alles weiß – Das Praxisbuch zum Wissensmanagement, Landsberg/Lech 1998.

Gronau, N. (2008): Potsdamer Wissensmanagement-Modell, in: *Kurbel, K./Becker, J./Gronau, N./Sinz, E./Suhl, L.* (2008): Enzyklopädie der Wirtschaftinformatik – Online Lexikon, Oldenbourg, online: http://www.oldenbourg.de:8080/wi-enzyklopaedie/lexikon/daten-wissen/Wissensmanagement/Wissensmanagement--Modelle-des/Potsdamer-Wissensmanagement-Modell, published: 28.09.2009, accessed: 29.06.2010.

Gronau, N./Weber, E. (2005): Analyse wissensintensiver Verwaltungsprozesse mit der Beschreibungssprache KMDL, in: *Klischewski, R.; Wimmer, M.* (Ed.), Wissensbasiertes Prozessmanagement im E-Government, Münster 2005, pp. 171–183.

Heisig, P. (2003): Business Process Oriented Knowledge Management, in: *Mertins, K./Heisig, P./Vorbeck, J.* (Ed.), Knowledge Management – Concepts and Best Practices, Second Edition, Berlin, Heidelberg, New York 2003, pp. 15–44.

Hufgard, A./Wenzel-Däfler, H. (1999): Reverse Business Engineering – Modelle aus produktiven R/3-Systemen ableiten, in: *Scheer, A.-W./Nüttgens, M.* (Ed.), Electronic Business Engineering – 4. Internationale Tagung Wirtschaftsinformatik, Heidelberg 1999, pp. 425–442.

Johannsen, W./Goeken, M. (2006): IT-Governance – neue Aufgaben des IT-Managements, in: *Fröschle, H.-P./Strahringer, S.* (Ed.), IT-Governance, HMD issue 250, Heidelberg, August 2006, pp. 7–20.

Krcmar, H. (2003): Informationsmanagement, Berlin, Heidelberg, New York 2003.

von Krogh, G./Koehne, M. (1998): Der Wissenstransfer in Unternehmen – Phasen des Wissenstransfers und wichtige Einflussfaktoren, in: Die Unternehmung, issue 5/6, 1998, pp. 235-252.

Linnartz, W./Kohlhoff, B./Heck, G./Schmidt, B. (2004): Application Management Services und Support, Erlangen 2004.

Maier, R./Hädrich, T./Peinl, R. (2005): Enterprise Knowledge Infrastructures, Berlin, Heidelberg, New York 2005.

Mertins, K./Heisig, P./Vorbeck, J. (2003): Knowledge Management Concepts and Best Practices, Berlin, Heidelberg, New York 2003.

Nonaka, I./Toyama, R./Konno, N. (2001): SECI, Ba and Leadership – A Unified Model of Dynamic Knowledge Creation, in: *Nonaka, I./Teece, D.* (Ed.), Managing Industrial Knowledge, Creation, Transfer and Utilization, London, Thousand Oaks, New Delhi 2001, pp. 11–43.

Probst, G./Raub, S./Romhardt, K. (2006): Wissen managen – Wie Unternehmen ihre wertvollste Ressource optimal nutzen, Frankfurt am Main, Wiesbaden 2006.

Rüter, A./Schröder, J./Göldner, A. (2006): IT-Governance in der Praxis, Berlin, Heidelberg 2006.

Santhanam, R./Seligmann, L./Kang, D. (2007): Postimplementation Knowledge Transfers to Users and Information Technology Professionals, in: Journal of Management Information Systems, vol. 24, no. 1, 2007, pp. 171–199.

Schmid, S. (2009): Wissensbasierte Konzeption der Wartungsorganisation im Betrieb komplexer ERP-Systeme, Göttingen 2009.

Schmidt, B. (2010): Wettbewerbsvorteile im SAP-Outsourcing durch Wissensmanagement – Methoden zur effizienten Gestaltung des Übergangs ins Application Management, Berlin 2010.

Takeuchi, H. (2001): Towards a Universal Management Concept of Knowledge, in: *Nonaka, I./Teece, D.* (Ed.), Managing Industrial Knowledge, Creation, Transfer and Utilization, London, Thousand Oaks, New Delhi 2001.

Taylor, S./Lloyd, V./Rudd, C. (2007): ITIL Service Design, Office of Government Commerce, London 2007.

Tornborn, C./Huntley, H. (2007): Best Practices for BPO Transitions, in: Gartner Research, online: http://www.gartner.com/DisplayDocument?ref=g_search&id=532509, published: 16.10.2007, accessed: 29.06.2010.

Towards a Reference Model for Risk and Compliance Management of IT Services in a Cloud Computing Environment

Benedikt Martens and *Frank Teuteberg*[1]

University of Osnabrück

---

1 The authors are indebted to Ms Anja Grube for fruitful discussions and substantive comments relating to this article.

1 Introduction and Motivation

Industry analysts have made several enthusiastic projections on how cloud computing will transform the entire computing industry. According to recent research studies it is on the verge of becoming an extremely lucrative business: the financial profit to be drawn from business and productivity applications as well as related online advertising is expected to amount to billions of Dollars.[2] However, the question arises whether there are any obstacles on the way to mature cloud computing environments. If one looks at IT outsourcing and the emerging field of cloud computing from an economic perspective, some obvious similarities between the two concepts strike the eye. In other words, already existing knowledge about the outsourcing of IT Services should be aligned with new arising obstacles and challenges created by the cloud. The objective of our paper is to support the improvement of decision-making processes by contributing to a better understanding of risk and compliance issues in the field of cloud computing and of their likely impacts. This can only be achieved by identifying the main risks and the necessary safeguards required.[3] The reference model presented in this article could help to accomplish this goal.

The paper is structured as follows: in section 2, we will give a short historical survey from the beginnings of IT outsourcing to the occurrence of cloud computing. Related work on the topic of risk and compliance management in IT outsourcing will be discussed in section 3. In section 4, we will introduce a reference model for risk and compliance management of IT services in cloud computing environments. The reference model consists of several types of models (IT service, risk, compliance and KPI model respectively). The implementation of this reference model by means of the software tool ADOit is described in section 5. Finally, in the concluding section we will discuss implications of our research work and point out some future work.

2 IT Outsourcing – From the Roots to the Clouds

The origins of IT Outsourcing date back to the year 1963, when EDS (Electronic Data Processing) and Ross Perot's company closed a contract on a data processing service.[4] However, other business companies showed very little interest in this agreement. Only the mid-1980s saw a growing acceptance of the concept of IT Outsourcing, with contracts closed between EDS and Continental Airlines, First City Bank and Enron. The signature of a USD 1 billion contract between Kodak and IBM-ISSC in 1989 can be regarded as groundbreaking for the degree of acceptance that IT Outsourcing is enjoying today. In the following, IBM, DEC and Businessland also entered into the contract. In the succeeding years, other renowned business companies followed this example. After a short time, the newly developed management concept of IT Outsourcing had established itself in Europe and has been the subject of recurrent debates ever since. With regard to the evolution of IT Outsourcing, three main di-

2 Cf. *Buyya* et al. (2008), p. 1, and *Meeker* et al. (2008).

3 Cf. *Bahli/Rivard* (2003), p. 211.

4 Cf. *Dibbern* et al. (2004), pp. 7 et seqq.

rections have emerged.[5] In the 1960s, IT Outsourcing was mainly looked at from a technological point of view. Contracts focused on mainframes, data centers and individual software that, in most cases, only large companies could afford. In the 1980s and 1990s, managerial aspects like cost benefit analysis, contract models and concepts of IT Outsourcing were at the center of attention. At the beginning of the 21st century, the research focus was laid more on software applications and industry-specific aspects. From this context, the concept of application service providing (ASP) emerged; i.e. the development, organization and hosting of software implementations by centrally localized services as part of a charge or rental agreement. Figure 1 gives an overview of the evolution of IT Outsourcing from the beginnings to Cloud Computing.

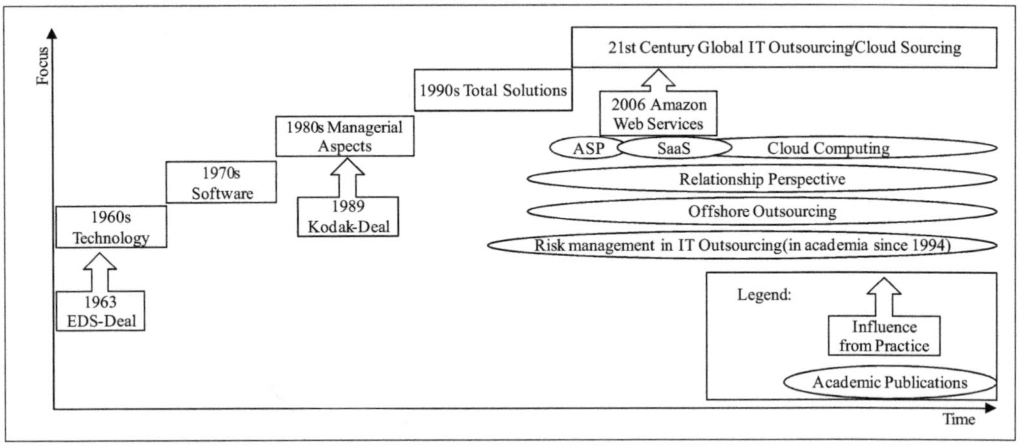

Figure 1: Evolution of IT Outsourcing[6]

A trend clearly indicated by the analysis is the special focus that researchers placed on offshore outsourcing in the year 2008. It is also apparent that IT Outsourcing is not location dependent any more, which creates new tasks and challenges. Two factors contributing to this development are certainly the globalization of IT and the improvement of ICT. The total number of papers on IT offshore outsourcing has continuously increased since 2001.[7] Indirect requests for research by several 'Calls for Papers' have influenced this development as well (cf. e. g. MIS Quarterly, June 2008). Other current developments show that Cloud computing is strongly influenced by technological trends like Grid Computing, Virtualization, as well as by current economic considerations that play a role for IT Service Management, service oriented computing, and the Software as a Service (SaaS) Model.[8] The notion of Cloud computing has been especially dominant in journals aimed at readers with a practical background. Cloud computing could cause major changes in IT business in the near future; several providers like Amazon, Salesforce and Google are already offering IT services via the internet which are processed by Cloud computing providers.[9] Along with the increasing spread of

5 Cf. *CURRIE/SELTSIKAS* (2001), pp. 123 et seqq.

6 Cf. *LEE* et al. (2003), p. 84, *DIBBERN* et al. (2004), pp. 9 et seqq., *MARTENS/TEUTEBERG* (2009a), p. 3, and *PÜSCHEL* et al. (2009), p. 3.

7 Cf. *MARTENS/TEUTEBERG* (2009b), p. 11.

8 Cf. *FOSTER* (2005), p. 815, *MEI* et al. (2008), p. 464, and *ZHANG* (2008), p. 67.

9 Cf. *HAYES* (2008), p. 10.

these concepts and technologies, new fields of activity entailing new risk factors emerge and require a new design of Risk and Compliance Management in IT Outsourcing.[10]

The authors of this paper did a Google search in order to determine and compare the interest factors of Cloud Computing, IT Outsourcing, Grid Computing, and Virtualization (cf. Figure 2). It is obvious, that there has been a strong upward trend of the number of search queries regarding the term "Cloud Computing" until the third quarter of 2007, a decreasing interest in terms like "Grid Computing" and "IT Outsourcing" for which the number of queries had remained more or less static until the middle of 2008, a continuing interest in the key word "Virtualization", and a general lack of interest in all of these topics by the end of 2008, which may have been caused by the outbreak of the financial crisis.

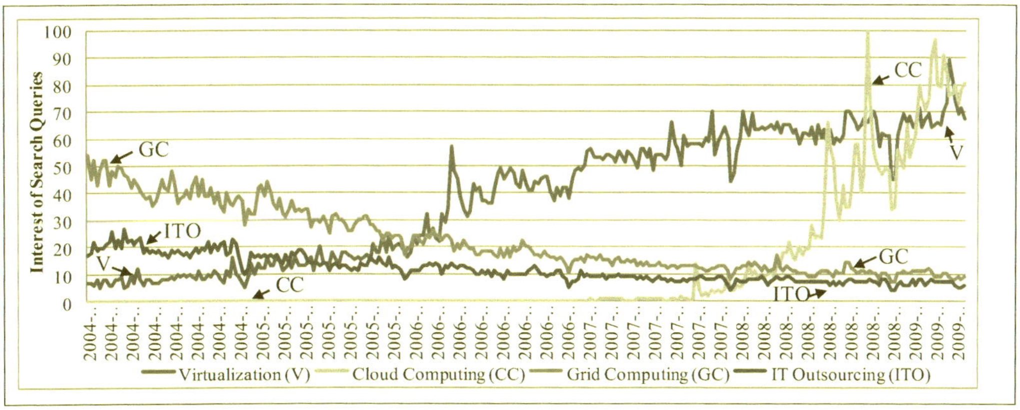

Figure 2: Interest of Search Queries Regarding Cloud Computing

3 Related Work

3.1 Framework of Analysis

To build this article on a solid basis, we applied the method of a systematic literature review.[11] In a systematic literature review, relevant work and current findings are analyzed with regard to a particular research question. Finally, a review should imply conclusions relevant for other researchers and managers alike. To improve the quality of the analyses, both authors of this paper were involved in reviewing and coding the analyzed articles. The inter-rater reliability was good (inter-rater percentage agreement: > 90 % in all analyses). The limitations of a systematic literature review lie in the paper selection and categorization process, which requires some judgment calls. To follow a proven course of action the process model depicted in Figure 3 has been applied. As a first step we defined the review scope by adopting the results from the systematic literature review on IT Outsourcing conducted by *MARTENS/*

10 Cf. e. g. *BUYYA* et al. (2008), p. 5.

11 Cf. *FETTKE* (2006), p. 257.

TEUTEBERG in 2009(b). The 97 articles were categorized by topic in order to select those that are relevant for this paper. To enlarge the number of articles we occasionally used forward and backward search. In *MARTENS/TEUTEBERG* (2009b) the WKWI ranking has been applied. This ranking was created by 54 German professors on the basis of 540 information systems journals and other relevant journal sources. To receive results that are more comprehensive we extended our review by also including those journals that are defined as high quality in the AIS journal ranking. In summary, we included all so-called A-journals from the WKWI ranking list and the top 16,8 % of all journals (all journals <=14,00 of the average rank points: 21 of 125) included in the AIS ranking list. The restriction of the source material to high-quality articles allows for reliable statements about the state of the art of Risk and Compliance Management in IT Outsourcing.

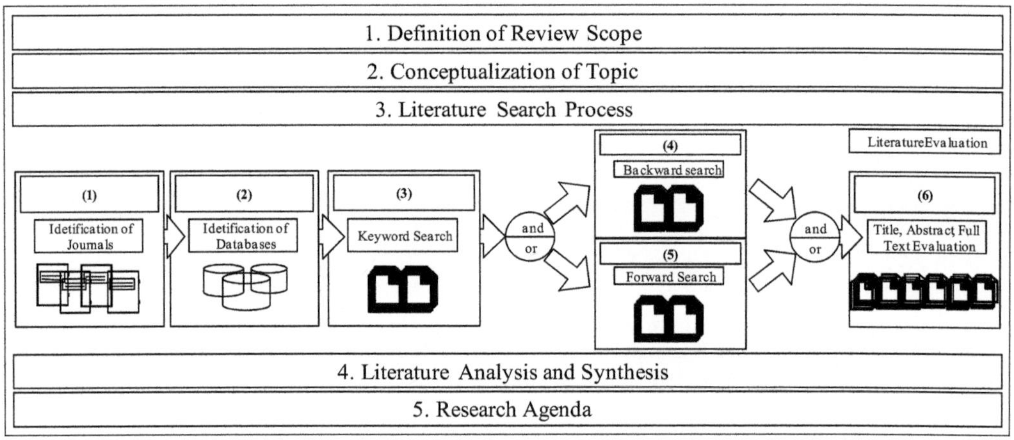

Figure 3: Process Steps of the Systematic Literature Review[12]

Table 1 contains the consolidated list of reviewed journals.

Journal	WKWI Ranking	AIS Ranking	Impact Factor
Management Information Systems Quarterly (MISQ)	(A)	(1.11)	(5.183)
Information Systems Research (ISR)	(A)	(2.67)	not Covered in the JCR
Communic. of the Assoc. for Comp. Machinery (CACM)	(A)	(2.75)	(2.646)
Management Science (MS)	(A)	(4.14)	(2.354)
Journal of Management Information Systems (JMIS)	(A)	(4.86)	(2.358)
Artificial Intelligence (AI)	(B)	(6.00)	(3.397)
Decision Sciences (DS)	(B)	(6.43)	not included in the JCR
Harvard Business Review (HBR)	(B)	(8.00)	not included in the JCR
IEEE Transactions Journals (IEEETrans)	(A)	(8.75)	Varying
AI Magazine (AIM)	-	(9.00)	(0.691)
European Journal of Information Systems (EJIS)	(A)	(10.17)	(1.202)
Decision Support Systems (DSS)	(A)	(10.67)	(1.873)
IEEE Software (IEEES)	(A)	(11.00)	(2.099)
Information & Management (I&M)	(A)	(11.89)	(2.358)
ACM Transactions Journals (ACMT)	(A)	(12.13)	varying
IEEE Transactions on Software Engineering (IEEETSE)	(A)	(12.17)	(3.569)
Journal of Computer and System Sciences (JCSS)	(B)	(13.00)	(1.244)

Table 1: Analyzed Journals (Part I)

12 Cf. *VOM BROCKE* et al. (2009), pp. 8 et seq., and *WEBSTER/WATSON* (2002).

Sloan Management Review (SMR)	(B)	(13.17)	not included in the JCR
Communications of the AIS (CAIS)	(B)	(14.00)	not included in the JCR
IEEE Transactions on Systems, Man, and Cybernetics	(A)	(14.00)	(Impact Factors: 1.350; 2.361; 1.375)
Journal of the Association of Information Systems (JAIS)	(A)	(17.75)	(1.836)
Organization Science (OS)	(A)	(18.00)	not included in the JCR
Information Systems Journal (ISJ)	(A)	(18.71)	not included in the JCR
Information Systems (IS)	(A)	(20.00)	(1.660)
Human-Computer Interaction	(A)	(20.67)	(2.905)
Journal of Strategic Information Systems (JSIS)	(A)	(22.57)	(1.484)
Informing Science (IS)	(A)	(24.00)	not included in the JCR
Wirtschaftsinformatik (WI)	(A)	(28.00)	(0.541)
Information and Organization (I&O)	(A)	(28.25)	not included in the JCR
Journal of Information Technology (JIT)	(A)	(31.50)	(1.966)
Electronic Markets (EM)	(A)	(34.50)	not included in the JCR
International Journal of Information Management (IJIM)	(A)	(37.00)	not included in the JCR

Table 1: Analyzed Journals (Part II)

All journals with a score of 14.00 or less points on the AIS ranking list were included in the review (the titles of these journals are set in bold type). The right column of the table lists the individual Impact Factors of the journals according to the Journal Citation Reports (JCR) of the ISI Web of Knowledge. The Impact Factor describes the average number of times that articles published in a particular journal within the time frame of two years were cited elsewhere within the span of one JCR year.[13] It is calculated by dividing the number of citations from a journal that occurs in the course of the JCR year by the total number of articles published by the journal in the two previous years. For example, an Impact Factor of 1.0 says that on average, the articles a journal has published during the last two years have been cited once a year. Accordingly, an Impact Factor of 2.5 means that over the last two years there has been an average of 2.5 citations from articles in a journal per year. Exceptionally, the citations as such may even appear in the same journal as the cited source.

3.2 Cloud Computing

Table 2 provides a survey of the different existing concepts of the Cloud computing paradigm. It lists the thematic fields, technologies and "as a Service"-terms that are dealt with in the reviewed articles, as well as the points of view taken by the authors. A few explicitly non-scientific contributions were also included in the analysis in order to cover a broad spectrum of opinions. However, these articles were checked for adequate scientific accuracy before their inclusion in the review. The results of the analysis show that to date, a common understanding of Cloud computing has not been arrived at.[14] One possible reason for this is that the topic attracts researchers and engineers from various backgrounds, as e. g. economic and technical perspective and client or vendor perspective. All of them approaching the topic from very different angles. The technologies which are relevant for Cloud Computing are not yet fully matured, but still in the process of development. Neither are the existing computing clouds suitable for large scale deployment. One can also draw from the table that the thematic field of risk management has not been as frequently discussed as topics from the area of Compliance Management. Generally, a stronger focus on the technical perspective of Cloud computing is recognizable. The following elements were described as central for Cloud Computing:

---

13 Cf. online *THOMSON REUTERS* (2009).

14 Cf. *WANG* et al. (2008), p. 825.

- Sourcing of particular IT Services or combined IT Services[15] (hardware, software) from Cloud computing providers (e. g. Amazon, Google) on demand.[16]
- Online delivery of IT Services which are hosted in huge high-scalable data centers (so-called Clouds).[17]
- IT Services from different providers could be flexibly selected and combined by means of short-term contracts and usage-based pricing schemes.[18]
- IT Service Management and Service Level Agreements (SLA) will play an important role for the definition of prices, qualities and characteristics of IT Services delivered by the Cloud.[19]
- A central aim is to hide the complexity of IT infrastructure from its users.[20]

One important first step in research has been taken by the Journal of IEEE Service Computing which incorporated the term "Cloud Computing" into its framework for the sorting and classification of Service Computing terms.[21]

15 Cf. *BUYYA* et al. (2008), p. 2, *THE ECONOMIST* (2008), p. 69, and *PÜSCHEL* et al. (2009), p. 3.

16 Cf. *WEISS* (2007), p. 22, *ARMBRUST* (2008), p. 4, *EYMANN* (2008), and *WANG* et al. (2008), p. 827.

17 Cf. *ARMBRUST* (2008), p. 4, *HAYES* (2008), p. 9, *KONDO* et al. (2009), p. 1, and *SURY* (2009), p. 183.

18 Cf. *BREITER/BERENDT* (2008), p. 625, *MLKA/TUMMARELLO* (2008), p. 82, and *SURY* (2009), p. 183.

19 Cf. *BUYYA* et al. (2008), p. 7.

20 Cf. *KONDO* et al. (2009), p. 1.

21 Cf. *ZHANG* (2008), p. 73.

Type of Reference	Author(s)	Year	Economical	Organizational	Risk	Compliance	Security	Privacy	Technical	Grid	SOA	Web Services	SaaS	IaaS	PaaS	Virtualization	Client	Provider	Neutral
A-Journal	*Weiss*	2007		X					X	X			X			X	X	X	
B-Journal	*Breiter/Berendth*	2008		X					X		X		X	X		X			X
Scientific Institution	*Buyya/Yeo/ Venugopal*	2008	X						X	X	X		X		X	X			X
Company	*Delic/Walker*	2008							X	X						X			X
Encyclopedia	*Eymann*	2008							X	X			X	X	X	X			X
A-Journal	*Hayes*	2008		X								X	X						X
Conference	*Mei et al.*	2008							X	X		X							X
Company	*Mika/Tummarello*	2008							X	X						X		X	
Conference	*Wang et al.*	2008							X	X			X		X	X			X
A-Journal	*Zhang*	2008	X						X	X						X			X
A-Conference	*Anandasivam/ Premm*	2009	X							X			X	X	X	X		X	
Scientific	*Armbrust et al.*	2009	X			X			X			X	X			X	X	X	
Conference	*Pearson*	2009				X		X								X	X	X	
A-Conference	*Püschel et al.*	2009	X							X								X	
B-Journal	*Sury*	2009				X		X					X				X		
A-Journal	*Vykoukal et al.*	2009	X	X	X		X			X		X							X

Table 2: Articles with a Focus on Cloud Computing

3.3 Risk and Compliance Management in IT Outsourcing

Articles with a topic of Risk and Compliance Management are shown in Table 3.

Author	Year of Publication	Journal	Risk Topic	Compliance Topic
Bahli/Rivard	2003	JIT	X	
Saeed/Leitch	2003	JMIS	X	
Adeleye et al.	2004	IJIM	X	
Murthy	2004	CAIS	X	
Singh et al.	2004	DSS	X	
Smith/Kumar	2004	I&M	X	
Cullen et al.	2005	JSIS		X
Oh et al.	2006	JMIS	X	
Cederlund et al.	2007	CAIS	X	
COBIT 4.1	2007	-	X	X
Goodman/Ramer	2007	CAIS	X	X
Hall/Liedtka	2007	CACM		X
ITIL V3	2007	-	X	
Sakthivel	2007	CACM	X	
Vitharana/Dharwadkar	2007	CAIS	X	
Xiong et al.	2007	ACMT		X
Braunwarth/Heinrich	2008	WI	X	
Gefen et al.	2008	MISQ	X	
Goo/Huang	2008	DSS		X
Iacovou/Nakatsu	2008	CACM	X	
Kauffman/Sougstad	2008	JMIS	X	

Table 3: Literature about Risk and Compliance Management in IT Outsourcing

The literature basis of this paper is formed by the extended results of the review conducted by *MARTENS/TEUTEBERG* (2009b) who identified 11 articles from the area of risk management. On the basis of the WKWI ranking list, further articles from the field of Compliance Management were identified for analysis. By including results of the AIS ranking, three additional articles on Risk Management and one more article on Risk and Compliance Management could be tracked down. In addition to the high-quality articles, the two frameworks ITIL V3 and COBIT 4.1 were also analyzed and drawn on for the construction of the reference model. In total, 19 articles of relevance for Risk and Compliance Management were identified. They are listed in Table 3.

Figure 4 illustrates the distribution of research methods applied in the articles. Besides empirical research, a formal, argumentative-deductive analysis is often the method of choice to validate theoretical concepts of risk management and to formulate formal models for risk management functions. Since the research topic of Compliance Management is very rarely worked on, the amount of papers dealing with this topic is too small to make a statement.

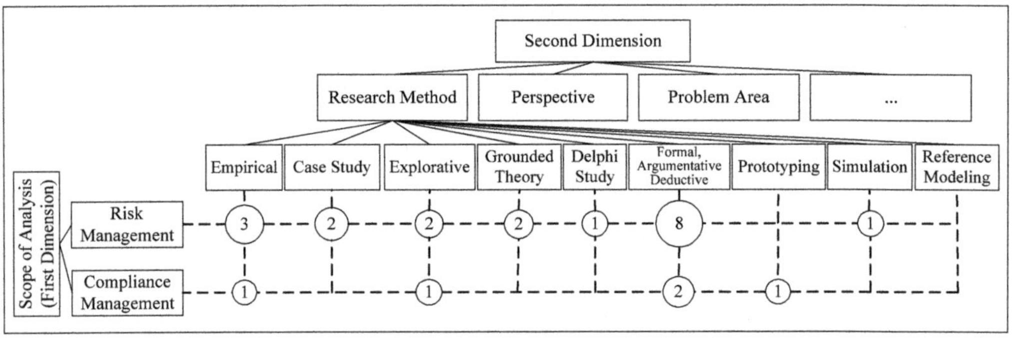

Figure 4: Research Methods Applied

As a result, one can summarize that the topics of Risk and Compliance Management in IT Outsourcing have only been in the focus of research attention since 2007. Existing works dealing with this thematic field were conducted at a very superficial level. Future research should explore both topic areas in more detail. There are no existing works known to the authors that examine the advantages of IT Outsourcing with a view to Risk and Compliance Management.[22]

3.4 Problems and Open Issues in Cloud Computing

In Table 4 problems and open issues in Cloud computing were extracted from the analyzed articles. One of the most frequently discussed problems are missing standards for protocols.

22 Cf. *MOSSANEN/AMBERG* (2008), p. 67.

	Problem/Open Issue	References
Economic/Business	**Overbooking**: If the computing center sells more computing and storage capacity than it actually has (overbooking procedure), not every costumer cloud exploit his reserved resources completely.	*ANANDASIVAM/PREMM* (2009), p. 5.
	Lock-In: Because of the lacking standardization of transport protocols and interfaces between the cloud platforms, a change of suppliers or platforms is economically unreasonable.	*BUYYA ET AL.* (2008), p. 7, and *ARMBRUST ET AL.* (2009), p. 14.
	Lack of applicable business models: Billing based on fixed prices and usage thresholds is too inflexible for companies and therefore does not conform to their needs.	*BUYYA ET AL.* (2008), p. 7, and *ARMBRUST ET AL.* (2009), p. 16.
Psy-chol.	**Trust:** Mutual trust between stakeholders (clients/suppliers) depends on the supplier's reputation. Standardized safety measures have not yet been established.	*WEISS* (2007), pp. 24-25, and *BUYYA ET AL.* (2008), p. 5.
Organiza-tional	**Different viewpoints:** Cloud computing as a topic attracts researchers and engineers from various backgrounds.	Wang et al. (2008), p. 825.
	Definition: There are still no widely accepted definitions of Cloud Computing.	*WANG ET AL.* (2008), p. 825
	Small and medium-sized Enterprises (SME): SMEs often have no access to new IT services, because of low spending power.	*BROWN/LOCKETT* (2001), p. 52.
	SLA-Management: Often, SLAs only contain clauses concerning basic service elements. Important aspects of IT/Corporate Governance (communication channels, joint decision-making and conflict resolution), experiences and changing business demands are not addressed.	*VYKOUKAL ET AL.* (2009), p. 207, and *BUYYA ET AL.* (2008), p. 5.
Legal/Compliance	**Data confidentiality, auditability and regulatory pressure:** It is impossible to know where exactly within the Cloud data processing takes place. The identification of potential subcontractors may be a complex and difficult task.	*BUYYA ET AL.* (2008), p. 8, and *ARMBRUST ET AL.* (2009), p. 15, and *PEARSON* (2009), p. 50.
	Privacy risk: The possibility of new privacy risks arises with the extensive use of Cloud computing services.	*PEARSON* (2009), p. 45.
	Supplier failure: Legal and financial damage caused by the supplier also affects the client (e. g. falling stock prices, inadequate compliance and reporting mechanisms).	*HALL/LIEDTKA*, (2007), p. 100.
Technical	**Technical Development:** It is difficult to make predictions about the future evolution and design of a service. Because of the paradigm shift in user requirements, a full design specification in advance is not always appropriate.	*PEARSON* (2009), p. 50, and *WANG ET AL.* (2008), p. 825.
	Velocity of up-and-down-scaling: The demand for IT services is mostly both dynamic and unpredictable. This could lead to performance problems because of slow up-and-down-scaling of IT service parameters.	*ANANDASIVAM/PREMM* (2009), p. 3, and *ARMBRUST ET AL.* (2009), p. 18.
	Data Transfer: The internet bandwidth could be a problem for transferring huge data volumes to the Cloud. Amazon has already started a service of shipping hard disk drives to the provider.	*ARMBRUST ET AL.* (2009), p. 16.
	Management and availability: It is not yet sure whether Cloud data centers will be able to handle high data volumes and data transfers in order to guarantee data availability. Also, the high numbers of applications and resources may lead to management problems.	*BREITER/BERENDTH* (2008), pp. 625, 628, and *ARMBRUST ET AL.* (2009), p. 15.
	Technical standards: Different interfaces and transport protocols slow down the development of a market infrastructure for trading in services. Standard protocols make it possible to interconnect several cloud instances.	*BUYYA ET AL.* (2008), p. 7, and *ANANDASIVAM/PREMM* (2009), p. 4.
Security	**Data governance models:** There is a lack of data governance models, which codify the accountability for binding rules that address privacy concerns (e. g.) in Cloud Computing.	*PEARSON* (2009), p. 50.
	Corrupt Cloud computing Server: IP addresses could be handled like SPAM to reduce white-collar crime.	*ARMBRUST ET AL.* (2009), p. 18.
	Data Security: The data privacy level is important for the outsourcing to an IT service provider. The use of encryption methods contributes just to a limited degree.	*GÜNTHER ET AL.* (2001), p. 558, and *JAYATILAKA ET AL.* (2003), p. 214, and *PEARSON* (2009), p. 3, and SURY (2009), p. 183.

Table 4: Open Issues in Cloud Computing

4 Reference Model

Reference models are used for the design of organizations and application systems. They are of recommendatory character for the selected application area.[23] They also have an explanatory function and serve as universally valid models for the purpose of comparison and for the deduction of recommended actions. It should be noted, however, that reference models usually need some organization-specific adjustments with regard to the selected application. Therefore, in each individual case a specialization of the models and KPIs discussed here will be necessary.

The particular reference model introduced in this section underwent several cycles of development. It is based on a combination of deductive and inductive elements, drawing on our own preliminary considerations, the systematic literature review (see section 2) as well as the results of expert interviews. Figure 5 illustrates this process of development and also presents future steps to be taken. At present, the project is at the stages of "Model construction" and "Validation and Improvement of Model". The iteration loop has already been run with the help of the expert interviews.

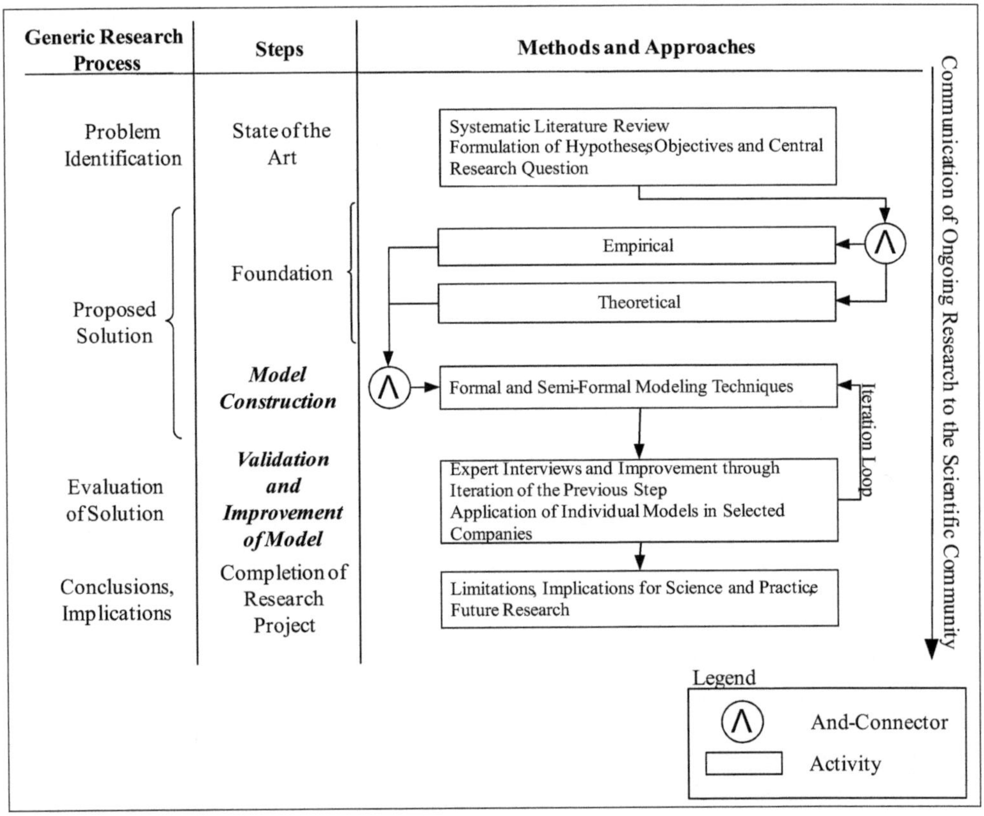

Figure 5: Research Process for the Development of a Reference Model

[23] Cf. *VOM BROCKE* (2007), pp. 47 et seqq.

4.1 Meta Reference Model and Sources for Construction

Figure 6 introduces a meta reference model which serves as a regulation framework to structure the application problem and its different aspects. The figure visualizes different types of models, their grouping and the interrelations between them. In the course of this article, the individual models will be explained in more detail. We chose UML as modeling language.

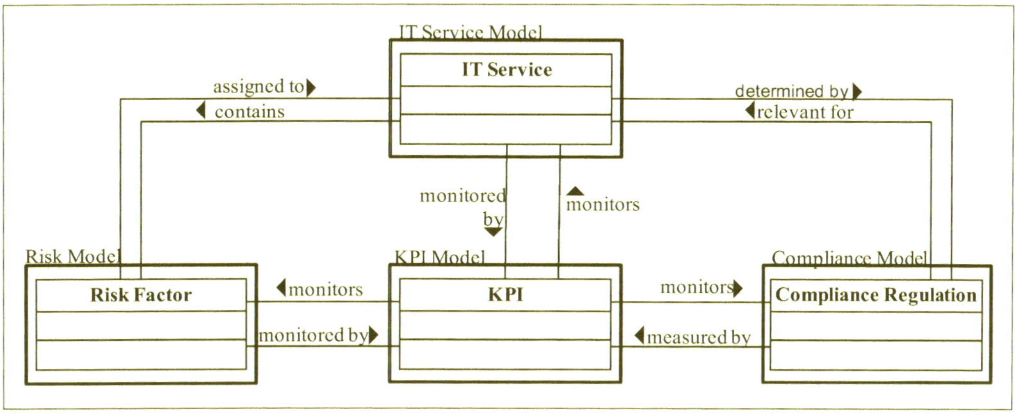

Figure 6: Meta Reference Model for Risk and Compliance Management in the Cloud

Table 5 lists the elements that served as a basis for the construction of the different models, including the most relevant sources from both the systematic literature review and the conducted expert interviews. It should be pointed out that not all scientific sources from the literature review were suitable for the construction of the models.

Model	References	Expert Interview
IT Service Model	*Braun/Winter* (2005), *Iqbal/Nieves* (2007), *Breiter/Berendt* (2008), *Buyya et al.* (2008), *Rohloff* (2008), *Matros et al.* (2009),	X
Risk Model	*Aubert et al.* (1998), *Aubert et al.* (2002), *Bahli/Rivard* (2003), *Aloini et al.* (2007), *Iqbal/Nieves* (2007), *Klotz/Dorn* (2008), *Martens/Teuteberg* (2009), COBIT 4.1, *Sackmann et al.* (2009),	X
Compliance Model	*Cullen et al.* (2005), *Knolmayer* (2007), *Müller/Supatgiat* (2007), *Brown* (2008), *Goo/Huang* (2008), *Karagiannis* (2008), *Kharbili et al.* (2008), *Mossanen/Amberg* (2008),	X
KPI Model	*Lacitiy/Willcocks* (1998), *Bernhard* (2003), *Braun/Winter* (2005), *Ngwenyama/Sullivan* (2006), COBIT 4.1 (2007), *Krause* (2008), *Blecken et al.* (2009), *Martens/Teuteberg* (2009),	X

Table 5: Sources drawn on for the Construction of the Respective Models

Table 6 outlines the corporate background of the experts interviewed for validating the reference model.

Company	Client/Vendor	Industry Sector	Notes
1	Client	Supplier for coating and lacquering of plastic parts	-Medium-sized company with 150 employees at two locations -One outsourcing experience mentioned was the development and implementation of an operational data acquisition system. The system is designed to conform to ISO 9000 (quality management)
2	Vendor	IT Service Provider	-Founded in 1994; staff size of 200 -Offers consulting, development and training services -Most employees are involved in IT development projects at the customer's location
3	Vendor	IT Service Provider for Supply Chain Management	-Software development (including web services) -Strategic and operative IT consulting -IT Outsourcing risks that affect the service quality are explicitly laid out in the contract
4	Vendor	IT Service Provider	-Founded in 1984, staff size of 70 -Networks, training, service and support -Specialized on archiving and document management
5	-	IT Consulting Company	-Founded in 2004; staff size of 70 -Management of IT Outsourcing projects -Improvement of development and service processes

Table 6: Corporate Background of the Experts interviewed

4.2 IT Service Model

The IT Service Model (illustrated in Figure 7) forms the center of the meta reference model and is linked to all other models via connectors. These connectors are marked by a frame and the model name. For example, an IT service is measured by means of one or several KPIs which are part of the KPI model and are further specified there. Since Cloud computing consists of generic IT services, as e. g. the provision of computing power, storage, platforms, infrastructure or standard software,[24] the IT Service Model is constructed on this basis. Such standardized IT services can be individually combined with the help of brokers. A broker takes up the function of a mediator. It can either be operated internally or externally on an automatic basis or be embedded in the company as a role. If the quality of relations to the supplier is important, human assistance is required.[25] The combination of IT services can result in economic advantages for the customer.[26] A very simple example is the combination of resources to create new "Software/Plat-form/Resource... as a service"-products. Correspondingly, an external broker can generate a profit by combining IT services. This profit can be defined as the difference between the company's added value and the original IT service costs.

24 Cf. *HAYES* (2008), p. 10.

25 Cf. *FLEMING/LOW* (2007), p. 95.

26 Cf. e. g. *SKILLICORN* (2002).

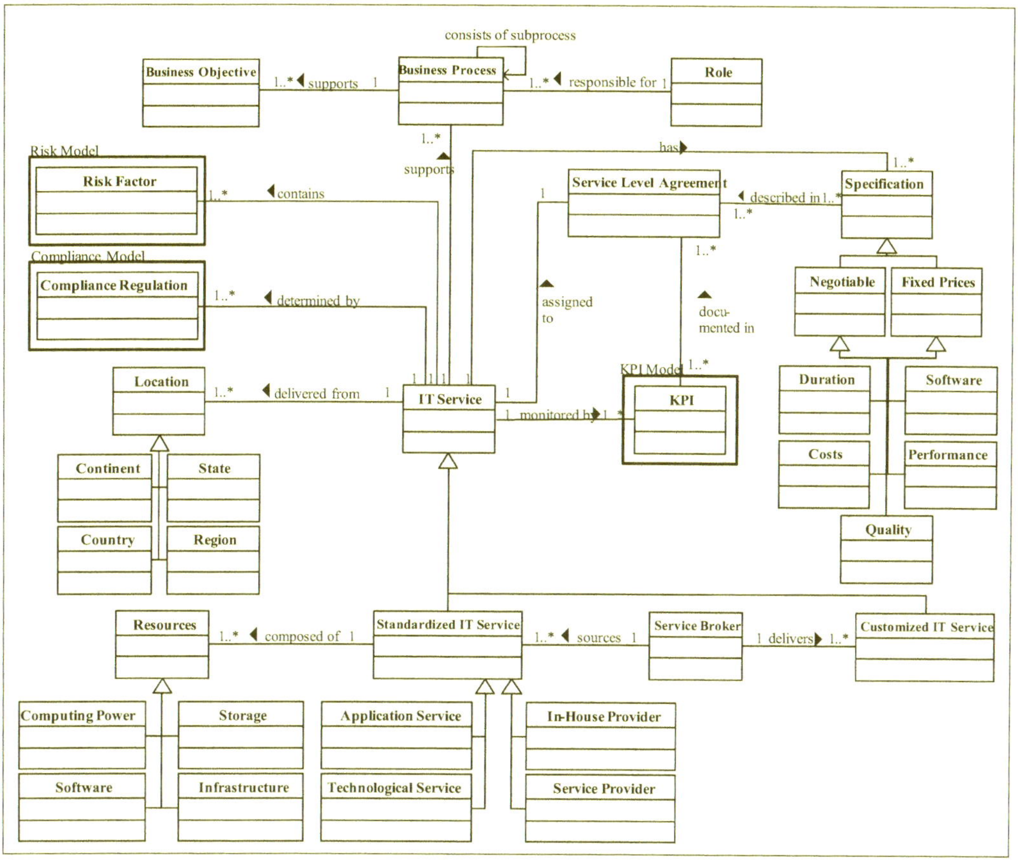

Figure 7: IT Service Model

Figure 8 shows one possible hierarchy of IT services from the Cloud. The illustration is more detailed than the model and integrates the broker into the architecture, whereas IT service, Risk and Compliance Management takes up a comprehensive function. Its task is to assess the customer's demands to the IT services with regard to risk, compliance and economic requirements. The identified IT services can then be distinguished in order to make well-founded decisions.

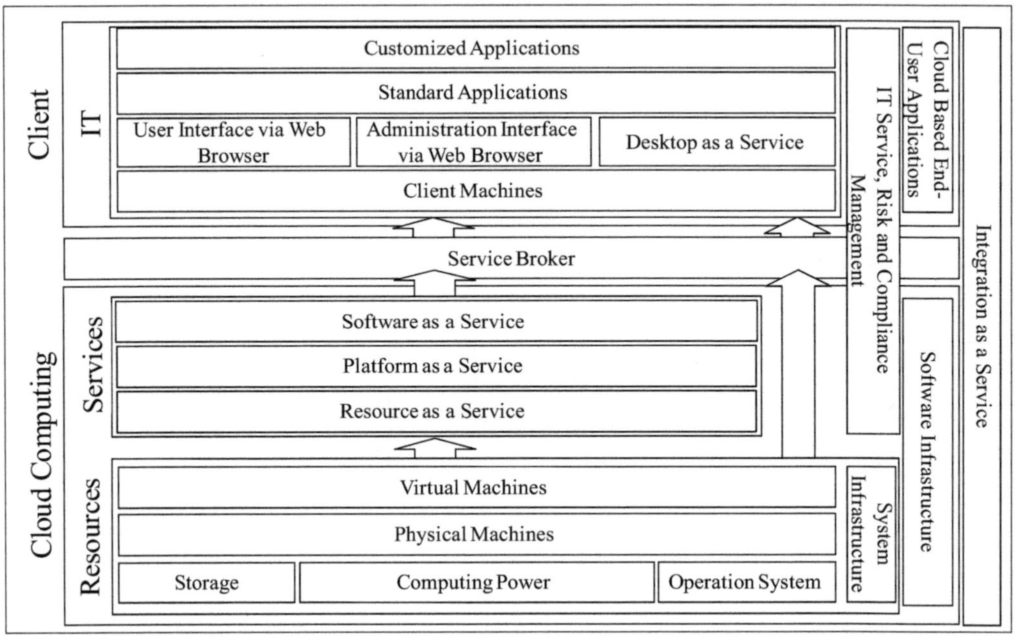

Figure 8: *IT Service Architecture for Cloud Services*

4.3 Risk Model

Figure 9 depicts the risk model. Risk factors are measured by a KPI and are assigned to IT services and compliance regulations. If a risk factor is assigned to a compliance regulation it should also be assigned to the risk category "Regulatory/Legal". The service broker operating within the IT Service Model assesses risk factors and has a certain risk attitude, as e. g. risk-averse, risk-neutral or risk-seeking. The probability of risks occurring can be assessed empirically by means of public risk databases[27].[28]

[27] E. g. the Common Vulnerability Scoring System (CVSS) (online: http://www.first.org/cvss/) or the Operational Riskdata eXchange Association (ORX) (online: http://www.orx.org/).

[28] Cf. *SACKMANN* et al. (2009), p. 360.

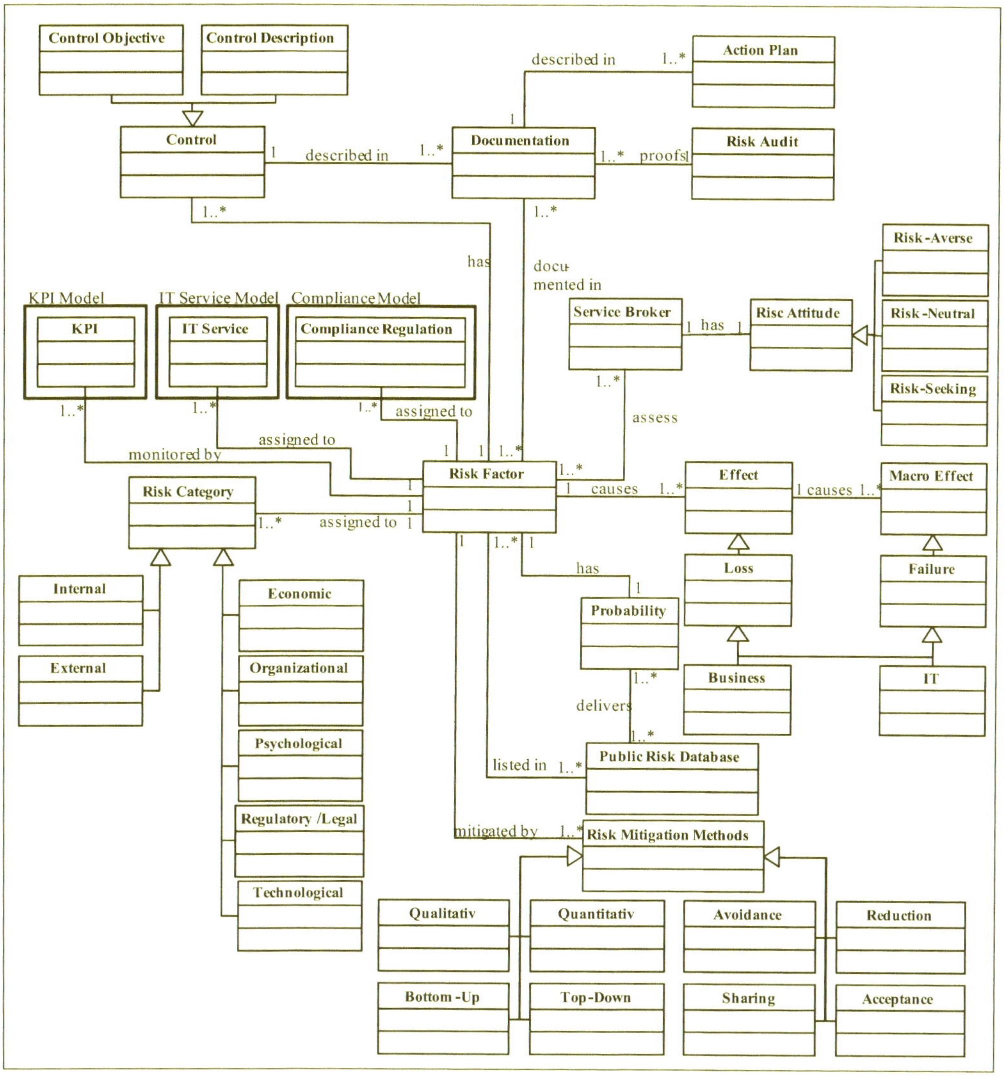

Figure 9: *Risk Model*

The risk factors listed in Table 7 were extracted from the IT Outsourcing articles analyzed in the systematic literature review conducted by *MARTENS/TEUTEBERG* (2009). The risk factors were then assigned to one of five categories (economical, organizational, legal, technical or psychological). These categories were adopted from the PEST analysis (Political, Economic, Social, and Technological) which identifies external factors for companies.[29] The categories were customized to fit our focus on IT risk factors. A total of 23 different risk factors were identified and assessed by the interviewed companies with regard to their relevance for Cloud Computing. Risk factors with a strong influence on Cloud computing are marked by "++", less important ones with "+" and risk factors with none or weak importance by "0".

29 Cf. *TURNER* (2008), p. 214.

	Risk Factor	Relevance for Cloud Computing
Economical	*1.1 Quality Inferior to Anticipation:* customer is not able to evaluate the quality of IT Services adequately (theory of adverse selection)	0
	1.2 Hidden Costs: costs which are not mentioned in contract; ICT (Information and Communication Technology) costs of securing efficient communication; transition/switching costs, post-outsourcing costs	++
	1.3 None/Poor Performance Measurement: lack of mutual monitoring and controlling of provider and customer	++
	1.4 Poor Cost Management: miscalculation and budget overrun because of poor cost management, unclear cost-benefit relationship	++
	1.5 Loss of skilled IT employees: loss of skilled IT staff and negative effects on employee morale	0
	1.6 High Moral Hazard: a company acts in an irrational way, since it does not bear the consequences of actions	+
	1.7 High Asset Specificity: overspending due to high transaction costs and a small number of providers on market	0
	1.8 Low Financial Stability: the provider's financial stability is important	+
Organizational	*2.1 Lack of Provider Expertise:* provider's experience with/knowledge of IT operations and IT Outsourcing projects	+
	2.2 Loss of Competence: if outsourced IT services are close to core competences, future actions could be threatened	0
	2.3 Low Customer Capability: customer experience with IT operations	+
	2.4 Poor Project Management: insufficient planning and management of IT Outsourcing projects	++
	2.5 High Performance Oscillation: provided performance after contract conclusion has high oscillations	+
	2.6 Excessive Dependence on Provider: customer has a limited scope of action	++
	2.7 High Task Complexity: the service or task complexity influences the achievement of objectives.	0
Legal	*3.1 Lack of Provider Expertise with Law:* gained provider experience regarding IT Outsourcing contracts: pricing clauses, liability clauses, renegotiation clauses	++
	3.2 Legality of Contract: scope/size/compliance/penalties of IT Outsourcing contract; poor contract management	++
	3.3 Lack of Customer Expertise with Law: gained customer experience regarding IT Outsourcing contracts	++
	3.4 Irreversibility of outsourcing decision: backsourcing is usually not economical	++
Tech-nol.	*4.1 Lack of Privacy/Data Security:* confidential data, intellectual property	++
	4.2 Lack of Flexibility: inability to adapt new technologies	+
Psychol.	*5.1 Cultural Disparity:* cultural barriers between customer and provider	0
	5.2 Poor User Integration: IT users have insufficient influence on the IT Outsourcing project/services	+

Table 7: Risk Factors[30]

30 Cf. *MARTENS/TEUTEBERG* (2009b), p. 9.

4.4 Compliance Model

The Compliance Model illustrated in Figure 10 shows the structure and interconnection of the three central components of Compliance Management. These three components are: Compliance Regulation (generally subdivided into internal and external regulations), Compliance Audit (monitoring of compliance) and Compliance Level (degree of compliance with a regulation). By means of different compliance levels the optimal degree of compliance (minimum costs and maximum profit) can be calculated[31]. This can be accomplished by regarding compliance as a continuous rather than a binary phenomenon. Striving for full compliance is usually not reasonable from an economic point of view, especially for large companies.

What remains significant both for IT Outsourcing and Cloud computing is the character of external data processing.[32] One can distinguish between Transfer of Operations and Commissioned Data Processing. This distinction plays in the Federal Data Protection Act an important role e. g.

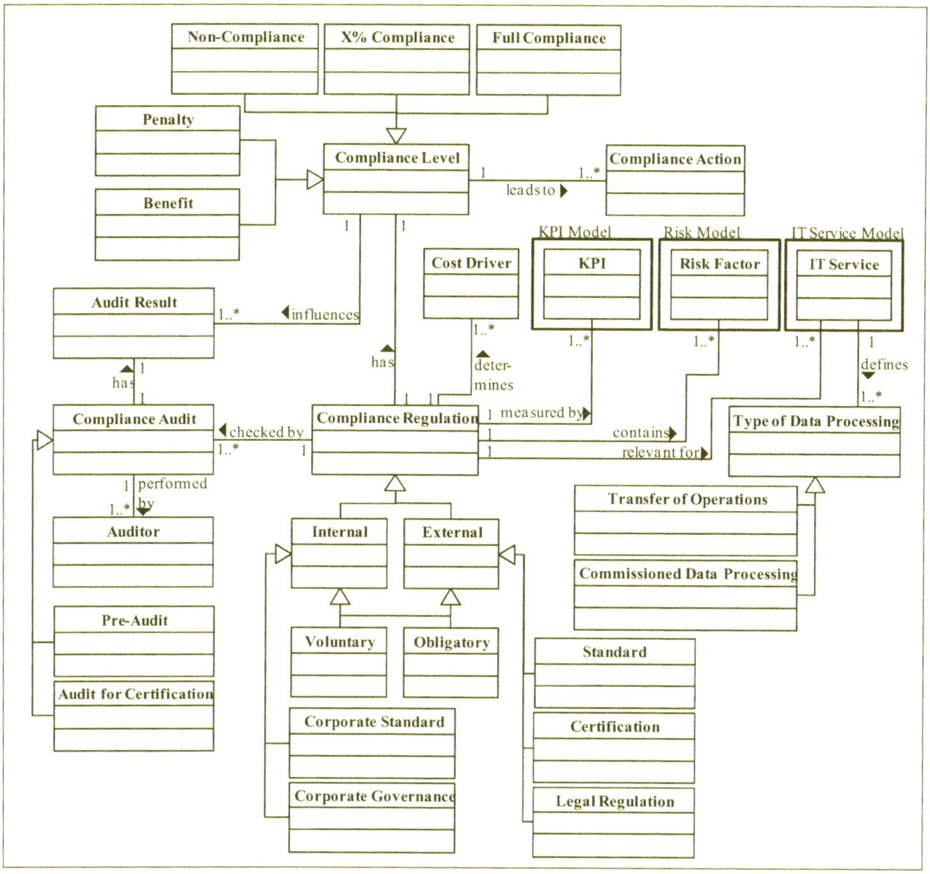

Figure 10: Compliance Model

[31] Cf. *MÜLLER/SUPATGIAT* (2007), p. 306.

[32] Cf. *MOSSANEN/AMBERG* (2008), p. 61.

A typical audit process for a SAS 70 report consists of five steps: 1. audit request to the client auditor; 2. reporting of requirements to the service provider; 3. transmission of audit request from the service provider to the service auditor; 4. creation of SAS 70 reports and transfer to the service provider, the client and finally to the client auditor; 5. client auditor creates audit report.[33]

4.5 Key Performance Indicator Model

The KPI model outlined in Figure 11 supports the operationalization of measures and strategic aims. KPIs measure the performance of IT Service, Risk and Compliance Management. The different values of a KPI, as the target value, the actual value and the lower limit value, trigger actions to improve the actual KPI value.

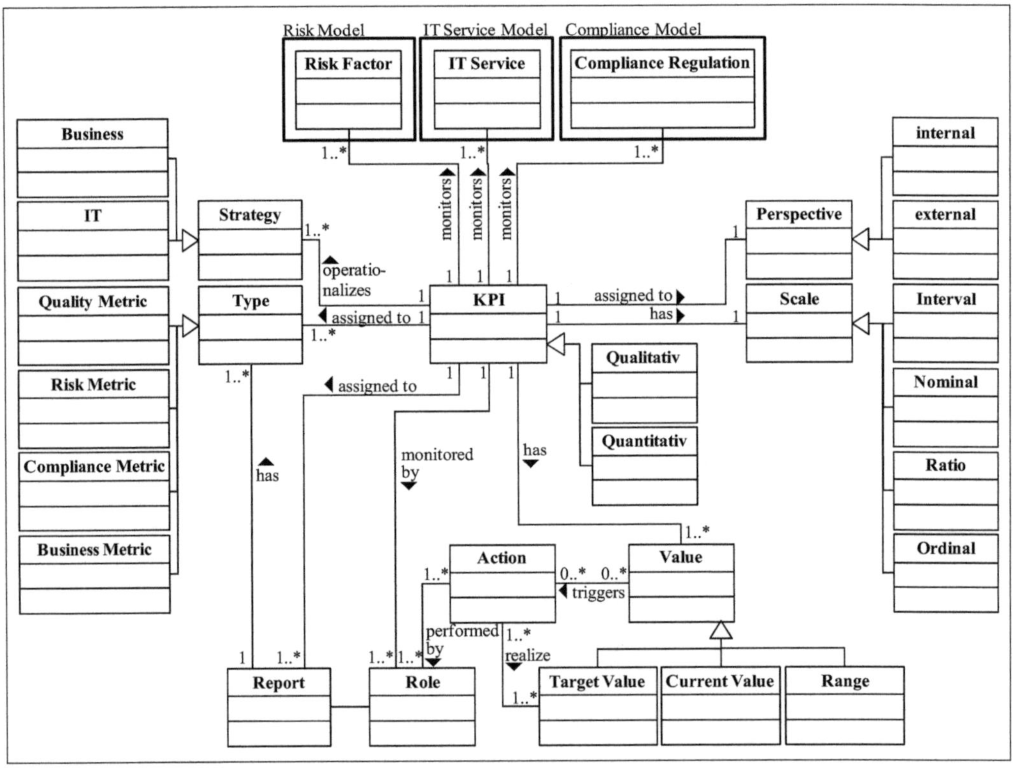

Figure 11: KPI Model

33 Cf. *KNOLMAYER* (2007), p. 98.

	Key Performance Indicator	*Strategic Goals*	*Actions*
Finance	- **percentage of total IT budget spent on outsourced IT services [*Kargl/Kütz* (2007)]** - **cost reduction rate for outsourced IT services [*Kargl/Kütz* (2007)]** - reduced unit costs of procured services [COBIT 4.1] - percent of IT budget spent on risk management activities [COBIT 4.1] - **cost of IT non-compliance, including settlements and fines [COBIT 4.1]**	- 20% cost savings for external IT services and non-compliance	- analysis and identification of cost drivers
Service Organizations	- **percent of major suppliers meeting clearly defined requirements and service levels [COBIT 4.1 , ITIL]** - percent of key stakeholders satisfied with suppliers (assessment of suppliers) [COBIT 4.1, *Kargl/Kütz* (2007)] - **number of procurement requests satisfied by the preferred supplier list [COBIT 4.1]** - number of request for proposals that needed to be improved [COBIT 4.1] - number of responses received to a request for proposal [COBIT 4.1] - number of supplier changes for same type of procured services [COBIT 4.1] - **number of formal disputes/incidents with suppliers [COBIT 4.1, ITIL, Kütz 2009]** - percent of major suppliers subject to monitoring [COBIT 4.1, ITIL] - percent of UCs with security specifications [ITIL] - number of suppliers/SLAs/contracts that have responsible employees in the organization [ITIL]	- improve supplier relationship for more efficient service delivery - bisect incidents with suppliers	- ABC analysis for suppliers - introduction of a supplier relationship management
SLAs	- **availability of IT Services [*Kargl/Kütz* (2007), ITIL]** - comparison of service deliveries with regard to quality, functionality [*Kargl/Kütz* (2007)] - percent of major suppliers subject to clearly defined requirements and service levels [COBIT 4.1] - percent of initial requirements addressed by the selected solution [COBIT 4.1] - **number of SLA violations caused by external service provider [ITIL, COBIT 4.1]** - number of Operating-Level-Agreements (OLAs) und Underpinning Contracts (UCs) covered by master agreements [ITIL] - **number of IT Services covered by an SLA [ITIL]** - **number of monitored Services and contracts [ITIL]**	- cover 95% of all IT services with an SLA - improve availability of external IT services	- establishment of SLA management process
Clients	- idle time for IT Service approval [*Kargl/Kütz* (2007)] - time lag between request for procurement and signing of contract or purchase [COBIT 4.1] - **satisfaction with IT Services [*Kargl/Kütz* (2007)]** - **number of user complaints due to contracted services [COBIT 4.1]** - level of business satisfaction with effectiveness of communication from the supplier [COBIT 4.1]	- improvement of IT service quality by 10% - improved effectiveness of supplier communication	- establishment of a supplier management process
Compliance	- percent of procurements in compliance with standing policies and procedures [COBIT 4.1] - number of significant incidents of supplier non-compliance per time period [COBIT 4.1] - **number of suppliers with certification [ITIL]** - **number of critical non-compliance issues identified per year [COBIT 4.1]** - frequency of compliance reviews/audits [COBIT 4.1] - number of open issues from the last service audit [ITIL] - **average time lag between identification of external compliance issues (new law or regulation) and resolution [COBIT 4.1]** - training days per IT employee per year related to compliance [COBIT 4.1] - audit and tracking of SLA, OLA and UC violations [ITIL]	- every IT employee should attend at least one compliance training - reducting the rate of non-compliance issues to 5%	- Establishment of a whistle-blowing system - Establishment of compliance levels
Risks	- **number of identified risks [ITIL, COBIT]** - number of risks of Service interruption [ITIL] - number of newly occurring incidents [ITIL] - percent of configuration objects covered by a business impact analysis [ITIL] - percentage of services that are covered by an operational risk assessment [ITIL] - **number of measures for risk reduction [ITIL]** - number of significant incidents caused by risks that were not identified by the risk assessment process [COBIT 4.1] - **percent of identified critical IT risks with an action plan developed [COBIT 4.1]** - frequency of review of the IT Risk management process [COBIT 4.1] - duration of risk analysis [ITIL] - percent of approved risk assessments [COBIT 4.1] - **percent of identified critical IT events that have been assessed [COBIT 4.1]** - percent of identified IT events used in risk assessments [COBIT 4.1] - number of actioned risk monitoring reports within the agreed-upon frequency [COBIT 4.1] - percent of Risk management action plans approved for implementation [COBIT 4.1]	- reduction of risks by 30% - covering 80% of all risks with an action plan	- improvement of the IT risk management process - establishment of an IT risk manager position

Table 8: BSC for Risk and Compliance Management of IT Services in the Cloud

The Balanced Scorecard (BSC), which is already a widely accepted Performance Measurement System, can be applied as a strategic management and controlling instrument.[34] The BSC was originally developed by *KAPLAN* und *NORTON* to augment the previously strictly finance-oriented performance measurement systems with a balanced number of financial and non-financial variables.[35] There have only been sporadic suggestions by researchers to apply the concept of the BSC to IT Outsourcing.[36] However, the authors of this article did not trace down any works proposing modifications of the BSC-concept to make it applicable to Risk and Compliance Management of IT services from Cloud Computing. The original four perspectives (Finance, Clients, Internal Business Processes and Learning/Development) were modified into the perspectives Finance, Service Provider, Service Level Agreements, Clients, Compliance and Risks (cf. Table 8). As opposed to the recommendations of *KAPLAN* and *NORTON* we provide a comprehensive, non-balanced BSC comprising more than 20 KPIs. Companies applying this BSC need to adjust it to their strategy and have to select individual KPIs. The KPIs printed in bold are the most important and fundamental ones.

5 Implementation of the Reference Model using ADOit

In this section we describe how the reference model and its internal object references can be implemented by means of a software tool. We decided to use the software tool ADOit by BOC GmbH for this purpose. The ADOit platform provides different types of models that visualize a company's IT architecture, processes and IT service structures.

A first implementation of the presented reference model is already available and is briefly described in this section. To provide a general overview, the interdependencies between the different parts of the reference model (model of the organizational structure, process model, IT service model, IT architecture model, strategy model, risk factor model and compliance model) are outlined in Figure 12.

Starting from the organizational structure, ADOit makes it possible to assign roles to process steps, processes, risk factors, compliance factors, IT architecture objects and strategy objects. For the sake of clarity we connected one role from each model to a process in the process model. This object takes up a central role in our example, being linked to risks, compliance regulations and IT architecture objects. The model reaches a higher level of detail by the attribution of objects to individual process activities in the IT service processes. The strategy layer can be regarded as a meta-level that is not directly linked to other models within the reference model and therefore does not have an impact on them in its context.

---

34 Cf. *BIBLE* et al. (2006), pp. 18 et seqq.

35 Cf. *KAPLAN/NORTON* (1997), pp. 41 et seqq.

36 Cf. *KRAUSE* (2008), pp. 253 et seqq.

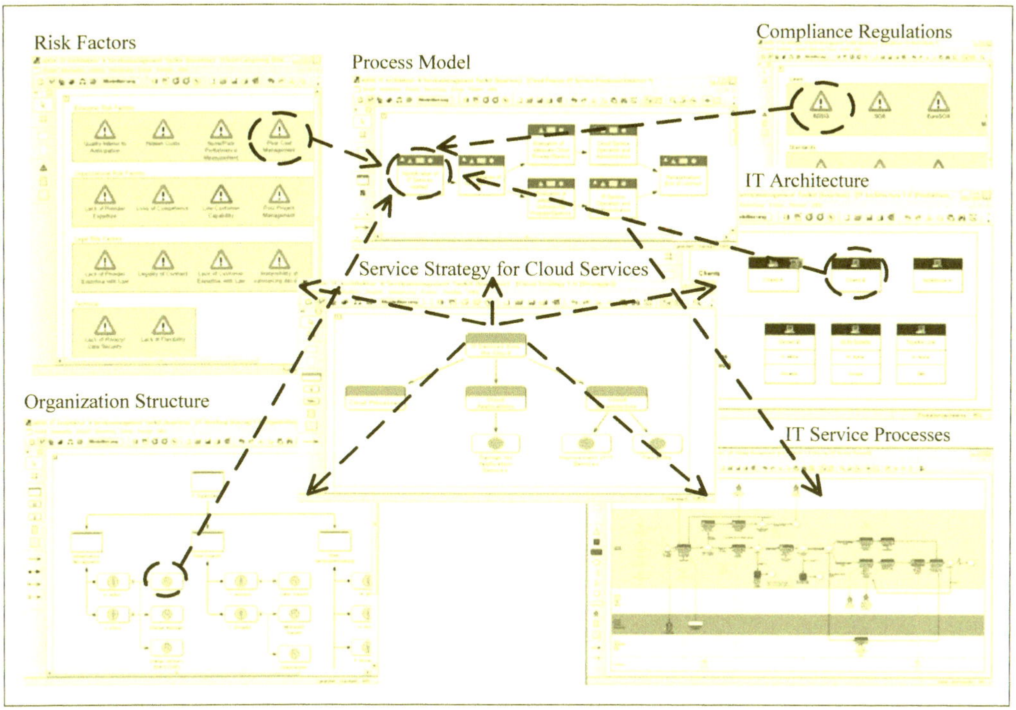

Figure 12: Model and Object References

6 Conclusions and Future Work

The results of our literature review and expert interviews have several implications for both Standard and Reference Model giving Organizations (SRMGO) and Standard and Reference Model Applying Organizations (SRMAOs):

Implications for Standard and Reference Model Giving Organizations: SRMGO typically hope that their work is spread widely. In this context, two maxims have to be considered: on the one hand, standards, frameworks and reference models for Cloud computing need to be precise and generally applicable. This leads to rather abstract and theoretical standard definitions and reference models. On the other hand, users expect standards to considerably help improve process quality, accelerate the introduction of new services and provide best practices. This is an impetus for more concrete standards and reference models. Furthermore, standards and reference models should be made more "configurable".[37] To prevent standards from being considered useless in practice, SRMGOs should ensure that their target groups are

[37] Cf. *FETTKE/LOOS* (2007).

sufficiently represented in the working groups that develop the standards and reference models.[38]

Implications for Standard and Reference Model Applying Organizations: SRMAOs should be aware that the application of standards and reference models solely does not lead to a better risk and compliance management of IT services. SRMAOs should carefully analyze which standard is most appropriate for their specific situation. It seems particularly reasonable to investigate industry-specific or service type-specific standards that are frequently more easily applicable and contain more specific best practices. Besides this, widespread standards and reference models are more likely to lead to synergies when executing inter-organizational Cloud computing projects. They also justify higher investments, since they will probably retain their relevance to IT services from the cloud and are more likely to be further developed. Yet the market for IT services from the sloud is not matured enough. The lock-in effect to one particular provider is currently the biggest issue in this field and could only be prevented by the establishment of standards and reference models. As well to protect SRMAOs, there are several open issues to be solved.

Implications for the Scientific Community in IS: Although standards and reference models in Cloud computing seem to be a topic for the IT Outsourcing and IT Service Management discipline in the first place there are some significant contributions the IS research community can make:

1. Software systems for Risk and Compliance Management need to be developed in accordance with the most important standards and reference models. This refers to terminology, methods and processes. Whenever researchers work on new concepts for IT service management software systems they need to take this into account. Moreover, it needs to be explored how software systems can be made configurable so that they can easily switch between different standards. This would allow the user to select a standard during the introduction phase of the software without the need for custom development.
2. While Grid Computing has been extensively driven by academia, the field of IT Outsourcing and additionally the field of Cloud computing is driven and developed by practice.[39] The conjunction of science and practice need to be extended by applying research methods like action research or field research to build a bridge for knowledge exchange.

The reference model presented in this article can help reduce the total expenditure for Risk and Compliance Management of IT services from the Cloud. At the same time, it can improve the quality and efficiency of IT Service Management through measurements based on the presented BSC. We are planning to develop an integral process model which shall be implemented by using the software ADONIS (BOC Group) and is meant to support the conduct of process simulation tests. The results shall be progressively integrated during the course of the project and shall also serve to improve the other models.

---

38 Cf. section 4.

39 Cf. *WEINHARDT* et al. (2009), p. 30.

References

ADELEYE, B. C. et al. (2004): Risk management practices in IS outsourcing: An investigation into commercial banks in Nigeria, in: International Journal of Information Management, 2004, 24(2), pp. 167–180.

ALOINI, D. et al. (2007): Risk management in ERP project introduction: Review of the literature, in: Information & Management, 2007, 44 (6), pp. 547–567.

ANANDASIVAM, A./PREMM, M. (2009): Bid price control and dynamic pricing in clouds, in: *NEWELL, P.* et al. (Eds.), Information Systems in a Globalising World: Challenges, Ethics, and Practices, Proceedings of the 17th European Conference on Information Systems, Verona 2009, pp. 1–10.

ARMBRUST, M. et al. (2009): Above the Clouds: A Berkeley View of Cloud Computing, online: http://www.eecp.berkeley.edu/Pubs/TechRpts/2009/EECS-2009-28.pdf, last update: 10.02.2009, date visited: 15.07.2009.

AUBERT, B. et al. (1998): Assessing the Risk of IT Outsourcing, in: Thirty-First Annual Hawaii International Conference on System Sciences, Band 6, Hawaii 1998, pp. 685–691.

AUBERT, B. et al. (2002): Managing IT Outsourcing Risk: Lessons Learned, in: *HIRSCHHEIM, R.* et al. (Eds.), Information Systems Outsourcing in the New Economy: Emergent Patterns and Future Directions, Berlin 2002, pp. 155–176.

BAHLI, B./RIVARD P. (2003): The Information Technology Outsourcing Risk: a Transaction Cost and Agency theory-based Perspective, in: Journal of Information Technology, 2003, 18, pp. 211–221.

BERNHARD, M. (2003): Der Werkzeugkasten für Service-Level-Kennzahlen, in: *BERNHARD, M.* et al. (Eds.), IT-Outsourcing und Service-Management, Düsseldorf 2003, pp. 295–312.

BIBLE, L. et al. (2006): The Balanced Scorecard: Here and back, in: Management Accounting Quarterly, 2006, 7(4), pp. 18–23.

BLECKEN, A. et al. (2009): Humanitarian Supply Chain Process Reference Model, in: International Journal of Services, Technology and Management, 2009, 12(4), pp. 391–413.

BRAUN, C./WINTER, R. (2005): A Comprehensive Enterprise Architecture Metamodel and Its Implementation Using a Metamodeling Platform, in: *DESEL, J., FRANK, U.* (Eds.), Enterprise Modelling and Information Systems Architectures, Proceedings of the Workshop in Klagenfurt, GI-Edition Lecture Notes (LNI), Klagenfurt 2005, pp. 64–79.

BRAUNWARTH, K. P./HEINRICH, B. (2008): IT-Service-Management – Ein Modell zur Bestimmung der Folgen von Interoperabilitätsstandards auf die Einbindung externer IT-Dienstleister, in: Wirtschaftsinformatik, 2008, 50(2), pp. 98–110.

VOM BROCKE, J. (2007): Construction Concepts for Reference Models – Reusing Information Models by Aggregation, Specialisation, Instantiation, and Analogy, in: *LOOS, P./FETTKE, P.* (Eds.), Reference Modelling for Business Systems Analysis, Hershey 2007, pp. 47–75.

VOM BROCKE, J. et al. (2009): Reconstructing the Giant: On the Importance of Rigour in Documenting the Literature Search Process, in: *NEWELL, P.* et al. (Eds.), Information Systems in a Globalising World: Challenges, Ethics, and Practices, Proceedings of the 17th European Conference on Information Systems, Verona 2009, pp. 1–10.

BROWN, D. H./LOCKETT, N. J. (2001): Engaging SMEs in E-commerce: The Role of Intermediaries within eClusters, in: Electronic Markets, 2001, 11(1), pp. 52–58.

BREITER, G./BEHRENDT, M. (2008): Cloud Computing Concepts, in: Informatik Spektrum, 2008, pp. 624–628.

BROWN, D. (2008): It is good to be green: Environmentally friendly credentials are influencing business outsourcing decisions, in: Strategic Outsourcing: An International Journal, 2008, 1(1), pp. 87–95.

BUYYA, R. et al. (2008): Market-Oriented Cloud Computing: Vision, Hype, and Reality for Delivering IT Services as Computing Utilities, in: Proceedings of the 10th IEEE International Conference on High Performance Computing and Communications, Dalian 2008.

CEDERLUND, J. et al. (2007): Global Sourcing of IT Services: Necessary Evil or Blessing in Disguise?, in: Communications of the Association for Information Systems, 2007, 19, Article 14.

COBIT 4.1 (2004): Control Objectives for Information and Related Technology Version 4.1, online: http://www.isaca.org/Content/NavigationMenu/Members_and_Leaders/COBIT6/Obtain_COBIT/Obtain_COBIT.htm, last update: 15.07.2009, date visited: 15.07.2009.

CULLEN, P. et al. (2005): IT outsourcing configuration: Research into defining and designing outsourcing arrangements, in: The Journal of Strategic Information Systems, 2005, 14(4), pp. 357–387.

CURRIE W./SELTSIKAS P. (2001): Exploring the supply-side of IT outsourcing: evaluating the emerging role of application service providers, in: European Journal of Information Systems, 2001, 10(3), pp. 123–134.

DELIC, K. A./WALKER, M. A. (2008): Emergence of The Academic Computing Cloud, in: ACM Ubiquity, 2008, 9(31), Article 1.

DIBBERN, J. et al. (2004): Information Systems Outsourcing: A Survey and Analysis of the Literature, in: The DATA BASE for Advances in Information Systems, 2004, 34(4), pp. 6–102.

EL KHARBILI, M. (2008): Towards a Framework for Semantic Business Process Compliance Management, in: Proceedings of the GRCIS'08 Workshop at CAiSE'08 - Governance, Risk and Compliance: Applications in IS, 2008.

EYMANN, T. (2008): Cloud Computing, in: *KURBEL, K.* et al. (Eds.), Enzyklopädie der Wirtschaftsinformatik, online: http://www.enzyklopaedie-der-wirtschaftsinformatik.de, date visited: 15.07.2009.

FETTKE P./LOOS P. (2007): Perspectives on Reference Modeling, in: *FETTKE P./LOOS P.* (Eds.), Reference Modeling for Business Systems Analysis, 2007, pp. 1–20.

FLEMING, R./LOW, G. (2007): Information System Outsourcing Relationship Model, in: Australian Journal of Information Systems, 2007, 14, pp. 95–112.

FOSTER, I. (2005): Service-Oriented Science, in: Science, 2005, 308(5723), pp. 814–817.

GEFEN, D. et al. (2008): Business familiarity as risk mitigation in software development outsourcing contracts, in: MIS Quarterly, 2008, 32(3), pp. 531–542.

Goodman, P. E./Ramer, R. (2007): Global Sourcing of IT Services and Information Security: Prudence before Playing, in: Communications of the Association for Information Systems, 2007, 20, Artikel 50.

Günther, O. et al. (2001): Application Service Providers: Angebot, Nachfrage und langfristige Perspektiven, in: Wirtschaftsinformatik, 2001, 45(6), pp. 555–568.

Hall, J./Liedtka, St. (2007): The Sarbanes-Oxley Act: Implications for large-scale IT Outsourcing, in: Communications of the ACM, 2007, 50(3), pp. 95–100.

Hayes, B. (2008): Cloud Computing, in: Communications of the ACM, 2008, 51(7), pp. 9–11.

Iacovou, C. L./Nakatsu, R. (2008): A risk profile of offshore-outsourced development projects, in: Communications of the ACM, 2008, 51(6), pp. 89–94.

Iqbal, M./Nieves, M..(2007): Service Strategy, 2. Auflage, London 2007.

Jayatilaka B. et al. (2003): Determinants of ASP choice: an integrated perspective, in: European Journal of Information Systems, 2003, 12(3), pp. 210–224.

Kaplan, R./Norton, D. (1997): Balanced Scorecard, Stuttgart 1997.

Karagiannis, D. (2008): A Business Process-Based Modelling Extension for Regulatory Compliance, in: *Bichler, M.* et al. (Eds.), Multikonferenz Wirtschaftsinformatik 2008, Berlin 2008, pp. 1159–1173.

Kargl, H./Kütz, M. (2007): IV-Controlling, 5. Auflage, München 2007.

Kauffman, R./Sougstad, R. (2008): Risk Management of Contract Portfolios in IT Services: The Profit-at-Risk Approach, in: Journal of Management Information Systems, 2008, 25(1), pp. 17–48.

Klotz, M./Dorn, D.-W. (2008): IT-Compliance – Begriff, Umfang und relevante Regelwerke, in: HMD – Praxis der Wirtschaftsinformatik, 2008, 263, pp. 5–14.

Knolmayer, G. F. (2007): Compliance-Nachweise bei Outsourcing von IT-Aufgaben, in: Wirtschaftsinformatik, 2007, 49, pp. 98–106.

Kondo, D. et al. (2009): Cost-Benefit Analysis of Cloud Computing versus Desktop Grids, in: 18th International Heterogeneity in Computing, Workshop, 2009.

Krause, E. (2008): Methode für das Outsourcing in der Informationstechnologie von Retail-Banken, Berlin 2008.

Kütz, M. (2009): Kennzahlen in der IT – Werkzeuge für Controlling und Management, 3. Auflage, Heidelberg 2009.

Lacity, M. C./Willcocks, L. P. (1998): An empirical investigation of information technology sourcing practices: Lessons from experience, in: MIS Quarterly, 1998, 22(3), pp. 363–408.

Lee, J. et al. (2003): IT outsourcing evolution: past, present, and future, in: Communications of the ACM, 2003, 46(5), pp. 84–89.

Martens, B./Teuteberg, F. (2009a): Ein Referenz- und Reifegradmodell für integrierte Fundraising-Managementsysteme an Hochschulen, in: *Hansen, H. R.* et al. (Eds.), Tagungsband der 9. Internationalen Tagung Wirtschaftsinformatik: Business Services: Konzepte, Technologien, Band 2: Anwendungen, 2009, pp. 543–552.

MARTENS, B./TEUTEBERG, F. (2009b): Why Risk Management Matters in IT Outsourcing – A Systematic Literature Review and Elements of a Research Agenda, in: *NEWELL, P.* et al. (Eds.), Information Systems in a Globalising World: Challenges, Ethics, and Practices, Proceedings of the 17th European Conference on Information Systems, Verona 2009, pp. 1–10.

MATROS, R. et al. (2009): Make-or-Buy im Cloud-Computing – Ein entscheidungsorientiertes Modell für den Bezug von Amazon Web Services, online: http://opus.ub.uni-bayreuth.de/volltexte/2009/552/pdf/Paper_45.pdf, date visited: 15.07.2009

MEEKER, M. et al. (2008): Morgan Stanley – Technology Trends, online: http://www.morganstanley.com/institutional/techresearch/pdfs/TechTrends062008.pdf, last update: 12.06.2008, date visited: 18.07.2008.

MEI, L. et al. (2008): A Tale of Clouds: Paradigm Comparisons and Some Thoughts on Research Issues, in: Asia-Pacific Services Computing Conference, 2008, p. 464–469.

MIKA, P.*/TUMMARELLO, G.* (2008): Web Semantics in the Clouds, in: IEEE Intelligent Systems, 2008, 23(5), pp. 82–87.

MOSSANEN, K./AMBERG M. (2008): IT-Outsourcing & Compliance, in: HMD – Praxis der Wirtschaftsinformatik, 2008, 263, pp. 58–68.

MÜLLER, P./SUPATGIAT, C. (2007): A quantitative optimization model for dynamic risk-based compliance management, in: IBM Journal of Research and Development, 2007, 51(3/4), pp. 295–307.

MURTHY, P. (2004): The Impact of Global Outsourcing on IT Providers, in: Communications of the Association for Information Systems, 2004, 14, Artikel 25.

NGWENYAMA, O. K./SULLIVAN W. E. (2006): Secrets of a Successful Outsourcing Contract: A Risk Analysis, in: *LJUNGBERG J./ANDERSSON, M.* (Eds.), Proceedings of the 14th European Conference on Information Systems, Göteborg 2006, pp. 1–10.

OH, W. et al. (2006): The Market's Perception of the Transactional Risks of Information Technology Outsourcing Announcements, in: Journal of Management Information Systems, 2006, 22(4), pp. 271–303.

PEARSON P. (2009): Taking account of privacy when designing cloud computing services, in: Proceedings of the 2009 ICSE Workshop on Software Engineering: Challenges of Cloud Computing, 2009, pp. 44–52.

PÜSCHEL, T. et al. (2009): Revenue Optimization Through Automated Policy Decisions, in: *NEWELL, P.* et al. (Eds.), Information Systems in a Globalising World: Challenges, Ethics, and Practices, Proceedings of the 17th European Conference on Information Systems, Verona 2009, pp. 1–10.

ROHLOFF, M. (2008): A Reference Process Model for IT Service Management, in: Proceedings of 14th Americas Conference on Information Systems, Madison 2008.

SACKMANN, P. et al. (2009): Selecting Services in Business Process Execution – A Risk-based Approach, in: *HANSEN, H. R.* et al. (Eds.), Business Services: Konzepte, Technologien, Anwendungen, Tagung Wirtschaftsinformatik (WI'09), 2009, pp. 357–366.

SAEED, K./LEITCH, R. (2003): Controlling Sourcing Risk in Electronic Marketplaces, in: Electronic Markets, 2003, 13(2), pp. 163–173.

Sakthivel, P. (2007): Managing risk in offshore systems development, in: Communications of the ACM, 2007, 50(4), pp. 69–75.

Singh, C., et al. (2004): Rental software valuation in IT investment decisions, in: Decision Support Systems, 2004, 38(1), pp. 115–130.

Skillicorn, D. (2002): The Case for Data-Centric Grids, in: Proceedings of the 16th International Parallel and Distributed Processing Symposium, 2002, pp. 247–251.

Smith, M./Kumar, R. (2004): A theory of application service provider (ASP) use from a client perspective, in: Information & Management, 2004, 41(8), pp. 977–1002.

Sury, U. (2009): Cloud Computing und Recht, in: Informatik Spektrum, 2009, 32(2), pp. 83–84.

The Economist (2008): When clouds collide, in: Economist, 2008, Volume 386 (Issue 8566), pp. 69–70

Thomson Reuters (2009): Journal Citation Reports, online: www.isiknowledge.com/jcr, date visited: 14.07.2009.

Turner, J. R. (2008): Gower Handbook of Project Management, 4. Auflage, Cornwall 2008.

Vitharana, P./Dharwadkar, R. (2007); Information Systems Outsourcing: Linking Transaction Cost and Institutional Theories, in: Communications of the Association for Information Systems, 2007, (20), pp. 346–370.

Vykoukal, J. et al. (2009): Services Grids in Industry -On-Demand Provisioning and Allocation of Grid-based Business Services, in: Wirtschaftsinformatik, 2009, 51(2), pp. 206–214.

Wang, L. et al. (2008): Scientific Cloud Computing: Early Definition and Experience, in: Proceedings of 10th IEEE International Conference on High Performance Computing and Communications, pp. 825–830.

Webster, J./Watson, R. T. (2002). Analyzing the past to prepare for the Future: Writing a Literature Review, in: MIS Quarterly, 2002, 26(2), pp. xiii–xxiii.

Weinhardt, C. et al. (2009): Business Models in the 2. Service World, in: IEEE IT Professional, 2009, 11(2), pp. 28–33.

Weiss, A. (2007): Computing in the Clouds, in: netWorker, 2007, 11(4), pp. 16–25.

Xiong, L. et al. (2007): Preserving data privacy in outsourcing data aggregation services, in: ACM Transactions on Internet Technologies, 2007, 7(3), pp. 1–28.

Zhang, L.-J. (2008): Introduction to the Knowledge Areas of Services Computing, in: IEEE Transactions on Services Computing, 2008, 1(2), pp. 62–74.

Learning over the IT Life Cycle – Advantages of Integrated Service Creation and Service Management

Irvathraya B. Madhukar and *Florian A. Täube*

Infosys and *European Business School*

1 Introduction

In this chapter we draw parallels between IT application development and management and the construction industry and internationalizing firms therein: while the construction life-cycle with its phases design, build, operate resembles that of IT, the internationalization of firms with a physical product – buildings – can be related to the virtualization of a digital industry – the recent trend to cloud computing. We are interested in different forms of learning between stages of multi-stage projects. In particular, we try to understand how to conceptually distinguish learning from mere trouble shooting. We build on research in the construction industry and lessons from a case study with a firm that integrates design, build and operation phase and internationalizes its operation through offshoring part of its value chain.

Organizational researchers have a long-standing interest in organizational learning and outcomes its antecedents and moderating effects[1]. Building on this literature, scholars have examined different types of learning in the context of project-based organizations, to show how firms try to build capabilities and achieve organizational learning through projects.[2]

Yet, there is an important gap that can be identified in the extant theoretical literature. Projects are often seen as sub-units of firms that are independent from one another. However, the organizational form of long-term and complex projects, especially when spanning national boundaries, incurs a series of interdependent sub-projects that can be separated into several distinct phases with fluid or permeable boundaries[3]. This interaction between different phases or sub-projects is not adequately researched from a theoretical perspective yet.

There are several Project management frameworks in popular use amongst corporates for IT projects such as Prince2 (of OGC) and Project Management frameworks by organizations such as PMI, APM etc While these frameworks cover the project and program lifecycle right from planning to closure, aspects such as organizational diffusion of learning garnered from one project into another is not adequately covered. Specific Frameworks that are popular used for Application development and management such as CMMi do emphasize and cover knowledge management and sharing to a certain degree. However, as is explained in further sections, aspects of cross-project knowledge diffusion and organization learning to cover business processes and methods is inadequately addressed.

For instance, engineering and construction firms, are increasingly involved in complex international projects.[4] Complexity arises because the projects are large-scale and geographically dispersed, have long timescales in design, production and operation and numerous sub-projects across different phases (design, build and operate), and involve multiple stakeholders with potentially conflicting interests [5]. This paper builds on research in construction industry and the challenges organizations working in international projects are facing as they try to capture and transfer knowledge in order to build capabilities and improve firm performance.

---

1 Cf. *LEVITT/MARCH* (1988), and *MARCH* (1991).

2 Cf. *PRINCIPE/TELL* (2001),and *BRADY/DAVIES* (2004).

3 Cf. *ERICKSEN/DYER* (2004), p. 440.

4 Similarly, large projects are taking place in other industries such as the Hollywood film industry. However, while this paper is largely conceptual, we confine our illustrations of projects to the construction industry.

5 Cf. *BRADY* et al. (2005a).

Construction has traditionally been perceived as a locally bound industry, for the obvious reason that pre- and post-construction services used to take place onsite or in close proximity to the construction site, which is by definition immobile. Yet, over the last decade or so there have been a number of people, both academics and practitioner-oriented, to argue that the improvement of information and communication technologies (ICT) led to an increasingly connected world[6] (or 'flat', in the words of Friedman, 2005) in which distance does not play a role anymore, in other words, the 'death of distance'[7]. This seems to be very plausible, given the recent spate of offshoring activities, mainly to India and China[8], which we illustrate below. In a flat world, we would also witness a lot of activities, often project-based, executed by teams that are spread across the globe, with everyone contributing to the delivery of a product or service. For the construction industry this would imply the possibility of shifting those parts of the value chain that are related to services provision and digitizable to offsite locations[9]. For example, design or maintenance phases can involve remote services from engineering offices in a number of different countries, such as India, through new technologies such virtual reality[10].

In recent years, traditional application and software development and management methodologies have been rocked by several industry trends that have the potential to cause fundamental shifts in the way IT has traditionally been consumed by corporates and individual users. Of course, we have all witnessed the growth of technologies around the internet and the consequent revolutionary effects it has had around collaboration, knowledge and information sharing and accessibility of digital assets. What is less obvious is the impact, usage and absorption of these technologies within the corporate world. Organizations such as UBS, Pfizer etc are currently relooking at the way they have been doing Application Management till date and bringing in a radically new approach to this long-considered a "developers only" arena. Several organizations are actively considering infusing Service Management disciplines into the way they manage their applications. This is also driven by the goal to move IT to a genuine "utility" model.

While the desire to move IT consumption to a "utility" model has been there for a long time in the industry, as also seen in it being one of the key stated goals when ITIL (IT Infrastructure Library) was being drafted by OGC back in 1981. However, with the coming of age of several technologies such as Datamining, HPC, Clustering, Web2.0, SOA, Grid Computing, BPM, SAAS, Virtualization etc, the right time and context for the evolution of cloud computing has arrived. These developments, in no small way, have helped IT organizations get closer to their goal of converting their IT infrastructure into an "On Demand" Utility model. There are important implications for international projects that can be drawn from these studies. The paper is structured as follows: the next section assesses the theoretical literature that we integrate in this paper; it starts with a brief review of the learning literature with an emphasis on project-based learning. We then offer international management as useful supplements for the international project context. Building on these literature streams we develop a framework to analyze the moderating effects of different types of distance on internationali-

---

6 Or 'flat', in the words of *FRIEDMAN* (2005).

7 Cf. *CAIRNCROSS* (1997).

8 Cf. *DOZ ET AL.* (2006), *THE ECONOMIST* (2007).

9 Cf. *MALHOTRA* (2003).

10 Cf. *WHYTE* (2003).

zation of economic activity in general. This is used to draw lessons for learning in international projects and is illustrated with case study evidence on temporary embeddedness.

2 Theoretical Background

In this chapter we study the interrelation between software application development and application management. We see these as two phases of long-term projects, comparable to, e.g., construction projects, in particular of hospitals, airports etc. where a long phase of service and maintenance follows the actual product delivery, the building.

2.1 Project Business and Organizational Learning

We are interested not in project management, but in project business, or the business of project-based organizations, for instance innovation in project-based firms[11]. These could be an entire firm (e.g. software, consultancy, construction and film production), a division and unit within a firm, or a network of several firms connected through a special purpose vehicle set up to complete an assignment. More specifically, we investigate how these firms develop capabilities in order to improve performance. In knowledge-intensive industries such as software development, engineering or construction services, a useful theoretical lens is organizational learning.

Studies of learning in project-based firms have found different types of learning, e.g., project-led learning and business-led learning[12], the former being bottom-up and the latter top-down in nature. We extend this established notion of learning by studying particular types of projects. In the case of large-scale complex projects one of the distinct features is the long timescale with numerous sub-projects across different phases design, production and operation[13].[14] Such projects are typically found in integrated solutions developed for public-private partnerships (PPP) but not always and not necessarily only there[15]. Such projects can be depicted in a stylized way as follows (figure 1)[16]. The figure shows nine sub-projects organized in the three different phases of three main projects. We can now identify three main directions of learning, horizontal, vertical and diagonal. However, both horizontal and diagonal learning can also occur through feedback mechanisms into projects that have started earlier than the one from which lessons are drawn – this is troubleshooting rather than actual learning. Therefore, there are at least five different ways of learning, upward vertical learning, and two-way horizontal and diagonal learning, respectively; in the case of diagonal this two-way can ac-

---

11 Cf. *GANN/SALTER* (2000), *ACHA* et al. (2005).

12 Cf. *PRINCIPE/TELL* (2001), *BRADY/DAVIES* (2004).

13 Cf. *DAVIES* (2004), *DAVIES* et al. (2006).

14 Given a time horizon of up to 25 or 30 years, these sub-projects can arguably be considered as 'regular' projects in their own right

15 Cf. *BRADY* et al. (2005b), *TRANFIELD* et al. (2005).

16 Cf. In reality, of course, phases can overlap in various forms.

tually be further classified in backward and forward, hence resulting in two different directions itself, adding up to a total of seven learning ways.

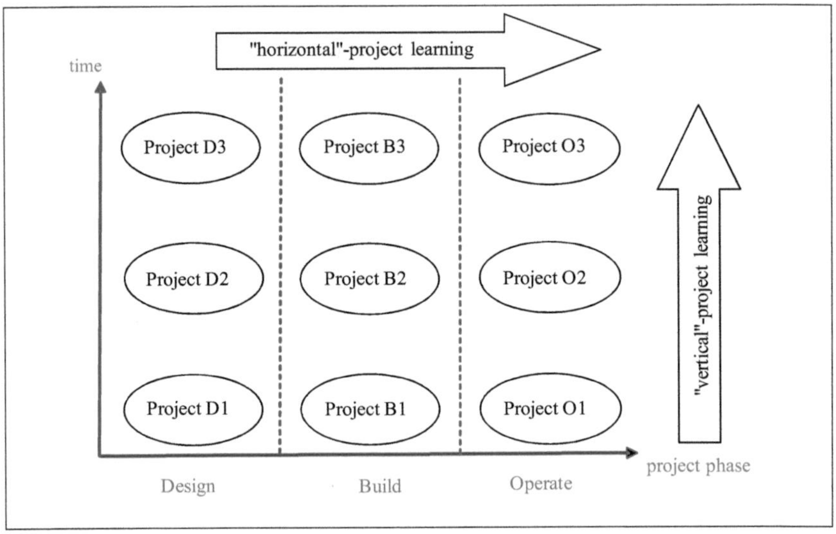

Figure 1: Learning in multi-phased, project-based organizations

The most important characteristics for organizational learning processes are whether the direction is backward or forward, and upward or downward. Thus, an interesting new feature of such projects that is understudied is a novel dimension of learning. We conceptualize the different learning types at the (sub-) project level, therefore they differ from similar notions that distinguish between individual, project and organizational learning for the vertical case[17]. In our case, vertical learning is probably most closely related to project-led learning[18] and diagonal learning somewhat similar to business-led learning. In other words, vertical learning is learning from one sub-project to another similar sub-project within the same project phase. Diagonal learning is related to more generic business knowledge, i.e. knowledge that can be re-used anywhere in the project-based firm. Reusability distinguishes tangible from intangible inputs, thus it is particularly relevant for knowledge components; it applies to all forward looking learning processes.

These learning models readily lend themselves when we talk of learning in the context of application development and management. There is a constant learning and knowledge management that happens around the technologies that are being implemented. These are akin to the vertical learning stages in the model above. As the application moves into subsequent phases and processes, increasing learning needs emerge. Below is the diagram of a typical lifecycle (and consequent processes) that an application (and its project teams) would need to pass through in an organization that has an ITIL V3 –based service management framework.

[17] Cf. PRINCIPE/TELL (2001), p. 1380.

[18] Cf. BRADY/DAVIES (2004).

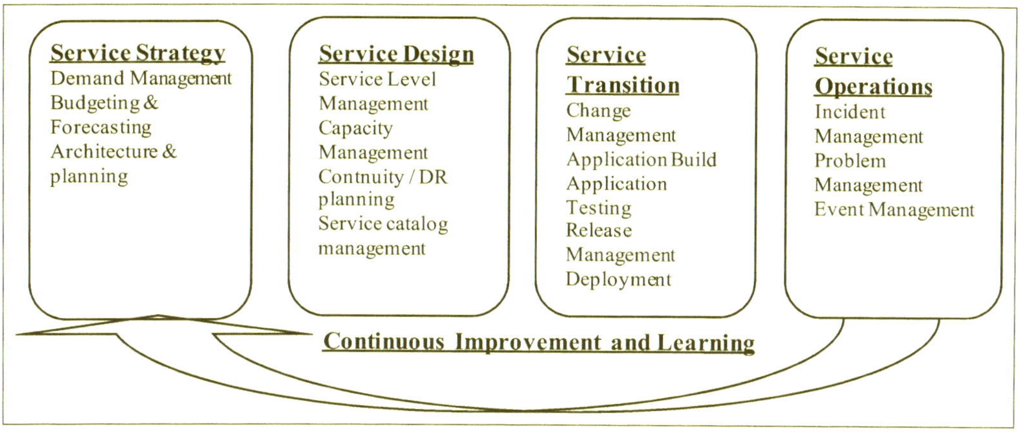

Figure 2: Learning across Application Management Lifecycle

Horizontal learning is learning between *different* project or service lifecycle phases; as mentioned above, this can happen both ways, either as the passing on of knowledge to downstream project (lifecycle) phases or through feedback loops from downstream to earlier phases. Feedback loops are backward looking in process terms, and hence, the most complex form of learning, because knowledge transfer has to occur against the usual direction or flow of a production process of a good or a service. It is most complex, because it not 'only' about codification and storage of knowledge about the output of a task in order to transfer it to the following stage; but it requires people to think more actively *how* earlier tasks could be improved in order to make the overall project more efficient through more effective interfaces between project or lifecycle phases.

Given the number of learning directions this is already a complex situation if the entire process took place in one location. However, once some of the project phases, or sub-projects are relocated to be produced from a remote location, things get more complicated; even more so, when such relocation happens internationally across long distances.

2.2 International Management

There have been a number of studies investigating organizational learning in project business settings. Yet, despite the growing importance of international – or even global - projects, the international dimension of project learning has not been studied yet[19], to the best of our knowledge. In particular, with reference to the construction and engineering industries, which have traditionally been conceptualized as 'local' industries almost by definition, hence the limited interest in taking an international perspective. The parallel to software application is that they traditionally have been customized rather locally – even in terms of implementation and maintained literally physically local.

19 For a recent exception see *SAPSED* et al. (2005).

This paper aims at closing this gap by introducing concepts from the international management literature. Since we are mainly interested in organizational learning and capability building in knowledge-based project businesses, our emphasis is on sourcing and transfer of knowledge and experience between sub-units of multinational companies, primarily as headquarter-subsidiary relationships[20].

Most studies in the field of international sourcing focus either on outsourcing and offshoring of manufacturing, or on simple standardized services[21]. In other words, sourcing seems to be predominantly associated with cost cutting and, therefore, with generic factor inputs, such as labor, or intermediate products[22] but rarely with innovation or R&D.[23]

More recently, some scholars have acknowledged that companies can gain more from offshoring than just cutting costs, i.e. access to knowledge not available elsewhere[24]. However, at this stage, there is little theory to provide an informed rationale how such knowledge-seeking can be explained in terms of firm strategy. Thus far, the distinction of MNCs' decisions to go abroad is usually between market entry and sourcing cheap labor, at least for emerging economies such as India[25]. One of the interesting challenges is to understand the evolution of Indian organizations that are moving up the value chain. This includes the ability of subsidiaries to evolve from competence-exploiting to competence-creating organizations within an international firm[26].

In the context of international projects, this evolution implies an increase in staffing teams with members located in remote locations such as India. An extension of the headquarter-subsidiary-literature is the emphasis on *collaboration*. Whereas most of the literature conceptualizes subsidiaries as either being exploiters of competences created in the 'West' or sole creators of new competences, there is a lot of anecdotal evidence that *exploration* is done in project teams that are dispersed geographically. We are interested in exactly this form of international division of labor and its implications for innovation in projects and dispersed team work. Potentially, the most important factor relates to the international dispersion of project team members and the increased difficulties for knowledge transfer and learning, due to the geographical and cultural distance between project team members. Such construct of distance or proximity have been studied by economic geographers and innovation scholars[27], hence it is worthwhile looking at it in more depth.

---

20 Cf. *GHOSHAL/BARTLETT* (1990), and *GHOSHAL* et al. (1994).

21 E. g. *MURRAY/KOTABE* (1999).

22 Cf. *GOTTFREDSON* et al. (2005).

23 R&D generates the new products, processes and services that give a company a competitive edge in the market. In other words, "research and development is the creation of the know-how and know-why of new materials and technologies that eventually translates into commercial development" [*WHEELWRIGHT/CLARK* (1992) p. 74].

24 E. g. *DOSSANI/KENNEY* (2003), and *MASKELL* et al. (2005).

25 Cf. *CANTWELL/MUDAMBI* (2005).

26 Cf. *BIRKINSHAW/HOOD* (2000), *CUMMINGS/TENG* (2003), and *WILLCOCKS/LACITY* (2006).

27 E. g. *LUNDVALL* (1988).

2.3 Economic Geography

Insights from economic geography serve as a moderating effect on the international dimension that we have just introduced to the project business. Simply said, economic geography is concerned with the locations of economic activity and distance or proximity between them.

Traditionally, distance, or proximity, was measured in geographical terms[28], but in recent years economic geographers have developed a whole range of proximity types, part of which has entered the management field under the distance label; for instance, literature on mergers and acquisitions that deals with cultural or institutional distance.

While there are many different notations for various dimensions of proximity, we argue that a synthesis would encompass four main kinds of space and proximity: geographical, cultural, organizational, and professional[29]. 'Proximity' is used in the sense of being close in terms of the respective dimensions. For instance, if a process requires organizational proximity – being organizationally close – you can actually not outsource it, because outsourcing by definition means 'sourcing externally'. Moreover, the notions of a 'flat' world or the death of distance hinge crucially upon the activities under study. In particular in the realm of knowledge-based industries a key question is *'what kind of knowledge do we talk about?'*[30]. Haas (2006), for instance, distinguishes between technical knowledge and country knowledge. Distinguishing between codified and tacit knowledge, improvements in ICT can contribute to the possibility of communicating codified knowledge over the distance. But it is questionable to what extent tacit knowledge can be exchanged between agents that are *not* in spatial proximity. Here it is important to analyze interdependences and interaction effects between different forms of proximity.

In this paper, we emphasize the moderating effects of professional and organizational, and to a limited extent cultural proximity, on geographic proximity. Both professional and organizational proximity are related to improvements in communication infrastructure. *Organizational proximity* exists between actors working in the same company regardless of their geographical location and thus gains a new relevance with the implementation of ICT[31]. It refers to firm-specific information and the way one deals with it: corporate identity, corporate philosophy, organizational rules and codes play a significant role[32]. In a similar manner, proximity between actors in the same type of job can bridge geographical and cultural distance to a certain extent. Actors in close '*professional proximity*' possess an understanding of each others' methods, practices and aims, share similar interests, and professional language. Both organizational and professional proximity facilitate the building up of trust and furnish a common background for the actors and hence a context for interaction, thereby simplifying knowledge exchange across geographical space by compensating for a lack of geographical proximity. They are based on shared conventions, thereby providing a common "framework of action [...] with other actors engaged in that activity"[33]. In contrast, the value provided by geographical and cultural proximity acts predominantly to keep activities within a certain

28 E. g. *ALLEN* (1977).

29 Cf. *GROTE/TÄUBE* (2007).

30 Cf. *CUMMINGS/TENG* (2003).

31 E. g. *YEUNG* (2005).

32 Cf. *BLANC/SIERRA* (1999).

33 Cf. *STORPER* (1997), p. 45.

territory. However, parallel to organizational proximity, cultural proximity can also create a common background and thus help in extending communication from a local, regional or national to a transnational dimension, in the form of ethnic networks as exemplified in the case of the Indian software industry and its connections with Silicon Valley[34].

In order to illustrate the different concepts of proximity, imagine five young British knowledge workers, e.g. application managers, sitting together in the same London office of their bank. Their exchange of information and knowledge is based on all four proximities: They are spatially very close together, share the same cultural background, work for the same firm, possessing organizational proximity, and do the same jobs and are therefore also professionally close to each other. Now, think of one them being moved to the Edinburgh office of the same bank. She is losing the spatial proximity, though she maintains cultural, organizational and professional proximity to her colleagues. The second decides to become a freelance IT Architect. He stays in London, visits the old colleagues frequently and delivers architecture consulting assignments on the very same technologies that he has designed before – his work has been outsourced but not offshored. He now shares only part-time spatial proximity, as well as cultural and professional proximity with his former desk mates but has lost organizational proximity. The third manager is fired. Part of her work is offshored (but not outsourced) and now done by a newly hired Indian colleague in the Bangalore office of the same bank. She will not have cultural proximity (e.g., to understand and interpret messages from Chief Financial Officers of Indian and UK companies respectively, different cultural backgrounds have to be taken into account) but shares organizational and professional proximity with the managers in the London office. Lastly, also the fourth analyst is fired. Her work is now done by a consultant in an Indian consultancy company in Mumbai, which is specializing in providing application management services. The work has been outsourced and offshored; the Indian analyst only has professional proximity to the analysts in London. These hypothetical reorganizations appear in order of their feasibility, with the last one, offshore outsourcing, being quite challenging.

2.4 Enforced Geographical Dispersion and the role of technology

As explained in earlier sections, the unfolding economics of outsourcing in the modern-day business context is challenging several established business processes. This is creating the need for newer theoretical organizational learning models and newer technology architecture frameworks to support the same. In this section, we take a look at the geographic dispersion of business processes, underlying infrastructure, associated intellectual property and people in the context of cloud computing.

Let us take a closer look at a real-life example (the company name not being disclosed here). This is a market-leading retail firm catering to the entertainment industry. As part of its efforts to adopt market-leading technologies to create a winning proposition in the marketplace, it is at the forefront in adoption of cloud computing technologies. One of the initiatives taken up, to improve their competitive positioning, is to migrate their collaboration and mail platform on a clould computing platform provided by Microsoft. A closer look at the underlying geographical dispersion of the supply chain involved with delivery of the IT services is interesting and offers revealing insights. As a result of the company decision to adopt a clould

34 Cf. *SAXENIAN* et al. (2002) and *TÄUBE* (2005).

computing platform, now the company does not own any servers or software or IP associated with the mail and collaboration platform. This will now be owned by the provider, in this case – Microsoft. This is being hosted thousands of miles away in the provider's datacenter. Further, the implementation and maintenance of this platform on behalf of the company is being done by a company based in India with software engineers sitting in India. This example of dispersion of the various aspects of the delivery chain across geographies is a key defining characteristic and a natural offshoot of the steady evolution of cloud computing.

This enforced dispersion in geographic terms leads to challenges around maintaining knowledge and learning throughout the supply chain. It is important to note that, as in the context above, in several situations, the learning and knowledge management needs to not only stretch across geographical boundaries but also across organizational and cultural boundaries.

Several technologies have been in use and being adopted in corporations worldwide to meet these learning needs. In-house adoption of Wiki technologies (of which the wikipedia on the internet is a famous example) is being used extensively amongst corporations worldwide. However, aspects of security, integrity and fidelity of knowledge stored on these wikis needs to be addressed effectvely before we see adoption of wiki technology in the corporate world on a scale similar to wikipedia. There are several other commercial technologies available in the technology marketplace such as Microsoft's Sharepoint, Lotus Notes groupware solution and Autonomy's Knowledge Management solution. While these technologies are adept at solving specific knowledge retention and retrieval requirements, large scale deployment of these technologies to harness the learning needs for international corporations is yet to happen. Most of the learning, as is also observed in the empirical evidence presented in subsequent sections, takes place through formal and informal modes of in-person or verbal interactions.

While discussing Geographical dispersion and its impact on learning, it is also important to acknowledge the highly audio-visual capabilities of modern-day conferencing systems and technologies. This is important from the perspective of their ability to help in substituting the need for geographical proximity, as discussed in the earlier section. However, when there is a wide geographical dispersion, as in the case of IT applications within the US being developed from India, there is the practical problem of time zone differences. What is day in one country is night in another. This has a big impact and limitation on the time that could be made available for complex learning modes such as all-day knowledge exchange workshops etc.

3 Empirical evidence

We will illustrate this with examples from ongoing research projects on international sourcing in knowledge-intensive industries. In previous research, we have been studying the financial services industry, in particular investment banks' research departments, and analyzed if and how they could use the potential of outsourcing and offshoring in their global value chains[35]. In addition, ongoing research uses case studies of UK construction and engineering firms to illustrate these points. In both industries, the firms we study have offices all over the globe, including wholly-owned subsidiaries in India that are integrated in their respective value

---

[35] Cf. *GROTE/TÄUBE* (2007).

chains. In fact, one of the key firms, for which we have completed the case study research, covers the entire construction value chain in both the UK and India. The core construction business is, of course, a local business, because buildings, infrastructure etc. is immobile. We used interviews in the UK headquarters and offices in India in order to understand how work is globally distributed between their offices – and why it is distributed, given that there are additional problems that arise from the international dispersion.

3.1 Methods and Data

We have conducted a case study with interviews in India at three subsidiaries of a UK construction firm – the name of which cannot be revealed and is henceforth called ConstructCo – and several other industry informants. ConstructCo India covers the entire construction value chain from just after architect drawings to post-construction (remote) facility management. We consider them as departments *within* one firm, although formally they are independent.

We interviewed the country head and CEO or MD, respectively, of all three companies. Most other interviewees were senior managers, but some project team members were included as well. Topics covered in the questionnaire are the interviewee's and team members' backgrounds; his (all interviewees were male) responsibilities within the firm; the organisation and staffing of projects; team objectives and tasks; the use of (information and communication) technology and learning within and across projects. For the present chapter, we have analysed field notes looking for broad patterns that can be observed.

3.2 Results

Preliminary findings from these field notes include the rare occurrence of teams that actually work in geographically distributed teams. We rather observed that staff from the Indian subsidiaries was assigned temporarily to work onsite with the client in the UK or the Middle East in order to understand thinking and work practices of the latter. After such an initial period of temporary co-location, future communication across distance and the usage of technology was highly improved. In other words, the strategy used to overcome geographical distance was to temporarily embed people in order to get a better understanding of each other. This is important when it comes to task partitioning which can be implicit, and in particular when this happens at an early phase of the value chain.

4 Discussion and Conclusion

4.1 Implications for software development and management

Analogous to offshoring, dispersion of projects across geographical space and into virtual clouds is more likely for those parts in the value chain of complex tasks that do not require cultural proximity and face-to-face contacts and where professional and organizational proximity ensures sufficient common background for clear communication via ICT across distance. In other words, more knowledge-intensive activities seem to require a higher degree of co-location in order to minimize geographical and cultural distance. Both of them are centripetal forces with regard to the locus of learning in international projects. However, they can be overcome by organizational measures that foster professional and organizational proximity. Figure 1 summarizes the conceptual framework with regard to project-based learning brought forward in the theoretical discussion.

The spatial dimension is not explicitly captured in the previous diagram. As we outlined above, any project team is affected by a number of forces facilitating and inhibiting dispersed collaboration. Arguably, the inhibiting factors are exacerbated once the collaboration extends to communication between two projects – and even more so once this collaboration and communication crosses different phases of an overall multi-phased, long-term project. Therefore, actual learning between application development and management, that goes beyond trouble shooting, can benefit from taking into account numerous forms of proximity. While learning is definitely possible, this chapter is a cautious reminder that it is far from an easy task. Further, as discussed in the technologies section, the ability of technologies available today to effectively substitute the need for proximity is limited.

The main lessons that can be drawn for international projects concern the organization of knowledge processes and learning therein. In particular, efficacy and efficiency of international project teams can be enhanced by understanding how proximities interact with each other. For instance, to build more effective teams across geographical space it can be useful to enhance professional, organizational, and cultural proximity between team members. This can be done through face-to-face meetings, such as induction or training events, early on through which later communication is facilitated. For instance, employees from the Indian subsidiaries of the construction firm were often sent to their clients' site in the UK in order to understand thinking and work practices of the latter. After such an initial period of temporary co-location, future communication across distance and the usage of technology was highly improved.

As for the somewhat ambivalent cultural proximity, it is not necessarily required to hire members from the same cultural background in terms of same nationality or ethnicity, although that certainly helps. Similar to increasing professional and organizational proximities between team members, putting them together in one location for a certain period facilitates a convergence of cultures or acculturation. When people learn to interact with different cultures, which has to happen in one physical location, they know how to better interact over distances later on. In fact, this was witnessed in the case of the Indian construction support workers who were sent to the UK.

4.2 Contribution and Limitations

Although we mentioned large-scale complex projects to take place in other industries such as the film industry, we largely concentrated our analysis on the construction sector. Moreover, we did not integrate our learning at the sub-project level with the way in which this is fed back into organizational learning, at the firm, or firm network level. However, to the best of our knowledge this is the first step towards integrating project learning and international business literature, and this opens up a number of interesting directions for future research. Not only the shortcomings mentioned above, but also empirical applications of this framework would help better understand how international projects could be made more effective in order to deliver better results.

We conclude with the outlook that a cloudy world seems rather unlikely, but a further cloudening does not seem unrealistic[36]. On the one hand, processes and tasks that are more complex and/or require intensive interaction through a customer interface are viewed as unlikely to be executed across geographical or virtual space[37]. On the other hand, we suggest that ever more processes will be executed in collaboration with remote locations and a simultaneous standardization allows for the integration of a larger share in the global division of labor to be executed in teams within, and across, organizations spread across the globe. Over time, learning on the part of remote locations could enable these to participate to a higher degree in innovative activities as well.

References

ACHA, V./GANN, D./SALTER, A. (2005): Episodic innovation – R&D strategies for project-based environments, in: Industry and Innovation, 2005, Volume 12(2), pp. 255–281.

ALLEN, T. J. (1977): Managing the Flow of Technology: Technology Transfer and the Dissemination of Technological Information within the R&D Organization, Cambridge MA.

BIRKINSHAW J./HOOD N. (2000): Characteristics of foreign subsidiaries in industry clusters, in: Journal of International Business Studies, 2000, Volume 31(1), pp. 141–154.

BLANC, H./SIERRA, C. (1999): The internationalisation of R&D by multinationals – a trade-off between external and internal proximity, in: Cambridge Journal of Economics, 1999, Volume 23, pp. 187–206.

BRADY, T./DAVIES, A. (2004): Building project capabilities – From exploratory to exploitative learning, in: Organization Studies, 2004, Volume 25(9), pp. 1601–1621.

BRADY, T./DAVIES, A./GANN, D. (2005a): Can integrated solutions business models work in construction?, in: Building Research and Information, 2005, Volume 33(6), pp. 571–579.

BRADY, T./DAVIES, A./GANN, D. (2005b): Creating value by delivering integrated solutions, in: International Journal of Project Management, 2005, Volume 23(5), pp. 360–365.

BRESNAHAN, T., & GAMBARDELLA, A. (Eds.) (2004): Building High-Tech Clusters – Silicon Valley and Beyond, Cambridge UK 2004.

CAIRNCROSS, F. (1997): The Death of Distance – How the Communications Revolution Will Change Our Lives, Harvard Business School Press 1997.

CANTWELL, J./MUDAMBI, R. (2004): On the geography of knowledge sourcing – a typology of MNE subsidiaries, Paper presented at the DRUID Summer Conference, Helsingør, 14–16 June 2004.

[36] Cf. *SVEJENOVA/VIVES* (2006).

[37] Cf. *DEUTSCHE BANK* (2006).

COWAN, R./DAVID, P./FORAY, D. (2000): The explicit economics of knowledge codification and tacititness, in: Industrial and Corporate Change, 2000, Volume 9(2), pp. 211–253.

CUMMINGS, J./TENG, B.-S. (2003): Transferring R&D knowledge – the key success factors affecting knowledge transfer success, in: Journal of Engineering and Technology Management, 2003, Volume 20, pp. 39-68.

DAVIES, A. (2004): Moving base into high-value integrated solutions – a value stream approach, in: Industrial and Corporate Change, 2004, Volume 13(5), pp. 727–756.

DAVIES, A./BRADY, T./HOBDAY, M. (2006): Charting a path toward integrated solutions, in: MIT Sloan Management Review, 2006, Volume 47(3), pp. 39–48.

DEUTSCHE BANK (2006): Indien spielt Vorreiterrolle, in: forum – Magazin für die Deutsche Bank, 2006, pp. 20–22.

DOSSANI, R./KENNEY, M. (2003): Went for Cost, Stayed for Quality? Moving the Back Office to India, Berkeley and Stanford: mimeo, 2003.

DOZ, Y./WILSON, K./VELDHOEN, S. et al. (2006): Innovation – Is global the way forward?, online: www.strategy-business.com/media/file/global_innovation.pdf, date visited: 28 September 2009.

EISENHARDT, K. M. (1989): Building Theories from Case Study Research, in: Academy of Management Review, 1989, Volume 14(4), pp. 532–550.

ERICKSEN, J./DYER, L. (2004): Right from the Start – Exploring the Effects of Early Team Events on Subsequent Project Team Development and Performance, in: Administrative Science Quarterly, 2004, Volume 49, pp. 438–471.

FRIEDMAN, T. L. (2005): The World is Flat – A Brief History of the Globalized World in the Twenty-first Century, London 2005.

GANN, D./SALTER, A. (2000): Innovation in project-based, service-enhanced firms – the construction of complex products and systems, in: Research Policy, 2000, Volume 29, pp. 955–972.

GERTLER, M. S. (2003): Tacit knowledge and the economic geography of context, or the undefinable tacitness of being (there), in: Journal of Economic Geography, 2003, Volume 3, pp. 75–99.

GHOSHAL, S./BARTLETT, C. A. (1990): The multinational corporation as an interorganizational network, in: Academy of Management Review, 1990, Volume 15, pp. 603–625.

GHOSHAL, S./KORINE, H./SZULANSKI, G. (1994): Interunit communication in multinational corporations, in: Management Science, 1994, Volume 40(1), pp. 96–110.

GOTTFREDSON, M./PURYEAR, R./PHILLIPS, S. (2005): Strategic sourcing – From periphery to the core, in: Harvard Business Review, February 2005, pp. 132–139.

GROTE, M./TÄUBE, F. (2007): When Outsourcing is not an Option – International Relocation of Investment Bank Research – or isn't it?, in: Journal of International Management, 2007, Volume 13, pp. 57–77.

HAAS, M. R. (2006): Acquiring and applying knowledge in transnational teams – The roles of cosmopolitans and locals, in: Organization Science, 2006, Volume 17(3), pp. 367–384.

LEVITT, B./MARCH, J. G. (1988): Organizational learning, in: Annual Review of Sociology, 1988, Volume 14, pp. 319–340.

LUNDVALL, B. A. (1988): Innovation as an interactive process – from user–producer interaction to the national system of innovation, in: *DOSI, G./FREEMAN, C./NELSON, R.R.* et al. (Eds.), Technical Change and Economic Theory, London 1988, pp. 349–369.

MALHOTRA, N. (2003): The Nature of Knowledge and the Entry Mode Decision, in: Organization Studies, 2003, Volume 24, pp. 935–959.

MARCH, J. G. (1991): Exploration and exploitation in organizational learning, in: Organization Science, 1991, Volume 2/1, pp. 71–87.

MASKELL, P./PEDERSEN, T./PETERSEN, B. et al. (2005): Learning Paths to Offshore Outsourcing – From Cost Reduction to Knowledge Seeking, in: DRUID Working Paper, 2005, No. 05-17.

MORGAN, K. (2004): The exaggerated death of geography – learning, proximity and territorial innovation systems, in: Journal of Economic Geography, 2004, Volume 4, pp. 3–21.

MURRAY, J./KOTABE, M. (1999): Sourcing strategies of U.S. service companies – A modified transaction-cost analysis, in: Strategic Management Journal, 1999, Volume 20, pp. 791–809.

PORTER, M. E. (1990): The Competitive Advantage of Nations, New York 1990.

PRENCIPE, A./TELL, F. (2001): Inter-project learning – Processes and outcomes of knowledge codification in project-based firms, in: Research Policy, 2001, Volume 30, pp. 1373–1394.

SAPSED, J./GANN, D./MARSHALL, N. et al. (2005): From Here to Eternity? – The Practice of Knowledge Transfer in Dispersed and Co-located Project Organizations, in: European Planning Studies, 2005, Volume 13(6), pp. 831–851.

SAXENIAN, A. (1994): Regional advantage – culture and competition in Silicon Valley and Route 128, Cambridge 1994.

SAXENIAN, A./MOTOYAMA, Y./QUAN, X. (2002): Local and Global Networks of Immigrant Professionals in Silicon Valley, Public Policy Institute of California, San Francisco 2002.

STORPER, M. (1997): The Regional World – Territorial Development in a Global Economy, New York 1997.

SVEJENOVA, S./VIVES, L. (2006): Quo Vadis, Europe?, in: Academy of Management Perspectives, 2006, Volume 20(2), pp. 82–84.

TÄUBE, F. (2005): Transnational Networks and the Evolution of the Indian Software Industry – The Role of Culture and Ethnicity, in: *FORNAHL, D./ZELLNER C./AUDRETSCH, D.* (Eds.), The Role of Labour Mobility and Informal Networks for Knowledge Transfer, New York 2005, pp. 97–121.

THE ECONOMIST (2007): High-tech hopefuls – A special report on technology in India and China, November 10th 2007.

TRANFIELD, D./ROWE, A./SMART, P. et al. (2005): Coordinating for service delivery in public private partnership and private finance initiative construction projects – early findings from an exploratory study, in: Proceedings of the Institution of Mechanical Engineers Part B-Journal of Engineering Manufacture, 2005, Volume 219 (1), pp. 165–175.

WHEELWHRIGHT, S. C./CLARK, K. B. (1992): Creating Project Plans to Focus Product Development, in: Harvard Business Review, March-April 1992, pp. 70–82.

WHYTE, J. (2003): Innovation and users – virtual reality in the construction sector, in: Construction Management and Economics, 2003, Volume 21, pp. 565–572.

WILLCOCKS, L./LACITY, M. (2006): Global Sourcing of Business and IT Services, Palgrave, United Kingdom 2006.

YEUNG, H. W. (2005): Organizational space – a new frontier in international business strategy?, in: Critical Perspective on International Business, 2005, Volume 1(4), pp. 219–40.

YIN, R. (1994): Case study research – Design and methods, Thousand Oaks, CA 1994.

Competitive Intelligence

Katja Wolter

Steinbeis-Hochschule Berlin

"It is pardonable to be defeated,
but never to be surprised."
FREDERICK THE GREAT

1 Introduction

The leading drivers of strategic chance in our current environment are globalization and technological innovation. According to *BRADLEY*, *HAUSMAN* and *NOLAN*[1], leading change in technology will be a fusion of information technologies and telecommunications, resulting in creating new industries, restructuring existing ones and changing the way companies compete.

Economies of scale, the foundation on which big companies have based their dominance in the Industrial Era, are no longer such an advantage. Changes in information technology, in the financial system, in just-in-time production techniques, and in the rise of companies offering distribution and support systems which previously only the largest companies could afford - remove the advantages of being big.[2]

The diseconomies of scale – overhead, inflexibility – are becoming increasingly powerful. Winning firms are organizations that most successfully master the business issues critical to their performance, and develop the most precise understanding of definitions and creation of value. Competitive advantage has a lot to do with leveraging the knowledge assets of the firm, while at the same time determining how competitors are likely to leverage theirs. A comprehensive and thorough understanding of competitors is thus an essential ingredient to developing and executing winning strategies. Organizations, therefore, need integrated analysis frameworks to identify and assess the current and potential strategies of current and future competitors.[3]

The general need for Competitive Intelligence (CI) in business is not controversial. But there is a vast range of attitudes about the importance of systematic intelligence efforts and an even wider range of practices for actually gathering, analyzing, and using intelligence information. On one hand, most firms do not have formal technical intelligence programs, they expect intelligence information to emerge as a routine part of all or some staff members' job.[4] On the other hand, a small, but growing number of firms have implemented introduction some form of deliberate technical intelligence effort in their organization.[5]

1 *BRADLEY/HAUSMAN/NOLAN* (1993).

2 Cf. *KAHANER* (1996), p. 15.

3 Cf. *FAHEY* (1999), p. vii.

4 Cf. *LANGE* (1994), p. 2.

5 Cf. *ASHTON/KLAVANS* (1997), p. 3.

In analogy to these considerations, a company also requires information on current and future markets, competitors, customers, technologies etc., so that it can position itself in an optimal way, make the "right" decisions and ultimately realize them at the most ideal point in time[6]. "A strategic plan can be no better than the information on which it is based."[7]

Competitive Intelligence can be described as a systematic process of information retrieval and -analysis, in which fragmented (raw) information on markets, competitors and technologies can be transformed into a vivid understanding of the corporate environment for the decision-maker. CI topics are usually future-oriented statements on competitive positioning, -intentions and -strategies. Intelligence is the final result of the process: the required knowledge on markets and competition. Especially statements on the expected effects on one's own firm and thereupon based recommendations are made.[8]

With using the concept of Cloud Computing, companies can avoid capital expenditure on hardware, software, and services when they pay a provider only for what they use. Consumption is billed on a utility (e. g. resources consumed, like electricity) or subscription basis (e. g. time based, like a newspaper) with little or no upfront cost. Cost is claimed to be greatly reduced and capital expenditure is converted to operational expenditure. This ostensibly lowers barriers to entry, as infrastructure is typically provided by a third-party and does not need to be purchased for one-time or infrequent intensive computing tasks. That means new competitors can easier access the market und there is a stronger need for analyzing the market and the competitors.

This article emphasizes analysis and assessment, the transformation of data – generated by attention to competitors – into outputs that are relevant for decision making. It therefore highlights the roles of Competitive Intelligence in adding value for decision-makers at all levels in the organization. Existing literature on CI is reviewed to brief the theoretical background and to find ideas to structure analysis.

2 Competitive Intelligence

The *Society of Competitive Intelligence Professionals* (*SCIP*) defines Competitive Intelligence as follows. "CI is a systematic and ethical programme for gathering, analyzing, and managing any combination of Data, Information, and Knowledge concerning the Business environment in which a company operates that, when acted upon, will confer a significant Competitive advantage or enable sound decisions to be made. Its primary role is Strategic early warning."[9]

---

6 *ZAHN/RÜTTLER* (1989), p. 35.

7 *MONTGOMERY/WEINBERG* (1979), p. 41.

8 Cf. *LANGE* (1994), *MICHAELI* (2005) and *FREIBICHLER* (2006).

9 *SCIP.ORG* (2009).

The current and upcoming competitors are those firms which the company considers rivals in business, and with whom it competes for market share. CI also has to do with detecting what the business rivals will do before they do it. Strategically, to gain foreknowledge of the competitors' strategies and to plan the own business strategy to countervail their plans. This involves many methods at the tactical collection level, but it also requires integration into the existing information infrastructure, analysis and distribution of the information, and finally, the support of business decisions on the grounds of that information and on the analysis thereof.[10]

Competitive Intelligence, also known as a sub-area of Business Intelligence, operates within the framework of Knowledge Management. It is sometimes also named as Business or Strategic Intelligence. Other synonyms like Strategic Planning, Competitor Intelligence or Competitor Analysis as well as Corporate Intelligence can be found in the literature. The objective of CI is not to steal a competitor's trade secrets or other proprietary property, but rather to gather in a systematic, overt (i. e. legal) manner a wide range of information that, when collacted and analyzed, provides a fuller understanding of a competitor firm's structure, culture, behavior, capabilities and weaknesses.[11] Regardless of where it resides, the ultimate goal of CI is to generate a greater awareness of the business environment in general, and competitor actions in particular, to support business planning. It is necessary to point out, that CI is not industrial espionage. [12] "CI is conducted legally and ethically whereas industrial espionage typically is not. Ethics and ethical behavior are concerns here and since the area is usually perceived as positive to a company's reputation and competitiveness, it would not be useful for a firm to undertake its intelligence activities without regard to ethical or legal considerations. It has become somewhat axiomatic in the field to say that 90 percent of the information needed for key decisions is available publicly.[13].

CI is not done, when data collection is finished. It has a broader scope. This section will show the environment within other concepts and their impact. The iterative process of these concepts is illustrated in Figure 1. Competitive Intelligence is not the same as market research. Market research is widely defined as primary, with results from surveys, questionnaires or focus groups. The focus of market research tends to be on the problems associated with the profitable marketing of a firm's products and services. Nevertheless market research builds a foundation to involve the primary data in the process of CI.

As already explained above the scope of CI is far broader. It draws on a wide variety of sources, with different expectations from the result. It targets anything in the Business universe that affects the ability to compete. Competitive Intelligence is a value-added concept on top of business development and strategic planning.[14]

---

10 Cf. *Johnson* (2000c).

11 Cf. *Sammon* (1985), p. 62.

12 Cf. *Lange* (1994), p. 72.

13 Cf. *Vella/McGonagle* (1988), p. 1, and *Gilad* (1994), p. 58.

14 Cf *Sharp* (2000), p. 37 et seq.; *Freibichler* (2006), p. 70;

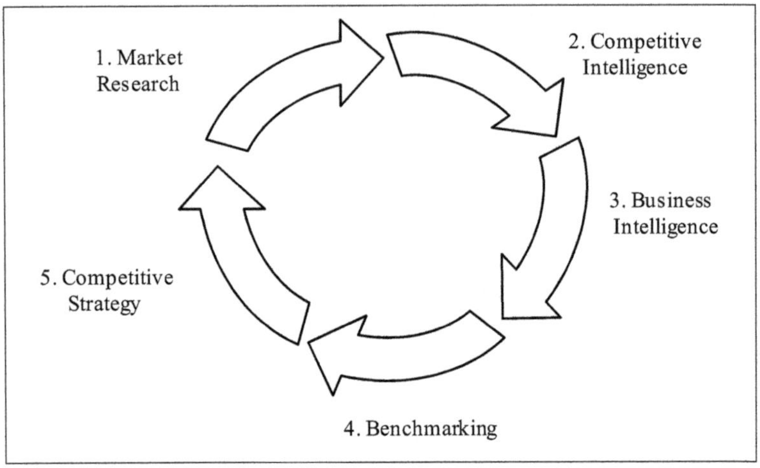

Figure 1: CI – an iterative process[15]

CI leads to Business Intelligence (BI). Particularly it is both a part and a basis for BI. Business Intelligence in this meaning is a broadening of CI. It supports BI and emphasizes all units of a company including strategic relevance.[16] The *GARTNERGROUP* defines BI as an interactive process for exploring and analyzing structured, domain-specific information (often stored in data warehouses) to discern trends or patterns, thereby deriving insights and drawing conclusions. "The BI process includes communicating findings and effecting change. Domains include customers, products, services and competitors"[17]. Besides, CI gives essential support in benchmarking activities. It is possible to investigate various subjects to compare the own firm with the best practice activities or processes of another company to find a field to generate competitive advantage.[18]

"The goal of competitive strategy for a business unit in an industry is to find a position in the industry where the company can best defend itself against the competitive forces (see Figure 3) or can influence them in its favour."[19] Structural analysis, as it is done within Competitive Intelligence, is the fundamental underpinning for formulating competitive strategy and a key building block for most of the concepts examined further in this work.

---

15 *GIESKES* (2000), p. 10.

16 Cf. *GIESKES* (2000), p. 10.

17 *FLUSS/HARRIS* (1999).

18 Cf. *KEUPER* (2001), p. 24 et seqq.

19 *PORTER* (1998), p. 4.

2.1 Purpose and Benefits of Intelligence in Business

The ultimate goal of any CI undertaking is to produce 'actionable' intelligence. Good research must invariably lead to good analysis - a better understanding of how external forces can benefit the firm in the future. The necessity of CI analysts to contribute to business decision-making is characterized most significantly in two ways. First, the need to make recommendations to one's constituents; and, second, to explain the implications of the alter-natives for decision makers.[20]

Data is the individual raw material like numbers, character strings, text, images, voice, video and any other form in which a fact may be presented. It is numbers or facts that are out of context, have no meaning and are difficult to understand. Data in context is facts that have meaning and can be readily understood, but it is not yet information because it has no relevance or time frame. Data is the first step in a process.

Information is data in context that becomes information when people are ready to accept that message as relevant for their needs. It is grouping data with meaning, relevance and purpose.

Intelligence is information that has been analyzed and suggests actions, strategies, or decisions.[21] Intelligence reveals critical information or insight and implications beyond the data. Data is a subset of information and information is a subset of intelligence. Without an appropriate basis for comparison, it is easy to make erroneous assumptions. Without suffi-cient information, it is easy to make mistakes about underlying causes or dynamics of the current industry. Converting information into actionable intelligence will end up winning the game.

The goal is to evolve from data to intelligence, to transform simple facts into valuable perspective that uncovers new patterns or emerging trends, or that sparks new ideas, new solutions and new possibilities. The purpose of CI is action.[22]

The product of the intelligence cycle is evaluated information. In practice, the intelligence product is unlikely to be created from perfect input. It is not possible to predict the future until events have already taken place and it is too late. The firm finds itself in a position where it can only react to the competitor's move, it has lost the advantage it might have had if the right intelligence had been available earlier. Although it cannot be known for certain that the exact details, plans and strategies can be discovered.[23]

Competitive intelligence's real value is to provide managers with the organizational tool to learn what the competitor will do, not what the competitor has already done. The bottom line benefits of CI are improved market knowledge, improved cross-functional relationships in the organization, greater confidence in making strategic plans, and improvements in product quality versus the competition. In short, better business performance by doing things better.[24]

---

[20] Cf. *Johnson* (2000b).

[21] Cf. *Keuper* (2001), p. 45.

[22] Cf. *Sharp* (2000), p. 37.

[23] Cf. *Johnson* (2000c).

[24] Cf. *Sammon/Kurland/Spitalnic* (1984), p. 16, and *Kahaner* (1996), p. 23 et seqq.

The value received from CI and the range of benefits realized can be broadly categorized along three dimensions (see Figure 2).

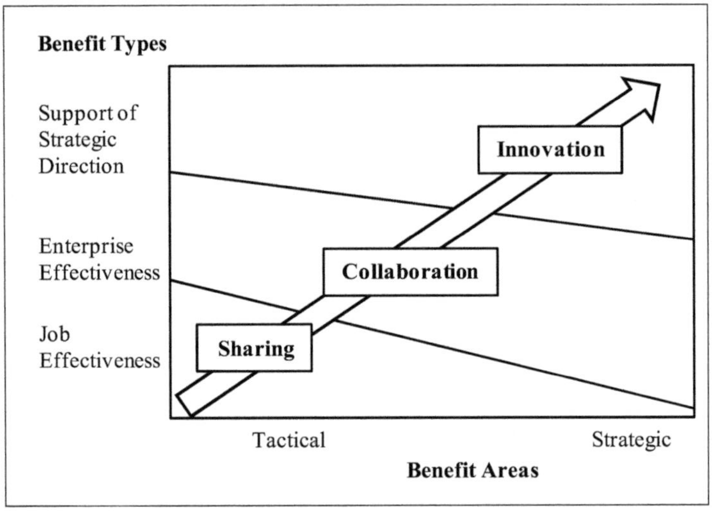

Figure 2: *CI Value and Benefits Framework*[25]

1. Benefit areas (plotted along the horizontal axis), which can be classified as tactical benefits, such as operational effectiveness or extending CI to customers and strategic benefits, such as cross-enterprise collaboration or formalized innovation.

2. Benefit types (plotted along the vertical axis), which are categorized by their area of impact. Job effectiveness describes the impact of CI on individual workers and their work. Enterprise effectiveness is the impact across business functions and operations. Finally, support of strategic direction is the impact on current and future strategic products, processes, services and business models.

3. Enterprise dynamics (represented by the diagonal arrow that runs from lower left to upper right of the framework chart) describe the degree of synergy created with CI programs and range from sharing to collaboration to innovation; further, each successively higher dynamic encompasses and builds on those preceding it. These dynamics are the source of increasing business value as the enterprise moves toward driving innovation with CI. As with all CI benefits, sharing, collaboration and innovation do not stand alone as business goals; they are most often a part of other business objectives, except perhaps in the case where the business objective is an initiative for greater innovation, e. g., product or service innovation. Sharing is the lowest-level dynamic and is defined as employees simply contributing their knowledge to be shared with others and relying on or applying the knowledge of others in their individual work. Collaboration is the second-level dynamic; in addition to sharing knowledge, colla-boration encompasses employees sharing activities, processes and accountability for work tasks and deliverables. Innovation is the final dynamic and is highest in both complexity and value. When an enterprise reaches this level of dynamism, employees and teams begin to use experience, insight,

25 *HARRIS* (2000).

information and collaborative activities as a source of ideas and tech-niques to innovate processes, products, services and business models.[26]

2.2 Competitive Technology Intelligence

R&D and strategic technology planning is an area where CI should be of particular interest to the technology transfer professional from industry, academia or government laboratories. Building in large measure upon technology forecasting methodologies that have existed for some time, competitive technology intelligence can provide the needed background into technology trends and competitor capabilities and needs. New developments in scientometrics (including patent analysis, literature citation analysis etc.), which rely on modern database technology, provide additional insight into the technological landscape. Such information is vital to strategic technology planning as well as the licensing and other commercialization activities undertaken by industry, universities and non-profit research institutions. Societal trends and regulatory activities impact all companies daily, whether they work in the profit or the non-profit sector of the economy. Anticipating societal needs, which are ultimately reflected in legislation and regulatory requirements, may help to minimize any adverse impact on the business. It may even identify future opportunities.

The degree of usage of Information technology is already a very important part of the business. That field is interesting during analysis since another competitor may have earned a reputation for leveraging its investment in superior information technology to gain a competitive advantage - it could be in the form of winning and retaining clients, improving the efficiency of internal processes, or delivering a more sophisticated service. It is important to benchmark the investments for each technology project and to make sure not to fall behind in this critical area.

3 Competitor Analysis System

The goal of a competitor analysis is to develop a profile of the nature of strategy changes each competitor might make, each competitor's possible response to the range of likely strategic moves other firms could make, and each competitor's likely reaction to industry changes and environmental shifts that might take place. Competitive Intelligence should have a single-minded objective - to develop the strategies and tactics necessary to transfer market share profitably and consistently from specific competitors to the company.[27]

---

[26] Cf. *Harris* (2000).

[27] Cf. *Johnson* (2000c).

Some common goals of a competitor analysis system are:[28]

- Detecting competitive threats
- Eliminating or lessening surprises
- Enhancing competitive advantage by lessening reaction time
- Finding new business opportunities

3.1 The Components of a Competitor Analysis

The intensity of competition is rooted in its underlying economic structure and goes beyond the behavior of current competitors. The state of competition depends on five basic competitive forces, that are shown in Figure 3. The Five Forces Model is the strategy model or framework created by *PORTER*.[29] A universally applicable model, describing how five industry forces affect an industry. The strengths of the competitive forces are determined by the key structural features of industries.

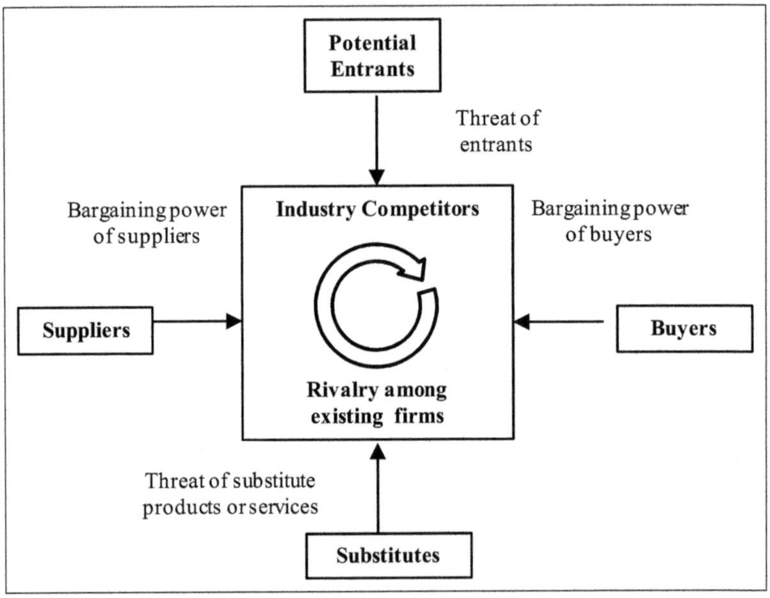

Figure 3: Five Forces[30]

---

[28] Cf. *RÖMER* (1988), p. 481, *AAKER* (1989), p. 69 et seqq., and *RIESER* (1989), p. 293.

[29] *PORTER* (1998), p. 4.

[30] *PORTER* (1998), p. 4.

The baseline for competitive analysis gives the next concept of *PORTER* in Figure 4. There are four diagnostic components: future goals, current strategy, assumptions, and capabilities. Answering the posed key questions will allow an informed prediction of the competitor's response profile. The driving factors on the left side, they often determine how a competitor will behave in future, are much harder to observe than the actual competitor behavior on the right side.

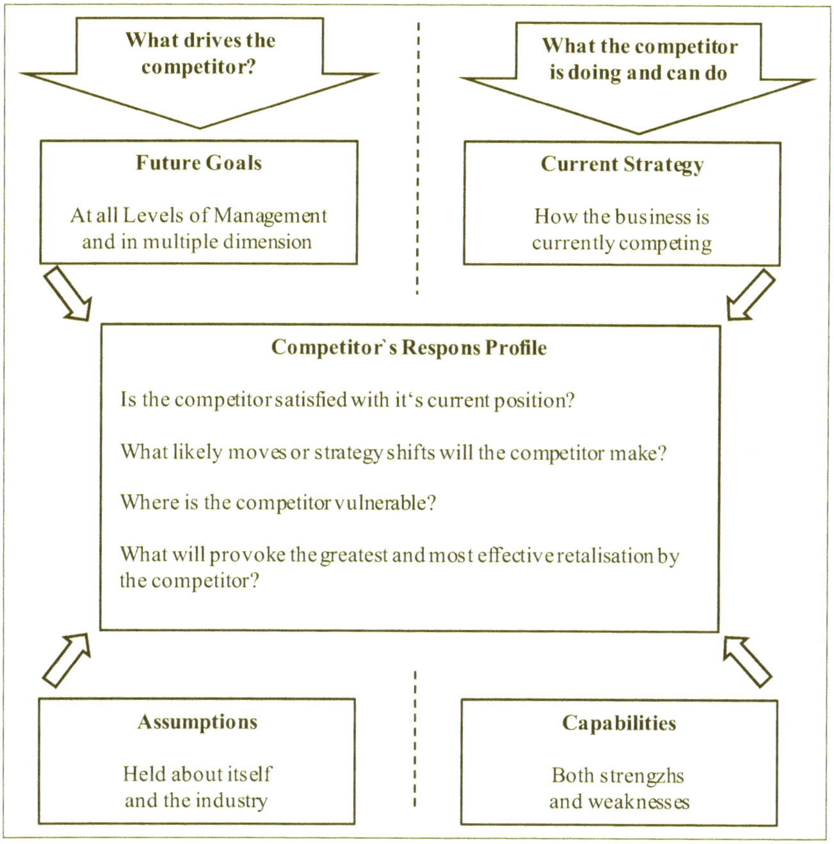

Figure 4: The Components of a Competitor Analysis[31]

The Competitor intelligence analysis describes the intelligence cycle as "the analytical process that transforms disaggregated competitor data into relevant, accurate and usable strategic knowledge about a competitors' position, performance, capabilities, and intentions."[32] The majority of authors in the CI-literature defining the Intelligence cycle with four steps (see Figure 5).[33]

31 *PORTER* (1998), p. 49.

32 Cf. *SAMMON/KURLAND/SPITALNIC* (1984), p. 91.

33 Cf. *FREIBICHLER* (2006), p. 70.

1. Planning and direction (establishing CI needs)
2. Data Collection (collection and research) and evaluation (processing and storage)
3. Analysis and Interpretation (analysis and production)
4. Dissemination and Intelligence Reporting (presentation and delivery)

The four-step description of how intelligence develops in a cyclical manner is shown in the next Figure.

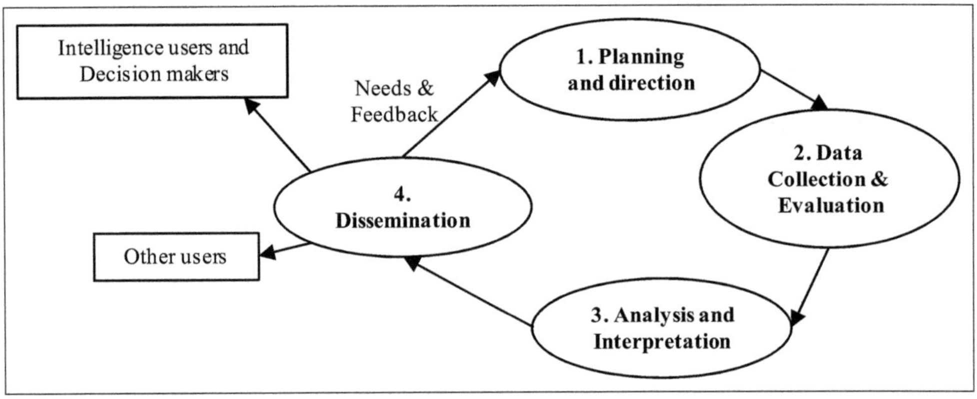

Figure 5: *The Intelligence Cycle*[34]

3.2 Planning and Direction

Planning and direction deals with the establishing of CI needs. As with virtually any business activity or project, a bit of preplanning is critical. The best is to start with the key question "What is needed to know?". This seemingly simple question can be terribly difficult to answer succinctly. Often, it will help to recast this question in terms of "What decision must be made?" or "What specific question should be answered after the fact?"[35].

Next, one really must look at who will make decisions using this intelligence? Is it for the benefit of senior management doing strategic planning or is it to support the tactical decisions of operating managers? The next critical issue to address is the time frame available for analysis. Fourth, one must identify the analysis framework or data reduction techniques that are suitable for providing the necessary intelligence. This really defines what is going to be done and how the question will answered. Fifth, identify specific targets for analysis if applicable. It might be wanted to know the plans of every firm in an industry but really only need to know about those of one or two specific competitors. Finally, using the results of the previous elements, determine precisely what specific information will needed for the decision at hand.

---

34 E. g. *DELTL* (2004), p. 55 et seqq., and *FREIBICHLER* (2006), p. 73.

35 Cf. *MARCEAU/SAWKA* (1999), p. 33.

The Focus is one key factor that drives successful development and use of Competitive Intelligence. The other factor is time.[36]

3.3 Developing a Competitor Analysis System

The expression Intelligence System is a catch-all phrase describing an on-going approach of developing and using intelligence throughout a company. While the word "system" appears to imply computer applications, in this case the phrase intelligence system should be considered as an intelligence process or a means to process intelligence. Any single corporate intelligence system may or may not have a computer-based network at its core.

To develop an intelligence system there is a strong need for a structured approach. The following Figure 6 illustrates this procedure of developing a Competitor system in ten steps.

Steps of developing a Competitor Analysis System		Steps of the CI cycle
Steps 1	Identifying Competitors	**Planning and Direction**
Steps 2	Definition of Core Issues	
Steps 3	Responsibility Matrix	
Steps 4	Identifying users	
Steps 5	Fixing sources and ways of obtaining data	**Data Collection & Evaluation**
Steps 6	Processing data and Evaluation	
Steps 7	Standardising Analysis	**Analysis**
Steps 8	Setting-up a reporting system	**Dissemination**
Steps 9	Security of performance of actions	
Steps 10	Checking feedback and internal communication	

Figure 6: Steps of developing a Competitor Analysis System[37]

[36] Cf. *BULLINGER* (1990), p. 12, and *KRYSTEK/MÜLLER-STEVENS* (1990), p. 336.

[37] Cf. *KAIRIES* (1997), p. 20.

In the originally version of *KAIRIES*[38] the "Responsibility matrix" was set behind the "Fixing of Sources and ways of obtaining data". In this paper it changed to step three, as it is seen as part of Planning and Direction. Furthermore the step "Identifying users" was originally step eight, behind the "setting-up the reporting system". It moved up to the Planning and Direction as well.

First of all, there is step 1 – "Identifying Competitors". The questions who the competitors and potential competitors are will be answered. Figure 7 shows an useful division of competitors. That will help to focus the following analysis, and support the delivery of intelligence. The best results will be obtained, if the focus lies on a limited number of competitors.

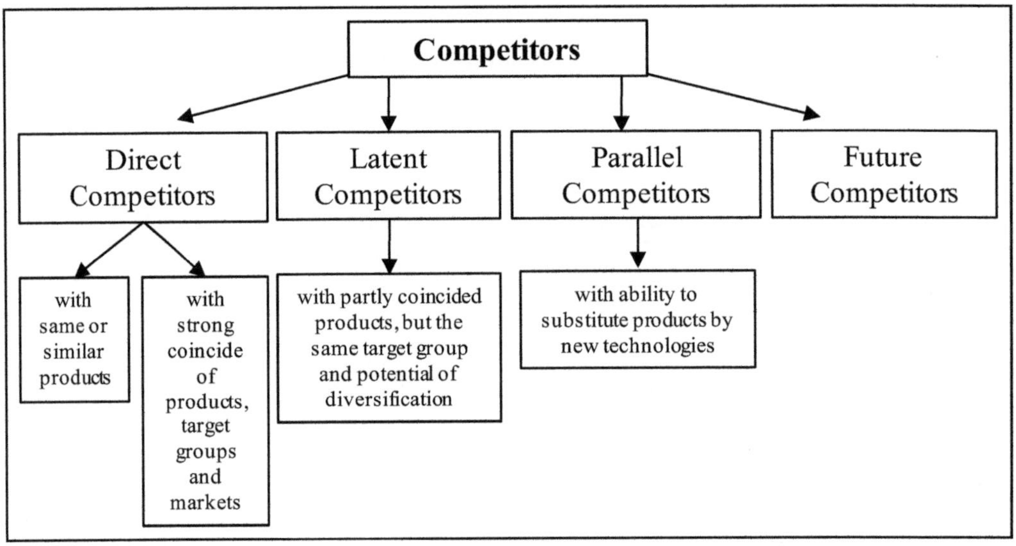

Figure 7: Categorization of Competitors

Step 2, the "Definition of Core Issues" or critical factors describe the key questions around which successful competitive analyses focuses on. Core issues often represent less than 10% of all the questions asked about a particular company or industry activity. They are a useful concept to apply when time and resources are limited.

For Step 3 – "Responsibility Matrix" – it is important to define the responsibility of each part of the system. Furthermore there must be a project leader and someone who takes the whole responsibility.

Step 4 is related to "Identifying users". It has been moved up to the Planning and Direction stage, because the users have to be identified in a very early stage of the process in order to concentrate on their demands of the users in every following step. Defining the intended audience will further narrow the search in the specific CI-topic. Users needs are largely determined by their responsibilities within the organization. Figure 8 lists some different clients within an organization and the types of information each might find most value.

---

38 Cf. *KAIRIES* (1997), p. 20.

User	Typical Information Needs
Scientists/engineers and technical managers	➢ Detailed technical data ➢ Technical objectives and approaches ➢ Technical results or progress ➢ Contracts/researchers
Marketing personnel	➢ Competitive product features ➢ Product sales ➢ Cost / price data
Senior executives	➢ Technical news ➢ New science and technology directions ➢ Contracts/researchers
Policy makers/ regulators	➢ Science / technology policy ➢ National science and technology goals and funding ➢ New science and technology directions

Figure 8: Information needs of different users[39]

3.3.1 Data Collection and Evaluation

The Data Collection is the second step of the Intelligence cycle. The first things to consider here are the types of sources. The data collected must be commensurate with the analysis to be performed. It must be decided upon the most promising sources and the employed data collection strategies. "Fixing of sources and ways of obtaining data" is Step 5 in Figure 6. How and where data and information can be obtained, is the key question for this step. The tools and techniques used in CI, as well as a detailed description of sources will be explained in the following. This section will also examine, which tools and techniques can be used to get the appropriate data in order to give input to the goals of CI. Different types of CI tools and techniques are available for different requirements of the CI process.

The action of watching and collecting information on a company's rivals and on the overall market is called environmental scanning.[40] This process involves regular, ongoing monitoring of direct competitors and their initiatives, so as to avoid surprises, as well as latent competitors (those who might backwards- or forwards-integrate to enter the market directly) and parallel competitors (those with replacement or substitute products or services) (see also Figure 7). Environmental scanning also involves monitoring other central issues important to the firm that might either present new opportunities or threaten the firm's position in the marketplace. This includes topics such as federal or state legislation and regulation, technological advances made outside the industry or investments made by the various industry organizations associated with the sector.[41]

39 *Ashton/Klavans*, (1997), p. 287.

40 E. g. *Aguilar* (1967), *Porter* (1998) and *Herring* (2001).

41 Cf. *Johnson* (2000a).

To generate intelligence and obtain important information, there is a multitude of ways in getting information. Conduits that are created during business transactions allow information to flow relatively free from the company involved in the transaction to the outside world. These conduits are called Information Bridges. No matter how small, how large or how secretive an organization, anytime a company enters into a business transaction it gives out information about itself.

The paths through which data and information flow are Information Channels. For example, when a brokerage firm opens a new office, it must contact a realtor, lease computer equipment and hire talent. Each transaction transmits information. Together they form a stream, a path, a channel. The most used publishing sources in CI are listed in Figure: 9.

Competitors themselves	
➢ Annual reports ➢ Credit reports/Company Brief	➢ Help wanted advertisement ➢ Brochures / advertisements
Other external sources	
➢ Daily newspapers ➢ Data bases (internal/external/online) ➢ Industry periodicals ➢ Import / export statistics ➢ Industry and government officials ➢ Industry experts and security analysts ➢ Corporate or Association directories ➢ University research centers ➢ Market and brokerage reports ➢ Trade associations ➢ Suppliers / vendor networking	➢ Vendor's promotional material / advertising ➢ Customers networking ➢ Buyers' guides ➢ Individuals at trade shows / conferences ➢ Journalists ➢ Sales trip reports ➢ Surveys ➢ Interviews ➢ Internal experts/professional colleagues

Figure 9: Sources[42]

The organized collection of Competitive intelligence is, similarly, divided into two types: primary intelligence (obtained from human sources of the competitor firms, from their customers, vendors, bankers, lawyers, et cetera) and secondary intelligence (culled from newspapers and online databases stocked by reports from those collecting primary intelligence).[43] Most critical, timely intelligence is derived from primary sources, with secondary sources frequently supplying the leads or expert names.[44]

A substitute source that offers similar information is called Information Proxy. For example, if a credit report does not have the number of employees at a site, then standing outside the property counting cars in the lot may offer the best. Tallying the percentage of patents in a certain technology would give the viewer a reasonable sense of the percentage of a company's R&D budget that it spends in this technology.

42 Cf. *LANGE* (1994), p. 268 et seqq.

43 Cf. *BERNHARDT* (1993), p. 171, *SULLIVAN* (1995), p. 25, and *HARKLEROAD* (1996).

44 Cf. *JOHNSON* (2000b).

Furthermore the literature makes distinction between the next four expressions. Local Sources, that refer to information sources physically located near the company or entity you are studying. Examples include a local newspaper, chamber of commerce, town hall, Competitor Analysis System nearby suppliers, customers and so on. Open Sources is a military intelligence term referring to information in the public domain, such as news articles. Traditional Sources, also known as standard sources, are for example, newspaper articles or results of database access or literature search.

Online Sources refer to all electronically available information resources, typically from the Internet or traditional online providers along with web-based information services – so called Alerting Services. Such push services provide the ability to receive automatically delivered electronic news on a specific competitor or topic, on a regular basis, or as the event occurs. Alternative terms include current awareness searches, selective dissemination of information searches (SDIs) and intelligent agents. They are widely available on commercial online and Internet database services. There are even free alerting services available from search service portals such as Google.[45]

As a Competitive Intelligence resource, the Internet serves both a source of information and a cost-effective means of sharing and disseminating information to decision makers. Internet technology utilized in intranets is also a major force reshaping the business environment – giving rise to new kinds of revenue opportunities, creating incentives for collaboration with existing competitors and providing niches for new kinds of competitors.[46]

Data obtained from the Internet used as raw material as quickly as possible are described below:

Company web sites describe products and services and contain information that can be used to evaluate corporate structure and market positioning strategies. They include job postings, also known as classified ads or help-wanted advertisements, which are potential indicators about the direction or plans of a company. They directly describe a company's employment needs to the public at large. While most companies do not advertise for more than one-third of their job needs through such ads, the ads themselves can reveal details on new product development, sales force deployment, product or service repositioning. In recent years, many newspapers have placed their help wanted advertisements directly onto the Internet at no charge to the user. [47]

Electronic discussion groups or newsgroups may uncover controversies, conflicts or rumors about competitors and these are starting points for further investigations that must be explored and validated.

---

45 Cf. *Kunze/Havemann* (1998), p. 24 et seqq.

46 Cf. *Rajaniemi* (2005), p. 158 et seq.

47 Cf. *Rajaniemi* (2005), p. 170 et seq.

Public and private company financial, corporate management and marketing information are necessary parts of every puzzle for learning about competitors. A Company Brief is a critical first-step information source in analyzing a company and indicates the markets a company competes in. It often reports details on privately-held companies or on subsidiary operations, including: cash flow, background on key managers, square footage, other affiliations, equipment loans or leases.[48]

- Patents which can be a strong indication of what new technologies, products, or markets a company is looking to enter in the near future.[49]
- Newly registered trademarks that reflect branding activities or product development and may also indicate a company's intentions of getting into a new market or industry.
- Newly registered Internet domains, which can point to the Internet tactics and provide a guide to general plans a company has for their online business strategy.
- Press releases with breaking news about industry reaction to a company's activities. A key use of the Internet is to track, monitor, and provide current alerting about competitors. Market research reports and industry and market statistics are useful for understanding the marketplace in which the company operates. News stories contain a wealth of information about a competitor's services, products and markets.
- A Message Board Summary shows the number of new messages on each board daily, the average number of messages, and the percentage of change. Large increases in message board activity can often indicate major financial or business changes.
- Analysts' reports with opinions, e. g., from the leading Wall Street firms about changes in the consensus recommendation and earnings estimates. These reports often provide insight into the financial well-being of a company and the path the company is headed in the near future.
- Speeches from company presidents and directors, which some people believe, provide good clues about insiders' outlook for the near future.
- Litigation including civil, class action, and anti-trust lawsuits which often indicate the activities or the business practices of a company and how the government or market is reacting to them. This information is often a gauge of difficulties or problems a company may currently face that could affect their business or financial state in the future.

Not all Competitive Intelligence tools and techniques are suitable for all CI objectives. The CI-unit has to use judgment in determining the relevant CI needs and the most appropriate tools and techniques. Specific tools and techniques are chosen depending upon various factors such as time constraints, financial constraints, staffing limitations, likelihood of obtaining the data, relative priorities of data, sequencing of raw data, etc.[50] While government sources have the advantage of low cost, online databases are preferable for faster turnaround time. Whereas surveys may provide enormous data about products and competitors, interviews would be preferred for getting a more indepth perspective from a limited sample. Therefore, human

---

48 Cf. *RAJANIEMI* (2005), p. 170 et seq.

49 Cf. *LANGE* (1994), p. 49.

50 Cf. *MCGONAGLE/VELLA* (1990), p. viii.

judgment is an essential element of the decision regarding which CI techniques to deploy in a specific situation.

Data are produced or released for a certain purpose, so that they have to be evaluated and analyzed for accuracy and reliability.[51] The reliability of data implies the reliability of the ultimate source of the data, based upon its past performance. The accuracy of data implies the [relative] degree of 'correctness' of data based upon factors such as whether it is confirmed by data from a reliable source as well as the reliability of the original source of data.[52]

Every attempt has to be made to eliminate false confirmations and to check for omissions and anomalies. Omission, which is the seeming lack of cause for a business decision, raises a question to be answered by a plausible response. Anomalies (data that do not fit) ask for a reassessment of the working assumptions. While the conclusions that are drawn from the data must be based on that data, one should never be reluctant to test, modify, or even reject one's basic working hypotheses. Very likely, the target competitor would be aware of the organization's CI moves and could make all possible efforts to thwart or jeopardize the organization's CI process. The competitor may have its own CI activities targeted at the organization. Or it might intentionally generate incomplete or inaccurate information designed to mislead the organization's efforts.[53] In fact, an organization's CI activities may find data which the competitor has 'planted' to keep the organization 'preoccupied' and 'off-balance'. There might be instances of false confirmation in which one source of data appears to confirm the data obtained from another source. In reality, there is no confirmation because one source may have obtained its data from the second source, or both sources may have received their data from a third common source. A company controls the information it places on the web. To round out CI research, it's necessary to use other sources that add depth and perspective. Although the Internet is a starting place, it is extremely important to continue using trusted vendors who provide much more in the way of analytical, historical information and peer reviewed professional and trade articles.[54]

There is no question that the Internet has become a significant tool and may be the only source to supply needed parts of a puzzle. Besides, it is also important to proceed with caution when gathering information from Internet. Any information must be questioned and confirmed for quality and reliability.

If processes are not in place to ensure knowledge content quality, there is high probability of a serious breach of user trust. This will result in low levels of content use or reuse and, ultimately, a risk of CI program failures. Enterprises should define their requirements for quality, commit to provide the infrastructure and processes to support those requirements and include reference points in all content that allow the user to determine relevance and quality.

---

51 Cf. *Meffert/Burmann/Kirchgeorg* (2008), p. 146.

52 Cf. *Lange* (1994), p. 71.

53 Cf. *Brockhoff* (1989), p. 50.

54 Cf. *Lange* (1994), p. 70 et seqq.

Considerable attention must be devoted to avoiding the errors in processes of collecting and evaluate data about competitors. To avoid these errors is a central topic of this section. The above mentioned target is to establish a supporting tool, that assembles the data into building blocks and generating information. It presents a framework, an analytical structure through which information is filtered and sorted. Ultimately an analytical framework's purpose is to develop intelligence. The tool will be an analytical device that allows for screening out unimportant or distracting information. This process of locating valuable information is part of the analysis process.

The objective is to gather relevant information that is valid and accurate. Incomplete or inaccurate information may jeopardize the organization's CI efforts. The failure to test and reject what others regard as an established truth can be a major source of error. The Data Evaluation (see Step 6 of Figure 6) is where the collected remaining instead of the unreliable or irrelevant data are organized, verified, collated, and otherwise transformed into meaningful input for the analysis yet to come.

First, it is important to gauge the reliability of both the data collected and the source of that data. Striving for corroboration wherever possible and trying to identify gaps in the data and eliminate misinformation. Then, assessing both the accuracy of the data and its relevancy to the project at hand. Various rating schemes have been proposed for these tasks, but generally the simpler the better.

Next, assembling the data into information building blocks. This step typically involves collating and organizing the data so that it provides useful input for the analyses yet to come. After this step the information will be assembled and abstracted again, categorized, and stored for easy retrieval. As seen the Data evaluation is the foundation to complete the analysis. To support the execution of this step the analyzing tables, developed in this work will represent a helpful tool.

3.3.2 Analysis

As already mentioned, Competitive Intelligence supports the market analysis when considering the key questions of what the short and long term trends impacting the industry are, and how these trends will impact the business, as well as how the competitors will likely respond to these trends, e. g., how the market responds to changes in price, distribution, or service. This section will define the market and the major trends, as well as possibilities of competitive advantage in this field.

To develop a competitive analysis system it is necessary to make the competitive fields of the company visible. To do this, in this paper an instantiation of the *PORTER* Five Forces model will be used to examine the characteristics of the competitive market the *Deutsche Boerse Group* is working in (see Figure 10).

Deutsche Boerse Group[55] provides access to capital markets for companies and investors. It combines the entire spectrum of services and system applications required to this from securities and derivatives trading through clearing and the provision of market information to systems development. Furthermore the *Deutsche Boerse Systems* acts as a provider for E-commerce platforms and other IT-solutions. The Xetra® trading platform has made *Deutsche Boerse* the second largest fully electronic cash market in the world. *Deutsche Boerse Systems AG (DBS)* is the internal technology supplier. It constructs and operates the trading systems for cash and derivatives markets as well as *Deutsche Boerse's* worldwide participant network connecting trading members. *DBS* develops, maintains and operates trading, and information systems which are used in the cash and derivatives market as well as in emerging markets. A new field of operations for market participants is the development of front-end systems allowing an Internet-based access for trading and clearing. The largest systems are Xetra®, the electronic trading system for the cash market and the Eurex® system for the derivatives market.

On the one hand, there is the financial market with all the exchanges and providers of alternative trading systems. On the other hand, there is the IT branch, because there is the global trend that exchanges become more and more IT solution- providers based on highly reliable hardware and software components. This future direction is supported by the continuation of the process of globalization and consolidation in the world markets. Europe has a single currency. Money and standardized financial products continue to flow more and more freely around the globe and will be traded on a global base. The world's biggest financial institutions, when not busily merging with one another, are already true global players.

Furthermore, there is the market trend of substitution of trading floors – with their so called "open outcry" procedures – with electronic trading platforms and systems. There is the explosive growth of the Internet – a growth in communication technology – as well as there exists encryption and identification technology that are suddenly widely available, well understood and will support to secure and authenticate transactions anywhere in the world. Lastly, there are the growing global recognition of the value of competition, recognition of the free market as a real force for the creation and destruction of enterprise and recognition of the importance of free and fair trade.

Individuals will be empowered to trade 24 hours a day, seven days a week, from almost anywhere on the globe in real time. Investors will continue to demand better service, more immediate information, faster results, lower costs and safer trading. The major stock exchanges face competition from online systems for over the counter trading. They have to offer similar levels of immediacy and efficiency as the new entrants, and have to create opportunities for vendors, exchanges and brokerages. All of this innovation will be driven by cost reduction through the use of communications and new computer systems.[56]

---

[55] Cf. *Deutsche Boerse Group* (2009).

[56] Cf. *Michelin* (1998).

The relevant suppliers, which are mostly IT companies, underlie the same IT market structure. A threat for *DBS* is the restructuring of the suppliers, when leaving product lines trying to create additional opportunities to develop competitive advantage such as the creation of new business interrelationships or change in service and product program as well as the expansion of industry scope regionally, nationally and globally.[57]

Considering the ever changing needs of the market, there is a need to devise methods by which intelligence can be brought back to the competitive strategy process – not just helping to compete day-to-day in the businesses – but make business leaders aware of where the competitors and the market will be in the future and take action to enter those markets at the right time.

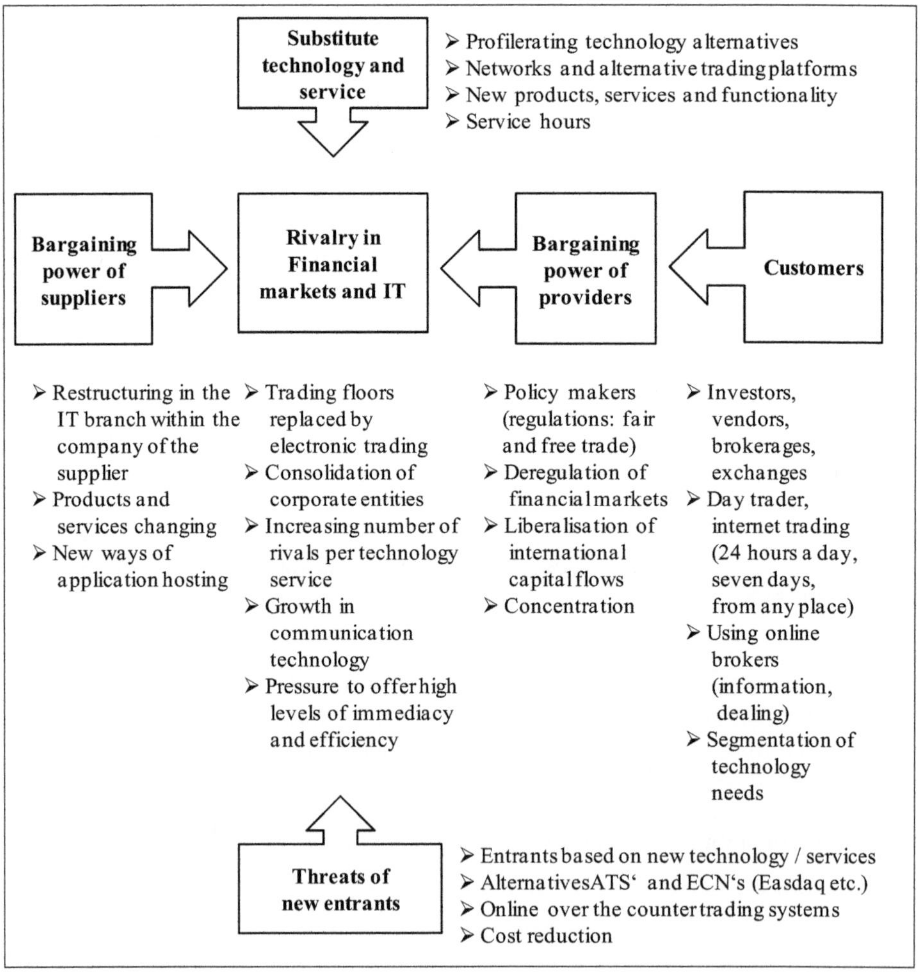

Figure 10: Sources of Industry Profitability (e. g. the competitive field of the exchange environment)

[57] Cf. *PORTER* (2000).

Analysis is the process by which information is interpreted to produce intelligence findings and recommendations for action. The keys to select and use effective analysis tools are the understanding of the user needs.[58] It is essential to find and analyze the most critical information in a timely fashion. The right moment would be that time when a major event takes place. That event could come from within the company or from without, such as the hiring of many new employees or a change in environmental rules. Any such event will generate a great deal of information on the target company and often on other affected subsidiary or affiliate operations. Next to the physical product, value for the company comes from the control of market information like customer preferences, comparative prices, and product data. Therefore these topics have to be analyzed.

The literature of Competitive Intelligence is discussing following analyzing tools:[59]

- Five Forces Model
- Growth-Share Matrix
- Critical success factor analysis
- Competitor profile
- Core competencies
- SWOT
- Value Adding Analysis
- Key data – Analysis

The SWOT analysis stands for assessment of Strengths-Weaknesses-Opportunities- Threats.[60] It is a useful framework for identifying a rival's weak spots, conversely, a useful tool to examine strategic opportunities. Strength is defined as the company's core competencies. Weaknesses are the company's drawbacks. Opportunities are the characteristics within the larger marketplace that can offer the company a competitive advantage. Threats are conditions in that same market that pose a threat to or block an opportunity for these firms. Figure 11 is a typical matrix with an example of a Company's SWOT analysis. The Matrix includes implications on possible scenarios. There will not be a one-to-one correlation on every cross factor nor will only one implication spring from each cross factoring of strengths, weak-nesses, opportunities and threats.[61]

---

[58] Cf. *Ashton/Klavans* (1997), p. 491.

[59] Cf. *Sammon/Kurland/Spitalnic* (1984), p. 124, and *Kahaner* (1996), p. 95.

[60] Cf. *Meffert/Burmann/Kirchgeorg* (2008), p. 237.

[61] Cf. *Kahaner* (1996), p. 100.

		Internal factors			
SWOT Matrix		**Strengths (S)**		**Weaknesses (W)**	
		1. Best technology	2. Skilled workforce	1. No management depth	2. Spotty distribution
External Factors	**Opportunities (O)**	**SO Implication**		**WO Implication**	
	1. Customers favor product application	keep technology current			
	2. Failing of other competitor,		might hire skilled workers from competitor	must satisfy growing market segments to remain competitive	
	Threats (T)	**ST Implication**		**WT Implication**	
	1. Possible regulation	might have to share technology to avoid regulation		management may not be able to thwart regulation	
	2. Growing of competitor		keep current workforce satisfied		competitor may take market share away

Figure 11: SWOT Matrix of Company A[62]

3.3.3 Dissemination

Dissemination and intelligence reporting is the last, but most important step in the CI process, when generating intelligence that users will find beneficial. Intelligence is useless if it is not available for decision makers to act upon.[63] In step one, it has been determined who will need to make decisions using the intelligence. The dissemination of results to other users in the organization who may benefit from having it may also be considered.

In short, dissemination is the process of distributing information throughout an organization. An essential benefit of this process is given by the setting up of a reporting system (see step 8 of Figure 6). To meet the needs of the users it has to be mentioned that identifying users must be included in the planning process, because it is the basis to develop the reporting system. The following questions have been answered before setting up such a reporting system. Who needs what pieces of intelligence and how do the users wish to use it? Who can use the data and who has access to information? What will be reported? How often will the basis information be delivered? How will exceptionally competitor information be delivered? When setting up a reporting system, a distinction has to be done between database organizations and reporting. Statistical data or standardized analysis and reports can be retrieved from the database (Pull-Service) and topical data have to be delivered immediately, e. g., by a newsletter (Push-

62 Cf. *KAHANER* (1996), p. 102.

63 Cf. *LANGE* (1994), p. 78.

Service). Everyone already suffers from information overload, so it must be avoided to blanket the entire organization with a report containing information needed only by managers in one division.[64] The mode of disseminating the intelligence product is equally important and must be appropriate to the situation. Various types of intelligence have to be used depending on the nature and criticality of the intelligence provided. The background of the users and how they like to receive information must be considered. It will do no good to present a voluminous report to a Chief Executive Officer who prefers to be briefed with a 10-minute presentation and provided with a one-page synopsis for future consideration.

The key manager can receive a monthly "Rival Report", which is electronically circulated internally. This very useful tool can include all the competitors, both at the parent company level and within a company's business units. Company Dossier is another tool which can be used. It provides a dynamic overview of a particular company – a snapshot of who they are, where they are headquartered, number of staff, financials and so on. It gives news, both as an archive and an update, on that particular company. The foundation to meet the demanded activity in Step 9 of Figure 6 is to secure the performance of precise actions that can be set by a well established reporting system.

The last point that has to be mentioned is the checking of feedback and internal communication (step 10 of Figure 6). There are still questions like "In which meetings will the delivered competitor intelligence be discussed?" and "How to organize continuous expert discussion/use groups?".

Furthermore the dissemination will involve recommendations of the Scenario Creation. As an example, an effective CI report might show through ongoing analysis, that the industry is being set by massive consolidation or predict which companies are likely to acquire other companies based on strategic fit and financing availabilty, as well as predict for each acquired company, what new strategies (marketing, financial, operational) will be adopted from their new parent. Visions will be build of what the new industry will look over the next five years with this consolidation. It quantifies the loss in market share and the reduction in industry profitability. An essential part is making recommendations detailing tactical action that could be taken to prevent loss of profitable market share. For example, if Company A acquires Company B, it is likely to supply B with its proprietary system software. B can now compete in the market with a new tool. If this development can be anticipated, the focal firm can move to thwart it.[65]

---

64 Cf. *Freibichler* (2006), p. 124 et seq.

65 Cf. *Pasemko* (2000).

Recommendations can take the form of Scenario-Creation, the providing of two or three likely outcomes under an envisioned change in the environment. It also includes the following forms:

- Prediction is the reporting on where the market could be going and in what direction it will be likely go in reality.
- Furthermore it covers the Contingency formulation – the evaluating of the current environment and assessing how the market will be likely react to a new product intro-duction.
- Formulating back up plans for reactionary events occurring 3 or 4 levels away from primary expectations.
- At last the early warning – providing information on likely competitive threats, competing products, and the direction of consumer desire and purchase power is contained as well.[66]

Scenario work is looking at what the competitors might do if the own company is doing the following steps. Their strategic intent is extremely important to analyze and assess. The need of doing scenarios is to know two years out, who the players will be, what their strategies will be and how that could impact the own business. It should not be planned for a time horizon of more than three or five years, because 18 months is a long planning horizon in the fast changing IT world.

The Scenario-Creation results are to support entrepreneurial decisions. The Scenario-Creation starts with the identification of key factors, which are characteristic for the development in the determination of the scenario field.[67]

Figure 12 shows a Matrix to evaluate Scenarios. The certainty of action is plotted on the horizontal axis and the impact to the company on the vertical axis. A wide range of environmental factors can lead to predetermined and unpredictable changes of a rival, including technological trends, government policy shifts, social changes and unstable economic conditions. Each should examine to see if and how it might affect the company.[68]

---

66 Cf. *PASEMKO* (2000).

67 Cf. *FINK/SCHLAKE* (2000), p. 39.

68 Cf. *PORTER* (1998), p. 452.

Scenario evaluation

Impact to the company		Certainty of action: high	Certainty of action: medium	Certainty of action: low
	high	Innovation, competitive threat	Transfer of technology	Acquisition of firms
	medium	Broadening of product segments	Changing markets, acquisition strategy	Marketing innovation
	low	Government policy changes	Changes in input and currency costs	Accumulation of experience

Figure 12: Scenario evaluation

The purpose of the scenario evaluation is to provide a checklist of the various ways in which the competitor can develop. Using the method leads to knowledge about which points have been considered previously. Strategic choices will be made by decision-makers. Formulating operational plans using a logical framework is a logical follow-up to strategic planning. A SWOT analysis and overview of existing plans and policies is needed to define strategic plans with responsibilities.[69] Doing the SWOT analysis on the competitors can be a good method to provide quarterly briefings. The frequently updated SWOT analysis indicates how competitors would see themselves and the level of "threat" with which they see the own company. It should be utilized within the process of the Scenario-Creation.

[69] Cf. MEFFERT/BURMANN/KIRCHGEORG (2008), p. 237.

Opportunity Matrix

Attractiveness \ Probability of Success	high	low
high	Company develops a more powerful system	Company develops a marketing innovation
low	Company changes buyer segments	Company changes input

Figure 13: Opportunity Matrix

Analysis of the potentials using insights from previous steps shown in the Figures above and a systematic approach (Opportunity-Attractiveness matrix) is to realize opportunities in which way the competitor may develop. The Threat Matrix in Figure 14 examines danger that can come from the rival.

Competitive intelligence also implies that information is presented to users in the context of the business processes in which they work. Users access any type of information through applications designed to support their work processes. Behind the scenes, the application supports a variety of data access engines that fetch the appropriate information and embed it transparently into the user's application. The methods for dissemination range from "low-tech" approaches, such as face-to-face meetings, alerts, reports and memos, as well as bulletin boards with news announcements to more sophisticated Intranet applications such as the use of GroupWare, e-mail briefings on competitors and situations in the market and even a Presentation Server within a company. The purpose of such a Presentation Server it to remain in close contact with intended users throughout the intelligence project and discussing the types of data being collected and the analyses being performed.

Threat Matrix

Seriousness / Probability of Occurrence	high	low
high	Competitor develops a superior system	Major prolonged economic depression
low	Higher costs	Tax's authority decision

Figure 14: Threat Matrix

4 Summary and Perspectives

This article describes the foundations, characteristics and methods of Competitive Intelligence. CI refers to the practice of collecting, analyzing, and communicating the best available information on competitors' moves and trends occurring outside one's own company. It produces actionable findings on threats and opportunities that are essential inputs to company managers.

Business has become increasingly technology dependent. The generation of new technological knowledge as a source of competitive advantage has become a bottleneck in many firms. A natural response to this trend might be to strengthen CI activities in the firms. For the company, CI should become an integral part of the strategy, because it is not just an exercise. It is important not just that the company has good CI resources and systems, but also that it tries to merge CI with the whole knowledge of the employees in the company.

This paper points out the potential long term benefits of the development of a Competitive Intelligence system. Furthermore, it has systematically explored different functions of CI that go beyond the creative development of new knowledge that may serve as a basis for future new products, services or processes.

The ultimate goal of CI is self-learning, how the focal organization can enhance its own marketplace strategy, and better manage its own activity/value chain(s) and other microlevel components. In order to support this self-learning process an understandable presentation will be designed to distribute intelligence results and analysis findings for users in many ways.

CI emerges as a discipline and as a profession and all indicators point to a rapid growth. The need to become competitive and stay that way is requiring technology-oriented organizations to operate in the rapid response mode. Decision-makers who must act under this pressure need real-time information upon which they decide. Improvements in computers and communications technology will change the way intelligence is produced, increasing the ease and effectiveness with which CI is collected, stored and analyzed.[70]

Many techniques from other fields are just emerging from fundamental development to the point where practical applications will soon be possible. For example, concepts and techniques that hold promise for intelligence analysis include computational linguistics, pattern recognition, fuzzy logic, group decision techniques, complexity/chaos theory, weak signal processing and war gaming.[71] A number of analysis tasks such as electronic brainstorming take advantage of computerized communication capabilities. Electronic brainstorming allows working groups to generate an abundance of ideas anonymously.[72]

Using Competitive Intelligence will present possibilities to create competitive advantage by providing the company with new ways to outperform their competitors. They can have a powerful effect on the cost structure of a business, increase opportunities for differentiation, and the benefits alter the competitive scope, increase economies of scale and opportunities for new customer relationships.

Next to the achievement of competitive advantage, the design stage is critical. A well-designed market intelligence analysis structure or map allows to create strategic plans to out-maneuver competitors by identifying their strengths and capitalizing on their weaknesses. Surprise attacks are prevented as far as possible. In the best case, the organization is able to equip itself to profitably capture market share.

Establishing and maintaining competitive advantage or market leverage is one of the most important issues that managers and leaders of enterprises ought to think about. The ability to compete and collaborate within the markets' ecosystem of an enterprise is brought about by core competency.

Finishing, it has to be said that Competitive Intelligence is a strategic imperative to move ahead, stay ahead or simply compete in the marketplace.

---

70 Cf. *ASHTON/KLAVANS* (1997), p. 506.

71 Cf. *ASHTON/KLAVANS* (1997), p. 496.

72 Cf. *ASHTON/KLAVANS* (1997), p. 497.

References

AAKER, D. A. (1989): Strategisches Markt-Management: Wettbewerbsvorteile erkennen, Märkte erschließen, Strategien entwickeln. Wiesbaden 1989.

ANSOFF, H. I. (1966): Management-Strategie, Munich 1966.

ASHTON, W. B./KLAVANS, R. (1997): Keeping abreast of Science and Technology – Technical Intelligence for Business, Columbus, Ohio 1997.

AGUILAR, F. J. (1967): Scanning the Business Environment, New York 1967.

BERNHARDT, D. (1993): Perfectly Legal Competitor Intelligence: How to get it, use it and profit from it, London 1993.

BRADLEY, S. P./HAUSMAN, J. A./NOLAN, R. L. (1993): Globalization, Technology and Competition, Harvard Business School Press, Boston, Massachussetts 1993.

BROCKHOFF, K. (1989): Schnittstellen-Management, Stuttgart 1993.

BULLINGER, H.-J. (1990): IAO-Studie: F & E – heute, Industrielle Forschung und Entwicklung in der Bundesrepublik Deutschland, München 1990.

DELTL, J. (2004): Strategische Wettbewerbsbeobachtung: So sind Sie Ihren Konkurrenten laufend einen Schritt voraus, Wiesbaden 2004.

DEUTSCHE BOERSE GROUP (2009): online: http://deutsche-boerse.com/dbag/dispatch/en/kir/gdb_navigation/about_us, last update: 2009, date visited: 2009-07-24.

FAHEY, L. (1999): Competitors: Outwitting, Outmaneuvering, and Outperforming, New York 1999.

FINK, A./SCHLAKE, O. (2000): Scenario Management – An Approach for Strategic Foresight, in: Competitive Intelligence Review, 2000, Volume 11 (1), pp. 37–45.

FLUSS, D./HARRIS, K. (1999): E-Business Glossary for Customer Service: Version 1.0, GartnerGroup Commentary, Stamford 1999.

FREIBICHLER, W. (2006): Competitive Manufacturing Intelligence, Wiesbaden 2006.

GIESKES, H. (2000): Competitive Intelligence at Lexis-Nexis, in: Competitive Intelligence Review, 2000, Volume 11 (2), pp. 4–11.

GILAD, B. (1994): Business Blindspots, Homewood /Il 1994.

HAMEL, G./PRAHALAD, C.K. (1994): Competing for the Future, Boston 1994.

HARKLEROAD, D. (1996): Actionable Competitive Intelligence, in: Society of Competitive Intelligence Professionals (Ed.), Annual International Conference & Exhibit Conference Proceedings, Alexandria/Va 1996, pp. 43–52.

HARRIS, K. (2000): KM Benefits: From building productivity to creating wealth, Gartner Group Commentary, Stamford 2000.

HERRING, J. P. (2001): Key intelligence topics – a process to identify and define intelligence needs, in: *PRESCOTT, J. E./MILLER, S. H.* (Eds.), Proven Strategies in Competitive Intelligence: Lessons from the Trenches, Wiley, New York 2001, pp. 240–56.

JOHNSON, A. (2000a): An Introduction to Knowledge Management as a Framework for Competitive Intelligence, online: http://www.aurorawdc.com/ekma.htm, last update: 2000, date visited: 2009-07-20.

JOHNSON, A. (2000b): The Core of Market Strategy: Turning Market and Competitor Knowledge into Actionable Intelligence, online: http://www.aurorawdc.com/marketstrategy.htm, last update: 2000, date visited: 2009-07-20.

JOHNSON, A. (2000c): What is Competitive Intelligence, online: http://www.aurorawdc.com/whatisci.htm, last update: 2000, date visited: 2009-07-20.

KAIRIES, P. (1997): So analysieren Sie Ihre Konkurrenz: Konkurrenzanalyse und Benchmarking in der Praxis, Renningen-Malmsheim 1997.

KAHANER, L. (1996): Competitive Intelligence: How to gather, analyze, and use information to move your business to the top, New York 1996.

KEUPER, F. (2001): Strategisches Management, München/Wien 2001.

KRYSTEK, U./MÜLLER-STEVENS, G. (1990): Grundzüge einer Strategischen Frühaufklärung, in: *HAHN, D./TAYLOR, B.* (Ed.), Strategische Unternehmensplanung – Strategische Unternehmensführung: Stand und Entwicklungstendenzen, Heidelberg 1990, pp. 337–364.

KUNZE, C./HAVEMANN, W. (1998): Das Internet als Instrument der Wettbewerbsanalyse, Wuppertal 1998.

KUNZE, C. W. (2000): Competitive Intelligence: ein ressourcenorientierter Ansatz strategischer Frühaufklärung, Aachen 2000.

LANGE, V. (1994): Technologische Konkurrenzanalyse, Wiesbaden 1994.

MARCEAU, S./SAWKA, H. (1999): Developing a World-Class CI Program in Telecom, in: Competitive Intelligence Review, 1999, Volume 10 (4), pp. 30–40.

MCGONAGLE, J. J./VELLA, JR., C.M. (1990): Outsmarting the Competition, Sourcebooks, Naperville 1990.

MEFFERT, H./BURMANN, C./KIRCHGEORG, M. (2008): Marketing – Grundlagen marktorientierter Unternehmensführung, 10th edition, Wiesbaden 2008.

MICHAELI, R. (2005): Competitive Intelligence, Heidelberg 2005.

MICHELIN, R. (1998): Globalization and Technological Innovation, http://www.barreau.qc.ca/publications/journal/vol30/no5/globalization.html, last update: 1998-03-15, date visited: 2009-07-20.

MONTGOMERY, D. B./WEINBERG, C. B. (1979): Toward Strategic Intelligence Systems, in: Journal of Marketing, 1979, Volume 43 (4), pp. 41–54.

PASEMKO, J. (2000): Competitive Intelligence for Beginners: Getting Started, in: Competitive Intelligence Review, 2000, Volume 3 (3), July – September 2000, pp. 44–46.

PORTER, M. E. (1998): Competitive Strategy: Techniques for Analyzing Industries and Competitors, New York 1998.

PORTER, M. E. (1998): Competitive Advantage: Creating and Sustaining Superior Performance, 2nd edition, New York, 1998.

Porter, M. E. (2000): Strategic Issues for Biotechnology Companies, Bio 2000 Economic Forum, http://www.isc.hbs.edu/BIO_2000_Strategy_03-27-2000.pdf, last update: 2000-03-27, date visited: 2009-07-22.

Rajaniemi, K. (2005): Framework, Methods and Tools for Acquiring and Sharing Strategic Knowledge of the Competitive Environment, Industrial Management 9, Diss. Vaasa 2005.

Rieser, I. (1989): Konkurrenzanalyse: Wettbewerbs- und Konkurrentenanalyse im Marketing, in: Die Unternehmung, 1989, Volume 43 (4), pp. 293–309.

Römer, E. (1988): Konkurrenzforschung, in: Zeitschrift für Betriebswirtschaft, 1988, pp. 481–501.

Rothblum, D. (2000): Wettbewerbsbeobachtung, Workshop of Siemens AG about their Competitive Intelligence, Frankfurt am Main 2000.

Sammon, W. L./Kurland, M. A./Spitalnic, R. (1984): Business competitor intelligence: methods for collecting, organizing and using information, New York 1984.

Sammon, W.L. (1985): Business Competitor Intelligence, New York 1985.

SCIP.ORG (2009): Glossary of terms used in competitive intelligence and knowledge manage ment,http://scip.cms-plus.com/files/Prior%20Intelligence%20Glossary%2009Jan.pdf, last update: Januar 2009, date visited: 2009-07-19.

Sheena S. (2000): 10 Myths that Cripple Competitive Intelligence, in: Competitive Intelligence Magazine, 2000, Volume 3 (1), pp. 37–39.

Sullivan, M. (1995): Fast Track Process Benchmarking: An Alternative Benchmarking Approach, in: Competitive Intelligence Review, 1995, Volume 6 (1), pp. 22–27.

Vella C./McGonagle, J. Jr. (1988): Improved Business Planning Using Competitive Intelligence, New York et al. 1988.

Zahn, E./Rüttler, M. (1989): Informationsmanagement, in: Controlling, 1989, Volume 1 (1), pp. 34–43.

Morphological Psychology and its Potential for Derivation of Requirements from Web Applications using Examples of Customer Self Care Instruments

CHRISTIAN SCHULMEYER and *FRANK KEUPER*

Schulmeyer & Coll. Management Consultancy
and *Steinbeis-Hochschule Berlin*

1 Psychological Dimensions of Web Applications and Customer Self Service Applications

In the following article theories and findings of recent research have been drawn upon to analyze the problems with respect to Usage Barriers which arise during handling Web Applications and the possible consequences. From this we can deduce which influencing factors with possibly high potential for explanation have been neglected till date during the research of the design of Web Applications. The aim of this article is therefore to highlight the potential of morphological psychology for deriving requirements for design recommendations of Web Applications using examples of Customer Self Service Applications.

The presentation of this theory potential builds the basis for an explorative, qualitative study of the effects of Customer Self Service under the transition of the concept of usage constitution from Pre Sales to After Sales Management. General requirements for designing Web Applications can be derived on the basis of such a broadly applied study.

2 Analysis of User Barriers of Customer Self Service Applications

The super-ordinated goals of Customer Service are understandably strikingly similar to those of Customer Relationship Management as Customer Self Service is to be considered an element of Customer Relationship Management. These goals are from the perspective of the Organization:[1]

- Collection and Use of Customer Knowledge (e.g. for Cross- and Upselling)
- Increasing Customer Retention and Differentiation in competition (on the basis of collected Customer Knowledge, amongst others)
- Reduction of Process Costs

Customer Self Service is meant to offer the customer greater flexibility, anonymity and autonomy. "The Organization reduces costs and the customer is in control"[2]

Parallel to the goals of the organization there exist several success stories.[3] From 1996 to 1998 Cisco increased the control of their Business to Business Service Requests from 4 % to 76 %. Cisco saved costs amounting to $365 Million and at the same time increased customer satisfaction by 25 %.[4] Apart from this IBM reportedly could transfer 99 Million telephone calls to Customer Self Service Usage which resulted in savings of $2 Billion.[5]

---

1 Cf. *ENGLERT/ROSENDAHL* (2000), p. 497 et seqq.

2 *STOLPMANN* (2000), p. 88.

3 Cf. *ENGLERT/ROSENDAHL* (2000), p. 497.

4 Cf. *ENGLERT/ROSENDAHL* (2000), p. 497.

5 Cf. *BURROWS* (2001), p. 94.

However such success stories are not to be understood as absolute justification of Customer Self Service as its introduction does not necessarily guarantee that customers will find, use, understand and accept the new Customer Self Service offerings.[6] According to a source an organization planned savings of $40 Million by introducing a new Customer Self Service System. However it had to book losses amounting to $ 16 Million because the new platform was not used to the extent expected.[7] In many cases the introduction of Customer Self Service Applications resulted in increased call volumes via the service lines instead of a reduction as planned. This can be explained as the result of a requirement for additional information due to deficiencies in the design of the Application itself and the information content.[8] *MONSE/JANUSCH* describe in an example how by introducing a Customer Self Service System the workload in the Call Centers increased by 57 %, which also resulted in increased costs.[9] The initial citation from *STOLPMANN* is to be critically viewed from this perspective; a Win-Win situation for providers as well as customers is often little more than a theoretical possibility.[10]

Customers do recognize the advantages of Customer Self Service but perceive it mostly not to the extent projected by the provider. The results of an analysis of *HOWARD* and *WORBOYS*[11] record that customers perceive an advantage in time.[12] However positive and negative perceptions with respect to steering, control, choice (flexibility) and price hold the balance and the absence of personal contact is actually evaluated negatively.

Customer Self Service therefore theoretically gives the organization great advantages for customer oriented processes, also particularly in After Sales Management but is not implemented effectively with the result that investments in Customer Self Service remain without the expected Return on Investment.

2.1 User Barriers in Self Service

The drastic change that Self Service brings with itself for the Provider-Customer-Relationship is the displacement of roles. The Self Service for the customers lies at the bottom of the automation of services. Automated service therefore always is synonymous with Self Service. To exemplify the connection between Self Service and the displacement of roles within the Provider-Customer-Relationship it must be clarified in which way Self Service changes the conventional interaction process between Provider and Customer. For this there are different theoretical observations[13], which are resorted to due to the lack of an empirical basis.

---

6 Cf. online *CHRIST* (2004).

7 Cf. *MEUTER ET AL.* (2005), p. 61.

8 Cf. *HOWARD/WORBOYS* (2003), p. 389.

9 Cf. online *MONSE/JANUSCH* (2003).

10 Cf. *HOWARD/WORBOYS* (2003), p. 382.

11 Cf. *HOWARD/WORBOYS* (2003), p. 382.

12 Cf. *HOWARD/WORBOYS* (2003), p. 382.

13 Cf. e.g. *VOSWINKEL* (2005).

A possible problem of Self Service is a greater *responsibility of the customer*, which may lead to *doubts* and *acceptance problems of self service.*[14] This is connected to the fact that the customer, for example in the case of purchase of groceries stands no longer only in front of the counter but can also examine the products and decide whether or not to initiate the purchase. In case of a wrong decision the responsibility lies with the customer.[15] This can also be transferred to the virtual area of Customer Self Service of the After Sales Phase: where the customer earlier only could speak personally to the customer care consultant for choosing an enhancement for a connection or plan, he can now configure it himself using Customer Self Service (Customer Center Application). Should he be dissatisfied with the enhancement at a later date, he will not be in a position to blame anyone for it as he had undertaken it at his own discretion.

According to *VOSWINKEL* Self-Service is "...a modern medium in which the customer is positioned as an autonomous subject. Self Service stands for an aspect of customer sovereignty, *customer autonomy*."[16] In connection with certain product and service categories, in particular even when the ideal of autonomy is at its limits, the other, older aspect of customer sovereignty becomes important for the customer, *dominance*. *VOSWINKEL* describes to illustrate "the paradoxical customer who gets irate when he is spoken to in a departmental store by a shop assistant and in the next second complains about the lack of service."[17]. Transferred to the area of After Sales Customer Self Service this would mean that customers definitely expect their service requests to be processed independently, comfortably and quickly via Customer Self Service (autonomy), but also expect in case there is a doubt that a dedicated point of contact is available to whom they could delegate requests (dominance). *SALOMANN/KOLBE/BRENNER* speak of a necessary balance between High-Tech and High-Touch.[18]

The examples show clearly the nature of the problem which can occur with the described displacement of roles. For offerings which have as prerequisites a "*Prosumer*" role and/or an empowerment of the customer, educating the customer is necessary for effective and efficient use. The customer has to first accept his changed role. Otherwise the enhanced autonomy in the form of additional options will not be understood by him as advantages.[19] The *DETICA*-Study showed that 75 % of 2000 respondents think that Organizations introduce Self Service purely out of their own necessities and not for the customers. Customers do not often understand how Customer Self Service can simplify the communication with their providers (51 %) and additionally feel that there is too little support from their providers (70 %).[20] In one of the few empirical studies in this area *MEUTER/BITNER/OSTROM/ BROWN* substantiate the unique meaning of the variable *Role Clarity*, in particular as a basis for a trial of Self Service Technologies.[21]

---

14 Cf. *VOSWINKEL* (2005), p. 93 et seqq.

15 Cf. *VOSWINKEL* (2005), p. 93 et seqq.

16 *VOSWINKEL* (2005), p. 90.

17 *VOSWINKEL* (2005), p. 91.

18 Cf. *SALOMANN/KOLBE/BRENNER* (2006), p. 65 et seqq.

19 Cf. *VOSWINKEL* (2005), p. 96 et seqq.

20 Cf. *DETICA* (2002), p. 3 et seqq.

21 Cf. *MEUTER ET AL.* (2005), p. 68 et seqq.

However empirical research on the meaning of displacement of roles and Role Clarity on the customers' side has till date been little.[22] It has to be noted that none of the available research (including the theoretical observations) matches the differentiations or restrictions regarding a definite usage context or usage situation of Self Service Offerings.[23] It has to be proven whether the displacement of roles which is described as a barrier for Self Service also has similar implications for Customer Self Service of the After Sales Phase. It is also possible that customers exhibit a different acceptance of a Prosumer role before the product purchase (Pre Sales Phase) during the configuration of product qualities as compared to problem handling *post product purchase* (After Sales Phase).

2.2 User Barriers of IuK based (Self) Service

The problem of the *missing inter-personal interaction* as well as the resultant problems there from have been extensively discussed and researched in connection with technology based (self) service.[24] It is postulated that the change in role of the customer from consumer to Prosumer is not the central problem – rather the change in interaction via the customer interface – from a *personal to a human-machine and/or human-computer interaction* is.[25] As a result of the discontinuation of the human interface the Provider-Customer-Relationship changes from a *triadic* (Provider organization, Provider personnel, Customer) to a *dyadic service relationship* (Provider Organization, Customer).[26]

Even in case of the provider organizations surveys regarding Self Service Technologies, the missing personal care is given as an important usage barrier.[27] *HANEKOP/WITTKE* emphasize through a qualitative study under the scope of which Customer Center Applications of a Mobile Phone Provider problems arise with navigation features (within the Customer Self Service Application), translation features (in case of technical terms) and interpretation features (in case of contractual passages) due to the missing personal care.[28] These are issues taken care of earlier by Provider Personnel. Only very few users are prepared to put in the effort required to learn these.[29] Those customers who are prepared to learn are called Early-Adopters[30], Innovation-Leader[31] or Pioneers[32].

---

22 Cf. *SALOMANN/KOLBE/BRENNER* (2006), p. 67 et seqq.

23 Cf. e.g. *VOSWINKEL* (2005).

24 Cf. e.g. *SELNES/HANSEN* (2001).

25 Cf. *SELNES/HANSEN* (2001), p. 87.

26 Cf. *SELNES/HANSEN* (2001), p. 87.

27 Cf. *SALOMANN/KOLBE/BRENNER* (2006), p. 74.

28 Cf. *HANEKOP/WITTKE* (2005), p. 214 et seq.

29 Cf. *HANEKOP/WITTKE* (2005), p. 214 et seq.

30 Cf. *DETICA* (2002), p. 9.

31 Cf. *SALOMANN/KOLBE/BRENNER* (2006), p. 73.

32 Cf. *WITTKE* (1997), p. 97.

Moreover the acceptance of Self Service technologies decreases with the increasing complexity of the structure as well as the use of the applications.[33] Very often a comparison is drawn between the acceptance and the complexity of the contents represented as well as the resultant application functions thereof. According to these sources Self Service Technologies are suitable only for simple tasks (e.g. withdrawing cash from an ATM) but in case of service requests of greater complexity, use of products which require intensive explanations, for technical problems or for consultation regarding charges personal contact is preferred.[34] A concrete example is given by *HANEKOP/WITTKE* in the form of the results of their study. The ask customers about their future usage intentions of Customer Self Service for different situations. The result: only 3 % of the respondents would want to find out their mobile plan charges using Customer Self Service and book through it, 47 % of the customers would *"definitely not"* use it. On the contrary 20 % of the customers say they would certainly find out account status and billing details *online* in the future and only 23 % would not use this Customer Self Service tool for the same.[35] These empirical findings show that *a differentiation regarding different usage contexts or usage situations* would need to be taken into consideration in general and in particular while designing Customer Self Service Applications. Disadvantages/Problems in case of Self Service Technologies are therefore:

- Absence of personal and/or interpersonal interaction
- Learning effort for the customer to use the technology
- Acceptance problems in case of increased complexity

The above mentioned acceptance barriers do not correlate to the usage requirements for Online Help and Support Applications, for Customer Center Applications the correlation is only partial. In case of online help it cannot be assumed that service requests in this context are simple in nature and repetitive. For Customer Center Applications individual usage situations e.g. tariff changes have to be observed critically. Generally it should be scrutinized if findings on acceptance barriers for different usage contexts (After Sales help and support) or usage situations (tariff change in the After Sales Phase) develop differently. It is doubtful if customers are prepared to make an effort to learn for certain usage contexts but not for others, or if the absence of personal consultancy is perceived and evaluated differently. *HANEKOP/WITTKE* make the assumption in their study that customers are more prepared to make the effort to learn in cases where they have a *strong personal interest in its success* and/or are *positively proven/connoted* (in case of Customer Self Service holiday bookings or shopping).[36]

In studies related to Online Service in general (not restricted to Customer Self Service) it has emerged that *Usability* of a website which is understood as *fitness for use* and *functionality*, as well as the look and feel (Layout, E-Scape) are important factors for acceptance. These underline the importance of design in general and design of the application interface in particular.[37] The *fitness for use* has to be *as high as possible* which can be achieved by creating a

33 Cf. *SELNES/HANSEN* (2001), p. 87.

34 Cf. *SELNES/HANSEN* (2001), p. 87.

35 Cf. *HANEKOP/WITTKE* (2005), p. 208.

36 Cf. *HANEKOP/WITTKE* (2005), p. 214 et seq.

37 Cf. *VAN RIEL ET AL.* (2004), p. 19.

user centric design.[38] The greater the complexity of the represented contents, the more complex are the functions and the menu items within an Online Service Application. This would make a user friendly design all the more important (and more difficult as well). Beside complexity of content, other usage barriers would also be the degree of confidentiality (e.g. in the Banking Sector or online purchases). This also stresses the necessity of a design which gives confidence.[39]

Summarizing the current status of research we can say that the disadvantages/problems while using online service which lead to declining acceptance are:

- Deficient *fitness for use*
- Deficient design
- Lack of confidence (due to contents which have a high degree of confidentiality/deficient design)

The absence of personal consultation in case of IuK based Self Service can therefore be compensated by approaches with user friendly designs and/or aesthetic and/or confidence building designs. This is applicable for all Web Applications.

2.3 Consequences for Customer Satisfaction and Customer Retention

Customer Retention is the primary goal of After Sales Management and Customer Satisfaction is the greatest factor in deciding and influencing Customer Retention. Many studies describe and substantiate that Self Service can have a negative effect on Customer Satisfaction and Retention. [40] *BARNES* describes how due to the introduction of Self Service Technologies in the banking sector (ATM, Internet banking and Phone banking), customers categorize their relationship as less close when compared to previous years.[41] *SELNES/HANSEN* could however ascertain *no negative effect* of Customer Self Service on *Social Bonds* (social bonding with a Provider) but *no positive effect* as well.[42] Customer Self Service from this perspective seems to have no effect on social bonding and therefore should be observed neutrally. On the contrary a strong positive influence of personal service on social bonding could be ascertained. Personalized service is important to create and maintain social bonding.[43] Therefore the authors argue that when personalized service is replaced by Customer Self Service the *positive influences on social bonding cease to exist.* This must lead to a reduction in bonding and ergo to a reduction in Customer Retention.[44] Even though Customer Self Service has no negative effects, here the absence of positive effects becomes a problem.

38 Cf. *BURMESTER/GÖRNER* (2003), p. 47 et seqq.

39 Cf. *HASSENZAHL* (2004), p. 33.

40 Cf. *BARNES* (2001), p. 133.

41 Cf. *BARNES* (2001), p. 133.

42 Cf. *SELNES/HANSEN* (2001), p. 87.

43 Cf. *SELNES/HANSEN* (2001), p. 87.

44 Cf. *SELNES/HANSEN* (2001), p. 87.

GENSLER/SKIERA analyzed the loyalty and readiness for change of customers while using different sales channels (Call Center for personalized service and Internet Shop for Customer Self Service) for purchasing different products. The results were constant for all three researched product categories: more customers were loyal to the sales channel Call Center, i.e. the probability for a repeat purchase via telephone is greater than via Internet (87.8 % as compared to 62 % for all three product categories). Additionally the telephone attracts potential *changers* to a much greater extent than the Internet (81.8 % as compared to 3.3 % for all three product categories).[45] The different values for both sales channels show a strongly divergent acceptance of personalized service as compared to Customer Self Service. Lower loyalty to online sales channels in converse argument also means deterioration in Customer Retention in the shifting from personalized service to Customer Self Service. *HOWARD/WORBOYS* came to the same conclusions after analyzing the difference between Telephonic Service and Customer Self Service: "Further analysis of the findings related to the insurance market also suggests that self-servers may be less loyal than other customers. This stands to reason, if they are more sophisticated and experienced, and less concerned about the personal touch, they are less likely to be attached to a particular supplier."[46] Instead of a Customer Service agent, the customer interacts with a user interface i.e. a technical interface. The assessment of this interface presumably strongly influences the evaluation of the core services as well as the additional and supporting features and finally also Customer Retention.[47] This has been substantiated by various studies:

CURRAN/MEUTER emphasize *Ease-of-Use* as the most important factor for Customer Satisfaction in case of Self Service Technologies.[48] *VAN RIEL/LILJANDER/LEMMINK/STREUKENS* demonstrate that *Usability*, *E-Scape* and *Customization* have a significant positive influence on customer loyalty as features of E-Service sites.[49] In a further study of *LILJANDER/VAN RIEL/PURA Site Design and Content* emerge as the most important factor for the perceived overall quality of the website and Customer Satisfaction.[50] In the study by *PARASURAMAN/ ZEITHAML/MALHOTRA* on Quality of E-Service, *Efficiency* and *Fulfillment* are the variables with the greatest significant and positive influence on loyalty.[51] *HOWARD/WORBOYS* come to the conclusion that Customer Self Service should first and foremost be quick and easy to use, i.e. it should be efficient and effective to ensure Customer Satisfaction.[52]

The relevance of usage context adequate and user friendly design can also be established by a study of *MEUTER/OSTROM/ROUNDTREE/BITNER* in which 823 usage situations of Self Service Technologies were categorized. 21 % of the customers were satisfied because the Self Service Technology functioned as it should have, i.e. it was effective. Anyhow in 36 % of the cases bad application design (meaning inefficiency or ineffectiveness) were responsible for Customer Dissatisfaction.[53] The quality of the core service is to be considered as being utmost critical because complications are particularly irritating for the customer (as there is also no

---

45 Cf. *GENSLER/SKIERA* (2004), p. 80 et seq.

46 *HOWARD/WORBOYS* (2003), p. 387.

47 Cf. *LILJANDER/VAN RIEL/PURA* (2002), p. 411.

48 Cf. *CURRAN/MEUTER* (2005), p. 107 et seqq.

49 Cf. *VAN RIEL ET AL.* (2004), p. 18.

50 Cf. *LILJANDER/VAN RIEL/PURA* (2002), p. 424.

51 Cf. *PARASURAMAN/ZEITHAML/MALHOTRA* (2005), p. 228.

52 Cf. *HOWARD/WORBOYS* (2003), p. 389 et seq.

53 Cf. *HOWARD/WORBOYS* (2003), p. 389 et seq.

competent point of contact available). The effects are also not only on the image of Customer Self Service but on the image of the organization as a Service provider.[54]

Beside purely *efficiency* and *effectiveness* of use other aspects should also be considered. References to this are to be found looking at the aspect of confidentiality and security with respect to sensitive content. LEE/SOHN could show that a significant positive influence of *Ease-of-Web-Use* (Usability) and *Web-Page-Design* (aesthetic look and feel) is there on the construct related to perceived security i.e. *trust*. This again has a strong significant influence on Customer loyalty.[55] Trust is therefore crucial for loyalty and can be created and designed like efficiency or effectiveness. If the results illustrated in the above passage were to be summarized, the following problems as mentioned earlier would be:

- discontinuation of personalized contact and
- bad design with respect to user friendliness, content and design.

These can have negative consequences for Customer satisfaction/loyalty and therefore also for Customer retention which has been partially proven by studies.

While drawing parallels to the preceding passages it is debatable whether these effects on Customer Retention are also specifically applicable for After Sales Customer Self Service and whether these are differently assessed for different phases of the Customer Buying Cycle or whether different usage situations are evaluated/assessed very differently. It is possible that the discontinuation of personalized contact in case of Customer Self Service has other (more difficult?) effects than in the case of Online Service where the communication is via e-mail which has some indirect personal contact. Similarly it is also debatable whether subjective constructs e.g. *trust* depend fundamentally on effectiveness and efficiency or are independent, or can create effectiveness and efficiency. This theory is supported by the assumption that subjective aspects of usage like trust, fear, insecurity, etc. (not only dependent on objective aspects like effectiveness) have considerable importance. Subjective aspects (barriers) not only arise from the design of the application but from the overall usage situation.

2.4 Interim Conclusions

The problems in connection with Self Service, Online Service and Self Service Technologies in general have been discussed using illustrations of results of different studies. In this scope studies have been introduced which deal directly or indirectly with Customer Self Service. Additionally possible consequences for Customer Satisfaction, Customer Loyalty, and Customer retention have been shown. The findings of empirical or theoretical analyses have been summarized once again in Table 1.

---

54 Cf. PARASURAMAN/ZEITHAML/MALHOTRA (2005), p. 230.

55 Cf. LEE/SOHN (2004), p. 218.

	usage barriers	negative effects	studies
self service in general (person centric perspective)	lack of role clarity on the customer's side (prosumer role)	lack of role clarity leads to deficient acceptance with respect to self service and as a result to rejection	➢ DAVIES/ELLIOT (2006) ➢ SALOMANN/KOLBE/BRENNER (2006) ➢ MEUTER/BITNER/OSTROM/BROWN (2005) ➢ VOSWINKEL (2005) ➢ DETICA (2002)
online service, self service technologies, customer self service	discontinuation of personal contact (interpersonal interaction)	discontinuation of personal contact has no positive effect on social bonding with the provider; regression in social bonding as a result	➢ SALOMANN/KOLBE/BRENNER (2006) ➢ HANEKOP/WITTKE (2005) ➢ SELNES/HANSEN (2005)
online service, self service technologies, customer self service	learning effort for use/application of the customer interface	leads to deficient acceptance with respect to self service and as a result to rejection. Negative effect on customer retention	➢ SALOMANN/KOLBE/BRENNER (2006) ➢ HANEKOP/WITTKE (2005) ➢ DETICA (2002) ➢ WITTKE (1997)
self service technologies, customer self service	high complexity of the contents represented	complexity of the content leads to complexity of the interface (more learning effort). This leads to deficient acceptance with respect to self service and as a result to rejection. Negative effect on customer retention.	➢ HANNEKOP/WITTKE (2005) ➢ PETERSON (2002) ➢ SELNES/HANSEN (2001)
online service, self service technologies, customer self, service	bad design of the interface and/or customer interface (usability, ease of use, site design, content, e-scape, efficiency and fulfillment, etc.)	negative effect on customer satisfaction and as a result on customer retention	➢ CURRAN/MEUTER (2005) ➢ PARASURAMAN/ZEITHAML/MALHOTRA (2005) ➢ VAN RIEL/LILJANDER/LEMMINK/STREUKENS (2004) ➢ BURMESTER/GÖRNER (2003) ➢ LILJANDER/VAN RIEL/PURA (2002) ➢ HOWARD/WORBOYS (2003)
customer self service	low attraction for repeat purchase or change to CSS provider as compared to personalized service	low loyalty to provider would mean low customer retention in general	➢ GENSLER/SKIERA (2004)
online service, customer self service	perceived deficiencies of the interface and/or customer interfaces with respect to "soft" variables like trust	negative effect on customer satisfaction and as a result on customer retention	➢ HASSENZAHL (2004) ➢ LEE/SOHN (2004)

Table 1: Summary of research on (customer) self service (technologies) and online service

The studies collated on the preceding topics relate only in exceptional cases to Customer Self Service. Customer Self Service functions are often handled only incidentally e.g. within the scope of Online Service. Additionally it must be concluded that none of the studies distinguish between usage contexts, usage situation or connotation of use and none of these studies concentrate specially on applications of the After Sales Phase of the Customer Buying Cycle. The mass of literature and/or research in the area of Self Service Technologies, Online Service and Customer Self Service relate to Pre Sales specific applications. In reality Pre Sales and After Sales applications in individual research papers are not separated, differentiated or differently evaluated.[56]

It has been assumed in this article however that particularly in the After Sales Phase that the different usage barriers and their negative effects on Customer Retention apply differently according to the different usage contexts and situation. As the studies put forward do not concern themselves directly with Customer Self Service, it should be examined which of the mentioned barriers are at all relevant for specific usage situations in After Sales Customer Self Service. Assumptions to that effect have been made in the preceding paragraphs. Negative effects (e.g. lack of role clarity, lack of will to learn or inefficient applications) on Customer Retention can thus manifest themselves very differently in Customer Self Service usage situations of the After Sales Phase (e.g. usage context Online help and Support; usage situation hardware operation problem) from a Pre Sales Customer Self Service Application.

[56] Cf. the research of *MEUTER et al.* (2000).

In this case, as shown in the studies discussed, a differentiation according to different usage situations (context, situation, etc.) has not been made. Therefore an inspection of the available literature does not provide enough evidence for these assumptions. This is also reinforced by the fact that the available studies almost never deal with Customer Self Service and in some cases only provide cursory observations.

Over and above it has been assumed that not only the usage barriers and acceptance problems with Self Service, Online Service and Customer Self Service that have been discovered till date are the ones that exist but that in case of a differentiation according to the usage situation completely new context specific or situation specific problems of Customer Self Service could arise. In this connection the focus is especially on *subjective* barriers and their effects which when compared to objective constructs (effectiveness, efficiency, ease of use, etc.) have been neglected till date. First indications on the importance of these "soft" variables provide evidence for the loyalty promoting effects of the construct trust.

Example: the most important subjective constructs are emotions and moods. A specific usage context e.g. Online help varies according to the emotions and/or moods the user associates (connotation) with Online help. This can be specified further for the usage situation: the user who books a new feature in the Online Customer Center is presumably differently disposed than a user who accesses his bill. Even if objectively similar procedural steps and environmental characteristics are present, two completely different usage situations may exist.

To answer the questions which arise regarding the requirements Web Applications in general and Customer Self Service Applications in particular need to fulfil, to be effective and efficient from the customers perspective a research approach is required which

- allows situation specific analysis of Customer Self Service of the After Sales Phase (differentiation of the situation according to usage context and situation) as well as
- analyses the usage situation macroscopically as multiple as well as different usage barriers (subjective and objective) have to be taken into consideration.

This results in the need for a wide ranging research focus for the explorative goals of which an adequate research design has to be found. As previous research designs for Customer Self Service, Self Service, Online Service or Self Service Technologies do not differentiate according to the usage situation and focus primarily on objective aspects, none of these designs can be taken over and used.

3 Relaxation Approaches for Overcoming User Barriers

To assess the implications of different usage contexts or situations within the After Sales Phase the use of suitable Customer Self Service Applications should be studied. This must be done macroscopically in each case as multiple aspects which are relevant (primarily to reveal new subjective problems, barriers, etc.) would need to be observed in the initial study.

Customer Self Service is an Internet based Self Service via Computer Applications (Web Applications) presented on Web sites. Approaches on Human-Computer interaction lend themselves to show how a Customer Self Service usage situation can be analyzed. These can be used also to observe individual usage situations which are under the scope of development and optimization of interfaces between human and technical components.[57]

Moreover findings may be available from studies of Internet usage patterns[58], as these relate to media and media contents which area part of media psychology. Media psychology deals with the research of short and long term media usage and effects of media.[59] In fact the technical disciplines tend towards media psychology due to the expansion of IuK Technologies, particularly the Internet.[60]

3.1 Approaches of Human-Computer Interaction

For a long time usage situations of computer applications e.g. websites have been studied within the scope of human-computer interaction.[61] In the so called *Usability-Tests* users are observed when directly interacting with the application so that they are able to give inputs on the usability. This procedure is widespread and is part of a standard process while developing new user interfaces.[62]

Because of this importance it is surprising that relatively few sources account for concrete suggestions for designing Customer Self Service elements and/or discuss Internet applications in general or provide derivations empirically.[63] The reason behind this is evident as post completion the Usability or user friendliness of interfaces is *checked specifically for a single application* in general. Non-controllable factors influencing different variables of the checked website play a role in this. Because of this usability tests cannot be classified as empirical experiments and their results cannot be generalized.[64]

In case of the existing question regarding an effective and efficient designing of Web Applications from the customer's perspective a classical usability test with a Customer Self Service application cannot therefore be in line with the set objectives. This is because only the usability of a particular website would be analyzed and generic observations with respect to usage context and usage situations of the After Sales Phase cannot be made. It would be much more helpful in this case if several Customer Self Service applications of the users could be observed to find out consistencies and general problems. Here it is important to pose further questions which are generic in nature and not only questions regarding aspects of functionality directly related to the applications. This would record subjective points of view as well as background aspects of the usage situation. The problematic aspect in case of conventional use

---

57 Cf. *Wandke* (2004), p. 326 et seqq.

58 Cf. *Wolfradt/Doll* (2005).

59 Cf. *Leffelsend/Mauch/Hannover* (2004), p. 52.

60 Cf. *Bente/Krämer/Petersen* (2002), p. 1 et seqq.

61 Cf. *Wandke* (2004), p. 326 et seqq.

62 Cf. *Wandke* (2004), p. 326 et seqq.

63 Exceptions are several approaches taken from the Pre-Sales sector, such as the usability questionnaire Ufos *Konradt* et *al*.(2003), available at URL: http://www.ufos-online.com/ufos/.

64 Cf. *Wandke* (2004), p. 335.

of the construct usability is that, as per the definition, the (subjective) satisfaction is part of the complete construct but is however neglected generally. *JORDAN* postulates on usability studies which have been conducted with a focus on functional aspects: "While these usability-based approaches certainly tackle some very important issues, they tend to take a view of people that is somewhat limited – perhaps even de-humanizing. The problem is that they tend to ignore or de-emphasize wider aspects of our humanness. What about our hopes, our fears, our dreams, our feelings, our self-image, the way that we want others to see us? All these things those are associated with the emotional and aspiration levels of a person's experience with a product or service."[65]

There is prior evidence shown in research results that *the subjective component "satisfaction" is not necessarily dependent on the supposedly objective components "effectiveness" and "efficiency"*:

BARTEL describes how in a usability test of a website for holiday homes all the test candidates dismissed a reference list of all available holiday homes calling it a clerical list; at the same time it was criticized that it would be insufficient if it were to restrict itself to a particular holiday.[66] Further evidence is provided in the study by *KRÄMER/NITSCHKE* in which an interface with a language input had high efficiency (the user did not have to type, he could just speak) but not high satisfaction/acceptance.[67] Similar doubts emerge in the study by *VAN MULKEN/ANDRÉ/MÜLLER* regarding the 1:1 dependency between satisfaction and/or acceptance on one side and efficiency and effectiveness on the other.[68] Here the test persons were explained a pulley tackle system using animation and language on a computer screen. In the first trial group the relevant parts of the system were explained by a virtual person with a pointer and in the second group only with a virtual arrow. The type of information and presentation did not vary otherwise between the two groups. The presence of the virtual person had no positive or negative effect neither on the objectively measured understanding nor the retention of the test persons. However there were significant differences between the test groups for *the subjective perception of comprehensibility and also entertainment value*. The test persons in the group where the presentation was done by the virtual person evaluated these points more positively. Thus in case of a subjectively high acceptance an objectively equivalent efficiency can also be perceived to be greater.[69]

Particularly also against the background of the first indicators to the significance of influences of constructs, such as reliance for example, aspects of subjective perception should be considered additionally to pure functional aspects. Social behaviour towards computers or comprehensiveness of the same in a mystical coherence is often reported within literature.[70] Overall, it is the issue according to the presumption of people that computers hold something irrational within: "Humans not only project aspects of their own psyche on other people and animals, but also on (objective) inanimate objects, such as teddies, cars and computers." [71]

---

65 *JORDAN* (2004), p. XI et seq.

66 Cf. *BARTEL* (2003), p. 72 et seq.

67 Cf. *KRÄMER/NITSCHKE* (2002), p. 245 et seq.

68 Cf. *VAN MULKEN/ANDRÉ/MÜLLER* (1998).

69 Cf. *VAN MULKEN/ANDRÉ/MÜLLER* (1998), p. 4 et seqq.

70 Cf. *MOLZBERGER* (1994), p. 58 et seqq.

71 *MOLZBERGER* (1994), p. 60.

Those subjective components which are neglected in the classical understanding of usability are primarily important for the existing debate as the functional usage barriers are relevant only at first sight. Additional usage barriers have to be discovered which result from the special usage situation (context and situation) on the customer's side. These are not directly connected with (objectively evaluable) functionalities. It is plausible that in the usage context online help and support specific subjective aspects (generally emotions and moods) vary fundamentally from those in online shopping. A study of Customer Self Service applications which restrict themselves to effectiveness and efficiency analogous to conventional usability tests would not be able to discover these differences in the subjective evaluation.

The observation or reconstruction of specific usage situations can therefore be taken from the basis of the standard process of Human-Computer interaction, i.e. the classical usability tests which could lead to success. In contrast to the usual procedure however

- *different applications* should be observed to be able to generalize the results for specific usage situations;
- besides the objective usage aspects taken into consideration in the conventional usability tests, *subjective aspects* of usage should also be considered;
- besides the characteristics of the application which are analyzed in conventional usability tests, the background aspects of the usage situation should also be considered.

3.2 Approaches of Media Psychology

Media psychology deals with aspects of media usage (also indirectly with respect to a particular usage situation) and the effects of media.[72] The following approaches for analysis of usage patterns (in which manner a person or group of persons uses a medium) have been broadly observed. These have arisen with respect to the new medium Internet in recent years. In doing so the suitability of different approaches for the questions in this article are evaluated.

3.2.1 Analysis of the quantitative Use of the Internet

There are primarily quantitative studies and/or research designs available for the research area of usage patterns of the medium Internet. Examples for such research are studies like *ARD/ZDF-Online-Studie*[73] or the *Digital Future Report* of the *Center for Digital Future* at the *USC Annenberg School* in Los Angeles.[74] The latter presents by way of example an annual list of most used web activities through a survey of 2000 households.

The most used offerings are indentified in these studies and changes in user numbers and usage patterns for the medium over a period of time can also be arrived at. Additionally relations can be drawn to the intensity and frequency of different offerings (usage contexts) with variables related to individuals like education, income, gender, etc. This again can shed some light on interpersonal differences for Internet usage. *WOLFRADT/DOLL* describe in their study the usage patterns of their test persons by a broad division of the activities: (1) Information

[72] Cf. *LEFFELSEND/MAUCH/HANNOVER* (2004), p. 52.

[73] Cf. online *VAN EIMEREN/FREES* (2005).

[74] Cf. online USC Annenberg School – Center for the Digital Future (2004).

(2) Communication and (3) Entertainment as well as recording the respective usage duration.[75] This type of study highlights different events regarding the above mentioned aspects (e.g. whether women use more informative offerings than men, whether income and Internet usage are related, etc.). It describes however the usage patterns of certain sociological or demographic groups in their super ordinate aspects and not for a specific usage situation, which is the aim of the following studies. This procedure is not factually adequate to answer the questions posed in this article. This is because the direct effects of the usage are not analyzed, nor can the *subjective aspects of usage* be taken into consideration in this quantitative analysis. It is possible to conduct a study of the usage frequency of the different After Sales Customer Self Service offerings. However such a study allows *very limited scope for conclusions regarding acceptance and potential usage barriers.*

3.2.2 Analysis of User Typology Analysis

Often *user typologies* are prepared after a quantitative analysis of different usage patterns. These present a special type of analysis of usage patterns. While compiling user typologies user types are differentiated on the basis of their respective characteristic user patterns.[76] *MAY-RING* explain the basic idea which is behind such typologies: "in case of typological analyses parts have to be filtered out of the material as per a previously fixed criterion and described in detail. These have to represent the material in particular."[77]

In case of the definitions of typologies for users of the Internet the basis of frequency of use is easily obtained. The differentiation is simply based on *heavy* users and *sparse* users, or according to the type of used offerings. This can lead to a further categorization in *Surfer* (online games, etc.) and *Information Seeker* (knowledge sites, news, etc.).[78] Besides the observed behaviour further variables are considered so that within a typology persons can be categorized in different types. These are demographic and socioeconomic features (e.g. gender, education, income, etc.) or psychographic features (e.g. attitude, motivation, etc.) as well. In this way a clear number of user types can be built which would allow us to draw *conclusions for the target audience specific designing* and offering of a website.[79] An example for a rather complex user typology can be found in the already discussed ARD/ZDF-Online-Study. In this study the Internet users have been categorized into nine different groups: (1) the young wild, (2) excitement seeking, (3) performance oriented, (4) oriented to new cultures (5) inconspicuous (6) open minded (7) homely (8) oriented to classical cultures and (9) reserved.[80] As recognizable from these type descriptions, how users go about the online offerings use them and how their socioeconomic and demographic background displays itself plays a role in the categorization. A user typology which restricts itself to how the users deal with the offerings in the Internet or with the contents and information is shown by *SCHANZE*.[81] He differentiates between four types (1) the input giver (2) the collector (3) the sorter and (4) the

---

75 Cf. *WOLFRADT/DOLL* (2005), p. 152.

76 Cf. *VON VERSEN* (1999), p. 60 et seqq.

77 *MAYRING* (1996), p. 105.

78 Cf. *VON VERSEN* (1999), p. 60 et seqq.

79 Cf. *VON VERSEN* (1999), p. 60 et seqq.

80 Cf. online *VAN EIMEREN/FREES* (2004), p. 353.

81 Cf. *SCHANZE* (2002), p. 25 et seqq.

replacer.[82] An example for a user typology which is similarly comprehensive as the ARD/ ZDF-Online-Study is the strategic customer segmentation by T-Online which is as follows:[83]

- Occasionals: Internet minimalists with very little usage and very little interest
- Stay at Homes: open minded surfers of high age group who do not use all the diversity of the Internet
- X-tra Light Surfers: narrow band surfers of middle age with very little online interest
- Light Surfers: advanced narrow band surfers with interest in further online products
- Professionals: well situated browsers who look at the Internet as an essential support for life
- Fun Seekers: entertainment oriented with medium Internet bonding
- Super Surfers: strong browsers who look at the diversity of the world of Internet as an important part of their life
- 24-7 Uppers and Downers: 'always online' is an essential part of their life

For answering the current questions a user typology on the basis of a quantitative compilation of Internet usage is less suitable. Particularly regarding the assumption made in this article that in different usage contexts and/or usage situations the user patterns also change. This is given that an "inflexible" typology has no or very little contribution to this discussion. *VON VERSEN* speaks exactly about this issue for the above categorization of Surfer and Information Seeker: the one and the same person can be a surfer or information seeker at different points in time or in different situations."[84]

There is less need of a typology approach which categorizes persons into usage types according to the criteria age, income, usage intensity, preferred offerings (chat, auctions, news, etc.). Instead of starting from the person, it should be from the usage situation (context and situation) to arrive at different usage patterns and effects of offerings for different situations (e.g. context help and support in general or for a change in tariff plan). This would mean that a typology is not compiled for the different users in the conventional sense but for the different usage patterns which each single user may display on using the tool. This is based on the assumption that the situation specific behaviour of the individuals is strongly shaped by recent or subjective influences (emotions, moods, feelings, etc.) than by stable qualities of the person (used offerings, income, age, etc.). From this derivations can be arrived at from psychological research on interdependencies between stable characteristics of the individual and the usage of media offerings.

---

82 Cf. *SCHANZE* (2002), p. 25 et seqq.

83 Internal documentation of T-Online International AG, to which the author has access to.

84 V*ON VERSEN* (1999), p. 64.

3.2.3 Analysis of the Stable Variables of the Individual

The paradox of consistency states that global personality qualities (e.g. extroversion, conscientiousness, etc.) of an individual are assessed consistently by different observers; however these qualities do not necessarily ensure consistent behaviour of an individual in different situations. [85] It can also be said therefore, that a differentiation of usage patterns of Customer Self Service in certain usage contexts can possibly *only give a partial explanation using super-ordinated personality qualities* (and/or stable variables of the individual). There is only a weak influence of personality on media usage and vice versa.[86] "Theories on interdependency between personality and media usage [are] not very elaborate".[87] Beside global personality qualities, other variables of the individual and/or their effects on computer and Internet usage have been analyzed, where primarily the variables gender and expertise have been named. It has been discovered that gender as a variable can be drawn upon only as an indirect and inaccurate causal variable for computer and Internet usage.[88] In contact with computer and Internet the variable expertise (experience and knowledge) is one of the decisive factors, if not the main factor for predicting behaviour.[89] Users are often divided into three groups (1) beginners/ novices, (2) advanced and/or average users and (3) professionals/experts.[90] In spite of the knowledge about the importance of expertise it is doubtful to what extent there is scope for a practical application. "Because in reality even in case of customized interfaces for certain [expertise] user groups only limited predictions can be made about the expected acceptance and efficiency".[91]

For this article this would mean that valid statements/conclusions regarding situation specific usage of Customer Self Service offerings cannot be made on the basis of personality qualities (like extroversion) or other stable variables of the individual (like expertise). This need not curtail the informational value, particularly for the variable expertise for different usage patterns. As mentioned in the preceding passages with respect to user typologies, the problem lies in *the low informational value of the stable variables of an individual for a specific usage situation*. As described already, first and foremost the usage situation, its effects on users and way of usage should be analyzed. Analyses of usage situations in media psychology are done primarily through cognition-psychological approaches, which originate largely from human-computer interaction.

---

85 Cf. *ZIMBARDO/GERRIG* (1996), p. 527.

86 Cf. *JACKSON ET AL.* (2005), p. 95 et seq.

87 *SCHMITT* (2005), p. V.

88 Cf. *KRÄMER* (2004), p. 658 et seqq.

89 Cf. *KRÄMER* (2004), p. 658 et seqq.

90 Cf. *KRÄMER* (2004), p. 659.

91 *KRÄMER* (2004), p. 660.

3.2.4 Analysis on Cognitive-Psychological Basis

"The description and explanation of human thought and understanding and the associated functional areas - for example perception, attention, memory, problem solving, conclusions – is the subject matter of cognitive psychology".[92]

Cognition psychologists assume the idea of man to be that of a rational decision maker.[93] Popular models deal with problem solving, processing capacity, and doing tasks successively amongst others.[94] Since there is a connection of computer applications and psychological aspects within human-computer interaction,[95] cognition psychologists also deal primarily with questions/doubts that arise.

It is a characteristic procedure for cognitive observation approaches of usage situations to *break up* actions into course of action, usage situation and sequence of actions so that they can be *observed successively and/or separately from one another*. A first step is mostly analyses of tasks which have to be executed to get an overview of the requirements when being in the preliminary stage of a product development.[96] Such analyses of tasks can be found with *DUFFY/PALMER/MEHLENBACHER* which analyses how the tasks for online help for software are done. This also fits in the scope of this analysis. *DUFFY/PALMER/MEHLENBACHER* structures the human work process as follows:[97]

- Representing the problem
- Accessing help
- Selecting a topic
- Searching for relevant information
- Obtaining the needed information
- Comprehending the information
- Navigating to other topics
- Applying the help information

It is doubtful whether usage situations in the context of online help and support can be really understood and explained through this procedure (breaking up of actions). The suitability of an early point in time in software development is not to be questioned. However, the direct effect of Customer Self Service Offerings as well as the perception and manner of use of the user possibly cannot be explained by this kind of situation and/or task analysis. Therefore the usage situation is assumed to be the basis of the analysis but this is objectively evaluated for all users equally. In reality it cannot be assumed that a user would find and understand the adequate help topic in each case or that he would then still be interested in further topics. Just

92 *SCHWAN/HESSE* (2004), p. 74.

93 Cf. also the concept of *Homo Oeconomicus*. Also cf. *FRANZ* (2004).

94 Cf. *SCHWAN/HESSE* (2004), p. 74 et seq.

95 *KRÄMER* (2004), p. 646 accounts that in 1973 the first article was published in this context, that covered the psychological research of two computer languages.

96 Cf. *BEU* (2003), p. 67 et seqq.

97 *DUFFY/PALMER/MEHLENBACHER* (1992), p. 185 et seqq.

the work package "Representing the Problem" may possibly turn out differently for different users.

Over and above the sheer (cognitive) activities of the user other determining factors are of importance. *BEU* describes by way of example the characteristics of the work environment which are to be analyzed: (1) organizational work environment (work group, management structure), (2) interruptions, (3) attitude and organizational culture (IT-principles, organizational structure), (4) work control, (5) hardware, (6) software, (7) physical environment, (8) work place design, (9) security and health.[98]

We can get the premises for the cognitive processing steps from these general parameters which the user uses to carry out his tasks. Except for the usability for a private usage context it seems to be doubtful whether besides the described objective features there are other relevant, *subjective* aspects for the explanation of usage situations. Here, in connection with service problems which take center stage in After Sales Customer Self Service, the assumption in the current study is that subjective aspects have considerable importance.

It can generally be highlighted positively in case of cognitive psychological analysis that the use of online offerings with respect to a certain usage context can be specified and analyzed (see the tasks analysis regarding online help). Situation specific basic parameters can also be included in the analysis (see characteristics of work environment above). However it is a disadvantage that the subdivision of work situations does not lead to an analysis of the usage situation in the intended sense. Not all sub tasks of a usage are executed or perceived by a user in the same way. The same is valid for the general parameters of the usage situation. Here we need to touch upon the importance of subjective aspects of the usage situation (e.g. fear, trust, etc.) which can close the gap in explanation. Exactly these parts - which are subjectively perceived differently and which map all users to objectively same usage situations, environment and work pattern - can only be observed inadequately. By cognitive psychological approaches. Particularly for the current debate subjective usage aspects are observed, which rules out a conventional cognitive psychological approach as an instrument of study.

3.2.5 Analysis of Subjective Components of the Usage Situation

Indications that emotions and similar subjective constructs for questions raised and goals of the questions raised are of considerable relevance are to be found in financial literature[99], as well as in literature pertaining to human-computer interaction.[100]

BENKENSTEIN/FORBERGER discusses that in case of quality evaluation of a service cognitive as well as affective components play a role *which cannot be clearly separated by the individual.* In recent times the idea that emotions and/or moods have a strong influence here has gained acceptance. Previous analyses of such processes were influenced by an understanding of the evaluation of the service as a *purely cognitive-rational process.*[101]

---

98 Cf. *BEU* (2003), p. 69 et seqq.

99 Cf. *BENKENSTEIN/FORBERGER* (2001).

100 Cf. *BLYTHE/WRIGHT* (2004).

101 Cf. *BENKENSTEIN/FORBERGER* (2001), p. 329 et seqq.

This relevance of the subjective components can be carried over to services like Customer Self Service and therefore to the areas of media psychology and human-computer interaction. Some authors call for a renunciation of the conventional observations of usage which are often influenced by focus on cognitive and objective aspects.[102] This is also the aim of the current discussion.

One of the main reasons for the current intensified emergence of requirements within human-computer interaction can be seen in the increasing prevalence of IuK technologies in the sphere of private life – *cognitive approaches anchored in industrial psychology* often cannot do justice to this phenomenon.[103] Here the existing assumption is that private users and/or customers do not search for functionally satisfying products which are simply characterized by effectiveness and efficiency; rather they *seek experiences which are satisfying*. The *subjective experience of the individual* is in focus.[104] To record this overall (macroscopic) observation of the product usage experience of the user is required which also takes emotional aspects into consideration and not only motorical and cognitive ones: "In other words: knowing, doing and feeling; the wholly trinity of interaction."[105] Even NIELSEN, who is known traditionally for a dominant techno-functional oriented design emphasizes: "In talking about a design's 'look and feel', feel wins every time.[106] The relevance of subjective components of the usage situation for the goals of this study is thus reinforced.

A mood is defined as a "relatively non-directional subjectively experienced mental state[107] or as a *prolonged emotional state which determines a person's view of life as well as his behaviour for a certain period of time.*[108] The last quote clarifies that the construct of mood becomes understandable by the construct of emotion: "Emotion. A complex pattern of changes; it encompasses physiological excitement, feelings, cognitive processes, and behavioural reactions as a response to a situation which is perceived as being of personal importance."[109] In spite of the complex structure of emotions and their far-reaching implications (physiological, unconscious, cognitive, etc.) a consensus has been arrived at to understand *moods as subjective components with longer durations than emotions and greater intensity.*[110] Additionally there is general consensus that emotions are directly related to objects, i.e. they can be easily assigned to their triggers and their behavioural consequences, which is difficult in case of moods.[111] Moreover it is certain that emotions and moods are unconscious to a considerable extent.[112]

---

102 Cf. *Knopp* (2001).

103 Cf. *Blythe/Wright* (2004), p. XVI.

104 Cf. *Overbeeke et al.* (2004), p. 7 et seqq.

105 *Overbeeke et al.* (2004), p. 8.

106 *Nielsen* (2004), p. 103.

107 *Silberer/Jaeckel* (1996), p. 20.

108 *Zimbardo/Gerrig* (1996), p. 521.

109 *Zimbardo/Gerrig* (2005), p. 547.

110 Cf. *Zillmann* (2004), p. 102.

111 Cf. *Zillmann* (2004), p. 102.

112 Cf. *Silberer/Jaeckel* (1996), p. 6.

Some authors also use the terms emotion and mood synonymously.[113] Other terms to be found in literature additionally are affect, feeling,[114] tonality of experience, evaluative judgment,[115] drive, passion, whim, temperament.[116] Even in English, there are different terms used which as per definition do not match their direct translations. This leads to additional problems in areas of definition and research (e.g. mood, feeling, emotion, etc.)[117] Due to the evident complexity of the constructs emotion and mood and the variety in constructs in the area of subjective components it becomes difficult to find a uniform definition and as a result an object of investigation which would be the focus of the observation. This vagueness of definition has always been problematic: "just as in the case of the definition of emotions none of the suggested definitions of moods so has found general acceptance.[118]

Within the current discussion subjective aspects to be analyzed cannot and must not be differentiated clearly, particularly in the scope of the aimed explorative observation of usage situations. The human experience (within the usage situation) should be analyzed macroscopically or globally to record as many facets as possible. A view already described by *SCHMALT:* "[It] seems that recently [source1982] The view has prevailed amongst many emotion theoreticians that <<feelings>> and <<ambition>, <<emotion>> and <<motivation>>, <<to feel>>and <<to want>> are inseparably connected to each other and in principle enclose the same phenomenon."[119]

Particularly because this article makes a first attempt to clarify the importance of subjective components of the usage situation in After Sales Customer Self Service a clear definitional separation of the subjective constructs is not compulsorily necessary. Rather this is about an initial collection of indications which should be comprehensive for the usage contexts and situations. Exactly this attempt speaks for a global observation of subjective components of the usage situation, the possible procedures for which are checked later.

There are several methods available for capturing moods and similar subjective components of a usage situation. One method is the measurement of physical indicators; however this is difficult irrespective of the type of indicator:

With respect to the indicator facial expression the problem is that it can be deliberately influenced. Further indicators like neuro-physical, endocrine (glandular secretion) or autonomous (autonomous nervous system) showed promise but could not differentiate even the basic emotions in studies.[120] In addition to this the necessary technical complexity often causes confusion among the test subjects and leads in as a consequence to erroneous measurements.[121]

---

113 Cf. *ABELE* (1995), p. 14

114 Cf. *SPIES* (1995), p. 13.

115 Cf. *ABELE* (1995), p. 14.

116 Cf. *ROST* (2005), p. 51.

117 Further insight on differing constructs in the field of subjective components is not further necessary, as merely emotions and moods are discussed. For an overview of the various descriptions and classifications cf. *ROST* (2005), p. 51 et seqq.

118 *MEYER/REISENZEIN/SCHÜTZWOHL* (2001), p. 40.

119 *SCHMALT* (1982), quoted from *ROST* (2005), p. 51.

120 Cf. *ZILLMANN* (2004), p. 108 et seqq.

121 Cf. *SILBERER/JAEKEL* (1996), p. 44 et seqq.

Yet another method is the verbal or written standardized survey. It should however be noted that people often cannot judge in which mood they are or which emotion they are feeling at the moment. Furthermore standardized recordings (e.g. by agreeing to statements) have limitations as it is not clear whether the respondents understand each question in the intended direction.[122]

Even without technical complexity and without the problems of a standardized survey and evaluation moods can be understood and captured from statements of a person, their manner of speaking and their body language as is observed in qualitative studies.[123] These indicators have however to be evaluated in a differentiated manner as statements basically do not have to be consistent with prevailing moods and emotions. This makes demands on the experience of the experimenter to capture subjective aspects or evaluations which are valid.[124] In light of the discussed background of the study as a first attempt at clarification in the field of After Sales Customer Self Service the conclusion is that of a qualitative and strongly interpretative procedure. From a standardized questionnaire for example, subjective aspects which have not been isolated till date cannot be initially analyzed.

Earlier conventional approaches of human-computer interaction and media psychology were analyzed, which lead to nowhere with respect to the instruments for analyzing and evaluating subjective components of the usage situation. In this paragraph unconventional new approaches from these research areas have been found and are used as instruments of analysis. These instruments aim to fulfil the existing prerequisites of a method of analysis for the questions which need to be answered, i.e. they observe the usage situation centrally while taking into consideration the subjective components.

According to *NIELSEN* the methods used to measure subjective aspects including relevant constructs – as in case of usability – of satisfaction or of emotions and moods within human-computer interaction are not elaborate enough.[125] The marginal consideration of subjective usage aspects are explained by *NIELSEN*: according to him the subjective components of the usage situation are much more difficult than objective aspects and can hardly be captured in a standardized manner,[126] which in turn leads to increased complexity of the analysis and supports the choice of a qualitative process for the course of analysis.

Measurements of subjective satisfaction within human-computer interaction are currently limited to a summary evaluation by the test subjects at the end of an unit of analysis (e.g. questionnaire: "Were you satisfied overall with the application?"), emotional evaluations are made from the individual statements of the test subjects (e.g. "cool" or "boring")[127]

---

122 Cf. *SILBERER/JAEKEL* (1996), p. 30 et seqq.

123 Cf. *SILBERER/JAEKEL* (1996), p. 5 et seq.

124 Cf. *SILBERER/JAEKEL* (1996), p. 6.

125 Cf. *NIELSEN* (2004), p. 104.

126 Cf. *NIELSEN* (2004), p. 104.

127 Cf. *NIELSEN* (2004), p. 104.

STEIN/TRABASSO[128] set up a process model which describes the emergence of emotions during Internet surfing. Within this approach, different components, their peculiarity and connection play a role through the build-up of basic emotions like joy, anger or surprise. These components are the emergence of new events, expectations about the achievability of goals due to these events, the subjective progress in the process of goal achievement, etc. amongst others.

HASSENZAHL set up a model which can be applied to the usage of a website and in its conception gives greater importance to subjective components in the scope of a usage situation: "Not only has the utility and usability of a product to be guaranteed, but also its attraction and an overall 'positive' usage experience. Over and above this the product should maybe even evoke emotions".[129]

Additionally in case of *HASSENZAHL* the usage situation has a strong effect on the evaluation of product quality. A vivid description is given by him in case of the example of an ATM which can be easily and intuitively understood, particularly for the first usages and which generates satisfaction for the customer. However, if the customer is in a hurry in a specific situation and moreover familiar with the machine, even small and easily understandable steps can prove a hindrance and even be frustrating. Even though the machine still possesses the quality 'easily understandable', this feature is irrelevant for the evaluation of the given usage situation. Usages therefore should be observed in a situation-specific and/or context-specific manner.[130]

A central parallel of the approach of *HASSENZAHL* to this debate and discussion is the assumption that *different usage situations have a considerable influence on the perception, usage and evaluation of a website/product.*

HASSENZAHL also differentiates between two situation-specific *Usage-Modes*[131]: the *Goal-Mode* and the *Action-Mode*. In the Goal-Mode the subject is strongly focused on a concrete goal in which effectiveness and efficiency come to the forefront; the type of behaviour is dominated by the goal aimed at. In the Action-Mode *the usage takes center stage* and the user lets himself be lead spontaneously and explores the product.[132]

These different Usage Modes imply in case of consequent observation different moods and emotions of the user as well. The theoretical framework developed by *HASSENZAHL* can thus be used for orientation. However *HASSENZAHL* uses standardized processes (questionnaires) to capture the diverse aspects of product usage, which for the purpose of an initial observation under the scope of this analysis has been evaluated as leading to nowhere.

---

128 Publication of *STEIN/TRABASSO* (1992). Quoted in the following after *OHLER/NIEDING* (2000), p. 230 et seq.

129 *HASSENZAHL* (2006), p. 147.

130 Cf. *HASSENZAHL* (2004), p. 33 et seq.

131 Cf. *HASSENZAHL* (2004), p. 39 et seqq.

132 Cf. *HASSENZAHL* (2004), p. 39 et seqq.

Similar to the mentioned Usage modes *COVE/WALSH*[133] described in 1988 in a theoretical observation different usage patterns of the Internet dependent on the respective usage context and differentiated between goal-focused information search (Search Browsing), searching for interesting information which could be understood as ‚browsing' (General-Purpose-Browsing) and a completely undirected search (Serendipity-Browsing)

An aimed situation specific analysis of Customer Self Service Usages with focus on subjective components can apparently happen by capturing the mode and/or mood in combination with the usage pattern of the user. The examples presented by *HASSENZAHL* (Goal-Mode/Action-Mode) as well as *COVE/WALSH* (Search-Browsing/General-Purpose-Browsing/ Serendipity-Browsing) can be understood as a typification of usage situations. The question which needs to be answered according to the adequate qualitative recording method still remains. An analysis from media psychology within which a typification of usage situations was conducted on the basis of usage situations is to be found at *AOL*. In this the concept of usage constitution was used.[134] In this way *AOL* presents seven different usage constitutions for the medium Internet as shown in figure 1.

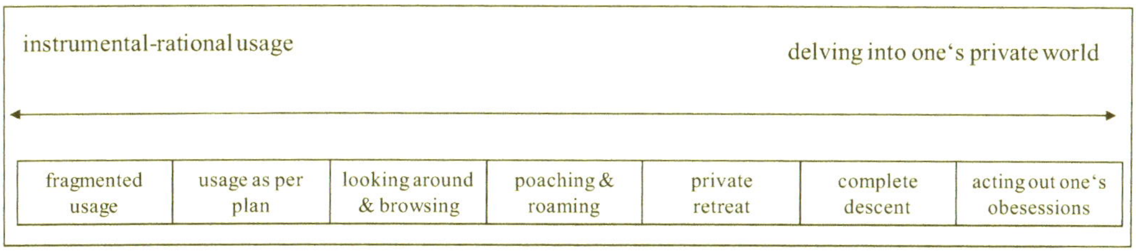

Figure 1: Usage constitutions during surfing in Internet[135]

The *fragmented usage* shows the usage of the Internet as a fast information medium. The user does not get distracted by side effects (e.g. advertisements, Pop-ups, etc.) and would like to finish it at the earliest (e.g. accessing the TV program). The usage as per plan describes similarly the strongly goal oriented behaviour of the user in which he is also able to exploit the diversity of the Internet as well as invest time. In an investigative fashion, the user searches for price comparison calculators, test reports, search engines, etc. (e.g. information before purchasing a new mobile phone). A type of drifting in the Internet is shown in *looking around & browsing*. The user follows his spontaneous thoughts and listens to some music on trial, looks at the costs of the CD, let's himself be lead by cross selling offers and loses track of time in doing all this. However he remains mostly on the Internet sites known to him. Similarly in case of *poaching & roaming* the interest of the user takes center stage as he kills time while browsing the offers and thematic diversity of the Internet. The user displays curiosity while searching for special and/or quaint sites which surprise him and which he can show to friends later. Usage as relaxation – this is how one could describe the central intention of *private retreat*. Similarly as many people do it in the case of television, the user searches for a place and/or an activity aloof from the daily rut to simply be able to switch off. This could lead to different Internet sites, varying as per the user. The *complete descent* is to be understood as a progression of private retreat in which the user dives deep into the offerings of the Internet. The possibility of continuously new configurations and options leads to the creation

133 Publication of *COVE/WALSH* (1988). Quoted in the following after *OHLER/NIEDING* (2000), p. 230.

134 Cf. online *AOL* (2003).

135 Online *AOL* (2003), p. 37.

of a kind of usage flow (e.g. online gaming). Finally the last usage constitution is shown in the *acting out of one's obsessions*. In complete anonymity the user can give in to his desires and preferences which would not be possible in the same way in daily life (e.g. sexuality, violence, death, etc.).

Basically for the usage constitution the basic principle of the A-identity is valid: "as a result the individual constitutions are also not strictly separable from one another. Under circumstances the user can even change the constitution during the usage; for example when during the necessity to inform himself he waits a little longer looking at an online offer and browses through the links on the page."[136]

This quality meets the assumption made here half way that the one and the same person can display different usage patterns at different points in time during the course of a day.

A usage constitution for the area of online help and support would presumably fall in the area of *fragmented usage*. Here the customer uses the Internet as an information and/or action medium. He has a clearly defined goal which he wants to reach and does not want to "look right and left or let himself drift into the colourful diversity of offerings of the Internet."[137]. It is to be assumed that while observing the usage for the usage contexts online help and online customer center as well as the subordinate usage situations, different usage constitutions will be discovered; these would be specific to Customer Self service Applications of the After Sales Phase (e.g. accessing a bill or searching for an instruction manual).

3.2.6 Interim Conclusions for the Analysis of the Usage Situation

It can be summarized that for the given question of this study the use of conventional methods of human-computer interaction and media psychology would only be partly practicable. Table 2 shows the advantages and disadvantages of conventional approaches as well as the discovered implications for the analysis methods to be applied. It can be summarized that for the given question of this study the use of conventional methods of human-computer interaction and media psychology would only be partly practicable. Table 2 shows the advantages and disadvantages of conventional approaches as well as the discovered implications for the analysis methods to be applied.

[136] Cf. Online *AOL* (2003), p. 37.

[137] Cf. Online *AOL* (2003), p. 38.

approach	Advantages/potentials	disadvantages/problems	conclusions for the method
usability testing	The usage situation is simulated and direct effects, aspects, etc. in interaction with an application are observed.	Usability is in principle evaluated by effectiveness and efficiency. Subjective aspects should however be observed separately; these influence the construct satisfaction/acceptance considerably and are independent of effectiveness and efficiency. This has been proven.	➢ Direct observation of the usage situation (simulation or reconstruction is evaluated as leading to results). ➢ Subjective aspects independent of effectiveness and efficiency should be observed as the stated new usage barriers can thus be discovered.
usage activities (-contexts) and socio-demographic features	The acceptance of different groups for different usage contexts can be arrived at through the quantitative capturing of internet usage.	The usage situation itself (particularly direct effects of the application, subjective perception and concrete usage patterns, etc.) cannot be analyzed.	➢ It is about a global analysis of usage patterns for the current debate. At the current pint in time this is not leading anywhere.
user typologies and stable variables of the individual	Through an analysis of the preferred usage contexts, the usage duration and diverse socio-demographic variables users can be mapped to certain types and predictions about future usages can be made. Similarly these predictions on the basis of personality characteristics of further stable variables can be made.	A user does not behave as per his type/personality etc. Rather different usage situations evoke different reaction and behavior patterns. This has been proven.	➢ For the given questions it would not make sense to start from the qualities of the user/person. ➢ Rather to the differentiate between different usage contexts and situations, the starting point, should be situative effects and short-term subjective perceptions. ➢ Therefore the goal is to arrive at a typology of usage situations and not a typology of users.
cognitive-psychological observations of the usage situation	There are cognitive approaches with touch upon characteristics of the usage situation (analysis of tasks) and capture further general conditions (e. g. environmental aspects)	Cognitive approaches see the human being as a rational decision maker an do not allow an analysis of subjective aspects of the use situation.	➢ Enquiring about general conditions in the background of the usage situation is evaluated as purposeful. ➢ A cognitive-psychological approach is no evaluated as purposeful. It is primarily problematic that subjective assessments are not taken into consideration, a s well as the division of the usage situation in objective individual aspects which are objective for all users.

Table 2: *Advantages and disadvantages of conventional approaches from human-computer interaction and media psychology*

A positive result of these preliminary considerations is that an adequate approach for analyzing different usage situations has been found through this procedure in usability tests. On the basis of the procedure for creation of user typologies the possibility of creating a typology of usage situations is considered. Additionally the assumption that stable variables of an individual are not primarily responsible for the situation specific perception and usage of a website has been reinforced. Rather situative aspects (characteristics of the situation, environment, situative subjective aspects, etc.) are responsible.

It should however be noted that general subjective aspects (trust, anxiety, anger, etc.) do not have much importance from the perspective of conventional approaches of human-computer interaction and media psychology. At the same time these are of considerable importance when it is assumed that a usage situation has not only objective parts but subjective ones as well.

To account for possibilities for capturing these subjective components, these have been touched upon separately again. The scope of definition for the subjective components of the usage situation to be observed has been laid out globally. One reason for this is due to the number of disputed definitions in the field of subjective constructs. The other reason is self-explanatory nature of the analysis as a first explorative search for indications.

It could further be shown that requirements for a strong consideration of subjective aspects already exist in financial writings (service evaluation) and those of human-computer interaction (e.g. website evaluation), which supports the intention of this article. In this connection the use of a standardized method has been evaluated as unsuitable as subjective components cannot be captured in a factually adequate manner. In case of an observation of previously subjective components of a usage situation within human-computer interaction and media psychology it was found that some "unconventional" (niche-) approaches exist which make allowance for subjective aspects. These workings come close to a typification of usage situations, however are to be found as desired in a qualitative method of capturing only for the approach of usage constitutions. Insofar this approach to follow is to be examined regarding its suitability in the connection of this analysis.

4 Analysis of Usage Constitution for Overcoming User Barriers

To follow the construct of usage, constitutions as well as its theoretical background will be presented to show to what extent this approach is suitable for arriving at conclusions regarding the designing of web applications in general and Customer Self Service in particular.

The approach of usage constitutions originate from the field of Pre Sales in which primary consumption habits as well as reception of advertisements were studies with respect to different media.

The basis for the morphological market psychology and therefore for the approach of usage constitution and/or constitution marketing is morphological psychology. As in case of the human-computer interaction in psychology as well it is partially rejected that this is too steeped in a cognitive-scientific tradition, in which the human being is considered to be a *computing machine*[138] and feelings only as *affective concomitant phenomena.*[139] In scope of the increasing relevance of subjective aspects of experience qualitative methods are however spreading fast as ascertained by *MAYRING*: "Purely quantitative thinking has become fragile; thinking which comes close to human beings and things by testing and missing, experimenting with them and examining their statistical representation without having previously understood the subject-matter and recording its quality."[140] *MELCHERS*, who complains about the usual procedure for measuring phenomena within the current market research, also argues similarly: "measurements serve the purpose of ascertaining which behaviours contained in the model in concrete cases will be given. Measurements without models make no sense."[141]

According to this a new orientation from the usual quantitative measurements to qualitative observations should take place which then can be used as a basis for quantitative measurements if desired. *JÜTTEMANN* discusses that the change in orientation of the academic psychology can be achieved by the introduction of morphology of human behaviour and experi-

[138] Cf. *ALLESCH* (2005), p. 168.

[139] Cf. *ALLESCH* (2005), p. 168.

[140] Cf. *MAYRING* (1996), p. 1.

[141] Cf. *MELCHERS* (1993), p. 34.

ence, i. e. a *morphological psychology*.[142] According to *ALLESCH morphological psychology WILHELM SALBER*s applies here[143]: "to bring these things to speech they must at first be seen in connection. A word has meaning only in a complete sentence. Only in 'context' can it be understood how something functions."[144]

From these preliminary observations two important points in the context of the study must be highlighted:

- The concept of morphological psychology supports the assumption made in this article that cognitive-psychological as well as quantitative methods are poorly suited for describing the subjective experience in concrete usage situations.

The origins of morphological psychology can be found e.g. in *GOETHE*[145] and within the psychology of coherent perception. *Morphology* is commonly defined as the doctrine of figures, shapes, forms and structure. According to *FITZEK* is such a definition too limited. It is rather of central importance for morphology to deal with "formation and alteration"[146], and the metamorphosis of figures. *SALBER* himself describes the morphological psychology as the method of *moving with the process of experience*. By taking the Goethian fundamental idea of metamorphosis into consideration "we can see directly how psyche arises from psyche".[147] Morphological psychology is a qualitative research method and in the tradition of *FREUD* shows a continuous further development and a strong, close bonding with its theoretical framework".[148] Besides being related to *GOETHE*s morphology and to *FREUDS* psychology morphological psychology has its origins in *the psychology of coherent perception*.[149]

Central in the psychology of coherent perception is the *principle of holism* which was first presented by *VON EHRENFELS*[150] in 1890 who used to work with musical melodies. According to this the whole is not the same as the sum of its parts: the same melody can be recognized in another tune; if the individual tones in the melody are arranged differently the form of the melody cannot be made out.[151] *WERTHEIMER* proved the fundamental idea of holism in 1912 by showing that two adjacent lines when shown at different times give the impression of movement: one line seems to move up and down.[152] The trials of *WERTHEIMER*s experiments were described as revolutionary as they showed that a new quality could arise without any physical basis for it; this proves the principle of holism.[153]

---

142 Cf. *JÜTTEMANN* (2004), p. 147 et seqq.

143 *ALLESCH* (2005), p. 170 et seq.

144 *SALBER* (1995), p. 6.

145 Cf. *GOETHE* (1987), (First edition 1796).

146 *FITZEK* (1994), p. 45.

147 *SALBER* (1965), p. 95.

148 Cf. *SALBER* (1965), p. 11.

149 Cf. *MELCHERS* (1993), p. 29.

150 Cf. *VON EHRENFELS* (1978).

151 Cf. *VON EHRENFELS* (1978), p. 11 et seqq.

152 Cf. *WERTHEIMER* (1925), p. 5.

153 Cf. *FITZEK/SALBER* (1996), p. 34.

This anchoring within the psychology of perception has given rise to the idea that the psychology of coherent perception is just the same as the psychology of perception.[154] In psychological reference material the laws of perception are usually simply presented where the psychology of perception is mentioned like the law of nearness, law of similarity or the law of good coherent perception for which the psychology of coherent perception is known.[155] That the psychology of coherent perception need not limit itself to the field of perception was primarily clarified by *LEWIN*: "It would be wrong to view the meaning of this holistically positioned theory as in the theory of coherent perception only restricted the narrow area of the psychology of perception from which the term 'form' originates (…). I would like to believe that we are at the beginning of a very dramatic catalysis of our psychological concept formation, based on of the concept of form in the sense of a dynamic-holistic system that can majorly change the complete structure of our basic psychological concepts and research methods".[156]

LEWIN postulates subsequently that units of observation should always be laid out holistically to able to analyze the *specific form of experience* (*LEWIN* speaks of actions as a whole) in all its facets.[157] The *outer surroundings* (objective general conditions) as well as the *inner surroundings* (subjective aspects *within* the individual) should be thereby taken into consideration. *LEWIN* clarifies this with the example of manual labour by describing studies which have shown that identical tasks lead to a dissimilar degree of tiredness, if their psychological signification is different.[158] This applies to the one and same individual in different situations.[159] At the same time *FITZEK/SALBER*[160] parallely discussed a further example, also introduced by *LEWIN*.[161] So thus the activity of writing can take different forms depending on the current context of action. Writing a letter in calligraphy stands out differently (e.g. accentuation of the motorical components) from compiling an official communication.[162]

The bases postulated by *LEWIN* were taken over by *SALBER* in the morphological psychology and correspond moreover with the basic assumptions made in this article. The relevance of the subjective components of a usage situation (inner surrounds) are also mentioned here and it is assumed that objectively same actions may be perceived subjectively differently. The example of a tariff change in comparison with accessing a bill can be mentioned. Even when the task steps are objectively very similar, the usage situation can be very different from a subjective viewpoint. This is why transposing research results from the Pre Sales Phase into the After Sales Management are doubtful.

---

154 Cf. *JUKL* (2001), p. 206 et seqq.

155 Cf. *ZIMBARDO/GERRIG* (1996), p. 130 et seqq.

156 *LEWIN* (1982), p. 101.

157 Cf. *LEWIN* (1982), p. 101.

158 Cf. *LEWIN* (1982), p. 101 et seqq.

159 Cf. *LEWIN* (1982), p. 103 et seqq.

160 Cf. *FITZEK/SALBER* (1996).

161 Cf. *LEWIN* (1982).

162 Cf. *FITZEK/SALBER* (1996), p. 97 et seqq.

Analogous to the holistic nature of actions as postulated by *LEWIN* so-called *units of effect* are observed in morphological psychology. This "wheelwork of conditions- with its points of disturbance and development–can be presented as a hexagram."[163] Within these units of effect the tensions of psychic occurrences can be visualized: "In all structural processes we find as basic forms adjustment, alteration, dispersion, alteration, equipment and adoption."[164]

The basic framework of each single effects structure, whether it is that of the Internet or of an activity, e. g. eating chocolate, is formed by the six described poles in the following figure:

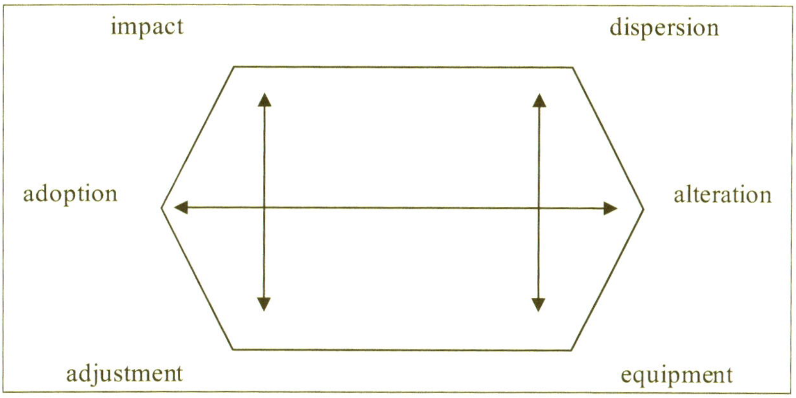

Figure 2: Units of effect of morphological psychology[165]

Within morphological market psychology units of effect on products (PWE) are discussed rather than just units of effect.[166] To help understand the principle of a unit of effect (on products) the model and the connection to the construct of usage constitution with a concrete example from morphological market psychology is used to illustrate the same. The units of effect on products of beer consumption are to be seen as in figure 2.

163 *SALBER* (1995), p. 36.

164 *SALBER* (1969), p. 64.

165 Cf. Online *VIERBOOM/HÄRLEN* (2009), p. 1.

166 Cf. *MELCHERS* (1993), p. 46 et seqq.

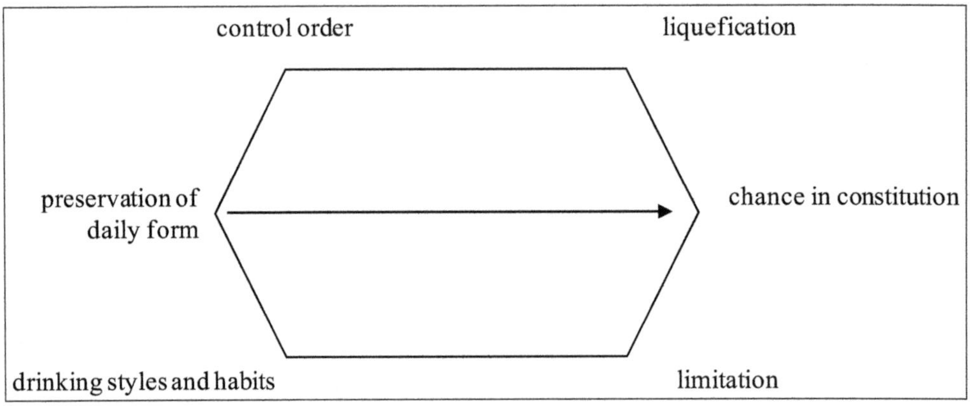

Figure 3: Units of effect on products for beer consumption [167]

The six poles of units of effect on poles are as follows:[168]

Adoption: *Adoption* describes how a person with aspirations of security, a need for used/known states, deals with a subject/product/activity. As shown in figure 3 in the case of drinking beer, this means that the consumer does not want to distance himself too far from a rational daily life usage constitution and/or wants to keep in the back of his mind what would await him the next day. The pole "adoption" of the units of effect on products is subsumed under the description "preservation of daily form".[169] This aspect of the units of effect stands mostly for the *wish for stability.*

Alteration: In *alteration* it is shown how the initial aspirations for stability and security are changed *willingly* or *unwillingly* by the subject/product and what develops as a result. The tension between adoption and alteration describes mostly the main character of a unit of effect on a product. The beer drinker would like to reach exactly this *change in constitution.* For example the *end-of-the-working-day beer* is very widespread to create distance from the stress of daily life. This aspect of the unit of effect on the product stands mostly for *willing* or *unwilling change*. In the example preservation of daily form and change of constitution are the contrasting tensions which the beer drinker has to reconcile.[170]

---

[167] Cf. Online *VIERBOOM/HÄRLEN* (2006), p. 1.

[168] Own elaboration under observance of *SALBER* (1969), p. 64 et seqq., *MELCHERS* (1993), p. 28 et seqq., and *IFM WIRKUNGEN+STRATEGIEN* (2001), p. 23 et seqq.

[169] Cf. *MELCHERS* (1993), p. 49 et seq.

[170] Cf. *IFM WIRKUNGEN+STRATEGIEN* (2001), p. 30.

Adjustment: In adjustment the rules, laws, etc. which need to be kept in mind for a successful and/or satisfactory interaction with the subject come forth. The mentioned phenomenon of the *end-of-the-working-day beer* already indicates that in case of beer drinking these are different drinking styles and habits which take effect. This aspect of the unit of effect on products stands mostly for *rules, structures and order, which a person must himself create while interacting with a product or submit to.*

Impact: In the case of *impact* it becomes clear in which manner the subject and the individual (in the scope of the existing rules) affect each other. In case of beer consumption a *control order* covers the drinking styles which in case of impact takes effect and communicates to the beer drinker that he should restrain himself. The drinking styles can accommodate the control order or make the control difficult. An example is given in case of someone who intends not to drink at all (support for the control order), however comes to a boisterous celebration (drinking styles work in contrast).[171] This aspect of the unit of effect of product shows, *how the individual interacts with the subject; this can be successful or unsuccessful.*

Dispersion: In *dispersion* it becomes clear which wishes and ideas appear in interaction with the subject as well as which intrinsic fears and apprehensions which remain unconscious take effect here. The distance to the daily life should disperse and increase during the consumption of beer which is described *as liquefaction*: "At first the speech becomes more fluent then social boundaries fluidize as well."[172] Exactly the fluidization of control is objectionable and displeasing while drinking beer and the consumer would like to avoid this as a rule. This aspect of the units of effect on products stands for *ideals and (often unconscious) fears in interaction with the subject.*

Equipment: In *equipment* limitations become evident which restrict the interaction with the subject. These restrictions could originate from the outer surroundings, and also be that of the subject or the individual. Beer drinkers therefore lay out limits which limit the fluidization or get these from the partner. There is also the possibility that "beer brands – particularly the premium brands – have given their brand image characteristics of limitation".[173] As the consumer of such a brand the fluidization remains in a limited area. This aspect of the unit *of effect on products shows limitations, to which the individual must comply or which are the prerequisites thereof.*

The units of effect on products with their six poles build the basis for an understanding of the different usage constitutions: in case of the different solution types (constitutions) certain aspects (poles) dominate the unit of effect on the products. E.g. in the case of the boozer the fluidization dominates (see below). As shown in figure 4 it is usual to show the solution types before the unit of effect on products and/or unit of effect to simplify understanding and sequence.

[171] Cf. *Melchers* (1993), p. 50, and *IFM Wirkungen+Strategien* (2001), p. 31.

[172] *Melchers* (1993), p. 51.

[173] *IFM Wirkungen+Strategien* (2001), p. 31.

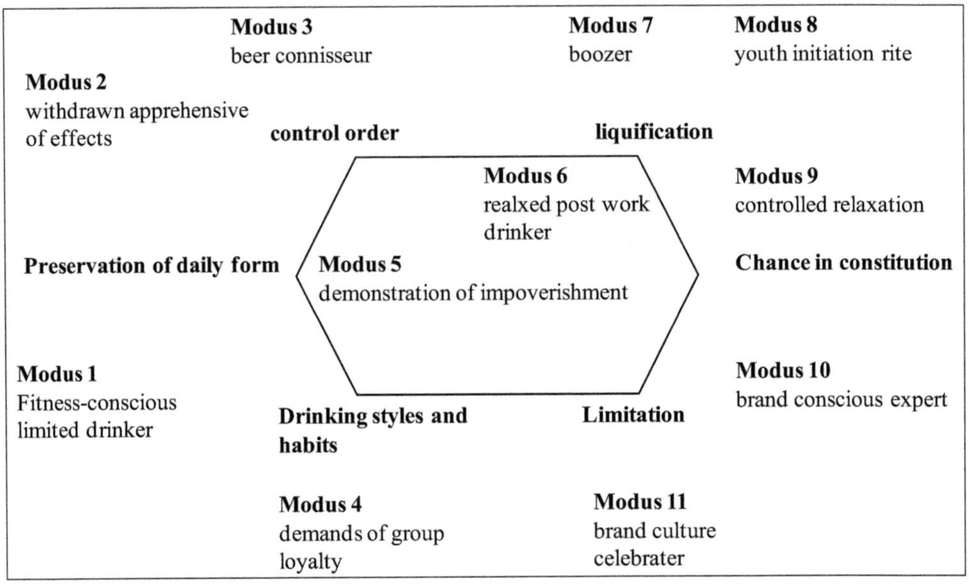

Figure 4: *Solution types in interaction with the units of effect on products for beer drinking*[174]

The different solution types and/or usage constitutions are "not personnel types, rather they are usage styles"[175], i.e. a user of a product is also not limited to a certain usage style. Each solution type is at the same time a certain usage style which is recognizable from the type descriptions (e.g. relaxed post work drinker or controlled relaxer). The presented solution types are ideally typical, particularly distinctive usage style in which all users can be arranged.[176] The morphological view of the markets on which it is based is shown in figure 5.

174 *IFM WIRKUNGEN+STRATEGIEN* (2001), p. 35.

175 *IFM WIRKUNGEN+STRATEGIEN* (2001), p. 35.

176 Cf. *IFM WIRKUNGEN+STRATEGIEN* (2001), p. 35 et seqq.

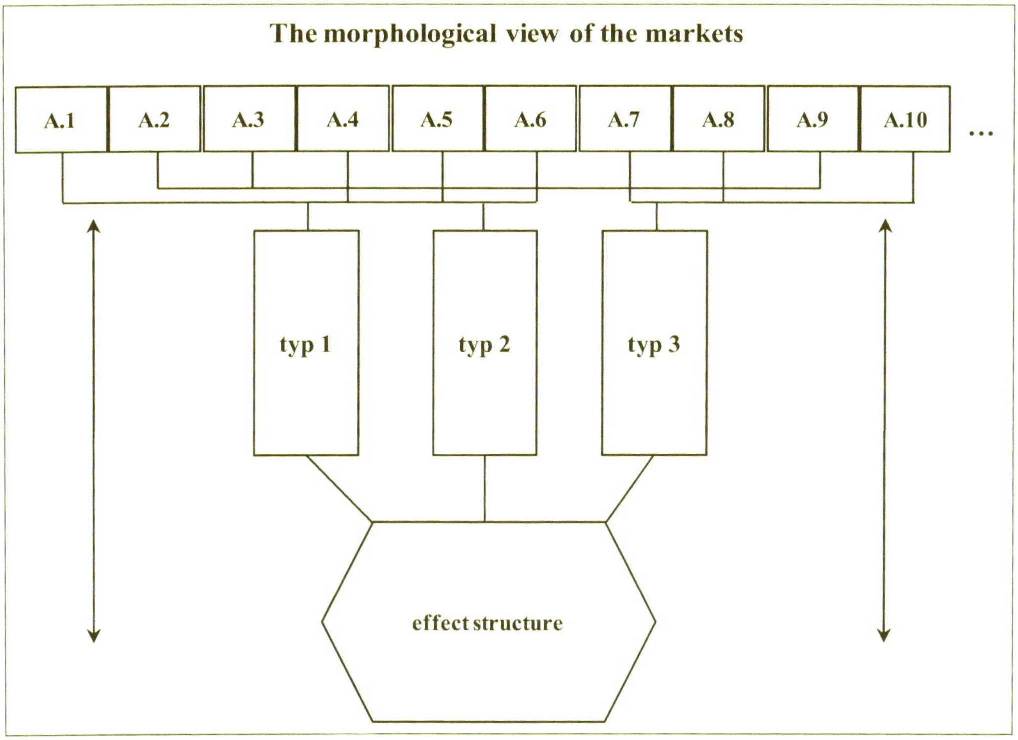

Figure 5: *The morphological view of the markets*[177]

Every customer shows a certain personal usage of a product (e. g. A.2). This type of usage can be mapped to the super ordinate usage type due to a corresponding and/or similar pattern (e. g. type 1). The discovered usage types are different solutions for the imminent tensions within the effect structure which each product has. Thus every person who uses a certain product is representative for PWE it is based on. This can be valid for persons who do not use the product because they do not want to deal with the effects thereof or do not want to be shocked by it.[178]

It is however important to stress that in connection with qualitative studies as well as with morphological psychology we cannot talk of statistical representativeness. Generally according to *DAMMER/SZYMKOWIAK* statistical representativeness in the scope of small sample checks as is normal in case of qualitative processes is not a relevant criterion. Statistical relevance has a very high importance in case of quantitative methods which are about ascertainment of the frequency of a feature within a population.[179] According to *LAMNEK* as well a quantitative-statistical evaluation is ruled out for qualitative interviews due to methodological and pragmatic reasons."[180]

---

177 *MELCHERS* (1993), p. 41.

178 Cf. *MELCHERS* (1993), p. 38 et seqq.

179 Cf. *DAMMER/SZYMKOWIAK* (1998), p. 34 et seqq.

180 *LAMNEK* (2005), p. 402

DAMMER/SZYMKOWIAK introduce in this connection the concept of the *functional-psychological representiveness* which is used in the morphological psychology:[181] "functional-psychological representiveness guarantees that all psychologically relevant principles that determine the market are considered."[182]

For this purpose a number of 30–60 respondents is sufficient. Morphological psychology requires that all possible effects are included in the effect structure which arise in interaction with a researched subject or could arise after thought experiments/in extreme cases. This would render quantifications unnecessary from the very beginning. The results are not any less valid due to the lack of statistic representiveness than those of quantitative designs. In contrast with a quantification of features factual events are to be clarified and understood.[183]

Should the PWE of a product and the corresponding usage styles or constitutions be known, these can be touched upon in the scope of constitution marketing. "Constitution marketing approaches the mood, the state or the conditions in which consumers and business customers are present, who come into contact with certain products and services. These moods, conditions, states are described with the concept 'constitution'. The market is considered to be a psychic field of strengths. Should a human being (customer, consumer) enter this field, he comes under these conditions and strengths. With this knowledge I can enter, steer, change – that is constitution marketing."[184]

Examples for this are the different constitutions of champagne drinking. From this it becomes clear which aspects a champagne brand should touch upon. This cannot be in agreement within a single brand picture and should be noted. By such analyses it can be arrived at that supposedly similar products can be used in very different constitutions or for very different purposes. This prevents a direct competition between these products. In this way carbonated mineral water is seen by the consumers as a thirst quencher, but un-carbonated water is rather used for continuous hydration. The drinks - both water- are used in basically very different contexts, which even make a parallel use possible.[185] Different constitutions are touched upon also by Milka chocolate and Ritter Sport: "chocolate balls, mini salamis, bread with cheese or ham compete with Ritter chocolates in case of active constitutions and pralines, small cakes chocolate puddings with Milka chocolates in case of narcissism-enjoying constitutions."[186]

Beside the requirements of the basic postulates and the basic assumptions of this study the weaknesses of the study of theory and method must be pointed out. Morphological psychology is often criticized due to its theoretical postulates and practical procedures.[187]

181 Cf. auch *IFM WIRKUNGEN+STRATEGIEN* (2001), p. 81 et seqq.

182 *DAMMER/SZYMKOWIAK* (1998), p. 34

183 Cf. *MELCHERS* (1993), p. 42 et seq.

184 Online *LÖNNEKER* (2006).

185 Cf. *LÖNNEKER* (2007), p. 96 et seq.

186 *LÖNNEKER* (2007), p. 89 et seq.

187 Cf. *ALLESCH* (2005), p. 177 et seq.

5 Usage Constitutions in the Morphological Market Psychology

Usage constitutions or constitutions have increasingly spread primarily as subjects of study within the morphological market and media psychology.[188] In case of published studies[189] it related to those regarding (usage) constitutions in interaction with media as well as the respective type of media and advertisement reception.[190]

Each customer shows a certain personal use of a product (e.g. A.2). This type of use can be mapped to the super ordinate usage type due to a pattern which corresponds/is similar to that of other uses (e.g. type 1). This is the same as a typification of use for different usage constitutions. The discovered usage types (constitutions) are different solutions for the imminent tensions of the effect structure which a product has. Therefore each person who uses a certain product is representative of the effect structure which it is based on.[191] With respect to *AOL* the medium Internet would be based on an effect structure. For this there are different constitutions (type 1: fragmented usage; type 2: usage as per plan, etc.) to be seen. Constitutions and effect structures are worked out from the usage styles of individual users (A.1, A.2, etc.).

Constitution marketing is increasingly described as "the royal road to the modern consumer"[192] as it can explain different motivations, product usages and media usages much more clearly than the usual target audience models. The starting point here is not stable characteristics of the target audience but rather situative and subjective variables.[193] This is also the goal of this study: "Constitution marketing approaches the mood, the state or the conditions in which consumers and business customers are present, who come into contact with certain products and services. These moods, conditions, states are described with the concept 'constitution'. The market is considered to be a psychic field of strengths. Should a human being (customer, consumer) enter this field, he comes under these conditions and strengths. With this knowledge I can enter, steer, change – that is constitution marketing."[194]

Constitutions are described here as moods, conditions and states. Within an *AOL* study it is made clear that usage constitutions "depend closely on the respective needs, goals and states of mind of the user."[195] The concept of constitution is not clearly defined or defined in a limited manner and related *globally to the subjective experience of a situation.* This corresponds to the intended procedure for the first part of this study. This makes the approach of usage constitution appear suitable for the intended procedure.

---

188 Cf. *LÖNNEKER* (2007), p. 89 et seq.

189 Online *KÜHN* (2005), p. 2, describes that a great majority of high quality unreleased studies within the qualitative market research, have up to now remained not easily accessible to the public, such as research communities, because they have been exclusively assigned by companies.

190 *LÖNNEKER* (2007), p. 87 et seq. An example of morphological analysis of the use of media and the reception of advertising is given in the study of *DONNERSTAG/BUCHERT* (2004) relating to the function of media during the course of a day.

191 Cf. *MELCHERS* (1993), p. 38 et seqq.

192 Online *LÖNNEKER* (2003), p. 11.

193 Online *LÖNNEKER* (2003), p. 11.

194 Online *LÖNNEKER* (2006).

195 Online *AOL* (2003), p. 37.

As indicated earlier another important feature of constitutions is that they are impersonal in nature. Individuals can therefore accept different constitutions at different points in time. This also corresponds to the basic assumptions of this study. Here lies the origin of the current success of constitutions and usage constitutions within the Pre Sales research in market and media. They accommodate a comprehensive cultural phenomenon of our times in a special manner: "consumers want to be everything at the same time: young and old, familiar and detached, rich/famous and simple/normal at the very least they do not want to leave out any options of changing themselves any time they choose."[196]

Parallels or confirmations for this are available not only in the field of morphological psychology. *STOJEK/ ULBRICH* postulated for the field of the Internet: "If we seek to define the E-customer, there is no definite profile."[197] And *BARTEL* states the following for his usability study of a website: "regarding the usability tests the unique user could not be defined in spite of an analysis of the target audience."[198]

According to *DAMMER/ SZYMKOWIAK* these core cultural-psychological events and phenomena necessitate a development away from psychology of qualities of the user and in the direction of that of the product or service area and the corresponding usage, as shown by morphological psychology.[199]

The theory and methods of morphological market psychology are not different from that of the morphological psychology in general: "Morphological market psychology is an application of morphological psychology. It shares the latter's theoretical-methodological concepts completely." [200]

CHRISTOPH B. MELCHERS is seen as the founder of morphological market psychology which for the first time aimed at professional use of morphological psychology to clarify market mechanisms.[201] *MELCHERS* himself stresses however that morphological market psychology has been practiced not just since the end of the eighties but that the founder of morphological psychology *WILHELM SALBER* had studied market psychological questions over 40 years ago under the super ordinate concept psychology of daily life.[202]

---

196 *LÖNNEKER* (2003), p. 11.

197 *STOJEK/ULBRICHT* (2001), p. 12.

198 *BARTEL* (2003), p. 114.

199 Cf. *DAMMER/SZYMKOWIAK* (1998), p. 44 et seq.

200 *MELCHERS* (1993), p. 28.

201 Cf. *ALLESCH* (2001), p. 1.

202 Cf. *MELCHERS* (1993), p. 29.

6 Criticism of Morphological Psychology

Fitzek already postulates that morphology gets along only with a lot of difficulty with other instruments of science and "the prominent advocates of morphology are said to be opinionated, uncomfortable scientists."[203] Thus morphological psychology has established itself in the fields of psychological market research[204] and media psychology[205] but occupies only a marginal position in today's psychological knowledge society and is examined critically.[206] This rejection is explained by *Allesch* as being due to the strong unconventionality of the approach as well as the development of a unique language style which can be described as "almost hermetic" [207] and "provocative."[208] Morphological psychology corresponds in few ways to traditional science. Thus the quality of scientific methods is evaluated according to its precision; an approach which can be applied to morphological psychology only with difficulty as it describes phenomena as vague and presents it the same way.[209] Differences are noticeable in demotic descriptions and can be seen in this work as well. The majority of science works with clear-cut definitions of concepts so that facts are described without any ambiguity.

Moreover, importance is attached to precision in most scientific disciplines to measure dimensions of effects and influence, relationships, etc.; this again does not correspond to morphological psychology which is a qualitative method to understand ways of functioning and connections of effects without numeralizing them.

From statements (e. g. 'Usually experienced users fall under this constitution') the questions arises: what does 'usually', 'in rare cases' or 'increased' mean? The problem with such formulations is that scope of interpretation of the interviewer and evaluator increases immensely, particularly that of the sponsor of the study and relevant interested third-parties, to whom the results are communicated.

Just as subjective aspects on the side of the respondents have a strong effect, the same is the case for the evaluators and particularly the audience for the results. Scientific methods are characterized by objectivity, which is mostly guaranteed by quantifiable results. Morphological psychology welcomes the numerous subjective influences and in fact criticizes the *Cartesian view of the world.*[210]

Thoughts of this nature lead to scientific theoretic discussion on fundamental ideas,[211] which should not be the case at this stage. It is important however for the course of investigation to take into consideration the mentioned weaknesses of morphological psychology at all times during further elaboration and interpretation.

---

203 *Fitzek* (1994), p. 7.

204 Cf. *Lönneker* (2007), p. 87 et seq.

205 Cf. *Donnerstag/Buchert* (2004).

206 Cf. *Allesch* (2005), p. 177 et seq.

207 *Allesch* (2005), p. 178.

208 *Allesch* (2005), p. 178.

209 Cf. *Salber* (1965), p. 43 et seqq.

210 Cf. *Fitzek* (1994).

211 Cf. e.g. *Allesch* (2001).

7 Interim Conclusions

Going forward the approach of usage constitutions is presented in which the basic qualities of constitutions and theoretical background of morphological psychology as well as the weaknesses of the approach are touched upon.

It has been shown that the scope of definition of the construct (usage) constitution is laid out relatively globally and not delineated clearly, that the construct is similar to that of the mood and describes the subjective components of a situation also globally. Capturing these components is basically through qualitative methods as morphological psychology from which the construct *constitution* originates, aims to lead to an understanding of contexts and not the quantification of statements. From this point of view the approach of usage constitution corresponds to previously formulated requirements in case of development of web applications where usage context and usage constitution have to be taken into consideration.

It could additionally be arrived at that constitutions are basically impersonal. Whether a person comes into contact with a subject or another usage constitution is dependent on the specific usage situation. This also supports the basic assumption of this study that acceptance or satisfaction with a service and as a result customer retention cannot be explained by the characteristics of the customer/individuals but rather by those of the situation. This characteristic of constitutions can be explained by the origin of morphological psychology in the psychology of coherent perception. *LEWIN* proved in 1926 *that objectively same work situations differentiate themselves subjectively according to their psychological signification.* Thus this can lead to varying degrees of tiredness in the one and same person.[212] This corresponds to a basic postulate of this study that research results which for example relate to Customer self service Applications cannot be transposed to After Sales applications. This justifies the use of the approach of usage constitution and strengthens the purpose of this study which is to observe Customer Self service elements separately to discover new aspects, which deviate from known acceptance and usage barriers in previous research.

In case of all positive results of the examination of the approach of usage constitution for the design of web applications however, the weaknesses of the method has to be taken into consideration. These are primarily imprecision in the used definitions as well as imprecision in the measurements: as this is about a method which is strongly dependent on the interpretation of the experimenter, it should be ensured that the studies are conducted only by experienced experimenters. Furthermore it is of importance that the interpreted results are clearly presented and communicated. This is to ensure that third parties do not individually interpret the same and draw faulty conclusions. To ensure objectivity of the results a mandatory quantitative study is to be conducted constitutively.

212 Cf. *LEWIN* (1982), p. 101 et seqq.

8 Transition of the Concept of Usage Constitution in the After Sales Phase

As presented in the previous paragraphs the area of application of morphological psychology and therefore constitution marketing is in the Pre Sales oriented market and media research. [213] Therefore it serves primarily in the achievement of sales goals. This is reflected in the nomenclature of the concept *constitution marketing* which stands for marketing supported research as also in the points laid out by *LÖNNEKER* which cover the focus areas of morphological psychology:[214]

- Brand and product use
- Development of marketing and communication strategies
- Image analysis
- Evaluation of advertisement campaigns
- Analysis of media informants
- Naming and/or logo development for brands and products

The phases of the customer buying cycle which aims at a use of the concept of constitution are primarily 'stimulus' and 'evaluation' and partly also the phase 'purchase'. The After Sales Phase in Customer Buying Cycle has till date not been considered. Currently there are neither studies and experiments specially for applications, effects and acceptance of self service or Customer Self service offerings in the After Sales Phase nor are there studies and experiments regarding a use of the concept of constitution with respect to the After Sales context.

For the first part of a proposed future analysis which would have as a goal the observation of Customer Self Service Usage situations of the after Sales Phase and the discovery of specific usage and acceptance barriers, the usability of the approach of constitution or morphological psychology has been established as a context-sensitive method. Particularly the subjective components of which promise to discover new barriers, can be shown in all their facets; at the same time objective components are also not neglected.

For the further course or for the connecting qualitative part of the study the approach of usage constitution must be taken out from the context of questions of the Pre Sales Phase and applied to the questions of the After Sales Phase. A result of this transition should be After Sales specific usage constitutions for Customer Self Service usages, from which negative aspects of After Sales Customer Self service (usage barrier, etc) can be arrived at.

The questions during transition with which the subject of study is approached is different from the conventional procedure for Pre Sales questions. In the case of the current question primarily the question which usage barriers exist is followed and secondly how these can be deactivated. For questions of the Pre Sales Phase the experimenter is more interested in high-

---

[213] Cf. *LÖNNEKER* (2007), p. 94.

[214] Cf. *LÖNNEKER* (2007), p. 94.

lighting the positive aspects of the subject of study to strengthen the consumption need or purchasing need of the customer.

By a transition of the approach of usage constitution an initial, explorative search for indications becomes possible as is intended in the background of the question "how the web application Customer Self Service must be laid out in the background of usage barriers and usage constitutions to achieve as great a degree of customer acceptance as possible. During this numerous aspects of usage and as a consequence results from the arising constitutions can be arrived at:

- Characteristics of typical usage situations for After Sales Customer Self Service for the usage contexts online customer center (self administration of customers) and online help and support (self help for the customer) for different usage situations (customer center: e.g. base data maintenance; help and support: usage problems). This comes close to the typification of usage situations.
- Objective components of usage of After Sales Customer Self Service which are related to the Customer Self Service Application itself and to further components of the usage situation.
- Subjective components of the usage of After Sales Customer Self Service which are related to the Customer Self Service Application itself and to further components of the usage situation.
- Inputs regarding not yet discovered and/or considered usage barriers which are specific to the usage contexts and situations to be studied.

With the help of the prognosed results first hypotheses can be presented which can be verified in a qualitative study to be conducted at a later date.

9 Protohypothesis with Regard to the Relevance of User Barriers and Constitution while Designing Self Service Applications

On the basis of the results till date that Customer Self service offerings are not used in the form as prognosed in studies and experiments as well as the fact that the existing studies on the range of topics do not differentiate regarding usage context and situation, particularly regarding the phase of Customer Buying cycle (pre Sales vs. After Sales), the *first protohypotheses* are formulated here.

These are protohypotheses because the statistical informational value of the morphological value is limited or at the very least disputed. With the results of a qualitative study which will be concluded this year following this article more exact and adequate hypotheses for a conclusive study will be formulated. The verification of the protohypotheses should give a first substantiated statement that usage context and usage situation of Customer Self service offerings are important facts of influence for the expectations of the customer and therefore for the real usage of Customer self Service applications.

Protohypotheses I
Usage barriers exist for web applications and in particular Customer Self Service usage barriers, which result specifically from implications of the After Sales Phase, i.e. the usage context as well as the different activities i.e. the usage situation: the usage of Customer Self Service elements is influenced by and dependent on usage context and usage situation. The usage constitution can be globally differentiated into negative, neutral and positive connotation.

*Protohypotheses II*The usages of web applications and in particular *online customer centers* as well as *online help and support applications* are fundamentally different from one another. The usage of online customer centers has rather positive connotations as there are usage situations which partly similar to those in the area of Pre sales (e.g. add on booking options) and the complexity of the tasks is lesser (e.g. viewing the bill). The usage of online help and support applications has rather negative connotations as new basic moods arise due to the emergence of problems with a product and the complexity of the tasks is greater (e.g. solution for a configuration problem).

References

ABELE, A. (1995): Stimmung und Leistung – Allgemein- und sozialpsychologische Perspektive, Göttingen 1995.

ALLESCH, C. G. (2001): Einführung in die Kulturpsychologie – Die „Morphologische Psychologie“ Wilhelm Salbers, online: http://www.sbg.ac.at/psy/lehre/allesch/vlkps01.doc, last update: 2001, date visited: 22.09.2006.

ALLESCH, C. G. (2005): Seelische Wirklichkeit als Gestaltwandel: Anmerkungen zum Thema 'Metamorphosen' aus Sicht einer Morphologischen Psychologie, in: *GOTTWALD, H./ KLEIN, H.* (Ed.), Konzepte der Metamorphose in den Geisteswissenschaften, Heidelberg 2005, pp. 167–179.

AOL (2003): Erfolgsfaktor Nutzungsverfassung – Eine qualitative Studie des rheingold Institutes zum Einfluss der Nutzungsverfassung auf die Wirkung von Online-Werbung, online: http://www.mediaspace.aol.de/downloads/studien/Erfolgsfaktor_ Nutzungsverfassung.pdf, Last update: 2003, date visited: 04.08.2006

BARNES, J. G. (2001): Secrets of Customer Relationship Management – It's all about how you make them feel, New York 2001.

BARTEL, T. (2003): Die Verbesserung der Usability von Websites – Auf der Basis von WebStyleguides, Usability Testing und Logfile-Analysen, Berlin 2003.

BENKENSTEIN, M./FORBERGER, D. (2001): Wirkung emotionaler Erlebnisse im Dienstleistungserstellungsprozess – eine konzeptionelle Analyse zur Intergration kognitiver und emotionaler Bewertungsprozesse, in: *BRUHN, M./STAUSS, B.* (Ed.), Dienstleistungsmanagement Jahrbuch 2001 – Interaktionen im Dienstleistungsbereich, Wiesbaden 2001.

BARTEL, T. (2003): Die Verbesserung der Usability von Websites – Auf der Basis von WebStyleguides, Usability Testing und Logfile-Analysen, Berlin 2003.

BENTE, G./KRÄMER, N. C./PETERSEN, A. (2002): Virtuelle Realität als Gegenstand und Methode in der Psychologie, in: *BENTE, G./KRÄMER, N. C./PETERSEN, A.* (Ed.), Virtuelle Realitäten, Göttingen 2002, pp. 1–31.

BEU, A. (2003): Analyse des Nutzungskontextes, in: *MACHATE, J./BURMESTER, M.* (Ed.), User Interface Tuning – Benutzungsschnittstellen menschlich gestalten, Frankfurt 2003, pp. 67–82.

BLYTHE, M. A./WRIGHT, P. (2004): From Usability to Enjoyment – Introduction by Mark Blythe and Peter Wright, in: *BLYTHE, M. A./OVERBEEKE, K./MONK, A. F./WRIGHT, P. C.* (Ed.), Funology – From Usability to Enjoyment, New York 2004, pp. XIII–XIX.

BURMESTER, M./GÖRNER, C. (2003): Das Wesen benutzerzentrierten Gestaltens, in: *MACHATE, J./BURMESTER, M.* (Ed.), User Interface Tuning – Benutzungsschnittstellen menschlich gestalten, Frankfurt 2003, pp. 47–65.

BURROWS, P. (2001): The Era of Efficiancy, in: Business Week 18.062001, pp. 94–98, online: http://www.businessweek.com/magazine/content/01_25/b3737701.htm, last update: June 2001, date visited: 20.05.2007.

CHRIST, P. (2004): Self Service May Come Back to Haunt Customers, online: http:// www.knowthis.com/articles/marketing/selfservice.htm, last update: October 2004, date visited: 04.04.2007.

CURRAN, J. M./MEUTER, M. L. (2005): Self-Service Technology Adoption: Comparing three Technologies, in: Journal of Service Marketing, 2005, No. 2, pp. 103–113.

DAMMER, I./SZYMKOWIAK, F. (1998): Die Gruppendiskussion in der Marktforschung: Grundlagen – Moderation – Auswertung – Ein Praxisleitfaden, Opladen 1998.

DETICA (2002): Self-Service Technology – Putting the Customer in the Driving Seat – A Detica Research Report – April 2002, online: http://www.ma-p.com/downloads/RR/Self-Service %20Technology %20- %20Putting %20the %20Customer %20in %20the % 20Drivi ng %20Seat.pdf, last update: April 2002, date visited: 02.12.2006.

DONNERSTAG, J./ BUCHERT, S. (2004): Mit Medien Emotionen in Aktion verwandeln, Universal McCann – Media Press, edition 3, p. 12–15, online: http://www.universalmccann.de/ _pages/newsletter/2004/0411036_mediapress_3.2004.pdf, last update: December 2004, date visited: 12.08.2006.

DUFFY, T. M./PALMER, J. E./MEHLENBACHER, B. (1992): Online help – Design and Evaluation, Norwood 1992.

VON EHRENFELS, C. (1978): On „Gestaltqualitäten", in: *WEINHANDL, F.* (Ed.), Gestalthaftes Sehen – Ergebnisse und Aufgaben der Morphologie – Zum hundertjährigen Geburtstag von Christian von Ehrenfels, 4. unchanged edition, Darmstadt 1978, pp. 11–43.

VAN EIMEREN, B./ FREES, B. (2005): ARD/ZDF-Online-Studie 2005 – Nach dem Boom: Größter Zuwachs in internetfernen Gruppen, online: http://www.daserste.de/service/ardon 105.pdf, last update: August 2005, date visited: 14.02.2007.

ENGLERT, R./ ROSENDAHL, T. (2000): Customer Self Services, in: *WEIBER, R.* (Ed.), Handbuch Electronic Business: Informationstechnologien – Electronic Commerce – Geschäftsprozesse, Wiesbaden 2000, pp. 317–329.

Franz, St. (2004): Grundlagen des ökonomischen Ansatzes: Das Erklärungskonzept des Homo Oeconomicus, in: *Fuhrmann, W.* (Ed.), Working Paper, International Economics, 2004, No. 2, Universität Potsdam, Potsdam 2004.

Fitzek, H. (1994): Der Fall Morphologie: Biographie einer Wissenschaft, Bonn 1994.

Fitzek, H./Salber, W. (1996): Gestaltpsychologie: Geschichte und Praxis, Darmstadt 1996.

Gensler, S./Skiera, B. (2004): Entwicklung eines Modells zur Analyse der Loyalität zu unterschiedlichen Vertriebskanälen, in: *Bauer, H. H./Rösger, J./Neumann, M. M.* (Ed.), Konsumentenverhalten im Internet, München 2004, pp. 371–384.

Goethe, J. W. (1987): Schriften zur Morphologie, neu herausgegeben von *Kuhn, D.* (Ed.), Frankfurt am Main 1987.

Hanekop, H./Wittke, V. (2005): Der Kunde im Internet, in: *Jacobsen, H./Voswinkel, S.* (Ed.), Der Kunde in der Dienstleistungsbeziehung – Beiträge zur Soziologie der Dienstleistung, Wiesbaden 2005, pp. 193–217.

Hassenzahl, M. (2004): The thing and I: Understanding the Relationship between User and Product, in: *Blythe, M. A./Overbeeke, K./Monk, A. F./Wright, P. C.* (Ed.), Funology – From Usability to Enjoyment, New York 2004, pp. 31–42.

Hassenzahl, M. (2006): Interaktive Produkte wahrnehmen, erleben, bewerten und gestalten, in: *Eibl, M./Reiterer, H./Stephan, P. F./Thissen, F.* (Ed.), Knowledge Media Design – Theorie, Methodik, Praxis, 2. revised edition, München 2006, pp. 147–167.

Howard, M./Worboys, C. (2003): Self-Service – A Contradiction in Terms or Customer-led Choice?, in: Journal of Consumer Behaviour, 2003, No. 4, pp. 382–392.

ifm Wirkungen+Strategien (2001): Morphologische Marktpsychologie – Ein Booklet zu Philosophie, Tools und Erhebungsmethoden, Köln 2001.

Jackson, L. A./von Eye, A./Biocca, F./Zhao, Y./Barbatsis, G./Fitzgerald, H. E. (2005): Persönlichkeit und Nutzung von Informations- und Kommunikationsmöglichkeiten im Internet: Ergebnisse aus dem HomeNetToo Projekt, in: *Renner, K-H./Schütz, A./Machilek, F.* (Ed.), Internet und Persönlichkeit – Differentiell-psychologische und diagnostische Aspekte der Internetnutzung, Göttingen 2005, pp. 93–105.

Jukl, G. (2001): Psychologische Aspekte des Webdesigns unter besonderer Berücksichtigung der Gestaltpsychologie, in: *Vitouch, P.* (Ed.), Psychologie des Internet: Empirische Arbeiten zu Phänomenen der digitalen Kommunikation, Wien 2001, pp. 206–241.

Jüttemann, G. (2004): Annäherungen an die menschliche Seele: Zur Bedeutung von ‚Drama' und ‚Wunsch' für eine konkrete Psychologie, in: *Jüttemann, G.* (Ed.), Psychologie als Humanwissenschaft – Ein Handbuch, Göttingen 2004, pp. 134–161.

Jordan, P. W. (2004): Designing great Stuff that People Love, in: *Blythe, M. A./Overbeeke, K./Monk, A. F./Wright, P. C.* (Ed.), Funology – From Usability to Enjoyment, New York 2004, pp. XI–XII.

Knopp, S. (2001): Aufbau, Gestaltung und Struktur bei Online-Hilfesystemen – Im Kontext der Mensch-Computer-Interaktion, Lübeck 2001.

Konradt, U./Wandke, H./Balazs, B./Christophersen, T. (2003): Usability in Online Shops: Scale Construction, Validation and the Influence on the Buyer's Intention and Decision, in: Behaviour & Information Technology, 2003, No. 3, pp. 165–174.

KRÄMER, N. C. (2004): Mensch-Computer-Interaktion, in: *MANGOLD, R./VORDERER, P./BENTE, G.* (Ed.), Lehrbuch der Medienpsychologie, Göttingen 2004, pp. 643–671.

KRÄMER, N. C./NITSCHKE, J. (2002): Ausgabemodalitäten im Vergleich: Verändern sie das Eingabeverhalten der Benutzer?, in: *MARZI, R./KARAVEZYRIS, V./ERBE, H.-H./TIMPE, K.-P.* (Ed.), Bedienen und Verstehen – 4. Berliner Werkstatt Mensch-Maschine-Systeme, Düsseldorf 2002, pp. 231–248.

KÜHN, T. (2005): Qualitative Forschung: ein Nibelungenschatz, den es zu bergen gilt, Tagungsbericht BVM-Fachtagung "Qualitative Marktforschung – State of the Art und Ausblick", online: http://www.qualitative-research.net/fqs-texte/3-05/05-3-5-d.htm, last update: September 2005, date visited: 04.10.2006.

LEE, D. I./SOHN, C. (2004): Trust and Switching Cost as a Way to build e-Loyalty in Internet Markets, in: International Journal of Internet and Enterprise Management, 2004, No. 3, p. 209–220.

LEFFELSEND, S./MAUCH, M./HANNOVER, B. (2004): Mediennutzung und Medienwirkung, in: *MANGOLD, R./VORDERER, P./BENTE, G.* (Ed.), Lehrbuch der Medienpsychologie, Göttingen 2004, pp. 51–71.

LEWIN, K. (1982): Gestalttheorie und Kinderpsychologie, in: *WEINERT, F. E./GUNDACH, H.* (Ed.), Kurt-Lewin-Werkausgabe, Band 6 – Psychologie der Entwicklung und Erziehung, Stuttgart 1982, pp. 101–109.

LILJANDER,, V./VAN RIEL, A. C. R./PURA, M. (2002): Customer satisfaction with e-Services: The Case of an Ondine Recruitment Portal, in: *BRUHN, M./STAUSS, B.* (Ed.), Electronic Services – Dienstleistungsmanagement Jahrbuch 2002, Wiesbaden 2002, pp. 407–432.

LÖNNEKER, J. (2003): Jenseits aller Zielgruppen: Der Konsument auf der Suche nach neuen Verfassungen, in: Rheingold Newsletter, edition 1/03, p. 11, online: http://www.rhein gold-online.de/rheingold-online/upload/Newsletter/1-03.pdf, last update: 2003, date visited: 14.08.2006.

LÖNNEKER, J. (2006): Das Ende aller Zielgruppen? Verfassungsmarketing als Königsweg. Verfassungen prägen heute das Konsumverhalten, online: http://www.rheingold-online. de/rheingold-online/front_content.php?idcat=38, last update: August 2006, date visited: 12.08.2006.

LÖNNEKER, J. (2007): Morphologie – Die Wirkung von Qualitäten – Gestalten im Wandel, in: *NADERER, G./BALZER, E.* (Ed.), Qualitative Marktforschung in Theorie und Praxis: Grundlagen – Anwendungsbereiche – Qualitätsstandards, Wiesbaden 2007, pp. 75–102.

MAYRING, P. (1996): Einführung in die qualitative Sozialforschung – Eine Anleitung zum qualitativen Denken, 3. revised edition, Weinheim 1996.

MELCHERS, C. B. (1993): Morphologische Marktpsychologie – Eine neue Sicht auf Märkte und Verbraucher, in *FITZEK, H./SCHULTE, A.* (Ed.), Wirklichkeit als Ereignis – Das Spektrum einer Psychologie von Alltag und Kultur, Band 1, Bonn 1993, pp. 28–58.

MEUTER, M. L./BITNER, M. J./OSTROM, A. L./BROWN, S. W. (2005): Choosing among alternative service delivery modes: An investigation of customer trial of self-service technologies, in: Journal of Marketing, 2005, pp. 61–83.

Meyer, W. U./Reisenzein, R./Schützwohl, A. (2001): Einführung in die Emotionspsychologie, Band 1 – Die Emotionstheorien von Watson, James und Schachter, 2. revised edition, Bern 2001.

Molzberger, P. (1994): Der Computer als Kommunikations-Partner?, in: *Beuscher, B.* (Ed.), Schnittstelle Mensch: Menschen und Computer – Erfahrungen zwischen Technologie und Anthropologie, Heidelberg 1994. p. 47–68.

Monse, K./Janusch, M. (2003): Enterprise Self Services – Wege aus der Kostenfalle?, online: http://www.ecin.de/state-of-the-art/selfservices/, last update: February 2007, date visited: 14.01.2007.

van Mulken, S./André, E./Müller, J. (1998): The Persona Effect: How Substantial Is It?, online: http://mm-werkstatt.informatik.uni-augsburg.de/files/publications/46 /hci98.pdf, last update: 1998, date visited: 23.10.2006.

Nielsen, J. (2004): User empowerment and the Fun Factor – Questions and Answers with Jakob Nielsen, in: *Blythe, M. A./Overbeeke, K./Monk, A. F./Wright, P. C.* (Ed.), Funology – From usability to enjoyment, New York 2004, pp. 103–105.

Ohler, P./Nieding, G. (2000): Kognitive Modellierung der Textverarbeitung und Informationssuche im WWW, in: *Batinic, B.* (Ed.), Internet für Psychologen, Göttingen 2000, p. 219–239.

Overbeeke, K./Djajadiningrat, T./Hummels, C./Wensveennd, S./Frens, J. (2004): Let's make Things Engaging, in: *Blythe, M. A./Overbeeke, K./Monk, A. F./Wright, P. C.* (Ed.), Funology – From usability to enjoyment, New York 2004, pp. 7–17.

Parasuraman, A./ Zeithaml, V. A./Malhotra, A. (2005): E-S-QUAL – A multiple-item Scale for Assesing Electronic Service Quality, in: Journal of Service Research, 2005, No. 3, p. 213–233.

van Riel, A./Liljander, V./Lemmink, J./Streukens, S. (2004): Boost Customer Loyalty with online Support: The Case of Mobile Telecomms Providers., in: International Journal of Internet Marketing and Advertising, 2004, No. 1, pp. 4–23.

Rost, W. (2005): Emotionen – Elexiere des Lebens, Sonderausgabe der 2. edition 2001, Heidelberg 2005.

Salber, W. (1965): Morphologie des seelischen Geschehens, Ratingen 1965.

Salber, W. (1969): Wirkungseinheiten: Psychologie von Werbung und Erziehung, Wuppertal 1969.

Salber, W. (1995): Wirkungsanalyse: was, wie, warum; Medien – Märkte – Management, Bonn 1995.

Salomann, H./Kolbe, L./Brenner, W. (2006): Self-Services in Customer Relationships: Balancing High-tech and High-touch Today and Tomorrow, in: e-Service Journal, 2006, No. 2, pp. 65–84, online: http://www.alexandria.unisg.ch/Publikationen/30035, last update: 2006, date visited: 23.05.2007.

Schanze, H. (2002): User Families. Von der ‚Gesellschaft des Geistes' zu einer Typologie der Nutzer interaktiver Mediensysteme, in: *Schanze, H./Kammer, M.* (Ed.), Interaktive Medien und ihre Nutzer, Band 4, Theorie der Nutzerrolle, Baden-Baden 2002, pp. 24–34.

SCHMITT, M. (2005): Geleitwort aus persönlichkeitspsychologischer Perspektive, in: *RENNER, K-H./SCHÜTZ, A./MACHILEK, F.* (Ed.), Internet und Persönlichkeit – Differentiellpsychologische und diagnostische Aspekte der Internetnutzung, Göttingen 2005, pp. V–IX.

SCHWAN, S./HESSE, F. (2004): Kognitionspsychologische Grundlagen, in: *MANGOLD, R./ VORDERER, P./BENTE, G.* (Ed.), Lehrbuch der Medienpsychologie, Göttingen 2004, pp. 73–99.

SILBERER, G./JAEKEL, M. (1996): Marketingfaktor Stimmungen – Grundlagen, Aktionsinstrumente, Fallbeispiele, Stuttgart 1996.

SPIES, K. (1995): Negative Stimmung und kognitive Verarbeitungskapazität, Münster 1995.

STOJEK, M./ULBRICH, T. (2001): E-Loyalty – Kundengewinnung und -bindung im Internet, Landsberg/Lech 2001.

STOLPMANN, M. (2000): Kundenbindung im E-Business: Loyale Kunden – nachhaltiger Erfolg, Bonn 2000.

VON VERSEN, K. (1999): Internet-Marketing, Berlin 1999.

VIERBOOM, C./HÄRLEN, I (2006): Forschungsinstrumente, online: http://www.wirtschaftspsych ologen.de/archiv/forschungsinstrumente.pdf, last update: unknown, date visited: 04.10.2006.

VOSWINKEL, S. (2005): Selbstbedienung: Die gesteuerte Kundensouveränität, in: *HELLMANN, K.-U./SCHRAGE, D.* (Ed.), Das Management der Kunden – Studien zur Soziologie des Shopping, Wiesbaden 2005, pp. 89–109.

WANDKE, H. (2004): Usability Testing, in: *MANGOLD, R./VORDERER, P./BENTE, G.* (Ed.), Lehrbuch der Medienpsychologie, Göttingen 2004, pp. 325–354.

WERTHEIMER, M. (1925): Drei Abhandlungen zur Gestalttheorie, Erlangen 1925.

WITTKE, V. (1997): Online in die Do-it-yourself-Gesellschaft? – Zu Widersprüchlichkeiten in der Entwicklung von Online-Diensten und denkbaren Lösungsformen., in: *WERLE, R./ LANG, C.* (Ed.), Modell Internet? Entwicklungsperspektiven neuer Kommunikationsnetze, München 1997, pp. 93–112.

WOLFRADT, U./DOLL, J. (2005): Persönlichkeit und Geschlecht als Prädiktoren der Internetnutzung, in: *RENNER, K-H./SCHÜTZ, A./MACHILEK, F.* (Ed.), Internet und Persönlichkeit – Differentiell-psychologische und diagnostische Aspekte der Internetnutzung, Göttingen 2005, pp. 148–158.

ZILLMANN, D. (2004): Emotionspsychologische Grundlagen.,in: *MANGOLD, R./VORDERER, P./ BENTE, G.* (Ed.), Lehrbuch der Medienpsychologie, Göttingen 2004, pp. 10 1–128.

ZIMBARDO, P. G./GERRIG, R. J. (1996): Psychologie, Berlin 1996.

Part 4:

Application Management – Case Studies

Case Study – Successful Outsourcing Partnership

ANJALI ARYA

Siemens AG – Siemens IT Solution and Services

1 Introduction

Application management support (AMS) is becoming a key strategic element for success of major businesses across the world. This initiative allows businesses to focus and concentrate solely on their core business strategies. In an ever changing competitive and technological world, AMS and outsourcing to trusted partners ensures that a business maintains pace.

Outsourced AMS allows a business to maintain competitive edge in a competitive globalized world while ensuring that current technological advances and resources are being leveraged to the best advantage of the business.

In this article I have presented a successful case study where outsourcing of AMS was deployed for a pharmaceutical industry major. Strategical decisions that helped this initiative to be a success have been covered in detail in this case study.

2 Scenario

A global company launched as a private equity acquisition needs transaction services agreement between its customer and former parent company for applications development and support, service desk, networks, desk side support and data center. The nature of the carve out was basically centered on manufacturing and consequently there were limited corporate support functions including information security (IS).

During the first few years of business operations, the company had to carve out operations to be independent of its parent company, develop full standalone business capabilities and also migrate to a new IT outsourced provider. Given the complexity of managing all these aspects within a short timeframe and prior to the spun off, the services were delivered in-house by the parent company. Hence the company decided to remain in a fully outsourced model and transition to a new provider.

Multiple companies were screened during the request for information (RFI) process. Initially there were 12 companies that were screened down to 6 at the time of RFI with request for proposal (RFP) issued to 4 finalists. Siemens IT Solutions and Services was selected to meet the need of an outsourcing IT partner who could provide an end-to-end technical solution within the stringent mandated structures of the industries.

The contract was awarded based on:

- Experience in buyers Industry
- Value proposition
- Superior processes and methodologies
- Service providers willingness to " put skin in the game"
- Cultural fit

Company's mission critical statement was to have a service provider that was robust, capable, and able to meet their growing needs.

Quality resources were rebadged as their roles were critical to the success of the engagement. Rebadging associates increased confidence with the customer that we could handle the compliance requirements as some of these resources were specifically trained in that area.

And to address concerns related to compliance and processes, we committed to on-boarding appropriately skilled staff and to on-going training. A complete detailed on boarding process was formulized to gain the confidence with appropriate training matrices.

3 Transition

The approach – primary objective of transition management was to minimize business disruption during a critical period of change by using proven methods & tools and demonstrable domain competence to effect a rapid transition with minimal cost and risk exposure.

In the overall application management services (AMS) engagement roadmap, transition management was positioned between the bid management cycle and steady state operations (see figure 1). Transition management is the process of transferring the responsibility for delivery of in-scope services from a customer's service provider to another service framework within defined time-lines and budget. The transition management service element details the methodology and processes followed to manage people transition, asset transition, partner transition, in-flight project transition & knowledge transition from the customer organization to the application management provider.

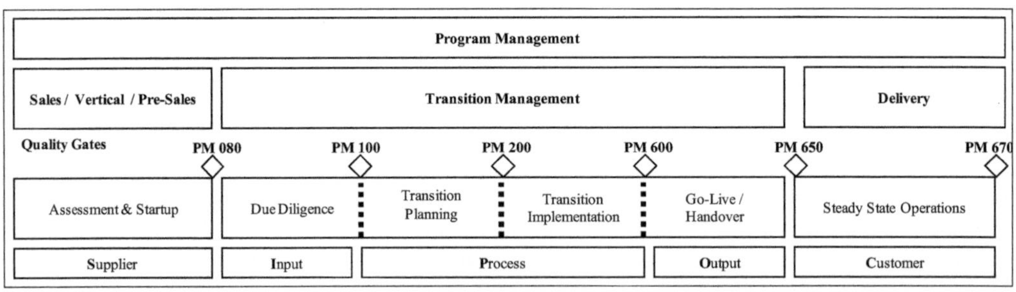

Figure 1: Transition management process

In our case transition management was focused on implementing large change, modification, innovation affecting the existing service delivery engagements. The aim of this process was to rapidly create and secure the application management service which would then, from a position of stability, be improved and innovated to progressive value generation for the customer.

The transition from existing internal service provider (from the parent company) was key to our successful delivery model. This handover acted like a strong base of the building block for future smooth steady state operations. This process was managed as part of a program. In line with the principles for practical project management methods, the transition activities were planned within the framework of individual phases. The activities were target-based which were jointly defined during contract phase between the teams. These activities were allocated to predefined service delivery tower, where a 'service delivery tower' is defined as a logical grouping of services offered. Application management services (AMS) were only a component of the entire transition. The service delivery towers included were defined under five areas:

- Applications devlopment and support
  - Included the assessment, selection, and ongoing modification and improvement of standards for application methodologies, standards, and architecture, which govern all development efforts
  - Control and maintenance of application software support agreements
- Service Desk
  - Served as a single point-of-contact for all types of support, including support for general software and/or hardware products and highly customized applications.
- Networks
  - Manages networks, third-party management and coordination of services, planning and design, performance monitoring and management.
- Deskside support
  - Transition of all desktop and print services
  - Establishment and distribution of all customers product standards for end users
  - Distribution of regular updates and development of the standards for EUC
- Data Center
  - Installation, testing and validation of quality, development and production environments,
  - Installation, testing and validation of operating system software products
  - Hosting all the servers

3.1 Major Contributors

- Governance: set of protocols, procedures, best practices and guidelines that can be of assistance to make better decisions. IT strategic governance is required to efficiently manage IT investments (programs, projects, services and resources). Governance took care of the following: applications development and support

  - Delineated the rules of engagement for management of the relationship, defined responsibilities needed, institutes regular communication between the teams, and set up protocols to manage changes to services and to escalate issues included the assessment, selection, and ongoing modification and improvement of standards for application methodologies, standards, and architecture, which govern all development efforts
  - Provided the activities, processes and tools needed to manage the relationship and presented scenarios for how these activities could be mapped to organizational structures
  - Cultural change management – The appropriate teams were empowered and motivated in order for real change to take place. Workshops were conducted with the management and user community to be able to gracefully accept the change
- Security & compliance: A control is defined as the policies, procedures, practices and organizational structures designed to provide reasonable assurance that business objectives will be achieved and that undesired events will be prevented or detected and corrected.
  - Implemented the initial policies and governance for customers information security management system
  - Created a security framework to facilitate transition of information security services to us.
  - Remediate quality assessment items identified during vendor evaluation process
- Communication: communication by definition is a two-way process. It encompasses not only information traveling from IT to other parties, but information coming into IT from these sources as well.
  - The organizational communication was necessary to effect consistent leadership from the senior management and the steering committee.
  - By leveraging structured and organized use of various media focused on keeping end users and management informed of progress and impending events occurring throughout the program duration

3.2 Transition Team

Transition management interfaced with diverse external and internal stake-holders in the organization value-chain and therefore this service element demanded multiple roles during the period of transition. The roles used during transition execution were as follows:

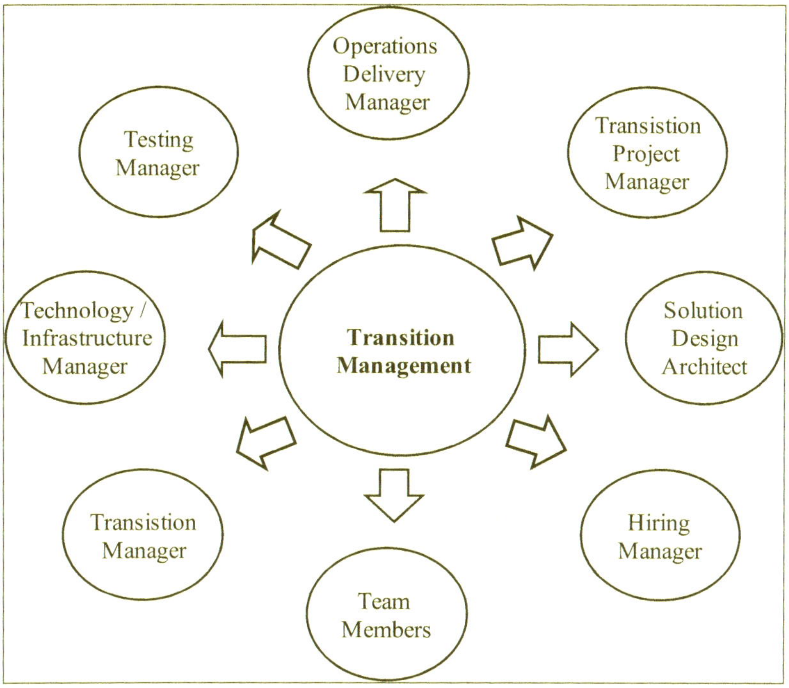

Figure 2: Transition team

Each role had specific responsibilities. The responsibilities were:

- Transition/project manager – The effective transition of all services included in the transition scope from the customer to the steady state service provision by delivery. Contract and budget mgmt. Check implementation of the transition within the specified time, cost and quality framework
- Technology/infrastructure manager – Understanding the project technology & infrastructure requirements, planning procuring and setup of the same at the delivery location within budgets and timelines
- Hiring/sourcing manager – Understanding the project manpower, skill requirements, planning and hiring of the same within budgets and timelines
- Solution design architect – Responsible for designing the solution which would lead the operating model through the transitional phases and for mapping the processes to standards
- Team member – Responsible for delivery of services, are actively involved in the knowledge transfer phase of the transition project
- Testing manager – Responsible for managing all testing requirements of the transition project. Assumes more importance in case the transition includes migration/upgrades/ enhancements

- Customer service manager – Responsible for managing all the requirements from a steady state delivery perspective of the project. Assumes responsibilities of customer service level agreements (SLAs) and key performance indicators (KPIs) during transition handover and provides sign-off on transition deliverables/documents

Upon completion of the transition and knowledge acquisition, we began to construct an IT platform for the company's future growth. Supporting the building of internal capabilities for new functions within the company's business functions were a critical next step. This included tax, treasury, accounts receivable, business development, and accounting.

Existing functions such as human resources, communications, regulatory affairs, corporate ethics and compliance were significantly transformed. During this timeframe, installations of high even applications were also completed.

New supply chain management and technology acquisitions also provided complexity during the transition. These innovations were critical to protecting the health and safety of the consumer.

3.3 Project Governance and Quality Management

The major cornerstone of quality management focuses particularly on quality gates. Quality gates are particularly important because of the preventive role that they play within our business. They enable the objective assessment and safeguarding of key interim and mandatory results of the project.

A quality gate is a point along the process chain at which a check is performed to determine whether all project goals and requirements have been fulfilled, or whether they can be fulfilled using the planned procedure. A quality gate is located at a selected milestone within a process/project at which previously agreed services and (interim) results are checked and are assessed with regard to their quality and completeness so that decisions can be made about the next steps. Quality gates are placed at points in the process where critical decisions relevant to quality are expected. Figure 3 documents the quality gate process.

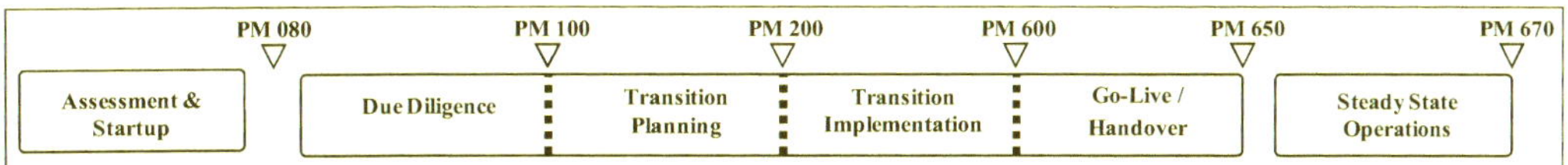

PM 080	This is the initial milestone marking the start of the transition project based on the results of the previous sales / bid project handed over to the transition project.
PM 100	This milestone marks the end of the project initiation and the clarification of the project scope, requirements, internal and external interfaces, planning, risk assessment and staffing.
PM 200	This milestone defines the end of the detailed planning including all supporting plans and results of the data gathering
PM 600	This milestone defines the end of Transition Implementation and the transfer of assets, people, contracts, knowledge etc
PM 650	This milestone defines the Handover from Transition Management & acceptance of the project results by the customer and by the service delivery manager responsible for the on-going operation.
PM 670	This milestone marks the end of the project, including the administrative finalization of the project, the release of project staff and lessons learned documentation.

Figure 3: Quality gates

4 Steady State Operations

Operations started with a successful handover from the transition team. The first and foremost building block was the program management office and governance model. The approach to program management and account governance was driven from the implementation of a program management office (PMO).

The PMO, headed by the program executive, provided a single point of contact for all account-related governance, program management and service delivery issues. This relationship management approach was integral to provide customer-centric and value-based solutions and services to the customer. The size and depth of the PMO was determined based on the independent consolidated services contracted.

A formal, annual account planning process was enforced focusing on business planning, alignment to current IT business value requirements, and improvement based on the customer's satisfaction and performance. So the PMO was the principle management and implementation vehicle for the innovation roadmap and transformation roadmap developed for the customer.

Account personnel met with the customer and our executives to periodically review, modify and enhance processes and procedures that were specific to the customer's needs. The account management team also served as the change management agent/facilitator for changes to the contract, service additions, and modifications.

The PMO committed to:

- Deliver, maintain and improve the quality of service delivered to the customer's corporate and user community
- Achieve contract compliance
- Ensure customer satisfaction through service-level attainment, thought leadership/value added and service delivery improvements

4.1 Governance

A three-tiered communication model was implemented to provide for ongoing operational, tactical and strategic communications at all levels of management.

- Account governance processes

A critical component of a successful account governance model is its processes. The following processes were implemented as standards and best or notable practices that were mutually agreed to by both parties.

- Relationship and communications plan (meetings, reporting, etc.)

The relationship and communications plan was collectively defined to the routinely scheduled meetings, participant lists, forums, etc, this has been instrumental / key between the customer and us to support communications and manage the outsourcing relationship.

The communications meetings made up the three tiered governance communication structure and included joint executive council board meetings (quarterly and semi-annually), account management/governance leadership operation/board meetings (monthly) and operations/service delivery management meetings (daily and weekly).

Some of the key outlines of these plans were:

- Finalize and maintain the relationship and communications plan process and updates about operations
- Distribute the plan to all change approvers and upon request
- Maintain the contractual meetings agreed to with the customer

Figure 4 graphically depicts the governance process.

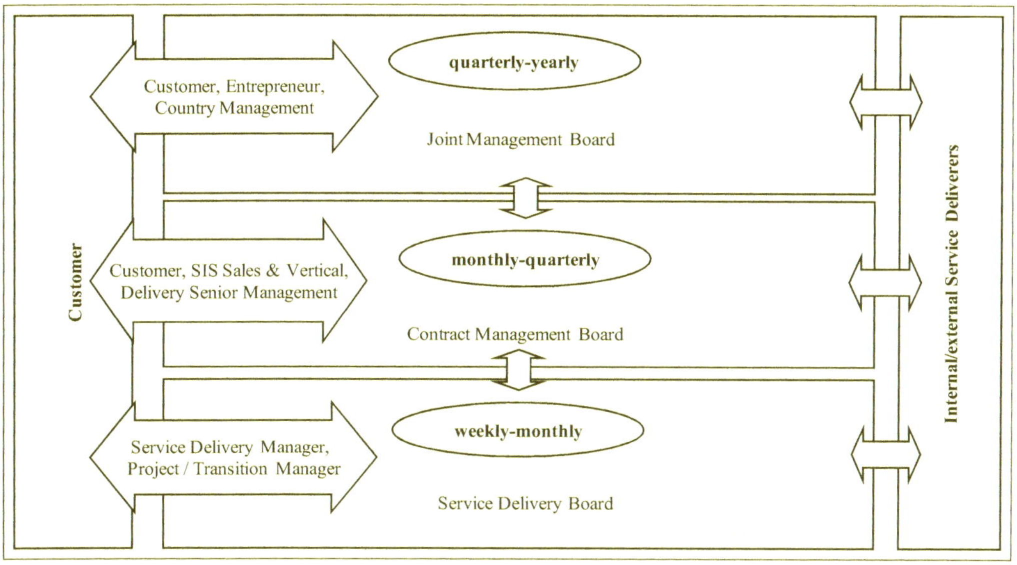

Figure 4: Project governance – governance structure

4.2 Incident and Problem Management

An incident is an unplanned interruption to an IT service. Failure of a configuration item that has not yet impacted service is also an incident, for example failure of one disk from a mirror set. Incidents are a secondary classification from event management.

According to ITIL an 'incident' is defined as an unplanned interruption to an IT service or reduction in the quality of an IT service. The primary objective of the incident management process is to restore normal service operation as quickly as possible and minimize the adverse impact on business operations, thus ensuring that the best possible levels of service quality and availability are maintained. 'normal service operation' is defined here as service operation within SLA limits.

Incident management is initiated by an end-user through help desk or by monitoring system in the production environment. An incident that is recurring and or has impacted business is classified as a problem, which is handled through the problem management operational support process. Incidents can range in level of priority from minor complaints that are reported by end users to the service desk top priority 1 (P1) and priority 2 (P2) problems that impact critical systems or have a significant financial impact to the company. For incident management, the help desk is the first and most important contact for the customer.

There are multiple different types of incidents occur, such as:

- Incidents reported to the service/ help desk, where an incident is defined as when programs, interface, batch jobs or transaction codes are not functioning as designed and performance is compromised

- Incidents identified from monitoring of the infrastructure such as alerts or events

Detailed operational procedures for recording, tracking and managing the above types of incidents focus on:

- For any P1 or P2 incidents the process defining key contacts / communication to the business if there is significant impact / and escalation process
- A clear process for any Batch Job failure what is the severity and who all should be notified since most of them run at night after office hours and do have a ripple effect.
- Problem management process, participants in these interactions, and tools and templates used during the process
- The mechanism for governing and providing oversight of the incident and mroblem management process in terms of periodic reviews of the process and any problems related thereof

4.3 Change Control

The change management team has the oversight responsibility for the change control process, to ensure any changes made to the production environment are tracked and approved prior to implementation; this would include changes to individual components and coordination of changes across all applications. The change management team monitors/tracks /owns the process through which change requests and projects will be scheduled for any changes to the production environment.

Below describe the key interactions between customer and service provider in the change control process, participants in these interactions, and tools and templates used during the process:

- The mechanism for governing and providing oversight of the change control process in terms of periodic reviews of the process and any issues related thereof
- Changes are initiated as a change request by either customer or by service provider. The stages involved in the change control process are:
  - Change request initiation
  - Assessment and design (impact analysis)
  - Approval and assign the release cycle
  - Implementation
  - Post change review
  - Closure
  - Post implementation review
- Types of changes

Changes are categorized by the following change types :

- Emergency: Changes needed to resolve ongoing and/or customer-impacting incidents. Qualifying emergency changes are break / fix which are accompanied with a Priority 1 or Priority 2 ticket.
- Expedited: Changes that can cause undue harm if not performed in an expedient manner. These changes follow the Normal change process at an accelerated pace.
- Planned: Changes that have been planned and scheduled in advance. Depending on the release cycle assigned and task it is assigned a priority of high, medium or low. A normal change will have different lead times.

4.4 Escalation Management

Functional escalation
As soon as it becomes clear that the service desk is unable to resolve the incident itself (or when target times for first-point resolution have been exceeded – whichever comes first!) the incident must be immediately escalated for further support.

Hierarchic escalation
If incidents are of a serious nature (for example priority 1 incidents) the appropriate IT managers must be notified, for informational purposes at least. Hierarchic escalation is also used if the 'investigation and diagnosis' and 'resolution and recovery' steps are taking too long or proving too difficult.

The objectives of escalation management are:

- Resolve issues in a timely and effective manner
- Communicate issues and status to PMO and customer executive management
- Proactively engage PMO and customer management as support for resolution
- Facilitate resolution of cross-functional issues from other processes
- Maintain historical records of issue resolution for consistency

Issues may be initiated by the customer or by the service provider are managed in a manner to facilitate quick resolution at the lowest possible organizational level. The escalation management process addresses issue recording, assignment, escalation, review and tracking to closure.

The escalation management process provides for the management of issues at all levels of the program. All issues are managed using the same process, regardless of priority.

4.5 Service Level Agreement

Service level agreements (SLA) are the management of all contracted services which ensure an attainment of all service levels. The SLA targets for overall incident-handling and resolution times need to be agreed with the customers and between all teams and departments – and targets need to be coordinated and agreed with individual support groups so that they underpin and support the SLA targets

Service level agreements (SLAs) are an important aspect in any business engagements. A service level agreement sets the parameters for deliverables, priorities, responsibilities and guarantees/warranties. SLAs are critical where the customers need assurance about the services and software's providing mission-critical services to their business. A single malfunction in IT operations can severely damage the working structure of the business. Siemens IT Solutions and Services has a clearly defined set of rules (SLA's) and strict regulation to ensure that the promised services will be delivered to the customer.

SLAs are usually scripted and cover most important aspects like:

- Application availability
- Response times
- Resolution time
- Estimation accuracy – schedule to actual variance, new applications delivered within +/- 10 % of scheduled delivery

SLA's			measurement
Problem Resolution - Performance Category	expected	minimum	window
Severity Level 1 problem response < 30 Clock minutes	95 %	90 %	rolling 3 months
Severity Level 1 rroblem resolution < 4 Clock Hours	96 %	92 %	rolling 3 months
Severity Level 2 rroblem resolution < 8 clock Hours	96 %	92 %	monthly
Severity Level 3 problem resolution < 24 business hours	96 %	92 %	monthly
Severity 1 applications availability	99 %	98 %	monthly
Estimation accuracy - achedule to actual variance, new applications delivered within +/- 10 % of scheduled delivery	98 %	90 %	monthly
KPI's			measurement
Key Performance Indicator	expected	minimum	window
rework required on new applications as a result of user acceptance testing	95 %	90 %	monthly
Estimation accuracy – budget to actual variance, new applications delivered within +/- 10 % of budget	95 %	90 %	monthly

Figure 5: sample SLA matrix

A service level agreement is applicable to both the service provider and the customer. Some of the important advantages of having SLAs are as follows:

- Documented evidence of the agreement
- Sets a framework for quality expectation and implementation
- Makes the rules clear in case of a disagreement between us and customer
- Makes goals and methodology crystal clear
- Creates a standard in the level of service
- Becomes a basis for improvisation of services

4.6 Contract Management/Service Request Management

Change management – Where a change is required to implement a workaround or resolution, this will need to be logged as an RFC and progressed through change management. In turn, incident management is able to detect and resolve incidents that arise from failed changes.

The PMO, customer service manager's (CSM's) and change management team are responsible for the change management process which ensures application service requests. Any change request which is a change to an existing mapped process which falls outside the scope of base operational service is taken as a service request. This means negotiating the terms and conditions and ensuring compliance, as well as documenting and agreeing on any changes that may arise during its implementation or execution. A change request is initiated to request additional services.

Change requests may be triggered by an event (or collection of events) such as the following:

- New service
- Elimination of a service
- Changes to scope
- Changes in process
- Implementation of automation or new tool
- Upgrades

In response to the change request, an estimate is provided to the customer who is responsible for reviewing and approving it. If approved, the Service Provider through PMO completes a change order with detailed terms, conditions and specifications of the work to be performed. The change order becomes effective only when signed by both parties.

4.7 Risk Management

The risk management process is in place which provides for a systematic approach to identifying, analyzing and responding to delivery risks. The process provides for a systematic approach to identifying, analyzing and responding to risks. The objective of the risk management process is to maximize the probability of occurrence and consequence of adverse events and minimizing that risk.

A risk is typically managed at the lowest level and affects at least one of the three constraints: time, cost and function. A risk becomes a program level risk when mitigation planning requires PMO and/or customer involvement.

- Project level risk – managed at the PMO level. Risks can impact multiple projects or the program as a whole.
- Customer program level risk – managed at the contract level.

Figure 6: *Risk Management*

Risk identification and evaluation involves determining which risk might affect the contract and then documenting their characteristics, including monetary impact when applicable.

Risk mitigation is the process of developing options and determining actions to enhance opportunities and reduce threats to the contract's objectives. For a risk with a low exposure, the risk management team can "accept" the risk without the need to put in place a formal mitigation plan. The alternative solutions to a risk is understood to a level that will allow the team to effectively analyze the potential success and the monetary impact to the contract if the risk occurs and the degree to which the mitigation solution "cures" the risk's impact.

4.8 Ressource Management

The resource management provides standards, policies and procedures regarding hiring, personnel development, human resources management, time reporting travel expenses and billing approval.

The PMO applies these standards, policies, and procedures with the focus on providing service delivery excellence.

The resource management approach focuses on the following elements:

- Developing a cost-effective, efficient human resource solution
- Communicating the customer clear target dates for each milestone
- Gaining employee support and addressing concerns
- Providing an environment that attracts and retains employees
- Enabling empowered and motivated employees to achieve the highest levels of performance
- Accurate time reporting and billing

Successful operations depend on the integration of technology and human talent. Resource Management commits to the following fundamental principles in managing their employees:

- To treat employees respectfully, fairly, and equitably in accordance with the laws and customs of the countries where from we deliver the services
- To value the rich diversity of the worldwide workforce, recognize employees as individuals, and give them opportunities to contribute to the Company's business success
- To implement policies and programs to attract, develop, motivate, reward, and retain diverse and talented employees in line with our global business strategies and objectives
- To create an environment that supports the development and well-being of every employee

It is important to retain critical systems and process knowledge throughout the contract term, beginning with transition. To decrease risks created by employees ceasing to service the account in their current role, the PMO insures the support team documents all relevant systems and processes. A succession plan is also implemented to ensure that we as the service provider have a methodology to fill key positions as they become vacant and offer ongoing challenges to deserving employees.

Retaining quality employees at the corporate level is a top focus of the service provider. True solutions require focus, attention, resources, and effort when managing employees. We addressed this issue at every stage of the employment cycle: selection, orientation, performance management, training and development, and communication.

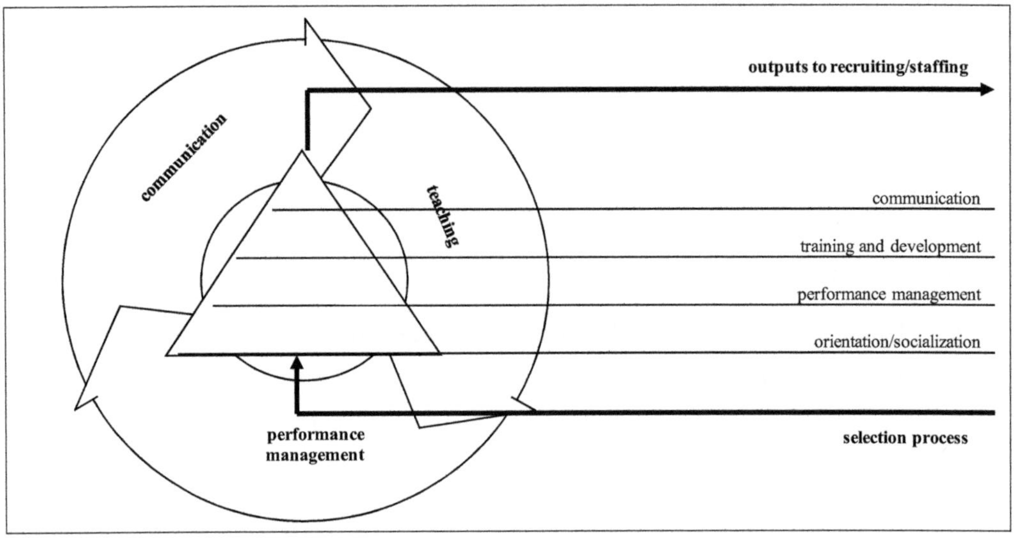

Figure 7: Ressource management

4.9 Knowledge Management

The global competition is getting fiercer and players are now increasingly emphasizing more on building and sustaining competitive advantages. Given the nature of the business, the source of competitive advantage in long run will be the work-force and their competence as a whole. Therefore we started focusing on systems and processes that helps consultants in keeping their knowledge abreast and thereby, become more productive and effective for our customers.

Knowledge management (KM) systems aim to ensure consistent, efficient, effective and smart services to customers by enabling smart work-ways within our delivery units.

Our KM approach has supported and is helping provide improved services to our customers:

- Improves productivity of consultants
- Ensures error-free / first time right (FTR) work-ways
- Ensures new joiners adapts faster and thereby reduces impact on delivery to customer
- Enable Common delivery pool (CDP) model by offering common source of knowledge and documentation which results into higher flexibility
- Enhance chances for cross-selling and up-selling by sharing enhancement & offerings across all customer accounts
- Improved SLAs and response time due to reduced information search time
- Drive standardization across processes
- Help get access to global subject matter experts across organization

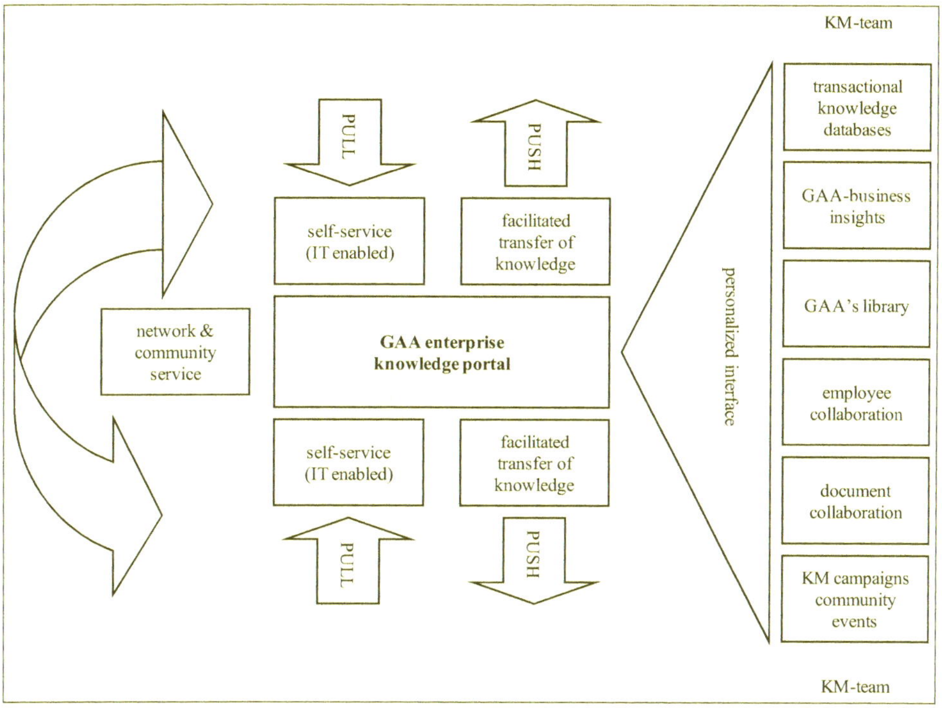

Figure 8: Knowledge management

Knowledge transfer process in place is designed to facilitate the successful transfer of knowledge between individuals, and it will provide a smooth handover of responsibilities, improve productivity through increased motivation, and lower risks through cross-training. The knowledge transfer process addresses two critical subject areas: business and technology. The business subject area includes an understanding of customer's business, commitments, and existing service levels. The technology subject area covers system access, libraries, standards, and other related topics.

In cases when an individual is no longer available, we use transition team members to reverse-engineer critical functions. In either case, the functions will be documented and incorporated into our normal procedures.

The PMO identifies areas of additional training, work sessions, and mentoring programs by frequent monitoring. The knowledge transfer process is considered completed when the sender and receiver agree that the receiver can perform the majority of the sender's work. Major by-products of the knowledge transfer process will be well-documented processes, exception criteria, and system functionality. This documented information is gathered and maintained in a shared environment.

We work closely with the customer on refining its strategic direction and introduction of new technologies into customer's environments. The teams supporting the customer participate in ongoing training that includes updates to existing technologies and information regarding new technologies. Trainings are made available through Web-based classes, classroom sessions, or other appropriate venues, depending on the scope and scale of the training need. For new hires, as a part of on boarding process all the topics are covered regarding the customer's environment, customer's technical objectives and goals, appropriate legal and regulatory considerations, and other appropriate topics.

4.10 Financial Management

Financial management encompasses the following activities: prepare budgets, prepare invoices, execute accounts receivable and payable activities, price new projects, application service requests, or contract addendums, and perform capital planning. PMO and CSM's are responsible for gathering and validating the billable metrics. The program management office is responsible for the day-to-day Administrative & Financial operations.

The main contract billing is set up in advance of the first billing date and generates automatically. Time card and work order invoices are also system generated. The invoice or credit request is set up and/or approved by the financial analyst, sent to operations for review, and forwarded by operations to the billing and collections center (BCC). Signed copies of contracts, change orders, and client approvals for miscellaneous out-of-scope billings have to be received by the financial analyst, operations specialist, and the customer care representative before invoice requests are processed.

- Fixed price invoicing – These are generated by system and are generated for the fixed fee for the steady state operation
- Time and material invoices – These invoices are generated based on the actual time spent logged via the time card system. Consultants record their billable time against the project or contract as they complete their weekly timecards in the system. The billable time entered is then reviewed and approved by the billing approval manager. Approved billable time is invoiced to the customer on a monthly basis.
- Additional resource charge (ARCs), reduce resource charges (RRCs), and SLAs – Any deviations from the baseline charges are invoiced or credited one month in arrears. ARCs and RRCs are calculated using the unit rates (ARCs and RRCs) as agreed in the contract and so are SLA penalties

4.11 Quality Management and continues improvement

In chapter 2.3 we have already touched upon some aspects of quality management. It is, however, worthwile to have a more detailed discussion on five critical areas of quality management as they relate to driving quality throughout the company:

- Quality assurance
- Continuous improvement
- Standards and consistency
- Quality development, and
- Customer integration.

Quality has been our benchmark for determining the degree to which our products, projects and services meet customer requirements. A key component of the quality management process is the accreditation program. Accreditation is the ability of a PMO to establish policies and procedures that meet quality and continuous improvement (QCI) best practices, quality, and standards and to demonstrate that personnel adhere to these guidelines.

Continuous improvement (CI) is key to ongoing operations. The CI program is supported by senior executives and has evolved a governance structure that facilitates identification, tracking, and resolution of improvement opportunities. The scope of continuous improvement efforts has steadily expanded to mirror customers' own growth and success. The customer's initial focus was on stabilizing and improving existing processes. Latter with the customer we have been jointly research and implement forward-looking technologies to strengthen and enable support of their business strategy.

Figure 10 depicts the quality management process

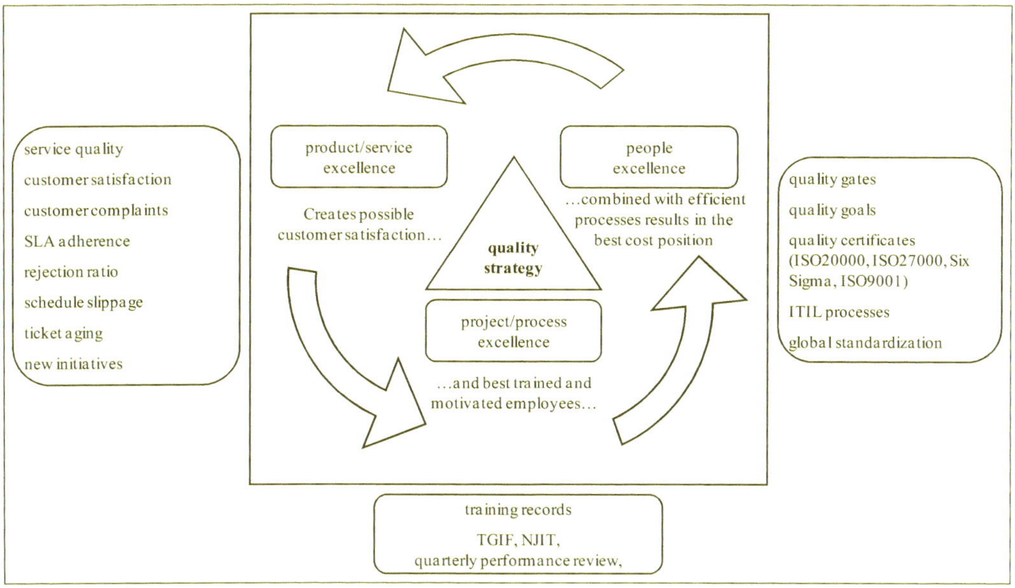

Figure 9: Quality management

5 Summary – The partnership

The partnership has established a strategic relationship that involves joint sharing of investment, risk and reward. The leadership of both organizations understands these elements and has intentionally designed the program around these core tenets.

We as the external service provider are viewed as an integral part of the customer's organization and are invited to management and all-hands staff meetings, participate in strategic initiatives, and have direct lines of access to customer's key leaders. The program has synchronized the IT strategies of both organizations, ensuring that priorities and capabilities are appropriately aligned and complementary of each other.

Key success factors attribute to the flexibility, support of an aggressive timeline and significant growth through the acquisition / build of a nationwide business, launch of business operations in across the globe, and support 50% revenue growth.

As partners the major joint contribution was on moving some of the onsite delivered services offshore, allowing them to reduce costs and maintain very high standards of service quality. The move was comprehensive and complex and the results most impressive. The joint planning group transitioned a high volume of services to be delivered remotely (from offshore) while continuing to meet existing SLA performance benchmarks and operate under existing governance models.

During the project, deliverables were often ahead of schedule and the transition group employed numerous best practices, including clear and precise project management practices, internal and external communication pathways, goals and expectation sharing, and a high degree of transparency.

Many a times customer felt that for minor changes our processes may have been a drag, however the company did acknowledge many a times that when it mattered the most we were not seen wanting. An example of this was the case of major application upgrade or bringing a Business unit under the umbrella of master agreement of existing landscape.

In all, everything transitioned is live and fully functional. Service is performing at or above anticipated levels of quality, as measured against monthly SLA reporting. Internal communications channels are in place and strong across all teams. The goal is to have geographic separation have zero impact on the operations.

Outsourcing has helped customer in multiple ways in achieving its objectives:

- Enabled their ability to grow business being able to focus on their core business
- Enabled taking advantage of new market opportunities
- Gained access to IT skills where they lacked in house
- Avoid Capital expenditures ; improved productivity and reduced costs
- Automate most of the in-house manual processes

The customer has achieved notable improvements in the IT cost structure as well. To improve customer quality and reduce costs, we have off-shored certain application management and information management services to one of our global production centers. This was done to benefit from low-cost delivery locations while maintaining high standards for language and cultural fit. Global production centers hold and maintain ISO quality, IT service management, and security certifications, so processes are transparent worldwide.

5.1 Highlights and Lessons-learned

- Due diligence of service provider to avoid any surprises
- Internal resistance to outsourcing, this can be can be managed by making sure to foster proactive and candid communications to succeed
- Transitions take time and is key to successful partnership / operations
- Well defined governance structure and proactive management
- Effective communication
- Have measurable SLA's and KPI's to evaluate performance
- Leverage resources with experience and skills that potentially help in developing own sourcing strategies and roadmaps

Successful Choreography for a Software Product Release – Dancing to deliver a final Product

Laurent Cerveau and *Freddie Geier*

Adventures GmbH

1 Introduction

1.1 The Impact of an Efficient Release Path

A never-ending problem in the software industry is to keep up an efficient path in term of products releases. There are many reasons for this: manage the customer's expectations, show a competitive spirit as well as a good reactivity, develop an aggressive marketing campaign and as an end result occupy the market. As one of the best examples, Apple releases over an approximately two years cycle a massive amount of software and hardware products: complete renewal of their hardware offerings, releasing of a major Operating System version for both desktop computer and mobile device product line, releasing of at least one new version of their consumer application software suite, as well as of their office application suite, shipping of their professional application software, security updates and many various updates in different areas.

Certainly, from inside a company, one will always see the negative aspects of such a high release rhythm: pressure on employees, impression of doing "half completed" work and associated frustration, feeling of always running after time. Additionally the more such an experience is negatively repeated, the more of a lack of confidence can happen within a team. Sentences like "We'll do it right later" are repeated, but their application never sees the light of day. Management is not anymore taken seriously, employees lose pride and self esteem, and a general lack of liability starts to appear.

On the other hand, overcoming such state can prove to be a benefit at all levels of a company. From a marketing side, the confrontation to the market is always useful to appreciate fully the impact of a product on its target audience and bring the necessary corrections. Releasing the product is also a way to move the pressure to the market and internally between different teams. For a development team, it can also be a positive challenge to develop software components in an incremental way, and learn to establish properly structured foundations that are always ready to be brought further even with very small incremental changes. The opposite danger exists namely in an "over designing/over predicting" approach. Work is invested in inappropriate areas of development and one can always be sure that a critical point will always be forgotten. Finally in a highly competitive environment as the software market (both consumer and business), "not or delay releasing" may send warnings and negative signals to customers who will turn to other solutions.

1.2 A Set of Software Methodologies

Certainly the desire for a "fast and no error recipe" has always been a constant in the software development area. Software methodologies and formalization methods have successively appeared, and their adoption has led to success in various degrees. For example, the Merise methodology appeared in France in the late seventies and was used heavily in the consulting area. As part of the family of the "waterfall" methodology, one of its characteristics was a relatively long and strictly defined process of documenting before starting practically the coding process. By itself such a method holds some potentials issue in the sense that the application of the method is requiring investment and time. Similar observations can be made of tools like the Unified Modeling Language (UML). Although ideally it can be seen as a common language to describe some computer-related idiosyncrasies, it can very fast become a topic of study and lead to a path diverging from the one of the original project.

A more recent wave of methods has appeared that are mainly based on the idea of "fast reaction" and creation of short cycle of introspection during the lifetime of a project. Examples are: XP Programming, Agile Programming, Scrum. They also try to put more focus on the individual, allowing each contributor of a project to express her/himself during regular meeting and thus avoiding creation of pool of frustration. But in a similar way as the "more formalized" category of development methods, they can also hold some of their limits and contradiction in themselves. For example, one of the lines of the Agile Manifesto is that it favors "Working software over comprehensive documentation". It can be sure than many developers will find here a legitimation to a complete lack of documentation inside the written source code.

A good summary of the problem of application of a method from either of those two high level categories can be a quote from one of the creator of the Merise method. "The name of Merise comes from "merisier", a special kind of cherry tree that can produces nice fruits only if one has grafted another variety onto it, just like the method can produce good results only if grafting it onto the company is a success".

1.3 To make a successful Graft

A method graft can be successful if one accepts from the start, that the field onto which it should be applied, that is the pool of human resources, does not obey to any kind of deterministic rules. In addition, there will always be a process in every team member of what can be called "minimization of cognitive dissonances". That is every divergence to a given method will be justified by a counter argument based on the problems that can happen in the project. For example, a common habit during the run of an agile process is to hold a "5 minutes daily stand-up meeting"; during such a meeting, every team member is present and briefly exposes what she/he has worked on the day before, what she/he will work on the present day, and if she/he is blocked by something. Through this way, essential information is rapidly conveyed to the complete team and necessary actions can be taken. If such a meeting is forgotten, there will always be someone to say that "bug fixes are more important", and legitimating the absence of meeting. At this point the application of the methodology is broken and bringing it back requires a lot of effort.

The role of the team manager is crucial here. For her/him, the real challenge does not lie only in the completion of the project, but also in maintaining a movement towards the method during the whole project. This should naturally take in account the diversity between team members, both in experience and cultural background. By enforcing a process of knowledge and experience sharing, a global movement in a team will happen, in which everyone will find a natural place and role as a contributor.

Proper use of the increasing project speed needs also to be made so that the global level of a team is raised; when the project is over, solid foundations should have been built, from where another cycle can be taken. For this, every team member should also accept a self-commitment to the method to be followed and not see it as an order coming from the manager.

The remaining part of this article will go in more details about how practically such a growing environment can be put in place and describe a set of tools that are necessary for this.

2 A Basic Set of Interaction Rules

2.1 Imply the whole Company

"Dogfooding", also known as "eat your own dog food" is a process happening in many American software corporations. Very early in the project, members of the team are required to use in a daily manner the product they are working on. As a benefit, the internal knowledge of what is being developed is growing and possible difficulties are seen in a short amount of time. Such process enforces also the idea that everyone in the company has a belief in the developed product.

A key point in establishing such a process is the "when" it happens. Too early, it generates frustration because of an unstable and buggy product. Rejection can happen, as well as the presence of a blaming attitude towards the development team. Too late, it may not be possible anymore to provide feedback that can be implemented in a seamless way. Often, a management decision is also needed to enforce the dogfooding process at one point in time and make sure it can bring its benefits.

Dogfooding brings also an advantage in the team building process as it forces to create a bridge between two main groups, technical and non technical, and reduce the risk of "dual disdain" process. Non technical people – in particular marketing and sales teams – sees the technical team as a "mean to implement their bright idea", while technical people consider their counterpart as "not understanding anything about how things work and thus should be". In the worst case this love/hate relationship ends up in a complete break of communication between those two groups or in a latent fight between "the technical incompetents" and the "geeky autistics"

Forcing the access to pre-release version of the product can help to have those two groups adopting mutual positions in regards to the development of the product. The "non technical" group plays the role of "first customers", acquiring an external black box functional vision of the product, while the technical one stops seeing it as a place for their own technical experimentation. In order to do so, it is necessary that, from the start, elements are put in place providing the conditions of what should be a real user experience. Technically this implies the creation of a proper internal distribution system with update notification mechanism and side elements (problem reporting infrastructure, versioning system, feature and milestone validation process).

2.2 The Teams in Presence

Going in more details than the "technical/non technical" separation, a common team set up for the development of a software product is the following.

The Research & Development team is globally responsible for the technical conception and development of the product. Although it is usually oriented "towards the company", when in development mode, it brings also an opening to the outside through a research activity requiring to watch, seek and try external technologies. Ensuring enough time for this Research part is essential to bring new concepts into a product line.

The Quality Assurance (QA) team is responsible for the monitoring of the product quality and stability, and the discovering and tracking of issues and bugs. A good practice is to give to the QA team a level of responsibility at the same level as the one of the Research and Development team, avoiding then a path of thinking that would consider it as "sub-engineer" group of people.

The Marketing team's main role is to provide a flow of input from the external word. One can quote the definition of the Cartered Institute of Marketing that defines marketing as "the management process responsible for identifying, anticipating and satisfying customer requirements profitability":

To this main, and cleanly segmented, trio can be added two roles acting also as a bridge between those three.

The Product Management/Product Design team is responsible for the conception of the product, mainly from a user point of view. It should then play the role of a natural bridge between the Research & Development and Marketing teams. In particular, a key responsibility is to understand how the balance should be oriented between the impact of customer's expectations and the creation of a strong internal identity for the product, which can then be pushed to become a potential market leader. As an example of such balance, the development of the iPhone by the company Apple, where some functionalities considered as major by the phone industry have been omitted from the first releases, helping also to focus on some specifics of what has become a strong product line.

The Project Management team is responsible for the planning, monitoring, issues anticipation – and if needed resolution – and status reporting during the project lifetime. One implication is very often to be in a "bad guy" role. There can be two possibilities as where the project manager should sit in a hierarchical structure. On "top" of the other team, it can provide a needed leadership. However another possibility is to enforce the role of the Project Manager as a cross functional one, being at the same level as the other ones. The role of project leader or mentor is then separated, and placed at the top of the hierarchy. To make a political analogy, a comparison could be the French Vth Republic: the project leader is the president; every team represents a ministry while the project manager would be the president advisor.

Out of this main pool, many teams are also usually contributing to the development of a software product, but not with such a fundamental role. Ideally they receive a document describing all requirements for a product at the beginning of a project, followed then by regular reports. For example, sales and business development will use this information to develop their planning and/or commercial forecasting, the operations team should provide an infrastructure for product development and delivery and finance plays its natural key role.

2.3 Commitment Seeking – Reviews

The commitment of a team to the project and product is essential for its success. From the moment that a part of the project team starts to think that the project is not what should be done (for justified or not reason), probability of failures dramatically increases. It is essential that at any time, every team member is proud of the product, themselves and their contribution to the product.

Adding the dimension of being in a "fast release" mode can help by offering the opportunity to create documented meeting points, also known as reviews, along the project development path. The Project Manager should write those after discussion with other project's team. Such review should always consider three axis of constraints, also known as boundaries: the product boundary concerns the definition of the product itself in all its aspects (R&D, Target audience, Supported configurations, Set of needed tools, External Dependencies, Quality criteria, Plan to Market...), the time boundary considers the schedule of development, the finance boundary how much the development costs. Every time a review is established, schedule and boundaries definition for the next review should be set up, as well as possible risks.

Reviews are different than regular reporting made by the Project Manager in the sense that they define macro goals and milestones inside the project. In their form, reviews can happen as a physical meeting happening around a presentation document, or be as simple as an email exchange. In both cases, reviews should be validated by a written approval of all managers of the project's team, avoiding thus a possible and negative "Nobody told me" syndrome.

Practically, and in particular during the concept phase, reviews should come with additional written deliverables providing more details about a team area (marketing requirements and expectations, pre-architectural White Paper, Test plan, cost spreadsheet...)

One can define different time periods that can be validated through a review.

During the concept phase, the team is assessing the feasibility of the project. At this point no commitment is firmly taken, but a direction is indicated and multiple roads inside this direction should be explored. It may even happen that the end of a concept phase has for result that the project should not be undertaken.

A proposal phase comes then where the project team is taking commitment towards the company. Things are not anymore in the field of possible, but in the one of doable. In some cases, usually when the concept phase has provided precise enough answers, the proposal phase is very short (or even none existing) and its validation review combined with the concept's one.
A development phase follows then. This is usually the longer one during the lifetime of a project. During this phase the project manager should fully play his role and provide weekly update about the project. The development phase is validated by a Release review, which describes the final state of the project, including possible known issues: its approval is then followed by the release of the product.

When emergency or divergence arises, additional reviews must happen during the development phase. They describe a state of broken (also known as out of bounds) boundary, and allow the project manager to raise openly an issue at the team management level, adjusting also the expectations. Broken boundaries can be of different nature. For example: the realization of a software component reveals to be more complex that thought and needs to be removed from the project; development time is taking longer than expected; planned number of contributors has been underestimated which results in a break of the finance boundary. It is very important that such a review also proposes solution and action that can be taken to address the situation, even if those can be difficult to accept internally in the team. Once a review has been validated, news boundaries are set for the project while previous ones are discarded.

2.4 The Art of Polyrhythm

While reviews provide a common high-level rhythm for a project, a fact is that each project team works with its own tempo. A good example resides in the interaction between Research and Development and QA. Very often, QA likes to have a certain time to fully assess the quality of a release, going through all its aspect and make sure no regression in behavior is found. On the other hand, engineers like to think that any bug fix or feature should be tested "now!" so they can move to the next problem without any worry. A case like this illustrates the fact that between all teams the interaction on the software can either follow a "push model" or a "pull" one, while both extremities of the production chain are only push or pull.

Trying to force a unique tempo is a potential source of tension and frustration within a team, in particular if brought too early in the project. Time should be given so that each functional unit organizes itself first internally, but also externally through meetings with other team managers and the project manager. It must namely be ensured that such preparation is not leading to a vast and inefficient compromise, but on the opposite to the discovery of possible friction areas.

Here also the project manager needs to play a role to slowly bring all teams together on the same rhythm for the final phase of a project. A way to do this is to enforce regular and time limited meeting points between all team members. For example weekly Bug Review Board can be an opportunity for everyone to not only get knowledge about what issues are in the software but also to appreciate different kind of reaction to a problem, and lead to a common understanding of what feature should be in a given version. In the tradition of Agile/Scrum software development methodology, daily five minute stand up meeting convey not only information about what people are working on, but also how they approach their work, although such information is more often in the "unsaid".

2.5 When the Music is over

A well known practice after a software project ends is to conduct a post-mortem where people can identify, among others, what went good, what went wrong and most of all where were the biggest sources of frustration. Without going in details (many articles are to be found on the Internet about the topic of post-mortem), there is however one element that is difficult to ignore: doing a post-mortem is not always easy, or a nice experience, especially for the first time participant. So that a post-mortem should really be effective, a special attention should then be paid that possible rancor disappears after it and do not appear in another form during a further project cycle.

3 Companion Tools

While the previous chapter has described more the principles of what should be a team configuration and interactions around a software project, this part will focus more on the practical implementation of tools needed to create such a configuration.

3.1 Internal Distribution Process

So that the "dogfooding" principle can be applied in the best conditions, providing a end user like distribution process will help a lot in the ingestion of the main course. Probably the main advantage in setting up such a process is simply to avoid many critics that could occur simply by its absence. Practically, the following elements are needed to establish such a process:

- An automatic software build environment.
- A well defined versioning system.
- A complete and systematical internal distribution infrastructure.
- An easy to use bug system open to the whole company.

3.2 Automatic Software Build Environment

"Continuous integration"[1] is a practice well known from software developers. It basically consists in the fact that software engineers should commit their work frequently, meaning at least once a day, preferably more often. Such an habit ensures mainly that no high divergence, leading to merging nightmare, is created in the source code of the software, and that a new version of the product can always be build in a minimum amount of time. Such a system can also be used to execute more tasks, like for example automatic tests, avoiding thus, to the maximum extent, regression in the developed product. As a result daily quality can only increase.

For non-software engineers, the main advantage of such system lies in the fact that it ensures availability of the product, and provides a feedback on the duration needed to build a complete fresh version. This information provides a useful contribution to the polyrhythm management needed between teams: a new version of the product cannot be available under a measurable amount of time. As a consequence, one can evaluate very fast if this build time is

---

1 *Fowler* (2000).

a critical factor in the software development process, and if more resources should be invested in a build system (parallel processing, addition of new build machine, different project structure).

Different type of software can be built. At the higher level, three main categories can be defined: native desktop client applications, dedicated clients for mobile devices, server based applications. If the first two ones are generally delivered through an end-user installer, the last one requires a deployment on a server. To respect the fact that each cross-functional team has its own working tempo, it is then necessary, as part of the set up of the build system, to create multiple server environments. Practically, it barely matters if those are available on multiple physical hosts, or on one unique host (in such case server speed can however be impacted).

To fully take advantage of an automated build system, this one should be able to provide notifications to a given group of people about the state of a build. When a build is done, a notification is generated (for example email, RSS feed or more "modern" ways like Twitter or IRC), so that the team members are aware of the presence of a new build. Such message should hold information like the name of the project being built, its version, the configuration used for building, a list of bug fixed in the release, and, if possible the originator for a bug fix. To respect fully the constraint of "user like experience", time should be invested in the formatting of such notification so that it is coherent and nice to read. For example mail message could contain images representing the logo of the company or use HTML formatting for better readability.

A practical build system has named "buildbot", and is available as an open source project. Buildbot is written in the Python language and has, among others, following advantages:

- Its deployment is scalable through the distributed use of multiple computers and every CPU resources in the company can contribute to the build system.
- Although it has been developed with obviously Unix based system in mind, it can also be used on Windows based computers.
- It respect the native way of building application and does not try to replace any of those, focusing more on its role as meta-structure using those native build system. Such native way could very well be the running of a set of unitary test.
- As an open source project it stays active and possible defects are fixed usually in a timely manner.
- It provides an HTML based interface, allowing to monitor easily the progress of very build happening on the global IT system (presence of a waterfall display mode) or see if a build has failed, giving thus access to the build log.
- It integrates seamlessly with different kind of source control management system.
- Finally buildbot allows the running of a build in multiple ways: through a trigger, like a change in the source code, in an automated way, or through a "on-demand" way. The combination of those possibilities is adding a contribution in the adaption of the use different tempo by different teams.

There can be also two ways of building: one would be called incremental, where only new elements of source code are built, while the other one would be called a "clean" way, which would build every component of the product from scratch. Incremental build should mainly be used in the case of a developer oriented continuous integration process and stay in this domain.

It has to be noted that if a component has not seen any changes and is built through a clean build, its version may stay the same.

3.3 Versioning

Although, evident at a first look, the issue and tracking of versioning is a critical one during a software development process. Miscommunication can have namely costly consequences like testers spending time on an improper release. Proper versioning is also at the root of the creation of a common team language; for example the presence of a defect/bug system can only be useful if it goes with a versioning system.

It is important also to separate the presence of a user readable versioning from the one of an internal, which may not be necessary "user friendly". Usually, user readable versioning has the following schema "M. m. b". Here "M" represents a major software version (often with a good part of new features), "m" a minor version (bug fixes, stability enhancement and maybe some improvements on a feature), "b" being reserved for very small bug fixes releases.

A complete project is also made of multiple software components. In a natural way, each of them is following its own path of progression. Therefore a two level versioning system should be used. A possible convention is the following

Every component has a version which is simply an integer incremented in a continuous way each time a new version of the component is build. A global, and separated, build number would also exist, representing the high-level project build number.

The complete schema for this global build number could be "D.L.Int" where "D" is a digit representing the major version, "L" is a letter (simply for readability reason) representing the minor version, and "Int" would be an integer incremented at each new build, if at least one change in any project exists (Such versioning system is inspired by Apple's MacOS X versioning convention).

The following diagram represents the way a build number would evolve.

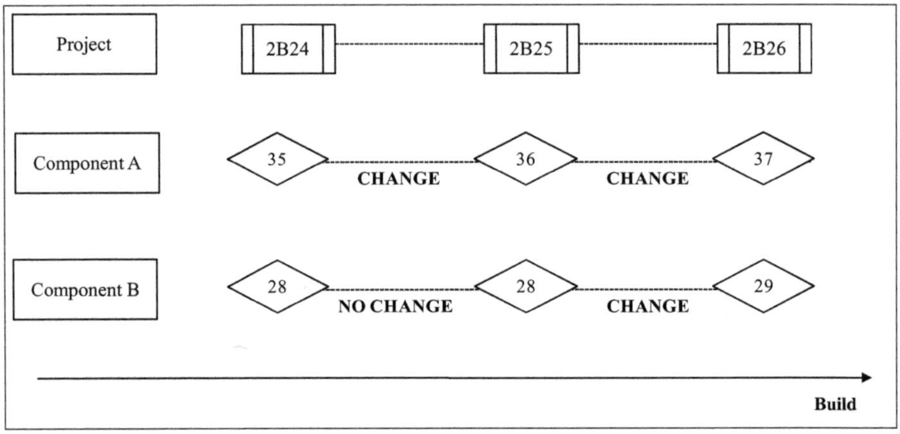

Figure 1: Project versioning organization and evolution

Cases can also occur of parallel project development. At the project version number this will very often translate into a change of minor version (letter in second position). At the component level, there can be 2 cases: either a used component should see its development going continuously, either 2 variants of it should be managed in parallel, and the source code be branched. In such cases, the branch is often versioned with a "dot" schema (e. g 67.45), where only the post digit number is incremented when a build is done. In practice, it is very rare than more than one branches is present and such schema is amply enough.

To ease the defect reporting process, all software components must have their version numbers accessible in a seamless way (About Box for native applications, footer on a web page), at least during the process of development. In an ideal way both the project number and the component number would be displayed.

Finally a minimal "team education" may be necessary to explain the impact of the development workflow on the release process. In particular, not all versions may be available to everyone in the company, as the Quality Assurance team may reject some of them.

3.4 Starting from the Source – Control Management System

So that the integration of a versioning system like mentioned above is possible, it s concept should be embedded at the root of the development process. This happens usually through source code organization inside the source control management system. Although a Subversion (commonly known in the industry as "SVN") system will be considered in the rest of the document, the principles described here can very well be achieved with other Source Control Management environment (Git, Perforce, CVS...).

Organizing source code is a never-ending task. It is also a necessity: when a new team member arrives in a Research & Development department, the first practical task should always be the following: get the source code of the project, build it, launch it in a debugger, find the "area of work", start the modifications. As projects evolve, so does the source code organization change: components become obsolete, others are grouped in logical entities, and new components appear. A key point in the choice of a Source Control System should always be its flexibility in proceeding for such organizations. As a testimony, until approximately 2005, the "king" of Source Control Management System was CVS; it was barely touchable. Since then Subversion has taken this role and mainly replaces CVS. There are many reasons for this (transaction support, easy transition path...) but certainly among the developers community the most appreciated one was the possibility to simply rename a file (without losing its history) allowing to finally get rid of some very short eight characters-long undecipherable name, coming from the dawn of the PC evolution.

Practically the organization needs for a project are translated into operations like branching and tagging. Due to its implementation for such features, SVN provides a lot of flexibility. A common organization can be the following:

- At the top level the main organization contains 4 main paths: one addressing the component organization, one addressing the higher level project organization, one being simply a "Playground" for each developer, where experimentation is possible, one containing the end results for each build version. Additionally a fifth path may be considered, holding the storage of the organization itself (build system related files, common delivery related code.)

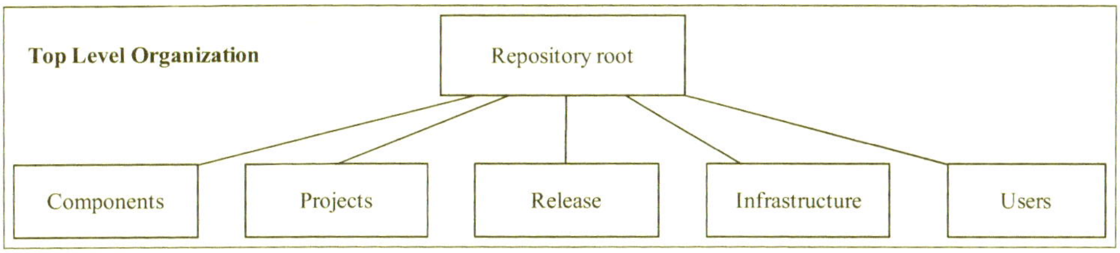

Figure 2: Example of a Source Control Management Repository organization

- The "Components" path is where the source code is really stored. Each component is broken down in a well-known schema: trunk (main development path), branches (for development of small sub releases, or on the opposite for the one of real major changes) and tags.
- The project related path consists then in a collection of links, also known as externals, to the needed components. A developer can then simply check out a project she/he is working on and proceed from here. Naming of a top-level project can be done using either a master version related schema, either product marketing version, or for new projects code names.
- The purpose of the "Releases" area is to keep a copy of the output of the build system. The organization of this area can very well reflect multiple organization structures. For example, in addition to the root "build versions", it is very well possible to add release paths linked to the functional organization inside the company/project. The content of those would be simply references to the "raw builds", after going through an approval process.

The following diagram shows a possible evolution along projects build.

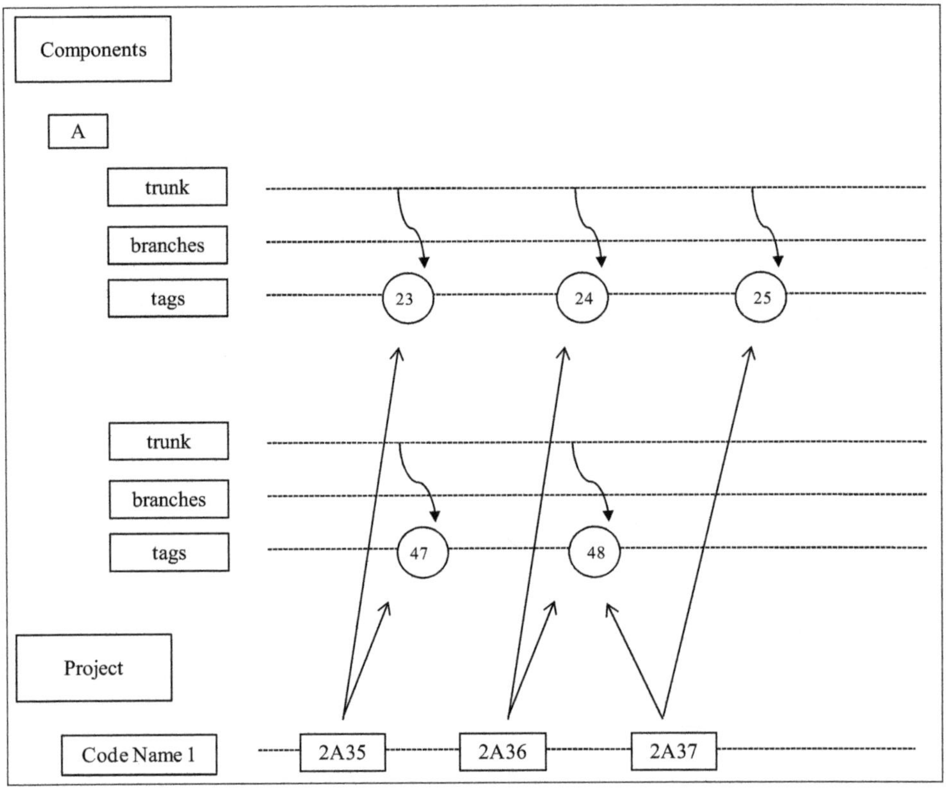

Figure 3: *Build Process related interactions inside a Source Control Management Process*

3.5 Packaging and the Distribution Process

Distribution is always the interface to the end customer, and this includes all members of a project teams. For server-based products, deployment is the main operation. For product that should be explicitly installed, efforts need to be dedicated so that such process is seamless. This general implies creation of an installer; as consequence, the Quality Assurance team should take in account multiple installation scenarios: first install, upgrade (including possible data migration). In both cases, document should be created like legal disclaimers, releases notes, company logo.

Internally distribution needs to happen following an easy to remember and coherent schema; a simple mean like a centralized distribution server is enough. In particular for server-based products, it can also be interesting to integrate in the product URL an indication of the "client team" and protect the access to the server (e. g.: people from the marketing team will not be able to log on to the server dedicated to the developer team).

3.6 Be ready for Feedback (and issues!)

As a project starts to progress, a process of feedback will take place and be part of the life of project. In general, the faster this stream is analyzed and processed, the better corrections can be brought to the project path. The Project Manager should first establish a few rules.

First, only one unique channel of feedback should be allowed on the project, that is a centralized bug system (also known as ticket or defect system). It is namely very common that some team members would favor other means like email, which at first looks certainly more convenient. The issue here is that email based communication does not lead to a standardized form of feedback which can be worked on later and in a convenient manner, by someone possibly not on the initial email distribution. Additionally when the management is in the position to use the bug system, they place themselves in a closer position to the team members.

Many open sources, or commercial, solution exists for such a system. To quote a few examples, some well known ones have for name Bugzilla, Trac, Redmine, or Mantis[2]. Even if the choice for one or the other is very often a matter of preferences, a few elements should always be taken in consideration. Those are:

- How to describe a defect/bug life cycle, and is such way parameter configurable? In general the main steps in the life of a bug are the following. First a bug as an "Unread" state, as long as it has not been reviewed by a Bug Review Board. Once done, the bug is given an assignee and a priority and move to an "In Work "state. When a fix is found, the bug will move to an "Integrate" state: that is, the solution has been found, needed changes committed to the source code, but no build exists yet containing the fix. Then the bug enters the "Build" or "Deploy" step, as soon as the automatic build system has started its process. This state has very often a short duration and can be seen more as a warning that "something is coming". After this the bug enters a "Verification" state, whose failure will send back to the In Work stage, and success in a final "Closed" state.

  It can happen however that those steps configuration does not work out in an efficient manner for a team. For example, more states can be needed instead of a unique "In Work", so one can guess how much the real work on the bug has progressed, or if is still staying as a non-processed entity in a pile of bugs, and if more resources should be brought to the Research and Development team. A bug system should allow such configuration.

- Can metadata be added easily to a bug description? Effectively the more a project is evolving the higher the number of bugs to process will be. To get a higher-level overview on the project advancement, bugs needs to be tagged across various dimensions (priority, component, nature, configuration where it happens.). In particular a very common habit is to have a field describing the nature of the bug along the following axis: real bug, enhancement request, feature (and as such all feature for a project should be entered in the bug system). It allows namely to manage the scope of a given release, avoiding undesired and costly changes of direction.

[2] Cf. *WIKIPEDIA* (2009).

- Can one do and save custom queries? Depending on the role of who is using the bug system, different approach to it will exist. For example, a member of the R&D team will first want to know how much defects are on her/his To-Do list. The manager of the QA team will want to know if tickets have been properly verified. The Project Manager would want to be able to track "hot potato" issues that are bugs that are changing of owner in a very fast way, usually because they are harder to find. The possibility to create and manage a pool of per user queries is then crucial.

  Another nice to use possibility is when the bug system can handle bug URL in a very systematical (RESTful) way. Practically it allows simply to read a report, click on a bug title and be led to a detailed description and can reveal to be a huge time saver

- How is the integration with the Source Code Management system (e. g. SVN). Both directions of communication should be considered here. That is first the bug system should have the possibility to easily know which source code change contains the resolution of the issue. Now if one considers a usage of the SCM system like described previously and containing the full management of the project, it is also very convenient to be able to attach a list of bug fixes to a given revision. The Subversion system offers for example the possibility to attach custom properties to a given file, or set of externals.

- Are the reporting capabilities convenient? In such case, more is very often not better. Very often the most practical and relevant feedback is namely a simple curve allowing to see if the bug count is increasing and decreasing. Such simple statistic and metrics should be available.

- Does the bugs system provide notifications? Although the centralized point for defect tracking should be the bug system, it may not be the main tool of a given team member. Therefore notifications features like Mail sending or RSS feed are very often the primary step on the path to the Bug System use.

- Does the bug system offer integration with the project time information? Although not mandatory, such feature can prove to be convenient, that is the possibility to relate the pool of bug to a timeline or schedule, allowing to see if a project is in advance or delayed. On the other hand, it may also add an additional and unnecessary complexity to the bug system.

- Finally, last but not least, a particular attention should be given to the usability of the bug system. This includes also the look and design of the user interface, if it can be customized, the speed of the system, if it can be accessed through on different devices (mobile access for devices like iPhone is definitely a plus). If one wants that the bug system becomes the centralized tool of the project, such features have to be there.

As a conclusion, it can be said that investigating time in the choice of a bug system, is usually having a high level of reward. A bug system should certainly not only a developer and QA tool, but more become the central meeting point for the complete project.

3.7 Additional Notifications

Although the problem of notification related to progress of the build system and ticket changes have already been mentioned, one should also mention an additional area where notification is required. That is source code changes. It may happen however that developers may not feel comfortable with the idea, as it basically "exposes all their work" to the rest of the world. In such case the manager of the R&D team has to enforce it as it can be a time saver in case of failure search.

For every set of notifications linked to a project, time should be invested in their formatting and display. For example, mail based notifications should have key information in their title so they can be searched easily. Presence of corporate identity elements inside the notification is also a plus and contributes to the team building.

Finally, it happens very often that once a few claims have happened because "no information is here", more complains exist because "too much information is here". That is team members have the feeling to be over-flown by notifications of any kind. At this point, the question is often asked to improve the system simply to "provide the right notification to the right people". Clearly a little can be done here with through the management of the distribution lists. However refusing to have a team and resources dealing with such issues is very often the best solution. Effectively, features like Mail filtering are easily usable on a end user machine, and one can always consider that it is part of the job of a team member to be able to manage the flow information and adapt it to her/his need.

4 Develop the Developers

While the previous chapters have focus on how to setup a complete team in order to be ready to face a challenging software project, one particular team to be considered is the Research and Development one, that is also the one at the root of the production line. For such a team the challenge is to be able to both deliver while growing both at the knowledge level and at the delivery's one.

A common pitfall in the management of an R&D team lies in the handling of the pressure applied to the team members. "Passing too much of it" is creating a feeling of insecurity, a loss of focus, and a lack of confidence in the management crew. It forces software developers to deal with costly interruptions, usually in a random and semi-chaotic way. On the opposite, "retaining too much of it" can also not goes unnoticed, and fails completely to consider the liability of team members. For the manager, a fine balance must exist where she/he should communicate and explain daily "micro-changes" in the project, but also their reasons, and how to deal with them technically and emotionally. Only then, team members will learn to deal with such interruptions in an effective way, while not losing the focus on the main target, as well as enforcing their motivation and comforting a feeling of common and individual growth.

4.1 The Meanings of "Growth"

There are a few ways an engineering team needs to manage its growth. At the basic level, the resource growth has to be considered. So that products can be delivered, new software developer needs to be hired in the most appropriate way. A very good practice for a team is to maintain a list describing all assets present in the team, and the one that would be needed to properly complete a project. By putting those two lists in parallel, it is then pretty straightforward to decide what capabilities are needed in a team. When an area of development is identified, there can be usually two possibilities. Either a team member would like to consider it for herself/himself, either new employees should be brought in. For a manager to take the appropriate decision, considerations of personality, schedule and current workload should be discussed in an openly manner. If an already present engineer is chosen to work on a different area, it might very well possible that still new head-counts are required, and in such a case one should consider the cost of a period of knowledge transition. When a new employee arriving in the team, the presence of an infrastructure like the one described above should ease the integration and make her/him feel form the start she/he can provide tangible contributions.

Another axis of growth is the one of the group homogeneity. Besides the different personalities, the manager of the development team should make sure that the team is becoming a consistent entity. In particular, attention should be taken so that any member of the team can leave at anytime (either for a short period of time, or in a definitive way). Naturally, a team consists of people with different backgrounds, experiences and seniority. But while "developing the homogeneity", the manager of the team should always ensure that here/his own requirement are the target for everyone, and integrates the experience of everyone in a way that enforces this set of "own" requirement instead of having them diluted through attempts to accommodate the personality of everyone.

It can also happen that even after some times, an employee is not in the position to contribute in the most efficient way. Such situation generates usually mutual frustration and even feelings of sorrow. If multiple attempts to correct the situation do not lead to satisfaction, painful decision like termination of the employee should be undertaken. Although difficult to take, it is always better when such event happens without delay.

4.2 Engineering Steps

Technical individual growth for each employee should also be a target for a team manager. Without going through an exhaustive list of practices, that can also be overwhelming and lead to no practical step, here are a few habits that can lead to positive results.

- Enforcement of a well know set of "pragmatic programmer"[3] habits: regular sitting with developer while working on a component, enforce code commenting, re-reading and if needed re-factoring, be strict on the naming conventions and coding style. Code reviews can naturally be considered as a way to tackle of all those issues, but may at first be appear too "time consuming" while working on a project. A "lighter" but regular interaction may lead to more concrete results.

3 Cf. *HUNT/THOMAS* (1999).

- Have the developer participate in open-source projects, even if those are not close to the current project. The simple fact to be confronted to "unknown" developers, and have to adapt to a different team (and usually without never seeing them) can only provide experience and help when working with in a "close situation".
- Enforce the idea of delivery and this through practical small deadlines. Very often software developers have a tendency to delay the commit of their work to the Source Code Management system, with the idea/excuse that "it can break the complete system". Practically progresses can happen only through continuous integration so that potential issues are detected as soon as possible. The role of a manager is to provide enough "rights to mistake" so that a team member does not have any apprehension in doing so. Such practice will contribute in the building of confidence and the process of fast reaction to a problem.
- Finally the organization of regular technical talk among developers is a very efficient way to spread the knowledge inside a team and to have people understanding the complete system. Those happen very often to be the places where an individual contributor ends up asking the "real" questions that can lead to the complete system understanding. In a similar way, it is essential to enforce that developer's copy the entire team on email, when they have fundamental questions.

5 Conclusion

Without giving any "ideal recipe" to manage software projects, the main aim of this article is to show that applying a software methodology requires to go through multiple small steps in many areas among the project team. From the definition of roles and communication between team members, to the set up of a practical technical infrastructure giving a tangible foundation and reference to everyone, as well as the regular development of practices that will help the global growth of a team.

As a result, tangible benefits should be seen inside a team project or the complete company: global increase in motivation and individual satisfaction, enhanced cross functional dynamic through a positive challenging behavior, gain in efficiency leading to cost reduction, better productivity leading to an increase of the company reputation and intellectual property.

References

FOWLER, M. (2000): Continuous Integration, online: http://martinfowler.com/articles/continuousIntegration.html, last update: 01.05.2006, date visited: 29.09.2009

WIKIPEDIA (2009): Comparison of issue tracking systems, online: http://en.wikipedia.org/wiki/Comparison_of_issue_tracking_systems, last update: 29.09.2006, date visited: 30.09.2009

HUNT, A./THOMAS, D. (1999): The Pragmatic Programmer: From Journeyman to Master, Amsterdam 1999.

Global Production Center in Latin America for Application Management Services

Maximo Romero Krause

Siemens AG – Siemens IT Solution and Services

1 Latin America – Emerging Region

Latin America has been emerging as a strong IT services market. This achievement has been of course very important for local and global service providers and also for several companies in the region; but specially for Latin American governments who are able to accelerate their economies with IT services as a very important pillar.

Instability in the region is greater than in Europe or North America, but less than in Southeast Asia or Africa. The region still has to overcome difficult challenges, such as wealth distribution, healthcare, education, unemployment, currency stability and, in some areas, even political strife and social unrest

But the significant information is that most of the economies in the region have been evolving at rates higher than world averages. The region has typically been an emerging market, moving to expand business and take advantage of economic opportunities. It has already attracted many major global corporations.[1]

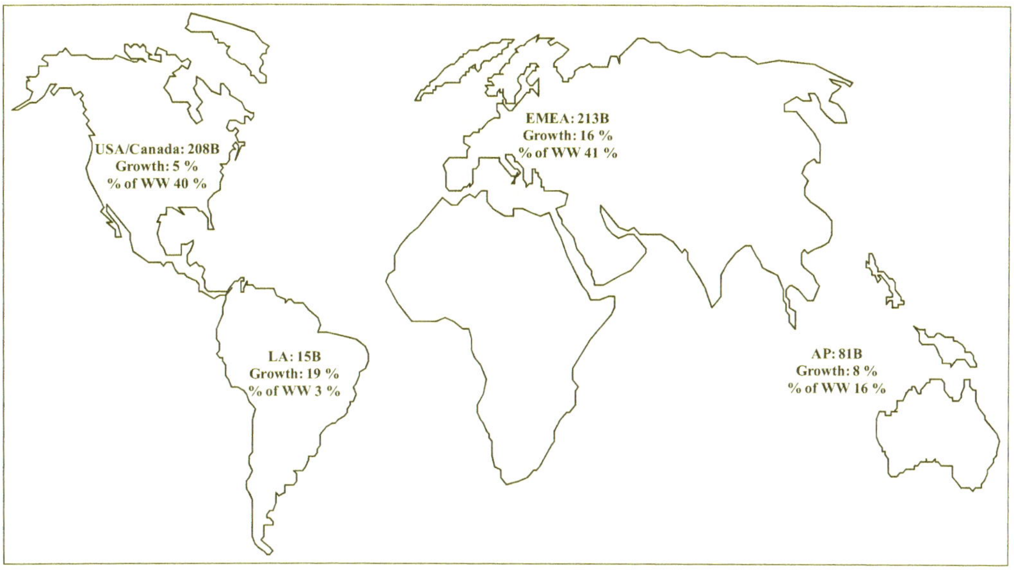

Figure 1: Worldwide Total IT Services Market Size, 2007[2]

Nowadays, IT service providers seeking to expand their global presence will consider the Latin American market as a potential growth opportunity. As a region, its businesses are increasingly participating in the global economy, global corporations invariably have a presence there, and technology adoption grows at record rates. However, to be successful in that market, service providers must understand its unique dynamics.

---

1 Cf. *GARTNER* (2005) p. 1.

2 *IDC* (2007).

In an increasingly globalized world, business practices tend to become more standardized and, in different geographic regions, you would expect that processes would be similar. Although different societies are capable of sharing business processes designed according to international templates, they still imprint in them the characteristics of their own habits, behaviors, cultures and beliefs. Below the level of appearances, different cultures, educational backgrounds, economic levels and business maturity shape different business environments.[3]

2 Focus on Application Management

In a globalized world, Latin America is an interesting destination for IT service providers as they look to expand their presence in different regions. Service providers can increase their share in the local market and also compete for offshore and nearshore business opportunities for clients elsewhere, making use of the delivery capabilities.

Global players, as shown in Figure 2, are already doing so in a wide variety of IT Services, such as Application Management Services.

Within Application Management Services we understand the effective support and maintenance of those applications. Moreover, the realization of the benefits of IT investment to make the Customer business more efficient and more profitable.
A key part of the Application Lyfecycle.

The following sections analyze the concept of a Global Production Center in Application Management Services considering the Latin American region as an interesting case, as well as specific characteristics that should be addressed when creating such a delivery center as part of a Global Delivery Network.

[3] Cf. *GARTNER* (2006), p. 4.

Figure 2: Selected Delivery Centers in South America[4]

---

4 *AMR Research* (2007).

3 Global Production Center in Latin America – (GPC)

Global Production Centers, commonly designated as GPC, provide standardized services which are performed around the world. Within these organizations, there are different "factories", each of them focusing on a single area of Application Management Services.

The Global Production Centers as part of an IT key player service organization, are usually more than one but only a few around the world, settled strategically in the most convenient cities in order to provide full industrialized and standard Application Management services to Customers all over the world.

Main characteristics of a Global Production Center are standardization, optimized resource utilization and advantages of low cost regions.

Standardization

- Global introduction of common tools and methods, based on an Application Management Framework.
- Global rollout of standard processes.
- More automation of processes.

Resource utilization

- Optimized resource utilization through capacity optimization and load balancing.
- Capacity optimization with common delivery pool, used for multiple customers.
- Performance Management for core delivery processes along service chain, globally standardized.

Low Cost Capabilities

- Delivery of new business mostly from global production centers in low cost locations.
- Overhead reduction in high- cost countries; Service Factory concept (shift centralized tasks to cost efficient locations).

In 2007 the Global Production Center Mercosur has been established in Latin America as part of the strategy of Application Management Services in *Siemens* IT Solutions and Services, including two main sites located in Buenos Aires, Argentina and Sao Paulo, Brazil;

Together with the GPCs located in Russia, India and Germany, the GPC in Mercosur completes the global delivery network of Global Application Management production centers within *Siemens IT Solutions and Services*, allowing to offer 7 days by 24 hours global customer's services, under the concept "follow the sun".

Additionally, the opportunity to serve a wide variety of Customers in the Americas time zone, in the same language (Spanish, Portuguese, English) and taking the advantage of cultural similarities and proximity. Specific characteristics of the business environment in Latin America and specially Mercosur, lead the decision to establish or increase their presence in the region.

- Mercosur (ARG, BRA) represents more than 50 % of the Latin America service market.[5]
- Buenos Aires and Sao Paulo open the entire Latin America market; the 5th largest market in the world (by GDP)[6].
- Latin America economic growth higher than the expected world growth.[7]
- International Data Corp (IDC) predicted that IT spending growth in the region would be a healthy 7–8 %, higher than in the U.S. and Europe.
- For the whole Mercosur the *SAP ERP* market share is 37 %.[8]

Additional factors have also influenced in the decision of the attractiveness of Latin America to settle a new Global Production Center such as:[9]

- Economic activity: A high level of economic activity in a country or region demands business solutions. This creates an active IT market, which in turn, increases IT maturity.
- Prepared workforce: An active economy will demand IT solutions, increasing market dynamics. That, in turn, will make a host of professionals available that have IT experience, not only from school books, but from using IT to solve real business problems or to support real business processes.
- Laws and regulations: The set of laws and regulations affecting the business of local and foreign suppliers is a strong factor in a globalized world. It may be the tipping point in a decision regarding the deployment of a new service unit.
- Educational infrastructure: The existence of an educational infrastructure devoted to creating (and retraining) IT professionals will guarantee the supply of new resources as the IT and IT services markets develop.
- Low Cost: Cost efficient locations provide an important advantage and interesting proposals to Customers.

On this regard, Gartner has provided analysis and rates of countries for their maturity and their potential as an option for the delivery of services.

---

5 Cf. *IDC* (2007), p. 14.

6 Cf. *Siemens IT Solutions and Services* (2008).

7 Cf. *IMF* (2009).

8 Cf. *Siemens IT Solutions and Services* (2008).

9 Cf. *Gartner* (2005) p. 3.

If services provided internally to the country and exported are considered, India is the leader in global IT services sourcing, and the countries in Latin America rank as:

- Challengers: Brazil and Mexico
- Up-and-covers: Argentina, Chile, Colombia, Costa Rica and Puerto Rico

Latin America is already an active region with regard to IT adoption, IT services and outsourcing. The region is maturing and behaving like more-developed regions as globalization advances.

The next figure offers an assessment of the usual factors taken into consideration when deciding where to locate in Latin America.

Criteria	Argentina	Brazil	Chile	Mexico	Colombia	Cost Rica
Cost attractiveness	●	◕	◑	◑	●	◑
Availability of skilled labor	◕	◕	◑	◕	◔	◑
Language capabilities	◕	◑	◔	◕	◔	◕
Political and economic stability	◔	◑	●	◑	○	●
Government support	◑	◔	●	◔	◔	●
Cultural affinity	◕	◑	◕	◕	◔	◕
Total attractiveness	◕	◕	◑	◑	◔	◑
Key highlights (pros and cons)	• Lowest wages for skilled labor in the region • Political and economic stability for a relatively short time compared to neighboring countries	• Significantly outnumbers country peers in call center and ITO industries, though it has a strong domestic focus • Limited number of English and Spanish speakers	• Remarkable stability of political and business environment • Limited availability of professionals fluent in English	• Closest to the United States • More developed market for BPO in the region, especially in finance and accounting • Key costs (salary, real estate) are higher than most peers	• Stable economy with available labor • Reputation impact, although crime rates in Bogots are lower than in Sao Paulo, the country's reputation reduces the inflow of investments	• Very good bilingual skills • Strong presence of large international (captive) service centers and vendors • Limited workforce availability given population size and potential saturation

○ least attractive ⟶ ● most attractive

Figure 3: *Latin America country attractiveness assessment*[10]

10 *AT KEARNEY* (2009).

3.1 Laborforce Availability in Latin America

In Latin America there is a motivated workforce and talented, which is a key factor when setting up a Global Production Center in IT.

In 2007, multinationals created thousands of new jobs in Colombia, Argentina, Chile, Costa Rica, Brazil and Mexico. The talented pool is key asset. People are entrepreneurial, driven to succeed, and acutely interested in technology and business. They have excellent work ethic and great interpersonal skills which make them desirable to many companies. In major cities, people are often bilingual, a skill necessary to work for the growing number of U. S. and multinational companies in the region.

RICHARD FEINBERG, a professor at the University of California in San Diego and former director of the Office of Inter-American Affairs for the White House National Security Council, notes that workplaces in Latin America tend to be social hubs. The region is known for its close-knit families, colorful traditions and offices which are not staid and quiet. "Latin Americans mix social lives with work. They are not happy in an environment where they stare at screen all day", he says. Latin American's have a drive to grow and discover. The region has a large number of people between the ages of 15 and 39, a group that comprises the core of its excellent labor force. Their drive to succeed contributes to attrition rates being much lower than those in India or Asia.

At least 11 major cities in Latin America with a minimum of 1.5 mi people to assure the workforce availability and numerous universities Argentina, Brazil, Chile and Mexico expanding university enrollment, IT graduates and quality certifications. Latin America has also developed some key IT and business services capabilities which cross a narrower set of competencies and in limited geographic locations. While the region has closer proximity to the US than other offshore, its potential as an offshore destination varies from country to country.

Among all countries in Latin America, Brazil stands out as an interesting IT center location characterized by the large workforce availability and local market size and Argentina by extremely competitive cost advantages and talented English speaking laborforce.

3.2 Brazil, Growth and largest Economy in Latin America

Brazil is a growth country and the largest economy en Latin America. In IT services it has a mature service market, currently represents about 40 % of *SAP* business in Latin America. *SAP* Professionals Program developing professionals for Latin America did incorporate more than 5000 new SAP consultants to the IT market in 2008.

With almost 200 million people, Brazil also represents a large segment of the total population of Latin America. Only six years ago, 54 % of the society was classified as poor. Now the figure is only 26 % which results in 50 million people joining the middle class. These people are consuming food, beverages, clothing, and cosmetics, which fuel the economy and create a new market.

Brazil does have a 60 % Tax barrier for service imports. To be competitive everybody has to offer the services from Brazil. The tax barrier compensates the higher price from Brazil. Brazil has traditionally hosted the large call center market in Latin America and now as well as Argentina; Brazil has developed some core competencies in providing application development and maintenance, and is now building a greater expertise in delivering other IT services.

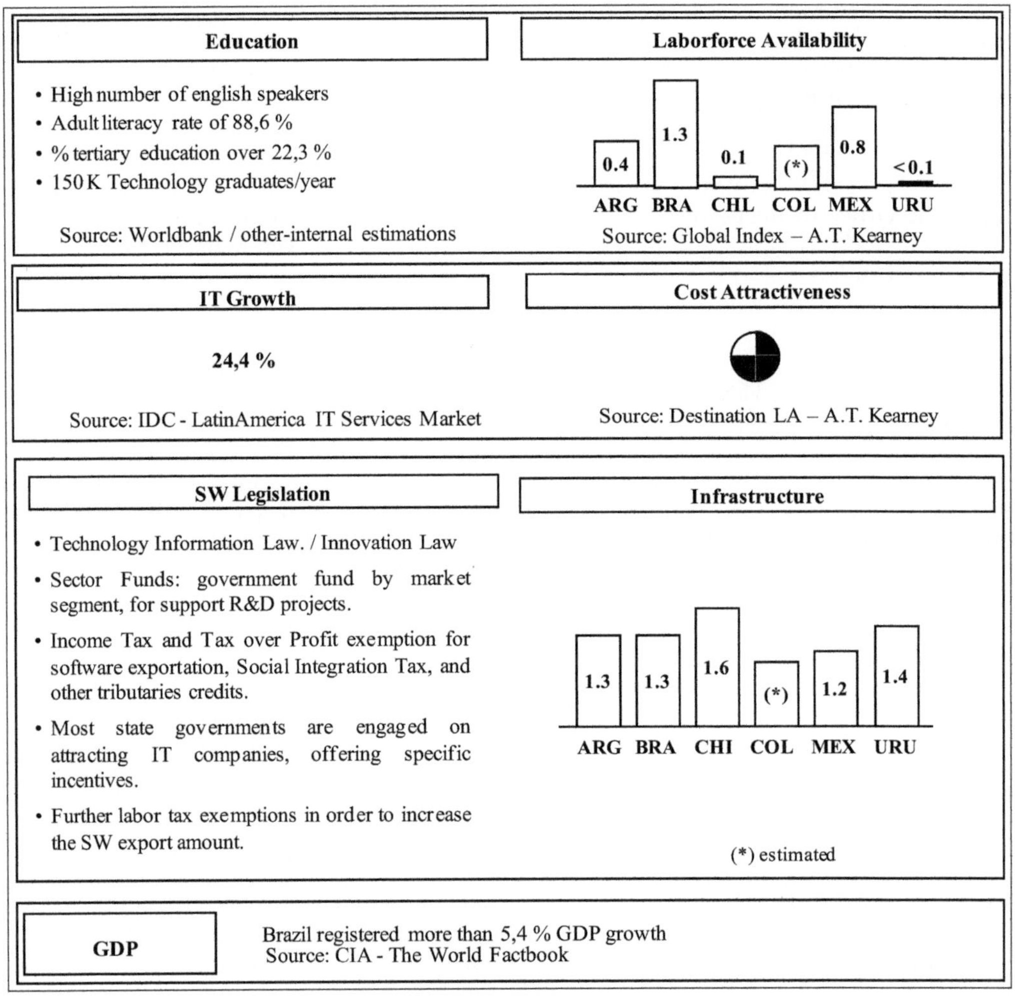

Figure 4: Brazil Country Profile[11]

11 Cf. *AT KEARNEY* (2007), *CIA* (2009) and *WORLD BANK* (2009).

3.3 Argentina, Substantial Potential for Offshoring

Argentina benefits from rich natural resources, a highly literate population, and a diversified industrial base. A large population of highly trained programmers and designers has helped the country stand out from its Latin American neighbors in the technology domain. Unemployment during Argentina's 2001 currency crash was a boom to outsourcing vendors in Argentina. These outsourcers are making their services available to the rest of Latin America and are starting to look at the US market. Argentina is attractive because of its time zone and culture similarities.

Argentina offers application development and maintenance as well as call-center support services. Though it has a reasonable infrastructure, English skills and a strong cultural compatibility, it suffers from political and economic instability. Argentina has developed significant advantages for IT service delivery:

- Highly qualified human resources
- Enhanced skills availability on recent technologies and languages
- Payroll costs below international average
- Reasonable telecommunications and information technology infrastructure
- Leader in Spanish-content products
- New laws for software industry development

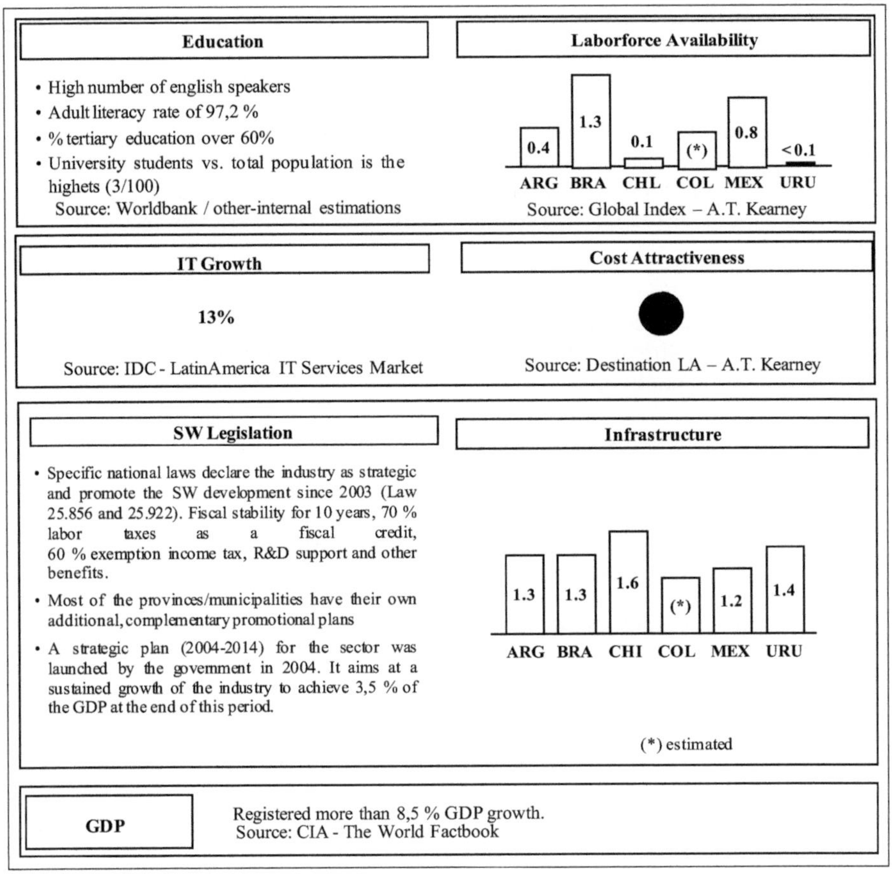

Figure 5: Argentina Country Profile[12]

4 GPC Mercosur, a Key Location in the Global Production Center network

The Global Production Centers (GPCs) are responsible for providing high quality technical delivery of services.

Adhering to ITIL best practice framework, the focus is to provide efficient technical services through the use of standardized tools, processes and roles across all GPCs. It's the factory concept bundles together highly skilled resources with similar skill sets aligned to vital business processes. This enables the GPC network access to a wide pool of technical expertise which offers in-depth knowledge and experience across functional clusters, as well as knowledge sharing and learning from each other.

[12] Cf. *AT KEARNEY* (2007), *CIA* (2009) and *WORLD BANK* (2009).

As they bundle together resources, factories are an important substructure within the GPCs. Current most common defined factories are: Business Intelligence (BI), Customer Relationship Management, (CRM), Financials (FIN), Logistics (LOG), Human Resources Management (HRM) and Technology (TECH).

The GPC Mercosur in Latin America, is integrated to the network by having the same and common processes among other GPCs within *Siemens* IT Solution and Services, such as the GPC Russia, India and Germany.

Processes mostly ruled by a standard and worldwide applicable Service Operation Handbook, describing a professional approach for Global Application Management Services and supported by commonly ruled initiatives such as: Incident Management, Change Management, Service Level Management among other ITIL processes, Common Delivery Pool and Follow the Sun Concepts, and commonly implemented tools.

4.1 Incident Management

The primary goal of the Incident Management process is to restore normal service operation as quickly as possible and minimize the adverse impact on business operations. This ensures that the best possible levels of service quality and availability are maintained.

- 'Normal service operation' is defined as service operation within SLA's
- Early detection and resolution of incidents resulting higher availability of services
- Capability to identify business priorities and dynamically allocate resources as necessary
- Identify potential improvements to services

Incident Management is highly visible to the business and it is therefore easier to demonstrate its value than most areas in Service Operation. For this reason, Incident Management is often one of the first processes to be implemented in service management projects.
The added benefit of doing this is that Incident Management can be used to highlight other areas that need attention. This provides a justification for expenditure on implementing other processes.

4.2 Common Ticketing Tool across all Global Production Centers

A unique tool globally available provides a standardized solution for the complete IT Service Delivery Process chain. This is the backbone for international service concepts enabling cross border business and the basis for the implementation of different ITIL processes such as Incident, Problem and Change Management.

Fully integrated platform and implemented in more than 300 Customers from *Siemens* IT Solutions and Services, the Operational Service Desk (OSD), a BMC ARS Remedy based tool, is the standard ticketing tool for *Siemens* IT Solutions and Services, for its worldwide IT services. Supporting the complete management process chain and enabling seamless cross border business.

Operational Service Desk (OSD) contributes to the integration of the existing tool landscape and allows the consolidation of many solutions into an international standard. Key benefits:

- ITIL Adherence – Complete adherence to ITIL aligned service management process.
- SLA Tracking – Easy Tracking of incident response times and service desk performance against pre-defined SLA
- Integration – Integrates well with Third Party Software.
- KNOX – Flexible integration of Knowledge Database

Additionally can offer the option where the key users are able to create also their tickets without the intervention of a first level consultant. For that purpose, the Global Production Centers usually provide customers with secure internet access to the ticketing tool. Once registered, users are able to enter incidents and query the status of previously reported incidents. That gives the customer visibility and also possibility to follow the progress of the GPC performance.

4.3 Common Delivery Pool (CPD) Concept

By using a Common Delivery Pool (or repository) of incidents worldwide as part of the Incident Management Process, all Global Production Centers and its resources can be combined together to provide a single service to the Customer.

One incident from a Customer can be resolved from one or another location; and also allowing the cooperation between each other. And, moreover consultants can work on incidents from several Customers.

The goal is to enable worldwide the collaboration within the Factories of each Global Production Center, thus enabling an excellent service and great efficiency.
In the Common Delivery Pool, project boundaries do not exist. Consultants are not assigned to a particular Customer and the consultants within a Factory are usually organized based on Global Service Areas.

A Service Area is a grouping of consultants within a Factory based on their core skills (Technical & Business knowledge).

Therefore, the tickets (Incidents) are moved from the Common Pool and resolved at Local Service Areas. Within a Service Area, any consultant who has the right skill sets (domain & technical) and the Business Process knowledge can resolve the ticket.

- Enablers to deliver the service by using a worldwide Common Delivery Pool:
  - Unified and worldwide Ticketing Tool
  - Knowledge Management (KM) Portal
  - Live Tools
  - Training

➢ Advantages of using the Common Delivery pool

Mission of CDP: To increase the effectiveness and efficiency of all value creating processes within GAA and between GPC:

Driver for the CDP concept	Enabler
Reduced delivery costs by increased utilization in GPCs	➢ Standardized Maximum flexibility in ticket assignment ➢ Use of cross-customer workgroups ➢ Implement pull-principle ➢ process and documentation (KM) ➢ Process improvement will impact all customers
Ensure business continuity independent from location and/or individuals	➢ Use of cross-GPC workgroups ➢ Enlarge group of enabled consultants ➢ Standardized process and documentation (KM)
Ability to provide 24/7 by follow-the-sun principle	➢ Use of cross-GPC workgroups
Optimize a seamless knowledge transfer	➢ Enlarge group of enabled consultants ➢ Implement 'Back-up' concept ➢ Standardized process and documentation (KM)
Increase attractiveness for consultants by job/task enlargement and experience leveraging	➢ Use of cross-customer workgroups ➢ Enlarge group of enabled consultants ➢ Implement 'Back-up' concept

Table 1: Driver for the CDP concept

4.4 Service Level Agreements (SLA) Management

The Service Level Management (SLM) process is responsible for ensuring Service Level Agreements (SLAs) and underpinning Operational Level Agreements (OLAs) or contracts are met, and for ensuring that any adverse impact on service quality are kept to a minimum. The process involves assessing the impact of Changes upon service quality and SLAs, both when Changes are proposed and after they have been implemented. Some of the most important targets set in the SLAs will relate to service availability and thus require Incident resolution within agreed periods.[13]

SLM is the hinge for Service Support and Service Delivery. It cannot function in isolation as it relies on the existence and effective working of other processes. An SLA without underpinning support processes is useless, as there is no basis for agreeing its content.

[13] Cf. *ITIL Foundations* (2009).

Ticketing Tools allows the definition of the each project SLA (Service Level Agreement). The SLA calculation and control takes into consideration the different time zones and countries where GPCs are established. This results in the ability to route tickets among Global Production Centers (GPCs) and still be able to control and achieve the Service Level Agreement (SLA) for a Customer.

Within the Service Level Agreement definition, the Ticketing Tool is able to:

- Differentiate between Response and Resolution time.
- Manage different Service Level Agreements (SLAs) for specific ticket types.
- Define Business and Services hours per day for the SLA calculation and control.

4.5 Description of "follow the sun" Concept

"Follow the sun" is the concept of a service designed to provide support all around the globe and timezones, delivered by a staff from Global Production Centers in different countries. The concept is: Service Delivery remains always "open".

Generally, 24 hours in-house operation is critical but it may not be an option that looks feasible for a Global Production Center due to several operational constraints. For that reason, the "Follow the Sun" model creates a 24 hours virtual workday for a Customer Organization. In this model when the operations of one GPC go off, the other GPC (in other timezone) takes over the responsibility for the next shift.

And within this shift in the delivery location, also the tickets are transferred. As an example, the Global Production Center in Mercosur will transfer the operation to India at the end of the day in the Americas and then viceversa at the end of the day in Asia.

The result for the customer is that their organization is On-Line 24 hours a day. This model creates continuous stream of production and reduce dramatically the calendar days required to deliver a project or product. Someone can say that with this concept, the sun never set down in GPC's around the world.

5 Customer Service Organization, Customer intimacy

As it was described in the first chapters, in an increasingly globalized world, business practices tend to become more standardized and, in different geographic regions, you would expect that processes would be similar. Although different societies are capable of sharing business processes designed according to international templates, they still imprint in them the characteristics of their own habits, behaviors, cultures and beliefs. Below the level of appearances, different cultures, educational backgrounds, economic levels and business maturity shape different business environments.[14] For that reason, its important in this Global Delivery Concept to count with local organizations or representatives.

The Customer Service Organization (CSO) holds a key function in the operational framework as the local in-country representative for customers and internal units responsible for the complete service delivery provided by the Global Production Centers.

CSO is responsible for the operational service delivery of customer specific, non-standardized services in an effective and profitable way to fulfill contract terms and meet customer expectations. Customer intimacy is key for the services and provides a local, highly effective, single point of contact (SPoC) interface for the customer.

The CSO organization has overall responsibility for service quality towards the Customer, to guarantee high quality delivery and services in accordance with the contractual SLAs and KPIs. The CSO in parallel fosters enhanced service quality throughout the service lifecycle which is derived from continuously introduced improvements, innovations and ensuring quality. Its broad business and application knowledge is thereby indispensable. In case of arising problems, the CSO is an escalation mechanism.

6 Key Findings – Why a GPC in Mercosur?

Latin America is already an active and fairly developed region with regard to IT adoption, IT services and outsourcing. The region is maturing and behaving like more-developed regions as globalization advances and local government efforts strive to develop a strong IT-services-based industry. As a result, we see global service providers positioning themselves to establish resources in different areas in the region, and delivering those resources to clients in the region as well as outside of it. At the same time, we see a strong base of local service providers emerging, not only to support local clients, but evolving as offshore alternatives to global organizations. This combination of positive growth occurring on the demand and supply sides of the market makes the future of IT adoption, IT services and outsourcing in Latin America very promising[15].

- The Global Application Management concept with common Ticketing Tool, Common Delivery Pool and Follow the Sun Concept enables the provision of value added Application Management Services to Global Customers with a need of 7x24 hours support service.
- Through the Global Production Center (GPC) in Mercosur Application Management Services can be provided in the US or Americas time zone.
- Also a great advantage because it enables to provide the service within the "Follow the Sun Concept" by serving the US Customers during the business hours time and during the night with services provided from other GPC; for example out of the Global Production Center (GPC) India.

---

[14] Cf. *Gartner* (2006), p. 4.

[15] Cf. *Gartner* (2005) p. 6.

- As it was mentioned, the talent pool is the key asset to provide Application Management Services. In this field, Latin America has great work ethics, professional, interpersonal and language skills .
- With the huge potential in IT markets in Latin America, it is essential to have an Application Global Production Center in Latin America.
- Among all countries in Latin America, Brazil stands out as an interesting IT center location characterized by the large workforce availability and local market size and Argentina by extremely competitive cost advantages and talented English speaking laborforce.

7 Key Findings – General Conclusions about Latin America?

Latin America is becoming a more inviting environment for IT and business service providers because the countries are politically more stable, the economy is evolving and IT spending is growing faster than in other areas of the world. Economic and business indicators are very favorable.

As with any other region, specific characteristics in the Latin American business environment require that providers abandon standardized approaches in favor of customized go-to-market strategies that leverage the region's positive characteristics. Latin America specifically requires from service providers the appreciation of diversity and the development of strong relationships.

- IT sector has been showing a strong growth in the last 4 years and many countries are already positioned as global delivery exporters.
- Governments are actively promoting and supporting IT activities by declaring national laws including benefits such as, labor taxes as fiscal credits, taxes exemption, R&D support and other subsidies.
- Today the picture shows that costs, cultural affinity, geographic and time zones proximity, labor resources are on the list of benefits of the region.
- Most Latin America countries present competitive and comparable costs and business environment over other common offshore destinations, such as India, China and Eastern Europe.
- Although Latin America is showing a promising future it is not as mature as India in terms of exporting software services.
- The actual conditions position Latin America as a key contender of traditional offshoring and near shoring locations. Near shore advantages in Latin America are increasing the attention of US companies due to geographic and time zones proximity and also considering the US has the second largest Spanish speaking population. Cultural affinity, geographic and time zones proximity are relevant additional differentiators of the region over other countries/regions.

- Many companies are not simply choosing between Asia and Latin America, they are choosing both.
- *Siemens IT Solutions and Services* local companies in Latin America have strong specific niches and vertical capabilities, an advantage to adapt and replicate their success stories across regions.

References

AMR Research (2007): Timezones Do Matter: Redescovering the Americas and Nearshore Delivery, s. l. 2007.

AT Kearney (2007): Destination Latin America – A Near-Shore Alternative, s. l. 2007.

AT Kearney (2009) Global Service Location Index, s. l. 2009.

CIA (2009): The World Factbook, online: https://www.cia.gov/library/publications/the-world-factbook/geos/xx.html, last update: 05.10.2009, date visited: 18.10.2009.

Gartner (2005): The Dynamics of Latin America´s service market, s. l. 2005.

Gartner (2006): Perspectives Business Issues and Best Practices Latin America-Primer for Service Providers, s. l. 2006.

IDC (2007): IDC Siemens special report, s. l. 2007.

IMF (2009): International Monetary Fund – World Economic Outlook, s. l. 2009.

ITIL Foundations (2009): online: http://www.itilfoundations.com, last update: n. a., date visited: 18.10.2009.

Siemens IT Solutions and Services (2008): Own analysis, estimations, s. l. 2008.

World Bank (2009): Countries & Regions, online: http://geo.worldbank.org/, last update: 15.06.2009, date visited: 18.10.2009.

List of Authors

AYRA, ANJALI: Masters in Engineering Computer Sciences with honors from *Lviv Polytechnic National University*, Lviv Ukraine; 1992–1997 Regional Manager Sales CIS for *Karya Intl*; 1997–1999 SAP – SD and CRM Consultant Optimos; 1999–2001 Siebel Certified Consultant *Siemens Information Systems Ltd*, India; 2001–2002 SAP CRM – SD Lead Consultant *Siemens Information Systems Ltd*, India; 2003–2005 Project Manager SAP Implementations *Siemens Information Systems Ltd*, India; 2004–2005 Regional Manager North India, SAP Implementations *Siemens Information Systems Ltd*, India; 2005–2006 Program Manager SIS US at Worldspace, *Siemens IT Solutions and Services*, Inc; 2006–2008 AMS (Application Management Services) Lead Customer Support Manager *Siemens IT Solutions and Services*, Inc US at Talecris; since 2009 Director Application Management System *Siemens IT Solutions and Services*, Inc, US.

BÖHM, MARKUS: Dipl.-Wirtsch.-Inf., born in 1981, Research Associate and PhD student at the Chair for Information Systems (www.winfobase.de), Department of Informatics, *Technische Universität München (TUM)*, Germany. From 2003 to 2008 he studied Information Systems at *Friedrich-Alexander Universität Erlangen-Nürnberg (FAU)*, Germany and at *Jönköping International Business School (JIBS)*, Sweden. He focused on General Management, IT- and Business Process Management, as well as Software Engineering. As intern he has been working for *BMW*, *Bosch*, *ContentServ* and *Siemens*. His research interests include information management, IT-related challenges of mergers and carve outs, and IT-enabled Value Webs.

BOSE, BHASWAR: A Bachelor in Production Engineering from *Jadavpur University*, Kolkata, India, with about 9 years in the Manufacturing Industry (*Eveready Industries* and *Gillette*), working in the Engineering Maintenance, Production shop floor and Quality Assurance and over 7 years of working experience in the Service domain (*Wipro Ltd* and *SIS*) with 2 years in Service Delivery and 5 years in the Quality Management domain. A certified "Six Sigma Black Belt" involved in setting up Quality Management systems for start-up operations and for Outsourcing projects in Service domain. Presently working as Head of Quality Management for Global Application Management in *SIS*, being responsible for deployment of *SIS* Quality principles and set-up for Continuous Improvement practices.

CERVEAU, LAURENT: Member of the Management at *Adventures GmbH*. Co-founded *mobileo* in 2008 where he led the Product Center team. 2005–2008 Senior Software Engineer on *Apple's Logic Pro* (Germany). 2003–2005 Engineering Manager for *Apple iSync Applications Apple* (France) . 2001–2003 Project Manager for *Apple's iCal and iSync applications* (France), 2000–2001 Engineering Manager of Audio CPU Software Team at *Apple* (California). Specialized in the development process for innovative software consumer products.

DEGENHARDT, ANDREAS: BSc in Business and Computer Science, *University of Applied Sciences and Arts Dortmund*, since 2005 Head of Global Application Management at *Siemens IT Solutions and Services (SIS),* before Senior Manager at T-Systems International and Partner at *PriceWaterhouseCoopers*.

ENDHOLZ, PETRA: MBA, Diplom-Betriebswirt (BA) at the *State Professional Business College Mannheim*; born 1974, HR Consultant for Education and Development at *Siemens Nixdorf Informationssysteme AG* in Frankfurt from 10/96-10/98; International Human Ressource Manager at *Siemens Corporate*, later *Siemens Shared Services LLC* (*SSL*) in New Jersey, USA, from 11/98–04/03 with project responsibility to standardize outbound delegation services by implementing a web based application; Senior HR Consultant and member in the HR organizational development project to streamline operative Human Resource function in Germany at *Siemens AG*, Munich, from 05/03–04/04; HR Line Manager at *Siemens Business Services GmbH & Co. OHG* (*SBS*) in Munich, 05/04–09/07, e. g. responsible for affiliated company in the banking business, project lead for a part of an international carve out deal of a unit of SBS; as of 10/07 heading up and responsible to set up and introduce Global Resource Management for Global Operation, Global Application Management at *Siemens IT Solution and Services* (*SIS)* in Munich, and responsible project manager for 'Competency Management' for Global Operations worldwide.

GEIER, FREDDIE: is member of the management of the adventure Ltd. Before he was active as General Manager Central European Region in Munich and among other things as a Senior Director Business Development in the Application Division in the headquarters in Cupertino for Apple.

KEUPER, FRANK: Prof. Dr. rer. pol. habil., Dipl.-Kfm., born 1966, is owner of professorship in Business Economics, in particular Convergence Management and Strategic Management (www.konvergenz-management.com) at the *School of Management and Innovation - Steinbeis-Hochschule Berlin*, editor and executive director of the business management trade journal *Business + Innovation – Steinbeis Executive Magazin*, executive director and Headmaster of the *Sales & Service Research Center Hamburg – Steinbeis-Hochschule Berlin* (co-operation partner: Telekom Shop Vertriebsgesellschaft mbH) as well as of the *Business School T-Vertrieb (*co-operation partner: Telekom Deutschland GmbH), visiting professor et al. at the *University Tai'an* (province of Shandong in China), various lectureships at European Universities, associated partner at *inRESTRUCT* – a member of the *iKnowledge Group*. 10/2002–08/2004 guest professor at the *Johannes Gutenberg University Mainz*. Doctorate and postdoctoral lecture qualification at the *University of Hamburg,* as well as studies at the *Münster School of Business and Economics*. Field of work and research: investment and financing theory, planning and decision theory, production, cost management, strategic management, convergence management, cybernetics, system theory, corporate planning and management, sales and service management.

KRCMAR, HELMUT: Prof. Dr., 1954, Full professor of Information Systems and holder of the Chair for Information Systems (www.winfobase.de) at the Department of Informatics, *Technische Universität München (TUM)*, Germany. He also is Academic Director of the *SAP University Competence Center* and *fortiss*, the research institute and innovation center for software-intensive systems at Technische Universität München. He studied at *Universität des Saarlandes*, Germany, where he also received his PhD and worked as Post Doctoral Fellow at the *IBM* Los Angeles Scientific Center, as assistant professor of Information Systems at the *Leonard Stern School of Business*, NYU, and at *Baruch College, CUNY*. From 1987 to 2002 he was Chair for Information Systems, *Hohenheim University*, Stuttgart. His research interests include Information and Knowledge Management, IT-enabled Value Webs, Service Management, Computer Supported Cooperative Work, and Information Systems in Health Care and eGovernment.

LEIMEISTER, STEFANIE: Dipl. rer. com., 1979, is a research group manager in Information Systems at *fortiss*, the research institute and innovation center for software-intensive systems at *Technische Universität München* (*TUM)*, Germany. From 2004 to 2009 she was a full-time Research Associate and PhD student at the Chair for Information Systems (www.winfobase.de) at *Technische Universität München*, Germany. Stefanie received her Master's degree in communication science from *Hohenheim University*, Stuttgart, Germany. She spent time studying and researching abroad at *Central Connecticut State University in New Britain*, CT, USA. Her research interests include IS outsourcing, relationship management, cultural studies, IT carve outs, cloud computing, IT business alignment, and IT governance.

MARTENS, BENEDIKT: Dipl.-Kfm., born in 1983, research assistant at the subject area Accounting and Information Systems (www.uwi.uni-osnabrueck.de), *University of Osnabrück*. Work and research areas: Risk Management in IT Outsourcing, IT Outsourcing and Cloud Computing, Recycling Networks.

OECKING, CHRISTIAN: Dipl. Ing. in mechanical engineering, *University of Dortmund*. He started his professional career as a consultant in software development, later moving to *EDS Electronic Data Systems* as a member of the German Management. He joined *Siemens Business Services* in 1998 as Head of German Outsourcing. In 2002, *CHRISTIAN OECKING* became head of Global Outsourcing of *Siemens IT Solutions and Services*. In this position, he has succeeded in making *SIS IT* operations best in class in European competition by setting up and enhancing a global delivery network, including the set up of several strategic offshore locations. He has introduced an Outsourcing Framework to *SIS* and enhanced its implementation on a worldwide basis. In addition to his role as CEO of Global Outsourcing *CHRISTIAN OECKING* is the Chairman of the Management Board of *Siemens IT Solutions and Services GmbH*. *CHRISTIAN OECKING* has been member of the Board of the German Outsourcing Community of *Bitkom* since 2003. He has published several books and papers focusing on IT outsourcing.

RIEDL, CHRISTOPH: BSc Computer Science, MSc Information Systems, 1981, Research Associate and PhD student at the Chair for Information Systems (www.winfobase.de), Department of Informatics, *Technische Universität München (TUM)*, Germany. He received a BSc in computer science from *TUM* in 2006 and an MSc in Information Systems in 2007. He spent time studying and researching abroad at *National University of Singapore (NUS)* and at *Queensland University of Technology (QUT)*. His research interests include IT-enabled Value Webs, open and service innovation as well as semantic web and web 2.0 technologies.

ROMERO KRAUSE, MAXIMO: Born in 1976, Dipl. Ing. in Industrial engineering, *University of Technology of Buenos Aires, Argentina (ITBA)*. Postgraduate in Marketing, *Catholic University of Argentina (UCA)*. Economy and Finance for Executives, *ESEADE Buenos Aires, Argentina*. He joined *Siemens IT Solutions and Services Argentina* in 2004 as the Portfolio Manager. From 2008 he has lead locally in the region the ramp up of the Global Production Center (GPC) Mercosur for Application Management (Argentina, Brazil) together in cooperation with *Siemens IT Solutions and Services HQ Germany* and after that responsible of Quality, Resource Management within the GPC Mercosur and Customer Service Management for different local and global projects. In 2010, he has been transferred to Germany as the responsible for the Transition in South West Europe for a *Siemens IT Solutions and Services'* Global Project and later on responsible of the Global Processes implementation within the same Project. Before *Siemens IT Solutions and Services*, he worked as a Senior Consultant for *Unisys Sudamericana* and *CITIBANK N.A.* In addition, guest professor on the field of Project analysis and investment in the *University of Technology of Buenos Aires, Argentina (ITBA)*.

SCHMIDT, BENEDIKT: Dr. rer. pol., MBA, Diplom Betriebswirt (BA), born in 1973 is CEO of a 100% affiliated *Siemens* Company called *Restart Gesellschaft für Back-Up Systeme mbH*. Doctorate at the *University of Potsdam* in 2009, Master of Business Administration at the *University of Würzburg* in Cooperation with the *Boston University* in 2002, Diploma in Business Administration at the *Berufsakademie Mannheim* in 1997. Work experience as international *SAP* Consultant and Project Manager in various international projects, from 2001 until 2006 Director of the Center of Competence for Application Management at *Siemens IT Solutions and Services* with a network of 15 countries and a responsibility for expert sales activities, portfolio management, knowledge management, application management consulting and international collaboration within the business unit Application Management Services. From 2006 until 2008 Program Manager for a large SAP harmonization program, since 2008 CEO at *Restart*. Fields of work and research: Business Continuity Management, knowledge transfer within Application Management, knowledge management and communication, international service management, ITIL and Offshoring.

SCHULMEYER, CHRISTIAN: Dipl.-Wirtsch.-Ing., born 1966, is an external postgraduate at the professorship in Business Economics, in particular Convergence Management and Strategic Management at the *School of Management and Innovation - Steinbeis-Hochschule Berlin*, lecturer at the *Pforzheim University* for e-commerce, internet applications and technologies. Owner of the consultancy *Schulmeyer&Coll.*; active in the fields of internet strategies, internet based service and support applications as well as internet related software and application development. Court-appointed expert witness for systems and applications of data processing within the internet field, web based applications and multimedia. Lecturer for e-commerce and internet technologies at the *Pforzheim University*.

TÄUBE, FLORIAN A.: Prof. Dr. rer. pol., M.A. in Economics (Diplom-Volkswirt) at Strascheg Institute for Innovation and Entrepreneurship, European Business School, born 1974. Before joining EBS in 2008, Florian was with the Innovation and Entrepreneurship Group at *Tanaka Business School, Imperial College London*. Moreover, he is external researcher at the *Entrepreneurship, Growth and Public Policy Group* of the *Max Planck Institute of Economics*, Jena. Florian has a Doctorate in Economics from *Johann Wolfgang Goethe-University*, Frankfurt, Germany for a thesis titled *Emergence, geography & networks of the Indian IT industry: evolutionary perspectives*. During his doctoral studies, he was a Visiting Scholar to the *Indian Institute of Science* and *The*

Wharton School. Florian's research interests lie at the intersection of entrepreneurship, economic geography, organization theory and international business. Using mainly qualitative methods, his empirical focus is on internationalization of project-based industries, in particular regarding IT, film, pharma and construction. His regional area of interest is India and, besides the role of local and non-local networks in the evolution of the Bangalore IT cluster, he is currently working on collaborative projects dealing with organization and networks in Bollywood, internationalization of project-based firms and growth strategies of Indian pharmaceutical companies.Florian has published in journals such as *Journal of International Management, Environment and Planning A, Journal of Financial Transformation* and several practitioner-oriented outlets as well as book chapters. He is an active member of the academic community as reviewer for journals and conferences and workshop organizer and session chair (e.g. *Academy of Management*, *Academy of International Business*). Recently, he has joined the editorial board of *Performance* (a publication by *Ernst & Young*).

TEUTEBERG, FRANK: Prof. Dr., Dipl.-Kfm., born 1970, has been head of the subject area „Accounting and Information Systems", which is part of the *Institute of Information and Business Management (IMU)* at the *University of Osnabrück*. *FRANK TEUTEBERG* is a member of the *German Association of University Professors and Lecturers* (Deutscher Hochschulverband, in short *DHV*), *Gesellschaft für Informatik e.V. (GI)* and the *German Academic Association for Business Research (VHB)*. He is part of the trustee board of the student-led consultancy *studentop* and a member of the *German Logistics Association*. He teaches at *Virtual Global University* (www.vg-u.de) and is a regular visiting professor at *ESCEM* (www.escem.fr) in Tours/Poitiers (France). Furthermore, *FRANK TEUTEBERG* is the founder and spokesman for science and research (in cooperation with *PROF. DR. FREDERIK AHLEMANN*) of the *Research Center for Information Systems in Project and Innovation Networks* (*ISPRI*; www.ispri.de). He was the leader of a subproject on Mobile Supply Chain Management (run from April 2004 to the mid of 2008) as part of the joint project "Mobile Internet Business" (www.mib.uni-ffo.de) which was funded more than 2 million Euros by the *Federal Ministry of Education and Research*. *FRANK* Teuteberg has published more than 80 scientific papers, many of which have appeared in leading German and international journals, including Zeitschrift für Wirtschaftsinformatik, Electronic Markets: The International Journal of Electronic Commerce & Business Media, International Journal of Project Management as well as International Journal of Computer Systems Science & Engineering. His main research interests are Supply Chain Management, Environmental Management Information Systems, Reference Modeling, and IT Risk Management.

WOLTER, KATJA: Dipl.-Betriebswirtin (FH), 1978, since 2009 Research Associate at professorship in Business economics, in particular Convergence Management and Strategic Management at the *School of Management and Innovation – Steinbeis-Hochschule Berlin*, 2008–2009 Director Finance/Controlling at listet *Deutsche Entertainment AG (DEAG)* in Berlin, 2002–2007 Administration Directorate at *Rundfunk Berlin-Brandenburg* (rbb) in Berlin/Potsdam, 2001–2002 Controller at *Lafarge Roofing GmbH* in Oberursel (Frankfurt am Main). From 1996–2000 Business Administration at *Fachhochschule Stralsund* and *John-Moores-University* in Liverpool (GB), 2000 Internship *Deutsche Börse Systems AG* in Frankfurt am Main, 1997 Internship *Siemens* in Greifswald.

Index

MIX
Papier aus verantwortungsvollen Quellen
Paper from responsible sources
FSC® C105338

If you have any concerns about our products,
you can contact us on
ProductSafety@springernature.com

In case Publisher is established outside the EU,
the EU authorized representative is:
Springer Nature Customer Service Center GmbH
Europaplatz 3, 69115 Heidelberg, Germany

Printed by Libri Plureos GmbH
in Hamburg, Germany